CliffsNotes®

AP® English Language and Composition 2021 Exam

CliffsNotes®

AP® English Language and Composition 2021 Exam

by
Barbara V. Swovelin, M.A.

Houghton Mifflin Harcourt
Boston • New York

About the Author

Barbara V. Swovelin taught AP and Honors classes at Torrey Pines High School in Del Mar, California, for 34 years before retiring in 2014. She is an experienced AP English Exam Reader and a College Board Consultant, working both nationally and internationally. Additionally, she prepares new AP English teachers at College Board Institutes and Workshops. She has also taught graduate-level test preparation classes at California universities since 1986, specializing in the GRE, GMAT, and LSAT exams. Swovelin is also the author of *CliffsNotes AP English Literature and Composition 2021 Exam*.

Acknowledgments

I am forever indebted to Dr. Jerry Bobrow, in memoriam, for believing in me.

Dedication

This book is dedicated to my husband, Jerry, who helped and encouraged me in every step of the process. I also dedicate it to the thousands of students I had over the years, who taught and inspired me more than I can express.

Editorial

Executive Editor: Greg Tubach

Senior Editor: Christina Stambaugh

Production Editor: Jennifer Freilach

Copy Editor: Lynn Northrup

Technical Editor: Jane R. Burstein

Proofreader: Heather Wilcox

CliffsNotes® AP® English Language and Composition 2021 Exam

Copyright ©2020 by Houghton Mifflin Harcourt Publishing Company

All rights reserved.

Library of Congress Control Number: 2020936239
ISBN: 978-0-358-35378-2(pbk)

Printed in the United States of America
DOO 10 9 8 7 6 5 4 3 2 1   4500802022

For information about permission to reproduce selections from this book, write to trade.permissions@hmhco.com or to Permissions, Houghton Mifflin Harcourt Publishing Company, 3 Park Avenue, 19th Floor, New York, New York 10016.

www.hmhbooks.com

Table of Contents

Text Permissions

The following excerpts have been reprinted with permission.

Gather Together in My Name by Maya Angelou. Copyright © 1974 by Maya Angelou. Used with permission of Random House, Inc.

"Do Public Subsidies Leverage Private Philanthropy for the Arts? Empirical Evidence on Symphony Orchestras" by Arthur C. Brooks, *Nonprofit and Voluntary Sector Quarterly* 28:32–45. Copyright © 1999 by *Nonprofit and Voluntary Sector Quarterly.* Reprinted with permission of SAGE Publications LTD and conveyed through Copyright Clearance Center, Inc.

"Athletes Salaries Too High? Sports Fans, Blame Yourselves" by Gene Callahan. Copyright © 2007 by *The Foundation for Economic Education.* Reprinted with permission.

"At What Cost Does Innovation Come?" by Ali Carr-Chellman. Reprinted with permission of the author.

"Catastrophe on Camera: Why Media Coverage of Natural Disasters Is Flawed" by Patrick Cockburn. Copyright © 2011 by *The Independent.* Reprinted with permission.

"The Culture War: When Government Is a Critic" by David Cole. Reprinted with permission of the author.

A Considerable Town by M. F. K. Fisher. Copyright © 1964, 1977, 1978 by M. F. K. Fisher. Used with permission of Alfred A. Knopf, an imprint of the Knopf Doubleday Publishing Group, a division of Penguin Random House LLC. All rights reserved. Any third-party use of this material, outside of this publication, is prohibited. Interested parties must apply directly to Penguin Random House LLC for permission.

Cities on a Hill by Frances FitzGerald. Copyright © 1986 by Frances FitzGerald. Reprinted with permission of Scribner, a division of Simon & Schuster, Inc. All rights reserved.

"Alerting America: Effective Risk Communication" by Ruxandra Floroiu. Copyright © 2002 by *The National Academies Press.* Reprinted with permission.

"Polling Isn't Perfect" by John Fund. Originally published in *The Wall Street Journal* 14 Nov. 2002. Copyright © 2006 by Dow Jones & Co., Inc. Reprinted with permission of *The Wall Street Journal.* All rights reserved worldwide. License number 4191530975654.

"Who Makes More Money: Athletes, Actors, National Leaders, or CEOs?" by Audrey Henderson. Copyright © 2017 by *Supermoney*. Used with permission.

"Bargain or Bust" by Cameron Hollway, as it appeared in the 8/3/2005 *St. Louis Post-Dispatch.* Reprinted with permission of the *St. Louis Post-Dispatch,* copyright © 2005.

"Who Should Pay for the Arts in America?" by Andy Horwitz. Copyright © 2016 by *The Atlantic Monthly.* Reprinted with permission of The Atlantic Monthly Group, Inc. and conveyed through Copyright Clearance Center, Inc.

"ISDR Joins Asia-Pacific Broadcasting Union to Boost Information, Education on Disasters." Copyright © 2005 by UNESCAP News Services.

"Why Do Conservatives Want the Government to Defund the Arts?" by Aaron Knochel. Copyright © 2017 by *The Conversation.* Reprinted with permission of the author.

"How Social Media Is Changing Disaster Response" by Dina Fine Maron. Copyright © 2013 by *Scientific American*. Reprinted with permission.

"Full-Time Virtual Schools: Enrollment, Student Characteristics, and Performance" by Gary Miron and Charisse Gulosino. Copyright © 2015 by the National Education and Policy Center. Reprinted with permission.

"The Disadvantages of Public Opinion Polling" by Lee Morgan. Copyright © 2010 by Leaf Group, Ltd., U.S.A. Reprinted with permission. All rights reserved.

Art Credits

Introduction

About the Exam

The AP English Language and Composition Exam is used by colleges to assess your ability to perform college-level work. Actual college credit (either for one semester or for an entire year) may be offered by colleges and universities. The exam lasts 3 hours and 15 minutes and consists of two major sections: multiple choice and free response.

The first section of the exam consists of 45 multiple-choice questions. This section contains two reading passages that address comprehension questions, plus three writing drafts that address composition questions. All of the questions in this section have equal value, and there is no penalty for an incorrect answer. You have 1 hour to answer the 45 multiple-choice questions.

The multiple-choice **reading questions** are designed to test your ability to analyze prose passages. These passages are drawn from a variety of sources, rhetorical modes, historical or literary periods, and disciplines. You will be asked questions about the passages' style, content, and rhetoric. Expect two reading passages with between 11 and 14 questions per passage. The multiple-choice **writing questions** will present three draft-quality passages from a variety of sources. You will be asked questions about editing, clarifying, and improving the passages' content and organization. Two of these writing passages will have between 7 and 9 questions; the third passage will have between 4 and 6 questions.

The multiple-choice questions are carefully written and screened by the AP Test Curriculum Committee and the Educational Testing Service (ETS). The committee is ethnically and geographically balanced, and its members represent public and private high schools as well as colleges and universities. The committee is responsible for choosing the passages for both the multiple-choice section and the free-response section. All of the multiple-choice questions are pretested in college classes before they are used on AP examinations.

In the free-response section, you are given three essay topics, and you must write an essay on each of the three topics in 2 hours and 15 minutes. The suggested time allotment for each essay is 40 minutes, with an extra 15 minutes for reading the essay prompts. Each of the essays is of equal value in your final score.

The free-response questions test your writing ability in a variety of modes and for a variety of purposes. These timed essays measure your expository and analytical writing skills, which are essential to success on many college exams. In general, the three essays will give you an opportunity to demonstrate that you can do the following:

1. Synthesize ideas from multiple short passages into an argument of your own.
2. Analyze how an author's rhetorical choices create meaning, based on one given reading passage.
3. Argue your position regarding the validity of an author's message in a short passage.

The essay responses are read and scored during a 7-day period in early June. More than half of the AP Readers are college or university instructors; fewer than half are high school teachers. Each Reader is assigned to score only one essay question during the reading session; therefore, each student's work is read by at least three different Readers. Some essays are read and chosen as samples to be examined by all the Readers, while others are checked by the table leaders and question leaders after individual Readers have scored them. You can trust that the essay scoring is as professional and accurate as possible. All Readers are thoroughly trained and retrained throughout the week of scoring.

Before the actual scoring session in June, a committee reads a large number of randomly selected essays and creates an analytic rubric on a scale of 0 to 6 for each of the three essay questions. You will likely have become familiar with these analytic rubrics during the year of study in your AP English Language course.

Overall, the entire exam is designed to show your awareness of how an author creates meaning through use of language, genre conventions, and rhetorical choices and how well you can do the same in your own writing. A qualifying score demonstrates your ability to perform freshman college-level work.

How the Exam Is Scored

In the multiple-choice section, you earn 1 point for each correct answer. No points are deducted for wrong answers. Unanswered questions do not count for or against your score. The multiple-choice section accounts for 45 percent of the total exam score.

The three essays are each scored according to a specific rubric that judges three components of essay writing: the thesis or central claim (0–1 point), the support (evidence and commentary) of the thesis (0–4 points), and the sophistication of the essay as a whole (0–1 point). These three subscores are totaled into an overall score between 0 and 6. The essay scores are then calculated to equal 55 percent of the total exam score. You can read more detailed information on how the essays are scored in Chapter 2, "The Free-Response Section."

The score for the multiple-choice section is added to the score for the free-response section to produce a composite (or total) score. This composite score is translated into a 5-point scale:

5   Extremely well qualified

4   Well qualified

3   Qualified

2   Possibly qualified

1   No recommendation

Scores are reported in July to you, your secondary school, and any college you designate.

Frequently Asked Questions

Q: Who administers the exam?

A: The Advanced Placement exams are sponsored by the College Board. The exam is administered through the Educational Testing Service.

Q: What materials may I bring to the exam?

A: Bring an identification card as well as plenty of pens for the free-response questions and pencils for the multiple-choice questions. You may not bring a dictionary, a thesaurus, or any other reference book.

Q: May I cancel my score following the exam?

A: Yes. You always have this option. Check the current AP Bulletin for procedures and deadlines, which is available at www.collegeboard.com/ap or from your school counselor.

Q: How can I prepare?

A: Practice! Become comfortable with the exam and its format. Take several practice exams to work on your timing. Learn new or unfamiliar terms that you might be expected to know for the exam. Practice your essay planning and timed writing. Practice paraphrasing what you read so that this skill becomes second nature before the exam.

Q: How do I register for an AP exam?

A: See your school counseling office for registration information. Schools must order all AP exams by November 15.

Q: Why are there two AP English exams?

A: Because not all colleges offer the same curriculum for freshman English. The two exams—AP English Language and Composition and AP English Literature and Composition—permit each college to designate the exam that best reflects its curriculum.

Q: What's the difference between the two AP English exams?

A: The two exams are similar; both test your ability to analyze the written word and to prove that you can communicate intelligent ideas on a given subject. However, the AP English Language and Composition Exam asks questions about nonfiction; it never presents poetry or fiction. The language exam also places more emphasis on rhetorical analysis and the study of *how* language works. In contrast, the AP English Literature and Composition Exam places greater emphasis on literary analysis; it includes poetry, fiction, and drama. You will be asked to analyze several poems on the literature exam.

Q: Which exam should I take?

A: The best way to decide which exam to take is to ask the college you plan to attend. A college may offer either one or two semesters of credit, depending on its freshman English curriculum. Generally, a school that has a literary component combined with expository writing skills in its freshman English course gives up to a full year's course credit for the literature exam. A school that has a full year of freshman writing in various rhetorical modes may give up to a full year's credit for the language exam. In addition, it helps to consider your own strengths and weaknesses and your likes and dislikes. If you enjoy reading prose and writing well-argued, analytical essays, then the language exam is for you. If you have a strong literary background, especially in American and British literature and poetry analysis, then the literature exam will be a better fit.

Q: Is one exam easier than the other?

A: They are equally rigorous.

Q: What is an average score?

A: At a typical exam administration, approximately two-thirds of all test-takers receive a score of 3 or higher. To earn an average score of 3, you must answer approximately 50 to 60 percent of the questions correctly on the multiple-choice section and also write three adequate free-response essays.

Q: Can I take both the literature exam and the language exam in the same school year?

A: Yes, they are administered on different days.

Q: How can I find out how much college credit I'll get if I pass the exam?

A: Contact the college and ask the admissions office for a clear, written response. Do not be surprised to find that this is a somewhat confusing issue, compounded by the fact that two English exams exist. Additionally, some colleges and universities consider an overall score of 3 as passing, while other colleges require a 4 or even a 5. Some colleges require that all freshmen take their freshman English class, usually a composition course. In addition, some schools or programs within a college have different requirements.

Q: Do colleges get separate scores for my multiple-choice and free-response sections? May I get the two separate scores?

A: No to both questions. Only your overall score, based on a scale of 1 to 5, will be released to you or to any college.

Q: What if my school does not offer an AP course or I did not enroll in the course? May I take the exam anyway?

A: Sure! Although an AP course is theoretically designed to prepare students for the exam, much of that "preparation" consists of reading quality literature—both fiction and nonfiction—and practicing analysis, critical thinking, and close reading, in addition to taking practice AP exams and understanding the format of the exam. You can do this on your own, especially if you have disciplined study habits. However, I do strongly recommend that you read this test-preparation book carefully and, if you can, explore the College Board website at https://apcentral.collegeboard.org.

Q: When will I receive my AP exam scores?

A: You will receive your scores at about the same time as the colleges do, in early July.

Q: How can I obtain previous exams to use for practice?

A: You may order previously released exams directly from the College Board; the AP section of College Board information can be found at the College Board website at https://apcentral.collegeboard.org.

Q: How often are previous exams released to the public?

A: Multiple-choice exams are released periodically; essay topics are released every year.

Q: How can I approximate my score from my practice tests into an AP-scaled score of 1 through 5?

A: Approximating your score is a bit more complicated than simply counting the number of right and wrong answers, but follow these directions. Additionally, a sample scoring worksheet is included in this book after each full-length practice exam.

> The total number of points on the exam is 150. Because the free-response and multiple-choice sections are weighted 55 percent and 45 percent, respectively, there are 82.5 points for the essays and 67.5 points for the multiple-choice questions. Because the three essays are graded on a 6-point scale, each point on your essay raw score is multiplied by 4.583. Three 6s total 18, and 18×4.583 rounds up to 82.5. For the 45 multiple-choice questions, each point in the raw score is multiplied by 1.5 to equal 67.5.

> The total number of points required for a final score of 3, 4, or 5 varies each year, but a very reasonable assumption is that you need to accumulate approximately 114–150 points for a score of 5, 98–113 points for a score of 4, and 81–97 points for a score of 3.

Multiple-Choice Questions

Q: Is there a penalty for a wrong answer to the multiple-choice questions?

A: No. As of 2011, no AP exams deduct any points for wrong answers.

Q: Can I still pass the exam even if I don't finish all the multiple-choice questions in time?

A: Yes! Many students don't finish all the questions and still receive a passing score. Naturally, if you don't finish, you need to do very well on the questions you do complete and write three strong essays. However, since you are not be penalized for any wrong answers, you should fill in something for every question if you see yourself running out of time.

Q: Should I answer the multiple-choice passages in the order they appear on the exam?

A: Most students choose to answer the multiple-choice passages in the order they appear on the exam, as it is a very systematic and logical approach. However, keep a steady pace and do not let one passage eat up too much of your time, subsequently causing you to rush on the last passage(s). Overall, remember that your score is determined by the total number of questions you answer correctly. If you prefer to "browse" the passages first and complete the questions in order of your personal preference, be sure to keep your eye on the clock to avoid running out of time. Also, of course, be very careful to bubble your answer choices next to the accurate question numbers.

Q: How many passages and multiple-choice questions should I expect?

A: As of 2020, the multiple-choice sections will have two passages with 11–14 reading comprehension questions each, plus three passages with 4–9 writing and composition questions each. You will get a total of 45 questions.

Q: The College Board–released exams document the percentage of students who got each question correct. How can this help me?

A: Use this information to help you recognize the difficulty level of each question and your ability as a test-taker. You'll want to always get the high-probability questions correct, like those that range about 75 percent or higher. Also notice the very low-percentage questions, like those in the 30 percent range or lower. These hard questions may be very time-consuming or very complicated. Don't let them eat up too much time; instead, concentrate on the questions you're most likely to get correct. This will build your score. Remember that, in any case, you will want to mark an answer for all questions since you will not be penalized for an incorrect answer.

Q: When should I guess on the multiple-choice section?

A: Answer as many of the questions as accurately as you can. Avoid mismanaging your time and spending too long on one passage or one question. Don't be afraid to guess if you can eliminate at least two of the five choices. If you are unsure of an answer, mark out the answers in the questions booklet that you know are wrong:

A.

B. ?

C.

D. ?

E.

The question marks indicate possible answers. If you come back to the question later, you will not waste time considering wrong answers you have already eliminated.

Q: Are there any trick questions in the multiple-choice section?

A: No. If you read the passage carefully, you should be able to answer the questions.

Free-Response Essay Questions

Q: Is paper provided for the essays?

A: Yes. In fact, you'll write all of your essays in a special book that conceals your identity from the AP Exam Readers who score it. You are permitted to write in the exam booklet itself, but nothing written inside the exam booklet will affect your score.

Q: Does the scoring give extra weight to one of the essays?

A: No, all three essays are counted equally. Because the free-response portion of the exam is 55 percent of your total score, each essay equals 18.3 percent of your essay score.

Q: Should I plan my essay in advance?

A: In general, yes, planning your essay in advance is a good strategy. An outline is never required and will never be seen by the Readers anyway, but clear and logical organization is, indeed, an important criterion on which your essay is scored. You need to at least organize what points you intend to make and the order in which you plan to present them. Your exam booklet has ample blank space for planning.

Q: How many paragraphs should I write for each essay?

A: Write as many paragraphs as you need to fully develop and present your ideas. Although the introduction-body-conclusion format is most frequently used, the number of body paragraphs presented varies from student to student and topic to topic. An introductory paragraph that contains a thesis is understandably an appropriate beginning, but don't worry if you don't get to the conclusion. Read more about essay organization and development in Chapter 2.

Q: How many pages should each essay be?

A: No set length is required; however, most high-scoring essays are *at least* two pages long. Naturally, some essays are shorter, and some are longer. Instead of worrying about length, concentrate on addressing all of the tasks of the topic and thoroughly developing your ideas. Be aware that very short essays, such as those that are only about half a page in length, are considered "unacceptably brief" and score very low; they simply do not demonstrate enough development of ideas to receive a passing score. In Chapter 2 and in all of the practice exams, you can read sample student essays and get a feel for length. A word count for all sample essays in this book is also included.

Q: How much should I worry about grammar and spelling?

A: Good news! You don't have to worry too much about your spelling. If you can spell reasonably well, no Reader will dock your score for occasional spelling errors. The Readers are remarkably tolerant; they want to reward you for what you do well. Grammar and punctuation can be another issue, though. The Readers are always willing to overlook what they call "minor errors" or "honest mistakes" that are made under time pressures. They understand that what you have produced is a first draft that is likely to have a few flaws. However, if your errors are persistent and serious, the Readers will have to lower your score.

Q: Should I write my essays in cursive, or should I print?

A: You need to write as legibly as you can, so use whatever is easiest to read. The Readers want to be able to reward you for your essay; to do so, they have to be able to read the words. If you know your writing is hard to read, try to separate your words with a little extra space; this helps the Readers. Please don't forget to use a nice black- or blue-ink pen; avoid ones that bleed through paper, because you'll want to write on the back of the page.

Q: Do the essays need a title?

A: Not at all. It will never affect your score. I can guarantee that Readers are bored by dull titles anyway.

Q: How much of the passage in the prompt should I quote?

A: No set, formulaic answer exists. Yes, you do need to refer to the passage appropriately in order to support your ideas, and many of those examples should take the form of quotations. However, a string of irrelevant quotations, glued together with a few of your own words, will not help your score. Read the sample essays in this book to get a feel for what's appropriate.

Q: Can I pass the test if I don't finish an essay?

A: Of course! Understandably, a radically unfinished essay will receive a very low score, so try to pace yourself accordingly, devoting approximately 40 minutes to each essay. Doing so should allow you time to finish each one. Also, practice your pacing many times before the test. I also advise practicing the planning period over and over. If, within approximately 10 to 12 minutes, you can organize what you're going to say and the order in which you're going to present it, you should have enough time to actually write the sentences. Finally, if you find yourself in a time crunch on test day, remember that body paragraphs are much more important than concluding paragraphs—especially conclusions that merely summarize. You should devote your time to getting your ideas down on paper.

Q: How should I begin my essay? Should I paraphrase or repeat the question?

A: Begin your essay in whatever way makes it easiest for you to write. If you simply cannot begin on your own without rephrasing the question, then do so; however, be aware that you will not receive a point for the thesis if you merely restate the prompt.

Some Successful Testing Strategies

1. Increase your awareness of the structure of the exam. Know how many questions you'll be asked, how much time you'll have, what basic skills you'll need, and so forth. Of course, these preliminaries are all covered in this book.

2. Understand the thought process behind the exam. If you understand what the test-makers have in mind when they write questions and answer choices, you'll avoid fighting the exam, and eliminating wrong answer choices in the multiple-choice section will go faster.

3. Read the exam directions carefully! Become familiar with the wording of the directions in advance so that you'll be as comfortable as possible on test day.

4. Mark your answer sheet carefully. If you skip a question, mark it in your exam booklet, and then carefully enter the next answer on your answer sheet.

5. Practice your pacing and timing skills. For multiple-choice questions, complete the easiest ones first; in the free-response section, follow your preplanned strategy.

6. Overall, be prepared! Become familiar with the exam. Remember that increased comfort builds confidence and relieves anxiety. The essential skills can all be improved by practicing frequently.

Chapter 1

The Multiple-Choice Section

The multiple-choice section is 1 hour long and consists of 45 total questions for five passages. It is broken into two types of questions: reading questions and writing (or composition) questions. The reading questions begin your exam by presenting two passages from previously published excerpts that represent a variety of rhetorical modes, such as narration, argumentation, persuasion, and description. These passages will vary in length from about 500 to about 800 words. Each of the two reading passages is followed by 11 to 14 reading questions based on its rhetorical content. The writing questions are presented in the last three passages, which are drafts on various subjects. These passages will be shorter, about 150–350 words. The first two of these passages will present 7–9 questions, and the last passage will have 4–6 questions, all based on how to improve the draft.

Remember that you're not expected to be familiar with the passage or its specific content. Any technical information crucial to comprehending the passage as well as unusual or foreign phrases will be defined for you.

You will be more comfortable with both the multiple-choice and the free-response sections if you are adept at reading works from many genres and time periods. For example, the exam can cover excerpts from autobiographies, biographies, historical writing, essays and literary criticisms, journalism, political writing, nature writing, and scientific writing. The exam passages can be up to about 400 years old, so you'll need to practice comprehending and appreciating the styles of older pieces as well as contemporary ones. A student who practices only with modern-day authors will not be as relaxed or efficient during the exam as one who has been exposed to John Milton, Cotton Mather, or Dr. Samuel Johnson.

Abilities Tested

The multiple-choice section tests your ability to analyze the linguistic and rhetorical choices of an author, plus your ability to understand methods for improving writing. You are expected to show an awareness of the stylistic effects created by specific word choices and syntactic decisions. These questions also test your ability to examine prose passages critically; to understand the author's meaning and purpose; to comprehend structural organization; and to analyze syntax, figurative language, style, and tone. The level of difficulty reflects college-level study.

Basic Skills Necessary

In general, you need to be able to glean the gist of a given passage, have skills in literary and rhetorical analysis, demonstrate an adequate background in grammar, and understand the elements of composition. Although the questions don't specifically ask for identification or definition of terms (such as *subordinate clause* or *syntax*), you should be familiar with terms that may show up in the question stems or in the answer choices. See "Terms for the Multiple-Choice and Free-Response Sections" in Appendix A for a review of the terms you may encounter on the exam. In addition, you need to be proficient in careful reading so you can analyze and interpret the passages.

Analysis of the Directions

The directions you see on the AP English Language and Composition Exam will look like this:

> **Directions:** This section contains passages from professional prose works with questions about their content, style, and form, plus unpublished drafts with questions about improving their content and clarity. Read each passage carefully. Choose the best answer of the five choices.

The following tips will help ensure your success on the exam.

- Use self-discipline to manage your time effectively during the exam. You can develop this skill through practice. You should divide your time for each passage accordingly. Do not let yourself fall further and further behind as the exam progresses.

- Answer all the questions to the best of your ability before going on to the next passage. This strategy prevents you from having to return to any passage at the end of the exam just to answer a few skipped questions. If you put yourself in the position of returning to a passage, you'll have to reread it, and that process is too time-consuming.

- Read each passage carefully and critically. First, paraphrase the author's ideas as you read; then, concentrate on the author's effective word choices. Avoid getting bogged down in diction, whether it's a word you don't know or the structure of a sentence that's confusing. Simply keep trying to get the main point, and then let the questions guide what you need to know.

- Read all the answer choices. Remember that the directions ask for the *best* answer, which means there can be more than one reasonable choice for each question. However, never forget that the wrong answer is wrong for a reason. The correct response will never have a single inaccurate word in it. Eliminate wrong answer choices as you go. You can become more proficient at eliminating wrong answer choices by practicing spotting the wrong word or phrase in the incorrect responses.

Test-Taking Strategies

You can do well on the AP English Language and Composition Exam by using some proven test-taking strategies.

Skim the Questions

First, skim the questions (especially in the reading questions) to find out what you should concentrate on. Skimming the questions before reading the passage helps you focus on what the test-makers found important. Skimming involves a very fast reading speed—approximately 1,000 words per minute—so be aware that during this skimming, you are really just glancing at the questions. Ignore any "generic" questions, such as ones that ask you the author's main purpose or main point; instead, try to find approximately three to five specific ideas that you can look for while you read the passage. Do not try to memorize the questions; you're just glancing at them to help you focus while you read.

This technique works well, but you must practice it frequently enough before the exam for it to become second nature. You should look for the specific content of each question. For example, don't merely note that a question asks you to draw an inference. You must also focus on the specific content included in the inference. Prior practice is essential for you to become comfortable with this strategy.

Read Each Passage Actively and Visually

Active reading means you should underline and mark key words and ideas (just the most important ones) as you read. Don't sit passively and merely let your eyes move across the page. Scientific studies support the idea that active readers gain higher immediate retention than do passive readers, and immediate retention is all you need in this case. You won't be concerned with long-term memory on the day of the exam.

Visual reading means you should picture any action of the passage in your mind; create a movie, if you will. Visual reading is a valuable tool for eliminating distractions while reading. It gives your brain a task to perform and helps keep your mind on the content of the passage. Most people are visual learners; they remember more after they have "seen" something, even if it's in their imagination.

Both of these strategies enhance your immediate retention and concentration—just what you need for this exam. Practice these skills daily and watch them become more effective with continued use.

Paraphrase While You Read

This technique also helps your immediate retention and understanding of the author's ideas. By definition, paraphrasing, like summarizing, means restating the author's ideas in your own words. This is an essential skill for comprehension, and, like visual reading, it gives your brain something to do that is on task while you read. Every question that asks about a passage's main ideas or an author's point can be answered correctly if you paraphrase accurately. Paraphrasing will help in the writing question passages because it helps you understand each passage's organization and know where ideas are located.

For any given passage, paraphrase each paragraph as a unit, and then paraphrase the author's overall point that covers all of the paragraphs. Initially, practice by writing down your concise statement of an author's point immediately after reading a paragraph or a whole passage. Later, you can develop this skill to the point that it's internalized, and you can paraphrase very quickly. You'll find that, eventually, you can paraphrase effectively while you're reading.

Read the Questions Carefully

Read the question carefully after you've read the passage. Don't assume from your earlier skimming that you know each question well. You must understand exactly what you're being asked. Students frequently choose the wrong answer because they have misread the question, either by reading too quickly or by not being sure what's actually being asked.

Read the Answer Choices Carefully

Eliminate a wrong answer choice as you read it by crossing out that letter in the exam booklet. Never waste time rereading the wrong answer choices. Make sure the answer choice you select is accurate according to the passage and that it answers the question.

Understanding how to eliminate incorrect answer choices saves time and increases accuracy. Of course, the test-makers are trying to mislead you. If you understand the tricks they frequently throw at you, you'll work faster to eliminate wrong answer choices and you'll be less likely to be deceived by them. When trying to eliminate wrong answer choices, remember to think like a test-maker, not a test-taker. Wrong answer choices can be:

- **Contradictory to the passage:** If you read the passage carefully and paraphrase it accurately, you won't be tricked into the time-consuming process of rereading it to decide whether the answer choice is consistent with the passage.

- **Irrelevant to the question:** These incorrect answer choices may sound good, but they simply do not answer the specific question. Be sure to read the question carefully, know what it asks, and select your answer accordingly. Many incorrect answer choices for the writing questions are irrelevant; they do not relate to the question or the passage.

- **Never addressed in the passage:** Again, poor readers are tricked into rereading to look for ideas that weren't there in the first place. Readers who are accurate at paraphrasing can quickly eliminate an answer choice that has no evidence in the passage.

- **Unreasonable:** If the answer choice makes you shake your head and ask, "Where did they get that idea?", it's unreasonable. You can learn to quickly spot unreasonable answer choices.

- **Too general or too specific for the question:** Understand the degree of specificity that you need for a correct answer and then eliminate incorrect answer choices accordingly. For example, if the question asks about the overall point of a passage, you need a general answer, one that encompasses the content of the entire passage. On the other hand, if you're asked about the author's use of a certain quotation, the correct answer is likely to be quite specific. In the writing questions, a general question may ask about something like what will make an attention-grabbing opening, while a specific question may ask for which ideas or details will make the writer's point stronger.

Finally, never forget that a wrong answer choice is wrong for a specific reason and will *always* contain an inaccurate word or phrase. Practice crossing out the exact word or phrase that is wrong, and you'll find you can perform faster and with greater confidence. The correct answer will not contain a single word that is inaccurate.

Leave the Most Difficult Questions for Later

Leave the most difficult questions until the end of each passage. From the practice exams, you can learn to recognize which questions are harder for you and which ones you can do accurately and quickly. Then use this knowledge as part of your personal strategy to get the most correct answers you possibly can. Remember to treat each passage as a unit and answer all the questions for that passage within your time limit before going on to the next passage. Because you will not be penalized for a wrong answer, be sure to choose an answer for each question.

One way to increase your score is to always analyze the questions you get wrong on the practice exams. Try to identify the specific reason why you selected each incorrect answer choice. Did you misread the question? Did you misread the answer choice? Did you work too quickly? Try to detect any trends; for example, a certain question type may always be challenging for you. Then you can study, analyze, and understand why the correct answer is better than your choice. This analysis will help you stop repeating the same mistakes.

Remember: Practice! With extensive practice, you'll increase your familiarity with the question types. Thus, you'll begin to think like the test-makers, not a test-taker, and your score will improve.

Question Categories: Reading Questions

Reading questions demonstrate your ability to read and comprehend what the author has said or implied and how the author has presented it. In general, the reading questions tend to fall into just a few categories. By becoming familiar with these, you can more quickly understand what you're being asked. Also, you'll be more comfortable with the exam format and able to work faster. As with all testing strategies, it is essential to practice recognizing the question types *before* the exam.

A brief analysis of these question types follows.

Note: Be aware that these question types do not constitute a complete list. You will encounter questions that don't seem to fit into a category. However, by understanding what question types appear most frequently, you will increase your familiarity with the exam and improve your understanding of how to find the correct answers. Don't be thrown off balance by questions that don't seem to fall into set categories.

Questions about Rhetoric

Many of the questions on the exam are about rhetoric and test your ability to understand *how* language works in each passage. These questions ask you to analyze the *syntax* (sentence structure and word order), *diction* (word choice), point of view, and figurative language and its effects. Your mere recognition of these elements is not enough; you must be able to understand precisely how and why the devices of rhetoric produce particular effects.

Here are some of the ways this question type may be worded on the exam.

- The shift in point of view has the effect of . . .
- The syntax of lines _____ serves to . . .
- Which of the following choices best describes what _____ symbolizes?
- The second sentence is unified by metaphorical references to . . .
- As lines _____ are constructed, "_____" is parallel to which of the following?
- The phrase "_____" has the effect of . . .

- The style of the passage can best be characterized as . . .
- The sentence "_____" is chiefly remarkable for which of the following stylistic features?
- In line _____, the word "_____" functions as a metaphor for . . .
- Compared to the rest of the passage, the diction of lines _____ is best characterized as . . .
- In lines _____, the author develops her rhetorical purpose by . . .

Questions about the Author's Meaning and Purpose

These question types also appear quite frequently on the exam. They measure your ability to interpret the author's theme, meaning, or purpose. As with questions about rhetoric, these questions are closely tied to specific word choices. However, now you must determine *why* the author chooses the wording, not what effect it produces. These questions demonstrate your understanding of the author's thematic reason for choosing certain phrases. They may refer to the passage as a whole or to a specific portion of the passage, such as only one paragraph or one sentence.

Here are some of the ways this question type may be worded on the exam.

- Which of the following best identifies the meaning of "_____"?
- Which of the following best describes the author's purpose in the last sentence?
- The main purpose of _____ is to make clear . . .
- The author emphasizes _____ in order to . . .
- The sympathy referred to in line _____ is called _____ because it . . .
- What is the function of _____?
- By "_____," the author most likely means . . .
- In context, which of the following meanings are contained in _____?
- In the commentary in the second footnote, the author's primary purpose is most likely . . .
- The author italicizes the word "_____" in order to . . .
- The author places quotation marks around the phrase "_____" in order to . . .

Questions about the Main Idea

These questions also appear quite frequently. They test your understanding of the author's ideas, attitude, and tone. To prepare for these questions, paraphrase everything you read. First, make yourself practice this skill in writing—literally write down an author's point in a sentence or two. After such practice, you'll be able to do it internally while you read, and you'll have greater comprehension.

Here are some of the ways this question type may be worded on the exam.

- The theme of the second paragraph is . . .
- The speaker's attitude is best described as one of . . .
- The speaker interests the audience by stressing the idea that . . .
- It can be inferred from the description of _____ that which of the following qualities are valued by the author?
- In context, the sentence "_____" is best interpreted as which of the following?
- The atmosphere is one of . . .
- Which of the following would the author be LEAST likely to encourage?
- Which of the following is true about the various assertions made in the passage?
- All of the following ideas may be found in the passage EXCEPT . . .

Questions about Implications and Inferences

These questions require that you read between the lines and consider ideas that are not expressed explicitly. To answer these questions, think about what is NOT stated directly, but rather what is logically *implied* in the passage. Remember that the correct answer has to be the very BEST answer choice; therefore, whenever you are asked to read between the lines, select the answer choice that is most obvious, most plausible, and most likely to be true. Test-takers sometimes think that the correct answer should be more obscure than it really is—beware of talking yourself out of the correct answer!

Here are some of the ways this question type may be worded on the exam.

- The passage implies that . . .
- The phrase "_____" suggests that . . .
- It can be inferred from _____ that . . .
- In context, the phrase "_____" is meant to indicate that . . .
- The image of _____ suggests that . . .

Questions about Organization and Structure

Appearing less frequently than the first four question types detailed here, these questions test your ability to perceive how the passage is organized. For example, you need to know whether the passage follows a compare/contrast structure or whether it gives a definition followed by examples. Other passages may be organized around descriptive statements that then lead to a generalization. These methods are just a few of the ones an author may use to organize ideas. You also need to understand how the structure of the passage works. For example, you must know how one paragraph relates to another paragraph or how a single sentence works within a paragraph. Pay attention to the passage's organization if you skim the questions before reading and spot one of these question types.

Here are some of the ways this question type may be worded on the exam.

- The quotation "_____" signals a shift from . . .
- The speaker's mention of _____ is appropriate to the development of her argument by . . .
- The type of argument employed by the author is most similar to which of the following?
- The speaker describes _____ in an order best described as moving from _____ to . . .
- The relationship between _____ and _____ is explained primarily by the use of which of the following?
- The author's discussion depends on which of the following structures?
- Which of the following best describes the function of the third paragraph in relation to the first two paragraphs?
- The organization of the passage can best be described as . . .
- When the passage transitions from paragraph one to paragraph two, it also moves from . . .
- The last paragraph signals a shift from _____ to . . .

Questions about Rhetorical Modes

You should expect only a few questions that ask you to identify and recognize the various rhetorical modes the author uses. You must know the difference between narration, description, argumentation, and exposition. Understanding *why* a particular mode is effective for the author's ideas is also helpful.

Here are some of the ways this question type may be worded on the exam.

- The pattern of exposition exemplified in the passage can best be described as . . .
- The author's use of description is appropriate because . . .
- Which of the following best describes the author's method?
- Because the author uses expository format, he is able to . . .
- The speaker's rhetorical strategy is to . . .
- The author develops the passage primarily through which of the following?

Question Categories: Writing Questions

Writing questions allow you to demonstrate your ability to understand the overall effect of the various choices that a writer makes. These questions allow you to think like a writer and to identify which changes will improve a draft. Consider the kinds of suggestions that an editor, teacher, friend, or classmate might offer to enhance and strengthen a piece of your own writing.

Like the reading questions, the writing questions tend to fall into a few categories. Once you are familiar with these categories, you can process the questions more efficiently and with greater comfort. Naturally, you need to practice recognizing these question types *before* the exam.

Writing questions often tend to be time-consuming because you are asked to make decisions about entire sentences, not just brief phrases or individual ideas. Most writing questions consist of more than one sentence. Therefore, you may find that they take more time than reading questions simply because of the quantity of words you have to read. To help you locate information, each sentence in the passage will be numbered. Additionally, the relevant sentence will usually be reprinted below the question so that you do not have to go back to the draft to find and reread it. Sometimes, a portion of the sentence will be underlined, and you will be asked about the best revision for just that underlined portion.

Some of the writing questions are worded essentially as yes/no questions; they ask whether the writer should or should not make some change to the passage. On occasion, an answer choice states that no change should be made; if so, this will always be answer choice A, and it will be worded parenthetically: (as it is now).

A brief analysis of these various question types follows.

Note: Keep in mind that the following categories do not constitute a comprehensive list; it is likely that you will encounter some questions that do not seem to fit into any preset category, but do not let this interfere with your concentration.

Questions about Organization

These questions test your ability to understand the overall organization of the passage: how the draft is put together and how the organization might be improved. For example, you may be asked about the best placement of a sentence within a paragraph or about a paragraph's placement within the passage.

Here are some examples of how questions of this type may be worded on the exam.

- In the context of the paragraph's overall argument, which of the following choices best describes the purpose of the second paragraph?
- The writer wants to add the following sentence to the third paragraph to provide further explanation. Where would the sentence best be placed?
- The writer is considering moving the second paragraph so that the sequence of paragraphs better reflects the logic used to develop the passage's argument. Where would be the best location for this paragraph?

- In sentence 2 (reprinted below), the writer wants an effective transition from the introductory paragraph to the main idea of the passage. Which of the following versions of the underlined text best achieves this purpose?
- The writer is considering what to do with the second paragraph (sentences 4 and 5). In the context of the passage's line of reasoning, what is best for the writer to do with the second paragraph?

Questions about Development of Ideas

These questions test your ability to determine the best method of developing ideas or furthering the argument in a passage. They may ask you to choose what information would best serve a writer's purpose or how a writer could improve the logical arrangement of ideas.

Here are some examples of how questions of this type may be worded on the exam.

- The writer is considering revising the third paragraph (sentences 4–6). In the context of the passage's overall flow of ideas, which of the following is the best version of the third paragraph?
- In sentence 5 (reprinted below), the writer wants to better illustrate the effects of _____ in order to show _____, as described in sentence 4. Which of the following versions of sentence 5 best accomplishes this goal?
- In order to fully develop the argument, the writer would most likely include all of the following examples in the third paragraph EXCEPT
- The writer is considering changing the method of development used in sentences 7 and 8 (reprinted below) to clarify the line of reasoning for the audience. Should the writer use a different method of development in sentences 7 and 8, and why or why not?
- Which version of sentence 6 (reprinted below) works together most effectively with the other sentences in the paragraph to help establish the thesis?

Questions about Adding Information

These questions test your ability to understand how the inclusion of additional information may help develop a writer's argument or support an idea. They may ask which information is most relevant or whether or not a writer should include new information.

Here are some examples of how questions of this type may be worded on the exam.

- In sentence 7 (reprinted below), the writer wants to add the phrase "_____" to the beginning of the sentence, adjusting capitalization as needed. Should the writer make this addition, and why or why not?
- The writer wants sentence 10 (reprinted below) to serve as evidence that reinforces the overall argument of the passage. Which version of the underlined portion of sentence 10 best accomplishes this goal?
- The writer wants to conclude the passage by supporting the specific claim made in sentence 15 with a quotation. Which of the following quotations, if placed after sentence 15, would best accomplish this goal?
- The writer wants to add more evidence to the second paragraph (sentences 5–8) to support the main argument of the paragraph. All of the following pieces of information help achieve this purpose EXCEPT
- The writer wants to add a phrase at the beginning of sentence 5 (reprinted below), adjusting the capitalization as needed, to set up a comparison with the idea discussed in sentence 4. Which of the following choices best accomplishes this goal?
- The writer wants to provide additional details in order to convey the significance of the narrative information provided in sentence 1 (reprinted below) and help develop the main idea of the passage. Which of the following sentences, if added after sentence 1, would best accomplish this goal?

Questions about Deleting Information

These questions test your ability to understand when less is more—which information may be irrelevant or unnecessary to a writer's argument or overall point. They usually ask whether or not information should be removed or which detail is least important.

Here are some examples of how questions of this type may be worded on the exam.

- The writer is considering deleting the underlined portion of sentence 9 (reprinted below), adjusting the punctuation as needed. Should the writer keep or delete the underlined text, and why or why not?
- The writer is considering deleting sentence 7 (reprinted below) from the passage. Should the writer keep or delete the sentence, and what is his or her reasoning?
- The writer wishes to delete any irrelevant information from the third paragraph. Which of the following sentences is the LEAST relevant to the writer's overall point and thus should be deleted?

Questions about Increasing Interest

These questions test your ability to understand how to increase the reader's interest in a passage, how to arouse the reader's attention, and how to help the reader focus on the writer's points in a passage. They may ask what would make a better opening sentence or what information relates best to the writer's overall point.

Here are some examples of how questions of this type may be worded on the exam.

- The writer would like to introduce the quotation in sentence 6 (reprinted below) in a way that best relates to the argument presented in the passage. Which of the following versions of the underlined portion of sentence 6 best supports this goal?
- In sentence 4 (reprinted below), the writer wants to allude to the example used in sentence 5 in order to better integrate it into her overall argument. Which of the following versions of sentence 4 best accomplishes this goal?
- Which of the following sentences, if placed before sentence 1, would help capture the reader's interest and also provide the most effective introduction to the overall topic of the paragraph?
- Which of the following sentences, if placed before sentence 1, would best provide an engaging contextualization for the argument that follows?

Questions about Clarifying Information

These questions test your ability to understand what information or which word choices help establish, clarify, or reinforce a writer's point. They may ask you to distinguish what revision best fits within a paragraph or what would most effectively explain the writer's point.

Here are some examples of how questions of this type may be worded on the exam.

- The writer wants to add a thesis statement after sentence 5. Of the following choices, which best reflects the writer's main claim?
- Which of the following sentences, if placed before sentence 1, would best provide engaging context for the argument that follows?
- Which version of sentence 5 (reprinted below) most effectively works together with the other sentences in the paragraph to help establish the thesis?
- Which of the following is the best statement of the writer's thesis about the subject?
- Throughout the passage, the writer wants to make sure to acknowledge the sources that are used as evidence. The writer should make which of the following revisions?

Questions about Refuting Information

These questions test your ability to understand not how to build up an argument but rather how to challenge or refute a writer's argument. They may ask you what new information best contrasts a writer's idea or which idea most strongly challenges a writer's argument.

Here are some examples of how questions of this type may be worded on the exam.

- To enhance the credibility of the overall argument, the writer wants to revise sentence 12 (reprinted below) so that it includes a rebuttal to the point made in the sentence. Which version of the underlined portion of sentence 12 most effectively achieves this goal?

- In sentence 14 (reprinted below), the writer wants to refute the idea presented in the first part of the sentence by offering a contrasting perspective. Which version of the underlined text best accomplishes this goal?

- In the fourth paragraph (sentences 9–11), the writer wants to expand on his concession that _____ may seem impossible. Which of the following examples would best achieve this purpose?

- In the third paragraph (sentences 4–7), the writer wants to provide further evidence to rebut the claim that _____ may not be feasible. Which of the following pieces of evidence would best achieve this purpose?

- The writer wants to add a phrase at the beginning of sentence 5 (reprinted below), adjusting the capitalization as needed, to set up a comparison with the idea discussed in sentence 4. Which of the following choices best accomplishes this goal?

Practice

This section contains two passages that are typical of the ones chosen for the multiple-choice section of the exam, followed by sample questions. The answers and their explanations follow.

Questions

Directions: This section consists of a passage from a prose work with questions about its content, style, and form, plus a draft passage with questions about improving its content and clarity. Read each passage carefully. Choose the best answer of the five choices.

Questions 1–14 refer to the following passage from a 20th-century British book of biographies.

Everyone knows the popular conception of Florence Nightingale. The saintly, self-sacrificing woman, the delicate maiden of high degree who threw aside the pleasures of a life of

(5) ease to succour the afflicted, the Lady with the Lamp, gliding through the horrors of the hospital at Scutari, and consecrating with the radiance of her goodness the dying soldier's couch—the vision is familiar to all. But the truth

(10) was different. The Miss Nightingale of fact was not as facile fancy painted her. She worked in another fashion, and toward another end; she moved under the stress of an impetus which finds no place in the popular imagination. A

(15) Demon possessed her. Now demons, whatever else they may be, are full of interest. And so it

happens that in the real Miss Nightingale there was more that was interesting than in the legendary one; there was also less that was

(20) agreeable.

What was the secret voice in her ear, if it was not a call? Why had she felt from her earliest years, those mysterious promptings towards . . . she hardly knew what but certainly towards

(25) something very different from anything around her? Why, as a child in the nursery, when her sister had shown a healthy pleasure in tearing her dolls to pieces, had she shown an almost morbid one in sewing them up again? Why was she driven

(30) now to minister to the poor in their cottages, to watch by sick-beds, to put her dog's wounded paw into elaborate splints as if it was a human being? Why was her head filled with the queer imaginations of the country house at Embley

(35) turned, by some enchantment, into a hospital, with herself as matron moving among the beds? Why was even her vision of heaven itself filled with suffering patients to whom she was being useful? So she dreamed and wondered, and

(40) taking out her diary, she poured into it the agitations of her soul.

A weaker spirit would have been overwhelmed by the load of such distress—would have yielded or snapped. But this extraordinary young woman

(45) held firm, and fought her way to victory. With an amazing persistency, during the eight years that followed her rebuff over Salisbury Hospital, she struggled and worked and planned. While superficially she was carrying on the life of a

(50) brilliant girl in high society, while internally she was a prey to the tortures of regret and remorse, she yet possessed the energy to collect the knowledge and to undergo the experience which alone could enable her to do what she had

(55) determined she would do in the end. In secret she devoured the reports of medical commissions, the pamphlets of sanitary authorities, the histories of hospitals and homes. She spent the intervals of the London season in ragged schools

(60) and workhouses. When she went abroad with her family, she used her spare time so well that there was hardly a great hospital in Europe with which she was not acquainted, hardly a great city whose slums she had not passed through.

(65) Three more years passed, and then at last the pressure of time told; her family seemed to realise that she was old enough and strong enough to have her way; and she became superintendent of a charitable nursing home in

(70) Harley Street. She had gained her independence, though it was in a meagre sphere enough; and her mother was still not quite resigned: surely Florence might at least spend the summer in the country. At times, indeed, among her intimates,

(75) Mrs. Nightingale almost wept. "We are ducks," she said with tears in her eyes, "who have hatched a wild swan." But the poor lady was wrong; it was not a swan that they had hatched; it was an eagle.

1. Which of the following best describes the structure of the first paragraph?

   A. It is divided into two parts, beginning with general statements, and moving to specific commentary.
   B. It is divided into two contrasting parts, with the division coming in line 9.
   C. It alternates a short sentence followed by a long sentence throughout.
   D. It moves from the presentation of Florence Nightingale's strengths (lines 1–9) to the presentation of her weaknesses (lines 9–20).
   E. It presents Florence Nightingale first in figurative language (lines 1–9) and then in literal language (lines 9–20).

2. In the first paragraph, all of the following words and phrases are used to present the popular conception of Florence Nightingale EXCEPT

   A. "saintly" (line 2)
   B. "self-sacrificing" (lines 2–3)
   C. "the Lady with the Lamp" (lines 5–6)
   D. "interesting" (line 18)
   E. "legendary" (line 19)

3. The first paragraph of the passage employs all of the following contrasts EXCEPT

   A. "the vision" and "the truth" (line 9)
   B. "fact" and "fancy" (lines 10 and 11)
   C. "another fashion" and "no place in the popular imagination" (lines 12 and 14)
   D. "the real" and "the legendary" (lines 17 and 18–19)
   E. "more that was interesting" and "less that was agreeable" (lines 17 and 19–20)

4. In the first paragraph, all of the following words have specific religious meanings EXCEPT

   A. "saintly" (line 2)
   B. "maiden" (line 3)
   C. "consecrating" (line 7)
   D. "Demon" (line 15)
   E. "possessed" (line 15)

5. In which of the following sentences from the first paragraph does the writer demonstrate effective use of parallel structure?

   A. the first ("Everyone knows . . .", lines 1–2)

   B. the third ("But the . . .", lines 9–10)

   C. the fourth ("The Miss . . .", lines 10–11)

   D. the seventh ("Now demons . . .", lines 15–16)

   E. the eighth ("And so . . .", lines 16–20)

6. All of the following words and phrases serve a similar purpose EXCEPT

   A. "popular conception" (line 1)

   B. "vision" (line 9)

   C. "as facile fancy painted" (line 11)

   D. "demons" (line 15)

   E. "the legendary one" (lines 18–19)

7. In which sentence in the first paragraph does the author use archaic diction and clichés?

   A. the first ("Everyone knows . . .", lines 1–2)

   B. the second ("The saintly . . .", lines 2–9)

   C. the third ("But the . . .", lines 9–10)

   D. the sixth ("A Demon . . .", lines 14–15)

   E. the eighth ("And so . . .", lines 16–20)

8. Which of the following phrases in the first paragraph employs BOTH hyperbole and metaphor?

   A. "the Lady with the Lamp" (lines 5–6)

   B. "the horrors of the hospital at Scutari" (lines 6–7)

   C. "consecrating with the radiance of her goodness" (lines 7–8)

   D. "as facile fancy painted her" (line 11)

   E. "no place in the popular imagination" (line 14)

9. The words "call" (line 22) and "mysterious" (line 23) in the second paragraph are related to the diction of the first paragraph because their meanings are associated with

   A. medicine

   B. religion

   C. social position

   D. psychology

   E. feminism

10. In the second paragraph, the sentence that is most likely to surprise the conventional expectations of a reader is the

   A. first ("What was . . .", lines 21–22)

   B. second ("Why had she . . .", lines 22–26)

   C. third ("Why, as a . . .", lines 26–29)

   D. fourth ("Why was she . . .", lines 29–33)

   E. fifth ("Why was her . . .", lines 33–36)

11. The significant difference between the syntax of the second paragraph and that of the rest of the passage is its use of

   A. both loose and periodic sentences

   B. parallel structure

   C. sentence fragments

   D. interrogative sentences

   E. connotative diction

12. The third paragraph implies a contrast between all of the following EXCEPT

   A. "weaker spirit . . . extraordinary young woman" (lines 42–44)

   B. "superficially . . . internally" (lines 49–50)

   C. "reports of medical commissions . . . histories of hospitals" (lines 56–58)

   D. "the London season in ragged schools and workhouses" (lines 59–60)

   E. "abroad with her family . . . slums" (lines 60–64)

13. Which of the following best describes the structure of the passage as a whole?

   A. The entire passage is developed chronologically.

   B. The first paragraph gives an overview, and the second, third, and fourth paragraphs develop chronologically.

   C. The first paragraph uses only the point of view of the author, the second and third paragraphs only that of Florence Nightingale, and the fourth paragraph only that of her mother.

   D. The first and second paragraphs generalize about Florence Nightingale, while the third and fourth paragraphs use specific detail.

   E. The first three paragraphs use a first-person narrator, while the fourth paragraph employs direct and indirect discourse.

14. Which of the following is the climactic contrast of the passage?

    A. "Three more years . . . the pressure of time" (lines 65–66)

    B. "independence . . . meagre sphere" (lines 70–71)

    C. "Harley Street . . . the country" (lines 70–74)

    D. "'ducks . . . wild swan'" (lines 75–77)

    E. "swan . . . eagle" (lines 78–79)

Questions 15–21 refer to the following draft.

(1) The rise of television in the 1950s brought many changes to the world, but one change rarely thought of deals with advertisements for children's toys: Suddenly toys became *things* that children believed they *needed* in order to play. (2) Until this time, children's play was largely unstructured, more or less unsupervised, freewheeling, and inventive. (3) Kids imagined lives as pirates and princesses, aristocrats and action heroes, doctors and explorers, improvising as they went, making their own rules and regulations.

(4) Play changed quite radically during the second half of the 20th century, as children were given ever more specific toys that implied or even required specific tasks and scripts. (5) Instead of playing pirate with a tree branch that morphed into a game of javelin-throwing in the ancient Olympics, the commercialization of toys began to shrink children's imaginative space. (6) Toys, like a Star Wars light saber, narrowed the scope of what children could do with it.

(7) As parents became more concerned with safety, children's imaginations took another hit. (8) When parents enrolled their offspring in karate classes, ballet, music lessons, and gymnastics, they hoped they were creating a safe environment for their children, but they were also inhibiting their kids' imagination.

(9) Psychologists believe that changes in what children do also affect their cognitive and emotional development. (10) Playing make-believe actually helps children develop a critical cognitive skill called executive function, which has as a central component the ability to self-regulate. (11) This trait helps one control emotions and behavior, resist impulses, and show self-discipline. (12) Poor executive function is associated with high dropout rates, drug use, and crime, while good executive function is considered a better predictor of success in school than a child's IQ. (13) It's simple: Children who can control their feelings and pay attention are better able to learn.

(14) One important aspect of children's playtime that helps develop self-regulation is called private speech, in which children talk to themselves about what they are going to do and how they are going to go about doing it. (15) This type of self-regulating language has been shown in many studies to be a predictor of executive function. (16) Unfortunately, the more structured children's play is, the more such private speech declines. (17) This, in turn, inhibits their ability to practice policing themselves.

15. Which of the following sentences, if placed before sentence 1, would best provide engaging context for the overall topic of the first paragraph?

    A. Children's playtime can be influenced by the toys they have at their fingertips.

    B. Children always like to play.

    C. Playtime is more important than previously believed.

    D. Advertising can change a culture.

    E. The history of children's toys took a surprising turn shortly after the advent of television.

16. The writer is considering adding the following sentence to the first paragraph (sentences 1–3).

Advertising budgets for children's toys soared after the Mickey Mouse Club debuted in 1955, and kids responded in droves.

Should the writer make this addition?

    A. No, because the information is redundant.

    B. No, because it distracts from the paragraph's main point.

    C. No, because advertising budgets in the 1950s are irrelevant today.

    D. Yes, because it reinforces children's desire to get toys they think they needed.

    E. Yes, because readers will relate to the Mickey Mouse Club.

17. The writer feels the need to add a transition to sentence 4 (reprinted below) in order to enhance the ideas of the second paragraph.

Play changed quite radically during the second half of the 20th century, as children were given ever more specific toys that implied or even required specific tasks and scripts.

Which of the following, if added to the beginning of the underlined portion and adjusted for capitalization, would best serve the writer's purpose?

   A. Therefore,
   B. However,
   C. Consequentially,
   D. Admittedly,
   E. Certainly,

18. The writer is considering moving the second paragraph so that the sequence of paragraphs better reflects the logic used to develop the passage's argument. Where would be the best location for this paragraph?

   A. (as it is now)
   B. Move it before paragraph one (sentences 1–3).
   C. Move it before paragraph four (sentences 9–13).
   D. Move it before paragraph five (sentences 14–17).
   E. Move it after paragraph five (sentences 14–17).

19. Which of the following presents the most plausible refutation of the argument in the third paragraph (sentences 7–8)?

   A. Children's imaginations cannot be restricted.
   B. Sales of children's toys have skyrocketed in recent decades.
   C. Such activities as karate and ballet can enrich children's minds.
   D. Children use toys for activities that the toy wasn't designed for.
   E. Parents who do not enroll their children in special classes are inhibiting their development.

20. The writer is considering deleting sentence 13 (reprinted below) from paragraph four.

It's simple: Children who can control their feelings and pay attention are better able to learn.

Should the writer make this deletion?

   A. No, because it articulates a general conclusion to the paragraph.
   B. No, because it is vital to the paragraph's overall point.
   C. Yes, because it is redundant and repeats information in sentence 12.
   D. Yes, because it provides no pertinent or interesting information.
   E. Yes, because its point has already been established in the paragraph.

21. The writer wants to add the following sentence to the fifth paragraph (sentences 14–17).

Children's self-regulating language is highest during make-believe play.

Where is the best placement for this sentence?

   A. before sentence 14
   B. after sentence 14
   C. after sentence 15
   D. after sentence 16
   E. after sentence 17

Answer Explanations

The first passage comes from Eminent Victorians, *a group of biographies written by Lytton Strachey and published in 1918.*

1. **B.** The first paragraph has two distinct parts, choice B. The first nine lines present the "popular" idealized notion of Florence Nightingale. The division is clearly marked by the sentence "But the truth was different." The rest of the paragraph begins the presentation of what the author claims is the "real Miss Nightingale." Choice A inaccurately claims the paragraph begins with general statements and moves to specific ones, but the whole paragraph has specific ideas. Choice C is incorrect because, although the paragraph uses both long and short sentences, the alternation is not consistent. Both the third and fourth sentences are short, and the fifth is long only because it uses semicolons in place of periods. Choice D misunderstands the progression of ideas; the contrast is not between Nightingale's strengths and weaknesses but between a romantic conception of her and a realistic account. Choice E is wrong because both sections of the first paragraph use figurative and literal language.

2. **D.** All but "interesting," choice D, are used to present the popular idea of Florence Nightingale. The author argues the *real* woman was "more . . . interesting" though less saintly than the woman of the legend. Choices A, B, and C are all located in the first section of the paragraph, which presents Florence Nightingale in her popularized depiction. Choice E, although it is located at the end of the first paragraph, refers to her popularized, "legendary" depiction.

3. **C.** Choice C offers the only pair of ideas that are consistent; "Another fashion" and "no place in the popular imagination" are both part of a sentence describing the "real" woman and are not contrasts. The remaining four options of these pairs are part of the legendary versus real contrast in the paragraph.

4. **B.** Though "maiden," choice B, might sometimes be used in a religious context, of itself it is simply the word for a virgin or an unmarried girl or woman, which applies to Florence Nightingale in this passage. The four other words have specific religious denotations. Choice A, "saintly," should be obviously wrong, as it carries a specific religious connotation. Choice C, "consecrating," has strong religious meanings that deal with dedicating one's life to religious thought or orders. "Demon" (D) also has religious connotations within the context of the paragraph. "Possessed" (E) is used (metaphorically) to mean controlled by a spirit.

5. **E.** The eighth sentence, choice E, is the only answer choice that employs parallel structure; it plays "in the real" against "in the legendary" and "there was more that was interesting" against "there was also less that was agreeable." None of the first four options uses parallel structure and can therefore be eliminated.

6. **D.** In choice D, the word "demons" does not refer to the popular concept of Florence Nightingale; instead, it refers to the way in which she was obsessed with her job. However, the word or phrase in all other answer choices specifically refers to the popular concept of the saintly Florence Nightingale. Choice A, "popular conception," refers to the well-known notions people had about Florence Nightingale. Choice B, "vision," refers to all of the visual images associated with Nightingale in the second sentence. Choice C, "as facile fancy painted," deals with the simplistic notions the public had about Nightingale. Choice E, "the legendary one," refers also to the popularized notions of Nightingale.

7. **B.** The second sentence, choice B, employs both archaisms like "maiden of high degree" or "couch" and clichés like "saintly, self-sacrificing," "delicate maiden of high degree," and "to succour the afflicted," as the author mocks the sentimental idea of Florence Nightingale. The other sentences avoid these excesses and are quite literal.

8. **C.** The overstatement is the claim that the "radiance" (a metaphor) of Nightingale's goodness "consecrated" the dying soldiers' deathbeds, choice C. She may have made the dying more comfortable, but she did not make them sacred. Choice A, "the Lady with the Lamp," is metaphorical but not hyperbolic. The "horrors of the hospital at Scutari" (B) is not hyperbolic or figurative, and "as facile fancy painted her" (D) is not hyperbole, though it is metaphoric. Choice E, "no place in the popular imagination," is neither hyperbolic nor metaphorical.

9. B. Though "call" and "mysterious" can be used without any religious reference, both have specific religious meanings, choice B. The word "call" can mean a religious vocation regarded as divinely inspired, and "mysterious" has several different religious meanings—for example, pertaining to that which only faith can explain. Within the context of the passage, these words carry religious connotations; they do not suggest medicine (A), social position (C), psychology (D), or feminism (E).

10. C. The third sentence in paragraph two, choice C, contains unusual images: Most modern readers are unlikely to expect the sister's pleasure in "tearing her dolls to pieces" to be described as "healthy," while Florence Nightingale's repairing the victims is "morbid." All other answer choices contain common images and childlike visions that do not buck convention.

11. D. Unlike the rest of the passage, the second paragraph depends almost entirely on the use of questions, choice D. Six of its seven sentences are interrogative. Choice A is incorrect because the second paragraph does not have both loose and periodic sentences. Choice B is wrong because all paragraphs use parallel sentences to some degree, not just the second paragraph. Choice C is incorrect; no paragraphs contain sentence fragments. Choice E is wrong because all of the paragraphs employ connotative diction.

12. C. The "reports" and "histories" noted in choice C are alike, not contrasted; they are both the subjects of Florence Nightingale's studies. The contrast of choice A is between "A weaker spirit," which refers to other women, and "this extraordinary woman," which refers to Nightingale herself. Choice B is inaccurate because "superficially" refers to Nightingale's social life in the upper class, while "internally" refers to her inner struggle to break free from the role she was expected to play within that society. In choices D and E, "the London season" and "abroad with her family" suggest situations associated with the high social position of Nightingale's well-to-do family, but her concern on these occasions is the world of poverty, of "workhouses" and "slums."

13. B. Choice B describes the overall structure, or organization, of the passage. The first paragraph establishes the basic contrast of the passage, that of the conventional view of Florence Nightingale with the realistic view that this passage presents. The second, third, and fourth paragraphs move chronologically from Florence Nightingale's youth, to her preparation, to her first success. Choice A incorrectly claims the entire passage is chronological, but the first paragraph is not. Choice C is completely wrong in describing the point of view; all paragraphs have the point of view of the author; none contains Nightingale's point of view or her mother's. Choice D is inaccurate because all paragraphs use specific detail, not only the third and fourth. The first phrase in choice E is inaccurate; the passage has no first-person narration.

14. E. This final metaphor, as seen in choice E, is the climax of the passage. The author emphasizes the contrast by the parallel construction of the sentence ("it was not a swan . . . it was an eagle"). The sentence is a final instance of the more genteel notion of Florence Nightingale ("a swan") and the author's vision of her strength and power ("an eagle"). Choice A merely explains the transition of time, as "Three more years" allows her family to come to terms with her decision to become a nurse; it is not a climactic climax. The phrases in choice B simply inform the reader that Nightingale gained her independence but on a small, "meagre" scale, which is not climactic. Choice C contrasts the "charitable nursing home in Harley Street" with Nightingale's summers in the country, but that contrast is not climactic. Choice D is incorrect because Nightingale's becoming a "wild swan" from her parental "ducks" may sound like a contrast, but it is not climactic. The final sentence of the passage provides the true climactic contrast.

The draft referred to in questions 15–21 discusses the importance of children's toys.

15. E. The opening paragraph explains how television advertising for children's toys in the 1950s changed children's perception of toys. Before TV advertising, children enjoyed mostly unstructured, unsupervised, and imaginative playtime, but children reacted to TV ads by clamoring for new *things* they thought they *needed* in order to play. Choice E articulates this surprising turn and prepares the reader for the information that follows; thus, it makes an appropriate opening sentence to the paragraph. Choice A is too weak to introduce the entire paragraph; while it may be true that children's playtime can be influenced by the toys they have available, the paragraph actually deals with the surprising change that occurred as a result of television advertising. Choice B is a true statement—children do like playtime—but that idea is irrelevant to the content of this paragraph, and thus it would not make a strong or appropriate opening sentence.

Choice C, which claims that children's play is more important than previously believed, makes a questionable judgment call that is not actually justified from the paragraph. Thus, it too would not make an engaging opening sentence. Choice D presents a true idea; indeed, advertising can change culture, but this idea is simply too general and too vague to be an effective first sentence of the paragraph.

16. D. The first sentence of the passage brings up the way in which children "suddenly" realized they needed specific toys in order to play, and this proposed new sentence reinforces how children "responded in droves" after seeing toy advertisements on the Mickey Mouse Club. Choice D is the best statement of this idea: it reinforces children's desire to get toys they think they need. Choice A wrongly discounts the new addition, claiming the information is redundant; however, the suggested addition is not actually present anywhere in the passage, so it is not repetitive. Choice B also erroneously votes for not adding the sentence, but it is wrong for a different reason; the suggested addition does not distract from the paragraph's point but enhances it. Choice C also votes to not add the new sentence, but for yet another wrong reason. Claiming that advertising budgets are irrelevant today demonstrates a misunderstanding of the importance of how "budgets for *children's toys* soared," and, in consequence, this changed the nature of children's play. Choice E correctly agrees with the addition, but for the wrong reason; whether or not readers can relate specifically to the Mickey Mouse Club does not help advance the passage's point.

17. B. The first paragraph initially states how children responded to the new TV advertising for toys in the 1950s before explaining how, previously, their play had been largely unstructured, unsupervised, and imaginative and improvised. Then the next paragraph marks a shift, claiming that "Play changed quite radically. . . ." The transition "However," choice B, is a perfect choice to alert the reader to this shift in thought. Choice A, "Therefore," makes no sense because the paragraph does not continue the thought of the first paragraph but instead changes the focus. Choice C also makes no sense; "Consequentially" requires a logical flow of cause-and-effect ideas, but that progression is not present in the passage. Choices D and E are off-the-wall ideas; beginning the paragraph with "Admittedly" (D) or "Certainly" (E) is akin to saying "definitely" or "indeed," neither of which makes an appropriate transition for this passage.

18. A. The writer would be wrong in moving the second paragraph to any other location in the passage. It is best located where it is now, choice A. Consider the overall organization. The opening paragraph introduces the main idea of children's toys, and it hints at how television advertising in the 1950s influenced children before exploring how children previously were used to unsupervised and unstructured play. The second paragraph transitions from unstructured play into toys that had a specific use that "began to shrink children's imaginative space." The third paragraph continues this idea by looking at other ways children's imaginations are inhibited, with highly structured and specialized classes, such as karate and ballet. The fourth paragraph moves into the realm of psychology and explores how make-believe play allows children to develop executive function, which increases their ability to learn. Finally, the fifth paragraph explores how the "private speech" that children employ during make-believe play helps develop executive function. The organization is clear, logical, and cohesive, and it would be distracting to move the second paragraph to any other location, thus making choices B, C, D, and E incorrect.

19. C. The third paragraph briefly explores the impact of parents enrolling their children in "karate classes, ballet, music lessons, and gymnastics," claiming the parents' main goal is safety. The paragraph states that while they are safe, these environments tend to inhibit kids' imaginations, so this point would be best contested by affirming that these same activities can serve to enrich children's minds, choice C; instead of inhibiting them, these activities can help children grow and mature. Choice A, that children's imaginations cannot be restricted, may sound like a potential refutation of the paragraph's point but is likely to be wrong in the real world, and therefore this is not a strong answer. One can think of many forces that can inhibit a child's imagination. The idea in choice B is irrelevant; whether or not sales of children's toys have skyrocketed is immaterial to the paragraph's point about parents' desire for a safe environment for their kids' spare time. Choice D, which states that every child uses toys for activities they weren't designed for, is probably true in the real world. However, this does not serve to refute the paragraph's point about safety; it is irrelevant. Choice E does not refute the paragraph, especially when taken in light of the overall passage. Because the overall point is that children need unstructured, creative make-believe time, it would make sense to think that parents who do not enroll their children in special classes are actually enhancing their development, not inhibiting it.

20. A. The sentence in question provides an appropriate conclusion to the fourth paragraph, choice A. The paragraph discusses how children's activities affect their development and how make-believe play enhances executive function. It further explains how self-regulation helps control emotions and behavior while acknowledging that a lack of executive function is associated with negative social behaviors and poor school performance. This final sentence sums it up well, stating that children who have the ability to self-regulate "are better able to learn." The ideas in the paragraph would be left hanging without this conclusion. Choice B may accurately vote for keeping the sentence in question, but its reasoning is weak; the sentence helps concisely conclude the paragraph's ideas, but it is not "vital" to the overall point. Choice C incorrectly votes to delete the sentence and mistakenly states that sentence 13 repeats information in sentence 12; it does not. Choice D wrongly claims the sentence "provides no pertinent or interesting information," when it indeed does by claiming children who can "control their feelings and pay attention are better able to learn." Choice E is wrong for the same reason as choice C; it claims the point has already been made, akin to being redundant, but the point in sentence 13 has not previously been made.

21. B. The potential additional sentence would be best placed between sentences 14 and 15, choice B. Sentence 14 introduces private speech that children use when talking to themselves about what they are going to do and how to do it. Then sentence 15 explains that this self-regulating language helps predict executive function. This additional sentence would provide a logical link between the two ideas by explaining that this self-regulating language is highest during make-believe play, connecting the idea in sentence 14 (private speech) to sentence 15 (developing executive function). Placing the new sentence at the beginning of the paragraph (A) makes no sense because it would discuss self-regulating language before it has even been introduced as private speech. Placing it after sentence 15 (C) also makes no sense and would leave the new sentence hanging, seemingly unrelated to the other sentences. Choices D and E are equally wrong because placing the new sentence after either of these sentences would be jarring and appear disorganized, as it does not relate to the ideas in these final sentences.

Chapter 2

The Free-Response Section

The free-response section of the AP English Language and Composition Exam offers you a wonderful opportunity! This section asks you to write three essay responses, giving you the opportunity to use your own voice, demonstrate how you organize your thoughts, show how your logic works, exhibit how you develop your ideas, and choose what you personally see as the most important aspects in specific pieces of prose. You should relish the chance to shine as you analyze the three prompts on this section of the exam.

The free-response section of the AP English Language and Composition Exam, also called the essay section, requires you to write three essays. You will be given 2 hours and 15 minutes to complete the essays. The suggested time for writing each essay is 40 minutes. The extra 15 minutes are allotted for reading the prompts and passages in the exam booklet and preparing your responses; you may begin writing in the answer booklet as soon as you are ready. Of course, you may jot any notes you want in the exam booklet as you read. You must complete all three essays within the 2 hours and 15 minutes time limit. Each of the three essays is equally weighted at one-third of the total essay score, and the total for the free-response section accounts for 55 percent of the entire AP exam score.

The free-response section always follows the multiple-choice section; it is never the first section of the exam. You will be given an answer booklet in which to write your essays, and it has more pages than you will need. Use your own pen, preferably one with black or blue ink. You may not use a dictionary or thesaurus. You can write the three essays in any order you wish, but the vast majority of students write the essays in the order they are presented. You will identify which prompt you are addressing by writing "1," "2," or "3" at the top of every page of each essay.

Abilities Tested

This section tests your ability to:

- Synthesize material from multiple sources to compose an informed and well-reasoned position on an issue.
- Construct a coherent and convincing argument.
- Demonstrate an understanding of *how* language works in developing ideas and arguments.
- Communicate intelligent ideas in essay form.

You should read the prose passages very carefully and then quickly articulate your ideas. Each essay should be written in approximately 40 minutes.

Basic Skills Necessary

The basic skill you need for the free-response section is the ability to articulate and prove a thesis through concrete examples. You must be able to write on any assigned subject. Your paragraphs should be well developed, your overall essay organization should make sense, and your writing should demonstrate college-level thinking and style. The basic writing format of presenting an introduction, body, and conclusion is helpful, but to achieve a high score, you *must* demonstrate *depth of thought*. Overall, you must show that you can read the prompt and any subsequent passages carefully, plan an intelligent thesis, organize and present valid and sufficient evidence while connecting your evidence to the thesis, and demonstrate college-level skill with your use of language.

Analysis of the Directions

The directions for the synthesis essay (question 1) will ask you to read material from six or seven different sources that all address an aspect of the same subject and then synthesize a discussion of at least three of the sources as you construct your position on the subject. Two sources will be visual, providing a photo, drawing, chart, or graph. The directions for the rhetorical analysis essay (question 2) will ask you to read an excerpt and then construct an essay in which you analyze how the writer's rhetorical choices help create the writer's point. The directions for the argument essay (question 3) will ask you to read a short excerpt or quotation and then write an essay in which you take a position and create a convincing argument based on the subject of the excerpt. Examples and more specific advice follow in "The Three Types of Free-Response Questions," later in this chapter.

Test-Taking Strategies

Remember the following as you practice writing your essays.

- Use the exam booklet to plan your essay. A poorly planned or an unplanned essay frequently reveals problems in organization and development.
- Consider using the standard format with an introduction, body, and conclusion, but do not force a formulaic and overly predictable five-paragraph essay.
- Clearly divide ideas into separate paragraphs; clearly indent the paragraphs.
- Stay on topic; avoid irrelevant comments or ideas.
- Use sophisticated diction and sentences with syntactic variety.
- Be organized and logical in your presentation.
- Be sure to address all the tasks the essay prompt requires.
- Develop your body paragraphs thoroughly with evidence, examples, and your analysis.
- Write as legibly as possible; the AP Exam Reader must be able to read your essay.

The following sections offer more specific strategies having to do with pacing, planning, and writing your essays.

Pacing the Essay

With an average time of only 40 minutes per essay, consider dividing your time as follows and then adjust your pacing appropriately after ample practice.

- **Spend about 10 minutes rereading the topic and the passage(s) carefully and planning your essay.** This organizational time is crucial to producing a high-scoring essay. In the first 10 minutes of your writing time, you need to follow the steps below. Do it efficiently, and you'll know what you want to write and the order in which you'll present your ideas. Although you are given 15 minutes at the beginning of the essay portion to read the topics, do not assume you don't need to skim the content again.

    1. Reread the prompt carefully and underline the specific task(s).
    2. Reread the passage(s) carefully, noting what ideas, evidence, and rhetorical devices are relevant to the specific essay prompt.
    3. Conceive your defendable thesis statement, which will ideally be placed in your introductory paragraph.
    4. Organize your body paragraphs, deciding what evidence from the passage(s) you'll include (using at least three sources in the synthesis essay) or what appropriate examples you'll use from your knowledge of the world. Know what relevant remarks you'll make about the evidence. Understand your body paragraph divisions—when you'll begin a new paragraph and what idea unifies each paragraph.

    The importance of this planning phase cannot be overemphasized. When your essay has been well planned, your writing flows faster, your essay stays on topic and is well organized, and the paragraphs are well developed. You must practice this essential planning step several times before you take the actual AP exam. On the day of the exam, you'll complete this planning in your exam booklet; it has ample space for it.

- **Take about 25 minutes to write the essay.** If you've planned well, your writing should be fluent and continuous. Avoid stopping to reread what you've written. Twenty-five minutes is sufficient time to produce all the writing needed for a good score. In general, most high-scoring essays are at least two full pages of writing, usually more.

- **Save about 5 minutes to proofread your essay.** Reserving a few minutes to proofread allows you time to catch the "honest mistakes" that can be corrected easily, such as a misspelled word or a punctuation error. In addition, this time lets you set the essay to rest, knowing that what you've written is the best draft you can produce under the circumstances. Then you can go on to the next essay prompt and give it your full attention. Don't try to rewrite or heavily edit your essay; don't attempt to move paragraphs around with arrows or numbers; trust your original organizational plan.

Planning the Essay

Your planning and organizing should be done in the exam booklet, which provides space for that purpose. Begin by reading the essay prompt carefully. Underline the key words and phrases of the prompt so that you *thoroughly* understand what your tasks are. Then read any accompanying passage(s) analytically, always keeping the essay prompt in mind. As you read, underline important ideas and phrases that relate to the topic. Your goals while reading are to:

- Understand and critique the author's point.
- Relate the passage to the prompt.
- Begin gathering evidence to support the points of your essay.
- Look for nuances of diction and syntax (for essay topics on rhetorical analysis).

After you've read both the prompt and the passage carefully, you're ready to plan and organize your essay. Again, use the space provided in the exam booklet. Organize your thoughts using whatever method you're most comfortable with—outlining, clustering, listing, and so forth. Planning at this stage is crucial to producing a well-written essay and should provide the following:

- Your defendable thesis statement
- A list of what you plan on addressing in each body paragraph (your topic sentence idea)
- A list of supporting evidence
- The order of presentation for that supporting evidence
- Notes on analysis or commentary to be added regarding the evidence (analysis that connects your evidence both to your thesis and to the essay prompt)

Be careful to manage your time during the planning stage. If you overplan, you may run out of time to commit all your ideas to paper. If you fail to plan sufficiently, you're likely to produce an unorganized essay or one that's not as thoroughly developed as it should be. Remember that you do not have time to write out full sentences for everything that is in the preceding list, with the possible exception of the thesis. Simply jot down phrases and ideas quickly. Your goal here is only to plan the essay; if you do that well, your writing will go much faster. You'll then need only to put it all down on paper in complete sentences, and you'll have produced a well-written essay.

Writing the Essay

A convenient format for essay writing uses the standard structure of introduction, body, and conclusion. The body should be made up of several paragraphs, but the introduction and conclusion need only one paragraph each.

The Introduction

In your introduction, make sure you include a strong, analytical thesis statement, a sentence that explains your main idea and defines the scope of your essay. Also, be sure the introduction lets the AP Exam Reader know that you're on topic; use key phrases from the prompt if necessary. The introductory paragraph should be brief—only a few sentences are necessary to state your thesis. However, do try to establish the importance of the topic, especially the central issue of the argument and synthesis essays.

Readers are aware that the thesis may appear anywhere in the essay, but placing it in the introduction lets the Reader know that you are in control and know what position you plan on defending. The most simplistic introductions merely repeat the prompt and will not earn a point, while the more sophisticated ones, those that do earn a point, engage the Reader's intellect while addressing the prompt with a thesis idea that can be defended. In other words, the thesis that earns a point is not obvious but instead arguable and defendable. The many sample student essays in this book's practice exams will demonstrate a wide range of introductions.

The Body Paragraphs

The body paragraphs are the heart of the essay. Each paragraph should be guided by a topic sentence idea that is a relevant part of the introductory thesis statement, although the topic doesn't need to be stated in the first sentence.

In the synthesis essay, be sure to cite at least three of the sources as you develop your paragraphs. For the rhetorical analysis essay, always supply a *great deal* of relevant evidence from the passage to support your ideas; feel free to quote the passage liberally (but not exclusively) as you analyze. In your argument essay, provide appropriate and sufficient evidence from the passage and your knowledge of the world. Prove that you are capable of intelligent civil discourse, a discussion of important ideas.

Always be sure to connect your ideas to the thesis. Explain exactly how the evidence you present leads to your thesis. Avoid obvious commentary. A medium- to low-scoring essay merely reports what's in the passage. A high-scoring essay makes relevant, insightful, analytical points about the passage. Remember to stay on topic.

AP Exam Readers give high scores to essays that thoroughly develop intelligent ideas. Students who notice more details and concepts in the prompt and present their relevant ideas in articulate, thoughtful prose receive higher scores than those who see only a few ideas to comment on and present them with simplicity. Therefore, strive to make your body paragraphs strong. Generously use examples from the passages, both implicitly and explicitly. In other words, sometimes weave direct quotations and phrases from the prompt into your own sentences and sometimes refer to the author's ideas in your own words. Thoroughly explore and explain the relationship between the text examples you present and your ideas; do not assume the Reader can also read your mind.

Additionally, understanding the writer's rhetorical appeal will help you analyze the persuasive tools the writer uses to sway an audience's response. Three appeals that are commonly referred to are:

- An appeal to **logos** uses logical reasoning, combining a clear idea (or multiple ideas) with well-thought-out and appropriate examples and details. These examples are logically presented and rationally lead to the writer's conclusion.
- An appeal to **ethos** establishes credibility in the writer. Because, by definition, "ethos" means the common attitudes, beliefs, and characteristics of a group or time period, this appeal sets up believability in the writer. He or she becomes someone who is trusted and concerned with the readers' best interests.
- An appeal to **pathos** plays on the reader's emotions and interests. A sympathetic audience is more likely to accept a writer's assertions, so this appeal draws on that understanding and uses it to the writer's advantage.

The Conclusion

Your conclusion, like your introduction, shouldn't be long-winded or elaborate. Even if it is only one sentence, be sure to separate it from the body paragraphs. In other words, do not simply tack your conclusion onto the last body paragraph; this will hurt your organization. Do attempt, however, to provide more than a mere summary; try to make a point beyond the obvious, which will indicate your essay's superiority. In other words, try to address the essay's greater importance in your conclusion. As one AP Reader remarked, "I ask my students to get *global and noble*."

Of course, you should also keep in mind that a conclusion is not absolutely necessary to receive a high score, and many students incorporate their concluding ideas in the last body paragraph. Never forget that your body paragraphs are more important than the conclusion, so don't slight them merely to add a conclusion.

Some Suggestions about Style

On the actual exam, you won't have enough time during your proofreading to make major adjustments to your style. However, as you practice, you can experiment with some stylistic devices that you can easily incorporate into your writing. Remember that top-scoring essays are stylistically mature and relevant to the essay's content, and your goal is to produce college-level writing. Carefully consider the following questions and then practice the suggestions, and your writing skills WILL improve. Remember that you can earn an extra point for sophistication throughout the entire essay, not just in one sentence.

- **How long are your sentences?** You should try for some variety in sentence length. Remember that the occasional concise, simple sentence can pack a punch and grab an AP Exam Reader's attention when it's placed among a series of longer sentences. If an essay's sentences are all of the same length, none will stand out.

- **What words do you use to begin your sentences?** Again, variety is desirable. Try to avoid "there is" or "there are" (or any other dull wording). Also avoid beginning every sentence with the subject. For variety, try such grammatical constructions as a participial phrase, an adverbial clause, and so on.

- **Does every word you use help your essay?** Some bland, vague words to avoid include "a lot," "a little," "things," "much," and "very." Additionally, phrases like "I think," "I believe," "I feel," "in my opinion," "so as you can see," and "in conclusion" are unnecessary.

- **How many linking verbs do you use?** A linking verb (usually a form of the verb "to be") has no action, is vastly overused, and produces unimaginative prose. Replace as many of these as possible with action verbs.

- **What sentence patterns do you use?** Again, you should aim for variety; avoid using the same pattern over and over. Also, try inverting the normal order. For example, try putting a direct object before the subject for emphasis. Poets frequently do this, as illustrated by Edward Taylor's line "A curious knot God made in paradise," which would normally be written as "God made a curious knot in paradise."

- **Are all your compound sentences joined in the same way?** The usual method is to use a comma and a coordinating conjunction (such as "and," "but," or "yet"). Try experimenting with the semicolon and the dash to add emphasis and variety (but be sure you're using these more sophisticated punctuation devices correctly).

- **How many prepositional phrases do you see?** Eliminate as many as possible, especially possessive prepositional phrases. For example, change "the words of Homer" to "Homer's words."

- **Do you use any parallel construction?** Develop your ability to produce parallelisms, and your writing will appear more polished and memorable. Parallel construction also adds a delightful, sophisticated rhythm to your sentences. You can find examples of parallelism in "Terms for the Multiple-Choice and Free-Response Sections" in Appendix A as well as in many of the high-scoring sample essays in this book.

- **Do you use any figures of speech?** If you practice incorporating the occasional use of alliteration, repetition, imagery, and other figures of speech, your writing will be more vivid and engaging.

- **What does your essay sound like?** Have a friend read your essay aloud to you and listen to how it sounds.

- **Is the title of the passage or source punctuated correctly?** Let the punctuation in the excerpt's introduction or description guide you. Also, always place commas and periods *inside* quotation marks in American usage. Only in British English are they placed outside.

- **Do you incorporate quotations smoothly and properly?** Avoid copying entire sentences from the excerpts; instead, for greater sophistication, embed the few essential words you need into your own sentences. Place brackets [ ] around any changes you make in a quotation for grammatical correctness or understanding. In your rhetorical analysis essay, you do not need to refer to line numbers parenthetically; this is a timed essay, not a research paper. Do not merely copy or reference line numbers, forcing the Reader to go back and reread the lines that you should have quoted. Avoid using quotations for every example; put some examples in your own words and only use quotations when you cannot say it as well yourself.

- **Do you merely summarize the excerpt?** Please don't. The Readers are already well acquainted with the passage(s).
- **Do you define technical terms?** Again, please don't. The Readers are extremely familiar with technical literary terminology.
- **Do you add a title to your essay?** Don't. It's not necessary. AP essays never need a title, and they frequently distract the Readers.

Vocabulary

Let's add another word about vocabulary. Of course, the use of sophisticated language is one of your goals, but do not use words you're unfamiliar with. In your practice, look up new words in a dictionary before you use them, especially if you find them in a thesaurus. Of course, you are not permitted to use a dictionary or a thesaurus during the actual exam. Variety in word choice is as essential as variety in sentences, but don't try to overload an essay with fancy, multisyllabic words. Use succinct words that specifically fit your purpose.

Use Strong Verbs

Select your verbs carefully; your choices can help you move toward deeper analysis, or, conversely, they can set you up to merely paraphrase the text. As an experienced AP Exam Reader, whenever I see strong, analytical verbs, I anticipate that the commentary will be insightful. On the contrary, when I see weak verbs, I expect that nothing more than mere summary will follow.

Some strong, analytical verbs include the following:

alludes to	creates	explores	probes
alters	criticizes	exposes	reflects
asserts	depicts	heightens/lessens	refutes
assumes	differentiates	hints at	repudiates
clarifies	dispels	ignites	reveals
conjures	elucidates	illustrates	shifts
conjures up	emphasizes	implies	stirs
connotes	enunciates	inspires	suggests
constrains	evokes	invokes	transcends
construes	examines	juxtaposes	

The following weak verbs merely set up paraphrasing:

basically says	considers	mentions	states
begins	continues	proceeds	tells
claims	ends	saying how	writes
concludes	expresses	says	

The following weak verbs merely point out what is in the piece:

demonstrates	produces	uses
exhibits	shows	utilizes

Scoring of the Free-Response Section

Each of the three essays equals one-third of the total essay score, and the entire free-response section accounts for 55 percent of the total exam score. (Remember that the multiple-choice section equals 45 percent of your score.) A sample scoring worksheet appears at the end of every practice exam in this book.

AP Readers will never know anything about you or your school location. Readers never know what scores your other essays received, nor do they know your multiple-choice score. Each Reader is assigned to read the same question over the entire week of scoring. The Readers do not get to choose which question to read, nor do they change from prompt to prompt.

Each essay is read by experienced, well-trained high school AP teachers or college professors. The essays are scored using an analytic rubric with a scale of 0 to 6. The Reader will assign a score based on the essay's claim and thesis, its evidence and commentary, and its sophistication and complexity. The Readers don't look for or count errors. (A student who doesn't even attempt to write an essay will receive the equivalent of a 0 score, but it is noted as a dash [—] on the Reader's scoring sheet.)

Although each essay prompt has its own analytic rubric based on that prompt's specific requirements, on the whole, high-quality essays encompass four essential points that all Readers look for in every essay. A well-written essay response should be:

- On topic
- Well organized
- Thoroughly developed
- Correct in mechanics and sophisticated in style

Analytic Rubric and Scoring Guidelines

As of the 2020 exam, the College Board is using a 6-point analytic rubric in place of the previous holistic 9-point scoring guide. This change is designed to help give you more precise and explicit information about what will help you earn more points and also what to avoid that would keep you from achieving a higher score. The rubric is also designed to add consistency over the years.

The new rubric for all three free-response essays is divided into three essential areas of composition, labeled Row A, Row B, and Row C:

- **Row A - Thesis: 1 point.** You can earn a point by presenting a defendable thesis; you will not get a point if you do not present a defendable thesis. This is the easiest point to earn; simply include a defendable thesis, and you get the point!
- **Row B - Evidence and Commentary: 4 points.** You can earn up to 4 points by analyzing textual evidence and by providing commentary that is relevant to the thesis and the subject of the prompt; you earn fewer points if your commentary is scant or nonexistent. You will earn at least 2 points in Row B by including textual evidence; read the **"AND"** statement under each point value to understand how to earn additional points.
- **Row C - Sophistication: 1 point.** You can earn a point by demonstrating sophisticated and complex thought and style that are appropriate to the thesis; you will not earn a point if you do not present such sophistication. This may be the hardest point to earn, but you can do so by incorporating at least one of the suggested techniques throughout your essay.

Each row is divided into three sections:

- The **Scoring Criteria** are the actual rubric, which presents specific information about what will earn point(s). The wording for this section will be consistent throughout the years for all three free-response essay prompts.
- The **Decision Rules and Scoring Notes** present relevant information to the specific prompt each year. This will be adjusted each year as necessary and will indicate how students actually performed on any essay prompt. These ideas describe what typical responses demonstrated at each level.
- The **Additional Notes** present supplemental information that clarifies parameters that apply to the scoring.

Sample Rubric for Question 1 (Synthesis)

While this sample rubric is specific to question 1, it is sufficient to give you an idea of what to expect in the other questions. Specific rubrics for each topic are provided for all sample essays in this book.

You can familiarize yourself with the wording of analytic rubrics by reviewing the many rubrics included in this book for each essay prompt. Finally, if you want additional information about this aspect, the website for the AP English Language and Composition Exam includes prompts, scoring guides, and sample essays with commentary for every exam since 1999. Visit https://apcentral.collegeboard.org/courses/ap-english-language-and-composition/exam. Remember that 9-point holistic scoring guides were used until 2020, when the scoring changed to a 6-point analytic rubric. (The College Board website includes adjusted scores and commentary, using the new rubric, for 2018–2019 prompts and sample essays.)

Row A: Thesis (0–1 point)	
Scoring Criteria	
0 points for any of the following: • Having no defendable thesis. • Only restating the prompt in the thesis. • Only summarizing the issue with no apparent or coherent claim in the thesis. • Presenting a thesis that does not address the prompt.	**1 point for** • Addressing the prompt with a defendable thesis.
Decision Rules and Scoring Notes	
Theses that do not earn this point • Only restate the prompt. • Are vague, do not take a position. • Equivocate or merely summarize others' arguments. • Simply state obvious facts rather than making a defendable claim.	**Theses that do earn this point** • Respond to the prompt (rather than restating it) <u>and</u> clearly take a position instead of simply stating pros and cons.
Additional Notes • The thesis may be one or more sentences that are in close proximity to each other anywhere in the essay. • A thesis that meets the criteria can be awarded the point whether or not the rest of the response successfully conveys that line of reasoning. • For a thesis to be defendable, the sources must have at least minimal evidence that could be used as support. • A thesis may present a line of reasoning, but it is not required to earn a point.	

Row B: Evidence AND Commentary (0–4 points)				
Scoring Criteria				
0 points for	**1 point for**	**2 points for**	**3 points for**	**4 points for**
• Simply repeating the thesis (if present). • **OR** restating provided information. • **OR** providing fewer than two references of the provided sources.	• Providing evidence from at least two of the provided sources. • **AND** summarizing the evidence without explaining how the evidence supports the thesis.	• Providing evidence from or references to at least three of the provided sources. • **AND** explaining how some of the evidence relates to the thesis, but the line of reasoning may be nonexistent or faulty.	• Providing specific evidence from or references to at least three of the provided sources to support all claims in the line of reasoning. • **AND** explaining how some of the evidence relates to the thesis and supports the line of reasoning.	• Providing specific evidence from or references to at least three of the provided sources to support all claims in the line of reasoning. • **AND** consistently and explicitly explaining how the evidence relates to the thesis and supports the line of reasoning.
Decision Rules and Scoring Notes				
Typical responses that earn 0 points:	**Typical responses that earn 1 point:**	**Typical responses that earn 2 points:**	**Typical responses that earn 3 points:**	**Typical responses that earn 4 points:**
• Are unclear or fail to address the prompt. • May present mere opinion or repeat ideas from a single source.	• Only summarize or describe sources instead of providing specific details.	• Mix specific details with broad generalities. • May contain simplistic, inaccurate, or repetitive explanations that do not strengthen the argument. • Fail to explain the connections between claims and to establish a clear line of reasoning. • May make one point well but fail to adequately support any other claims.	• Consistently offer evidence to support all claims. • Focus on the importance of specific words and details from the sources to build an argument. • Use multiple supporting claims to organize an argument and line of reasoning. • May not integrate some evidence or support a key claim in the commentary.	• Consistently offer evidence to support all claims. • Focus on the importance of specific words and details from the sources to build an argument. • Organize, integrate, and thoroughly explain evidence from sources throughout in order to support the line of reasoning.
Additional Notes				
• Writing that suffers from grammatical and/or mechanical errors that interfere with communication cannot earn the fourth point in this row.				

Row C: Sophistication (0–1 point)	
Scoring Criteria	
0 points for	**1 point for**
• Not meeting the criteria for 1 point.	• Exhibiting sophistication of thought and/ or advancing a complex understanding of the rhetorical situation.
Decision Rules and Scoring Notes	
Responses that do not earn this point:	**Responses that earn this point demonstrate one (or more) of the following:**
• Try to contextualize their argument, but make predominantly sweeping generalizations (*"Throughout all history . . ."* OR *"Everyone believes . . ."*). • Only hint at other possible arguments (*"Some may think . . ."*). • Present complicated or complex sentences or language that is ineffective and detracts from the argument.	• Present a nuanced argument that consistently identifies and examines complexities or tension across the sources. • Illuminate the significance or implications of the argument (either the student's argument or the arguments within the sources) within a broader context. • Make effective rhetorical choices that consistently strengthen the force and impact of the student's argument. • Develop a prose style that is especially vivid, persuasive, resounding, or appropriate to the student's argument.
Additional Notes	
• This point should be awarded only if the demonstration of sophistication or complex understanding is part of the argument, not merely a phrase or brief reference.	

The Three Types of Free-Response Questions

The exam presents three types of free-response questions: the synthesis essay, the rhetorical analysis essay, and the argument essay. Each prompt will have "stable wording," which means that the directions explaining your basic task will remain the same; only the specific topic for each prompt will change each year. This will give you comfort since you will know what to expect. All of the prompts in this book reflect the prompts you will get on the AP Exam. Become familiar with each type so that you can efficiently and quickly plan your essays on the day of the exam and stay on topic.

- **The synthesis essay:** This essay type presents six or seven sources on the same subject. Two of these documents will be visual (such as charts, photographs, art, or political cartoons). You need to read all the documents carefully and then, using at least three of them, synthesize the various authors' points while intelligently discussing their validity. Therefore, this essay is similar to the argument essay, only it asks you to incorporate more viewpoints from more sources to support your position on the issue. Incorporate explicit and implicit evidence from the sources, plus your own ideas based on your knowledge of the world. Your purpose is to present an intelligent and thoughtful discussion on a subject, acknowledging various viewpoints from the authors, while bringing in your awareness of the world. This is the first essay prompt in the exam booklet, also called question 1.

- **The rhetorical analysis essay:** This essay presents a passage and asks you to analyze the rhetorical and literary choices the author uses to create effect or meaning. Accurately identify the devices and strategies the author uses and evaluate *how* they create meaning. Be sure you understand the effect and author's meaning before you begin writing. Uncertainty results in muddled ideas. Refer to the passage liberally, incorporating quotations into your own ideas. Usually, this is the second essay prompt in the exam booklet, also called question 2.

- **The argument essay:** This essay presents one short passage; read it carefully and formulate an essay discussing your position regarding the author's claims. As with the synthesis essay, you will be well served if you intelligently address multiple sides of the issue and persuasively explore evidence from the passage, while incorporating examples from your understanding of the world based on your readings, observations, and experiences. Usually, this is the third essay prompt in the exam booklet, also called question 3.

The Synthesis Essay

Think of the synthesis essay as a variation of the argument essay in that you will be asked to take a position on an issue and then support it with sound logic and concrete examples. It differs in that you will be given multiple sources to peruse (six or seven instead of one), and you must incorporate at least three of these sources into your essay to earn a good score. Two of the sources will be visual (pictures, cartoons, etc.), and one of these two will be a quantitative source (chart or graph). The synthesis essay is like a mini research paper, wherein you demonstrate your ability to weave different ideas from the various sources into your discussion of the issue.

In crafting an intelligent response to the issue, keep in mind that the AP Readers (high school English teachers and college professors) are impressed by a student who can conduct civil discourse, demonstrating a good understanding of all sides while presenting a position. Avoid both oversimplification and jumping to conclusions. Remember the adage "Judgment stops discussion."

It's okay to let the Reader watch your ideas develop throughout the essay, instead of stating the conclusion up front and then spending the whole essay trying to justify it. Read the topic carefully and keep in mind that you may not have to take only one side in the issue. Frequently, a very good essay demonstrates a thorough understanding of multiple sides of an issue and presents a qualifying argument that appreciates these many sides.

The directions for this prompt will be organized into two paragraphs. The first paragraph will introduce the issue of the prompt and establish its importance. It will define or clarify any terms you may need. The second paragraph will narrow down the directions. You will be directed to read the sources (and their introductory material), then synthesize details from at least three of them into an essay that discusses your position on the issue(s) and examines their validity. Following that, you will find a list of the six or seven sources. Finally, you will see a bulleted list of what you should do in your response; these bullets will present generic guidelines that are reprinted each year. You will be reminded that your position, your stance on the issue, is central and must contain a defendable thesis. You will be reminded to select evidence from at least three of the sources to support your position. You will also be told that you should cite the sources appropriately, whether you do it parenthetically or within your sentences. You can use the author's name (when given), the name or title of the source (when given), or simply refer to it as Source A, Source B, and so forth. You will also be reminded to explain how the evidence you choose supports your reasoning, and, finally, you will be reminded to use appropriate grammar and punctuation.

Here are some specific strategies for writing the synthesis essay.

- While reading the sources, think about the following.
  - Pay attention to the introductory material for each source (enclosed in a box above the source itself). Try to draw inferences about who wrote it, what type of source it is, when it was written (and any related historical context), and what intended audience it may have had. Think about whether this information implies objectivity or bias in the author and/or the source.
  - To make sure you understand the gist and the content of each source, read actively, underlining key points and jotting brief notes in the margin as necessary.
  - Understand the author's attitude about the issue; is it positive, negative, or neutral? Perhaps put a + or – on the page.
  - You know in advance that the different sources will provide a variety of outlooks or attitudes on the issue. Think about this as you read, looking for evidence you can use to support your position.

- Every synthesis topic will include at least two visual documents, such as charts, graphs, photos, advertisements, or cartoons. One of the visual documents will have quantitative information. Carefully interpret the points in these sources and their relationship to the written sources.
- Think about your position on the issue as you judge the validity of each source, looking for examples that will strengthen your argument and counterexamples you can refute or minimize.
- When writing the essay itself, do the following.
  - Don't use only the sources that support your argument. Show that you understand the opposing sides and that you can intelligently dismiss them.
  - Use as many examples as you can from the sources, remembering that you must cite at least three different sources. Citing more sources can help your score if they are accompanied by intelligent discourse, but do not feel obligated to try to incorporate all the sources.
  - Discussing more than one source in any given paragraph helps demonstrate a greater awareness of how to synthesize materials; do not forget that's the name of the essay! In other words, avoid discussing only one source in each of your paragraphs.
  - Show fairness in your essay. Use undistorted language and avoid hyperbole. Also avoid using absolute words that can be inaccurate, such as "never," "only," "all," "must," "will," or "everyone." Instead, use more general terms that are much more likely to be accurate, such as "some," "often," "frequently," "might," "occasionally," or "likely."
  - Incorporate the sources into your essay with sophistication, variety, and style. You can use direct quotations (blending them into your own sentences for greatest effect), or you can paraphrase, summarize, and so forth.
  - Cite the source properly. You can refer to the source parenthetically at the end of your sentence, using either the author's name or the source letter designation, or you can refer to the author and/or the title directly in your sentence. *Always cite the source for every idea or quotation you incorporate.*
  - Embellish and expand your argument with concrete examples from your own reading, observation, and experience. Show that you can relate the issues in these sources to your knowledge of the world.
- Demonstrate your logical reasoning skills. Avoid logical fallacies, such as circular reasoning, non sequitur arguments, or begging the question.
- Be sincere. Show that you find the topic interesting and worthy of intelligent discussion.
- Know your audience. All Readers are high school English teachers or college professors.

A sample synthesis essay prompt follows, along with planning details, the scoring rubric, sample essay responses, and analysis of these responses.

Sample Synthesis Prompt

Online education has been increasingly incorporated into K–12 school districts and college programs in the past decade. In contrast to the many benefits of online education, such as its flexible learning schedule, many people argue that online education is tearing down the stability that has been traditionally found in the school academic structure.

Considering the pros and cons of online education, read the following seven sources (including any introductory information) carefully. Then, write an essay that synthesizes material from at least three of the sources and develops your position on the idea that the effects of online education are beneficial to students and the school system.

> Source A (Smith, D. Frank)
> Source B (Department of Education)
> Source C (Miron)
> Source D (Smith, Nicole)
> Source E (Carr-Chellman)
> Source F (DePaoli, et al.)
> Source G (What After College)

In your response you should do the following:

- Respond to the prompt with a thesis that presents a defensible position.
- Select and use evidence from at least three of the provided sources to support your line of reasoning. Indicate clearly the sources used through direct quotation, paraphrase, or summary. Sources may be cited as Source A, Source B, etc., or by using the description in parentheses.
- Explain how the evidence supports your line of reasoning.
- Use appropriate grammar and punctuation in communicating your argument.

Source A

Smith, D. Frank. "7 Telling Statistics About the State of K–12 Online Learning." *EdTech magazine.* 26 Nov. 2014. Web. 1 Sept. 2017.

The following article, written by a social media journalist, explores the availability of online learning opportunities and mentions some of the reasons for a lack of online educational opportunities in some states.

A new report on the state of K–12 online education shows growth in the world of connected instruction, but some states are still putting up barriers to bringing classrooms online.

"Keeping Pace with K–12 Digital Learning," the 11th edition of Evergreen Education Group's annual study, is a 176-page, detailed analysis on how schools across the country have been incorporating online instruction. The report reaches two conclusions: Students have more online learning options than ever before, but wide gaps remain in how these options are distributed among schools. The report also raises concerns about the lack of studies tracking digital learning activities.

"Online schools and courses are meeting needs for students in those cases where students do not have access to adequate physical school and course options. However, meaningful information and evidence are lacking for most digital learning activity," the report states. "Plenty of examples show that digital content and tools can assist in boosting outcomes, but the broad base of digital learning usage and effectiveness is unstudied."

Different grade levels incorporate online learning techniques in different ways. The online options at the elementary school level are often "deliberately designed to exclude online collaboration with other people," the report states.

High school students are afforded a wider variety of online course options and tools. The level of supervision is also different at the high school level.

"High schools are more likely than middle or elementary schools to have online courses in which the teacher is online, or the teacher of record is in the same building, but does not share a regular class period with students," according to the report.

Just as school policies on implementing online learning vary, so do state policies. Some 30 states and Washington, D.C., have fully online schools open to students statewide, while 20 states prohibit open enrollment in online schools. Various restrictions are not necessarily a result of outdated policies; some are the unintended consequence of strict standards meant to safeguard student data.

"New laws are being considered in many states—and too often are passing—that have the laudable goal of protecting student privacy, but are written in ways that will slow the spread of data usage in ways that will help schools and students," the report says.

Facts About the State of K–12 Online Learning

- **316,320** students attended online schools in the 2013–2014 school year
- **30** states offer fully online statewide schools
- **20** states prohibit open enrollment in online schools
- **26** states offer state virtual schooling
- **16%** of the U.S. K–12 student population is enrolled in online schools, charter schools, or private schools
- **20** states have enacted a combined total of 28 laws related to data privacy in 2014
- **11** states offer online course choice programs

> ### Source B
>
> "Reimagining the Role of Technology in Education: 2017 National Education Technology Plan Update."
> Department of Education, Office of Technology. N.D. Web. 2 Sept. 2017.

The following success story about an Iowa school district was published in chapter 3, "Leadership: Creating a Culture and Conditions for Innovation and Change," in the 2017 National Education Technology Plan Update.

John Carver, Superintendent of Howard-Winn Community School District, faced less than optimal conditions when he initiated a digital learning transformation project modeled on Future Ready Schools. The district was experiencing declining enrollment and was failing to meet the standards of No Child Left Behind in reading comprehension, and almost half of the district's students qualified for free or reduced-priced lunch. Many districts face similar challenges; what set Howard-Winn apart was the district's decision to view failure as an opportunity to learn and improve.

Despite a lack of funding and community reluctance to change, Carver successfully gained support by working closely with teachers, the school board, and the district's School Improvement Advisory Committee to set an ambitious goal: By the year 2020, children in Howard-Winn will be the best prepared, most recruited kids on the planet.[1]

Creating a new brand, *2020 Howard-Winn,* helped Carver communicate the district vision of technology embedded in all parts of instruction, social and online systems of support for district professionals, and active community buy-in and participation. Behind these three pillars are leadership attributes essential to change: the courage to identify challenges and create a sense of urgency; openness to invest time, build trust, and cultivate relationships with stakeholders; and constant availability, visibility, and ownership as the drivers and face of change.

Although the implementation is still in its early stages, the district has acquired 1,300 laptops and implemented a 1:1 program. Teachers are challenged to be digital explorers and are asked to seek professional development opportunities proactively by using technology and to teach their students to be good digital citizens.

Since implementing these measures, student attendance at Howard-Winn schools has improved 90 percent, and a tech-enabled partnership with Northeast Iowa Community College has saved students between $9,000 and $10,000 in tuition fees by allowing district students to access college coursework while still in high school. The district also has seen a 17 percent increase in students meeting and exceeding summative assessment benchmarks. With more than $250,000 in support from stakeholders, the district also has been able to implement sustainable and cost-saving measures such as solar-powered Wi-Fi routers and propane-powered buses. The district has also created and publicized #2020HowardWinn—which reflects their commitment to be a transformed 21st century educational system by the year 2020.

As the district continues to implement its vision of digital learning, Carver says he and other leaders have been driven by the following question: "Do we love our kids enough to stop doing the things that do not work anymore?"

---

[1] John Carver. (2015). 2020 Howard-Winn Admin Update. Retrieved from http://2020hwinnadminupdates.blogspot.com/2015/10/jcc-october-16-2015.html?_sm_au_=iVVZSvStrsDP4TqR

Source C

Miron, Gary, and Charisse Gulosino. "Full-Time Virtual Schools: Enrollment, Student Characteristics, and Performance." *National Education Policy Center*. 2015. Web. 11 Sept. 2017.

The following Executive Summary was published by the National Education Policy Center in its study titled "Virtual Schools in the U.S. 2015: Politics, Performance, Policy, and Research Evidence."

This section provides a detailed overview and inventory of full-time virtual schools. Such schools deliver all curriculum and instruction via the Internet and electronic communication, usually asynchronously with students at home and teachers at a remote location. Although increasing numbers of parents and students are choosing this option, we know little about virtual schooling in general, and very little about full-time virtual schools in particular. Nevertheless, the evidence suggests that strong growth in enrollment has continued. Large virtual schools operated by for-profit education management organizations (EMOs) continued to dominate this sector. While more districts are opening their own virtual schools, district-run schools have typically been small, with limited enrollment. This report provides a census of full-time virtual schools. It also includes student demographics, state-specific school performance ratings, and a comparison of virtual school ratings and national norms.

Current scope of full-time virtual schools:

- Our 2012–13 inventory identified 400 full-time virtual schools that enrolled close to 261,000 students.
- Although only 40.2% of the full-time virtual schools were operated by private education management organizations (EMOs), they accounted for 70.7% of all enrollments.
- Virtual schools operated by for-profit EMOs enrolled an average 1,166 students. In contrast, those operated by non-profit EMOs enrolled an average 350 students, and public virtual schools operating independently enrolled an average 322 students.
- Among the schools in the inventory, 52% are charter schools; together they accounted for 84% of enrollment. School districts have been increasingly creating their own virtual schools, but these tended to enroll far fewer students.
- Relative to national public school enrollment, virtual schools had substantially fewer minority students, fewer low-income students, fewer students with disabilities, and fewer students classified as English language learners.
- While the average student-teacher ratio was 16 students per teacher in the nation's public schools, virtual schools reported more than twice as many students per teacher. Virtual schools operated by for-profit EMOs reported the highest student-teacher ratio: 40 students per teacher.

School performance data:

- Most states have implemented school performance ratings or scores. These have typically been based on a variety of measures combined to produce an overall evaluation of school performance.
- In 2013–14, 28% of virtual schools received no state accountability/performance rating. Of the 285 schools that were rated, only 41% were deemed academically acceptable.
- Independent virtual schools were more likely to receive an acceptable rating than virtual schools operated by private EMOs: 48% compared with 27.6%.
- During the 2013–14 school year, charter virtual schools lagged behind their district-operated virtual schools in terms of acceptable school performance ratings by seven percentage points: 37.6% compared with 44.9%.
- As schools transitioned from the adequate yearly progress (AYP) measure to multiple performance measures under ESEA flexibility waivers, differences in performance outcomes of independent virtual schools and those run by private EMOs continued. In addition, full-time virtual schools continued to lag significantly behind traditional brick-and-mortar schools.
- Only 154 virtual schools reported a score related to on-time graduation in 2013–14. Based on data available in states' annual federal reports, the on-time graduation rate (or four-year graduation rate) for full-time virtual schools was nearly half the national average: 43.0% and 78.6%, respectively.

Recommendations:

- Policymakers slow or stop growth in the number of virtual schools and the size of their enrollment until the reasons for their relatively poor performance have been identified and addressed.
- Policymakers specify and enforce sanctions for virtual schools if they fail to improve performance.
- Policymakers require virtual schools to devote more resources to instruction, particularly by reducing the ratio of students to teachers. Given that all measures of school performance indicate insufficient or ineffective instruction and learning, these virtual schools should be required to devote more resources toward instruction. Other factors, such as the curriculum and the nature of student-teacher interactions, should also be studied to see if they are negatively affecting student learning.
- Policymakers and other stake holders support more research for better understanding of the characteristics of full-time virtual schools. More research is also needed to identify which policy options—especially those impacting funding and accountability mechanisms—are most likely to promote successful virtual schools.
- State education agencies and the federal National Center for Education Statistics clearly identify full-time virtual schools in their datasets, distinguishing them from other instructional models. This will facilitate further research on this subgroup of schools.
- State agencies ensure that virtual schools fully report data related to the population of students they serve and the teachers they employ.
- State and federal policymakers promote efforts to design new outcome measures appropriate to the unique characteristics of full-time virtual schools. The waivers from ESEA present an opportunity for those states with a growing virtual school sector to improve upon their accountability systems for reporting data on school performance measures.

Source D

Smith, Nicole. "An Argument Against Online Classes: In Defense of the Traditional Classroom." *Article Myriad.* 2010. Web. 29 Mar. 2011.

The following excerpt is from an online article about problems with online education.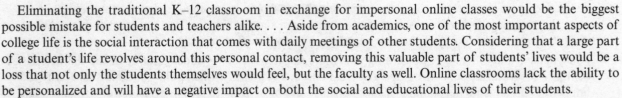

Eliminating the traditional K–12 classroom in exchange for impersonal online classes would be the biggest possible mistake for students and teachers alike. . . . Aside from academics, one of the most important aspects of college life is the social interaction that comes with daily meetings of other students. Considering that a large part of a student's life revolves around this personal contact, removing this valuable part of students' lives would be a loss that not only the students themselves would feel, but the faculty as well. Online classrooms lack the ability to be personalized and will have a negative impact on both the social and educational lives of their students.

Also of importance, students will lose the motivation necessary to actually complete the work necessary since there are no teachers "there" physically to ensure the student's success. "Motivating students can challenge instructors who have moved from traditional to online classrooms. Online student motivation can vary owing to difficulty with content, challenges with access to technology or technology itself, isolation, poor communication with instructors, English as a second language, and lack of connection between content and students' needs" (Beffa-Negrini, 2002). The points made here are certainly worth considering since they are far-reaching and don't just include teachers or students, but learners of different types. Aside from the lost social interaction mentioned above, this problem of motivation on both the parts of students and teachers alike would likely be an issue.

Works Cited

Beffa-Negrini. (November/December 2002). *Journal of Nutrition Education and Behavior.* Strategies to Motivate Students in Online Learning Environments. Vol. 34, Issue 6, p334, 7p, 2 charts.

Source E

Carr-Chellman, Ali. "At What Cost Does Innovation Come?" *Education Week.* 8 Feb. 2012. Web. 12 Sept. 2017.

The following commentary responds to a web-series discussion about the degree to which online learning is beneficial for students.

I have been teaching in an online environment for many years. But it wasn't without great trepidation that I approached the enterprise of online learning in higher education. The research here is pretty clear: meta analyses of empirical research studies have shown that really there is "no significant difference" between online and face-to-face in traditional measures of achievement in most contexts. This is good news, it means that online learning is "working."

While this may be true, there is a great deal of research on the other side suggesting that it will bring on the downfall of the university or school system. David Noble is among my favorite critics of online learning in terms of ways that this enterprise may serve to hasten some very nasty potential results, particularly for the "life of the mind" that has been the hallmark of university life. . . .

I believe that the research will show likewise—that K–12 online learning, when we carefully compare similar groups of children in terms of their achievement scores on standardized tests, will be very similar. We'll find again that there is little or "no significant difference" between the online mode and the face-to-face mode of delivery. But the question, particularly for our public schools, goes far beyond whether it "works." Is it good for us as a society, as a community?

Online learning in K–12 settings is a significant boon for Olympic-level skaters, severe asthmatics, and some ADHD children who really cannot exist within the confines of a traditional school setting for a variety of reasons. And for certain specific applications I can definitely understand the usefulness of this approach and medium.

However, I've been exploring a number of concerns within cyber charters and am quite concerned by several important issues. Did you know some of the following?

- Cyber charter schools have no limitations on the amount of money they can spend to advertise and/or lobby politicians (and these expenditures allow them to remain non-profit).
- Cyber charter populations tend to be bimodal rather than similar to the larger general schooling population with a large number of high achievement and special needs learners.
- Traditional public schools must pay cyber charters for every child who leaves their school for a cyber charter, and in PA alone, this amount now approaches $1 billion (with a B), leaving underfunded traditional K–12 schools.
- There is no real regulation on the ability of parents to include religious education in the regular school day, or to link religious lessons throughout the curriculum of a cyber charter if they wish to. That is, the separation of church and state in these schools cannot realistically be policed.
- Cyber charter schools use a great deal of their money on expensive curricular materials, which are generally published by the same company that owns the "non-profit" cyber charter school.
- There is very little ability of cyber charter schools to monitor cheating.
- Exercising choice for individual achievement in the form of cyber charter schooling will likely leave our most vulnerable children behind in underfunded schools. Research on school choice indicates that parents with more education and better resources are the most likely to exercise choice in any form.
- The CEO of the largest provider of cyber charter curriculum, sold specifically to their own non-profit schools, made more than $28 million last year.

These facts make me very concerned. Is capitalism really the way we want a publicly funded school system to function? I do believe that schools where significant losses of students have led to innovations of their own represent an exciting possibility for the future of school change. But I worry at what cost that innovation comes. If the trade-off is capitalist schooling models that create huge profits, religious education in public schools, unfettered lobbying and enormous advertising budgets within the realm of public schools, I fear we are no longer seeing any service of the public good from public schools, and instead are only concerned about our highest aspirations as individuals and not our greatest successes as a society.

Source F

DePaoli, J., Balfanz, R., and Bridgeland, J. "2016: Building a Grad Nation: Progress and Challenge in Raising High School Graduation Rates." *GradNation.* 12 May 2015. Web. 4 Dec. 2017.

The following chart compares graduation rates at different types of high schools.

Low-Graduation-Rate High Schools, High-Graduation-Rate High Schools, and Average Adjusted Cohort Graduation Rates (ACGR), by School Type, 2014

School Type	Percent of High Schools 67% and Below	Percent of High Schools 85% and Above	Average ACGR
Regular	7%	64%	85%
Alternative	57%	8%	52%
Charter	30%	44%	70%
Virtual	87%	4%	40%

Note: The high schools in the above table have a total enrollment of 100 students or more. "Regular" includes only district-run public schools that are non-charter and non-virtual. "Alternative" includes only district-operated alternative high schools. "Charter" includes only regular (non-alternative), non-virtual charter schools. "Virtual" includes only regular (non-alternative) virtual schools.

Sources: U.S. Department of Education, National Center for Education Statistics. (1998–2015). Public Elementary/Secondary School Universe Surveys. U.S. Department of Education through provisional data file of SY2013–14 School Level Four-Year Regulatory Adjusted Cohort Graduation Rates.

Source G

"Indian Online Education Would Be Worth $1.96 Billion by 2021." *whataftercollege.* 25 July 2017. Web. 6 Dec. 2019.

The following graphic depicts the variety of available online subjects.

Planning Your Response

Before we look at the scoring guide and sample student essays, let's first examine how one can approach this (and any other) synthesis essay using our previously listed suggestions. First, clarify the issue and your position on it. Next, understand what each source says and which ideas you can use from the sources to support your stance. Remember that your essay must reference at least three sources. Consider creating a quick chart to help your organization. The following sample chart is much more detailed (and time-consuming) than you should need. Try practicing with something like this, using abbreviations and phrases that you can easily understand.

The topic: Defend, challenge, or qualify the idea that online education (OE) is beneficial to students and schools.

Create a chart to organize your thoughts:

Source	Brief Summary	Does It Support or Refute the Idea?	What Might I Use?
A (Frank Smith)	30 states offer fully online school 20 prohibit open enrollment 26 offer state virtual schooling 16% of K–12 enrolled in online, charter, or private	Neutral/Both pros and cons	1-more OE options 2-wide gaps in how options are distributed 3-concerns about lack of studies tracking student activities
B (Dept. of Education)	Success story of one district in Iowa Superintendent worked closely w/ teachers, school board, and dist. committee Get 1,300 laptops, 1:1 program, teachers seek pro dev.	Defends/Supports	Attendance up 90% HS students can access college coursework at local CC +17% students meeting and exceeding summative assessments
C (Miron)	Studies full-time virtual schools only (students at home; teachers at remote location) VS = bad performance ratings Much more research and policy adjustments needed	Challenges/Refutes	VS enrollment growing; most enrollment at for-profit organizations (EMO) 52% are charter schools Far fewer minorities, disabled, and English language learners VS have more than twice student-per-teacher ratio EMOs only 27.6% acceptable rating! VS grad rate = half national avg!
D (Nicole Smith/ online article)	Eliminating traditional classroom for OE = biggest mistake; no social interaction; impersonal; possible loss of motivation	Refutes	Social interaction is important, but is anyone really proposing completely eliminating traditional classrooms? Not a strong argument; list of things that can lower motivation is good

Source	Brief Summary	Does It Support or Refute the Idea?	What Might I Use?
E (Carr-Chellman)	Likes OE, but has several worries	Defends but with qualifications	OE great for certain students, but . . . No regulations regarding separation of church and state Charter schools pay big $ for materials that are published by the co. that owns the charter Little ability to monitor cheating More students in cyber charters = leaves most vulnerable students in underfunded public schools
F (DePaoli/chart)		Refutes	Regular HS avg 85% grad rate Virtual schools avg 40%! All other schools lower than regular schools
G (visual graphic)		Defends	Demonstrates the variety of subjects available through online education

After creating your chart, you can then decide which sources you will use and the order in which you'll present your ideas. As you organize, don't forget to group ideas into coherent and logical paragraphs.

Scoring

Row A: Thesis (0–1 point)	
Scoring Criteria	
0 points for any of the following:	**1 point for**
• Having no defendable thesis. • Only restating the prompt in the thesis. • Only summarizing the issue with no apparent or coherent claim in the thesis. • Presenting a thesis that does not address the prompt.	• Addressing the prompt with a defendable thesis.
Decision Rules and Scoring Notes	
Theses that do not earn this point	**Theses that do earn this point**
• Only restate the prompt. • Are vague, do not take a position. • Equivocate or merely summarize others' arguments. • Simply state obvious facts rather than making a defendable claim.	• Respond to the prompt (rather than restating it) and clearly take a position on the idea that the effects of online education are beneficial to students and the school system instead of simply stating pros and cons.

continued

Additional Notes

- The thesis may be one or more sentences that are in close proximity to each other anywhere in the essay.
- A thesis that meets the criteria can be awarded the point whether or not the rest of the response successfully conveys that line of reasoning.
- For a thesis to be defendable, the sources must have at least minimal evidence that could be used as support.
- A thesis may present a line of reasoning, but it is not required to earn a point.

Row B: Evidence AND Commentary (0–4 points)

		Scoring Criteria		
0 points for	**1 point for**	**2 points for**	**3 points for**	**4 points for**
• Simply repeating the thesis (if present). • **OR** restating provided information. • **OR** providing fewer than two references of the provided sources.	• Providing evidence from at least two of the provided sources. • **AND** summarizing the evidence without explaining how the evidence supports the thesis.	• Providing evidence from or references to at least three of the provided sources. • **AND** explaining how some of the evidence relates to the thesis, but the line of reasoning may be nonexistent or faulty.	• Providing specific evidence from or references to at least three of the provided sources to support all claims in the line of reasoning. • **AND** explaining how some of the evidence relates to the thesis and supports the line of reasoning.	• Providing specific evidence from or references to at least three of the provided sources to support all claims in the line of reasoning. • **AND** consistently and explicitly explaining how the evidence relates to the thesis and supports the line of reasoning.

		Decision Rules and Scoring Notes		
Typical responses that earn 0 points:	**Typical responses that earn 1 point:**	**Typical responses that earn 2 points:**	**Typical responses that earn 3 points:**	**Typical responses that earn 4 points:**
• Are unclear or fail to address the prompt. • May present mere opinion or repeat ideas from a single source.	• Only summarize or describe sources instead of providing specific details.	• Mix specific details with broad generalities. • May contain simplistic, inaccurate, or repetitive explanations that do not strengthen the argument. • Fail to explain the connections between claims and to establish a clear line of reasoning. • May make one point well but fail to adequately support any other claims.	• Consistently offer evidence to support all claims. • Focus on the importance of specific words and details from the sources to build an argument. • Use multiple supporting claims to organize an argument and line of reasoning. • May not integrate some evidence or support a key claim in the commentary.	• Consistently offer evidence to support all claims. • Focus on the importance of specific words and details from the sources to build an argument. • Organize, integrate, and thoroughly explain evidence from sources throughout in order to support the line of reasoning.

Additional Notes

- Writing that suffers from grammatical and/or mechanical errors that interfere with communication cannot earn the fourth point in this row.

Row C: Sophistication (0–1 point)	
Scoring Criteria	
0 points for	**1 point for**
• Not meeting the criteria for 1 point.	• Exhibiting sophistication of thought and/or advancing a complex understanding of the rhetorical situation.
Decision Rules and Scoring Notes	
Responses that do not earn this point:	**Responses that earn this point demonstrate one (or more) of the following:**
• Try to contextualize their argument, but make predominantly sweeping generalizations (*"Throughout all history . . ."* OR *"Everyone believes . . ."*). • Only hint at other possible arguments (*"Some may think . . ."*). • Present complicated or complex sentences or language that is ineffective and detracts from the argument.	• Present a nuanced argument that consistently identifies and examines complexities or tension across the sources. • Illuminate the significance or implications of the argument (either the student's argument or the arguments within the sources) within a broader context. • Make effective rhetorical choices that consistently strengthen the force and impact of the student's argument. • Develop a prose style that is especially vivid, persuasive, resounding, or appropriate to the student's argument.
Additional Notes	
• This point should be awarded only if the demonstration of sophistication or complex understanding is part of the argument, not merely a phrase or brief reference.	

Sample Responses

Note: The following sample essays were not written by the student who brainstormed the above ideas.

High-Scoring Essay

Online education is one of the fastest-growing segments of education today; indeed, the rapid rise of online education is unprecedented in the American education system. There is no question that online education is growing exponentially; as more and more school districts offer online options, many more students are enrolled in such online programs than ever before, and these numbers grow larger with the beginning of every school year. However, one must question if such growth is justified. Many experts who have studied online education have come to the same conclusion: Online education does have the potential to offer many benefits, but because of the way it is currently implemented, its overall effect on the participating students, and on their school districts, is detrimental.

One cannot deny that the explosive growth of online education is well-documented. One example is the report "Keeping Pace with K–12 Digital Learning" (Source A), a very extensive report on the state of online education throughout the country. One of the report's two major conclusions is that "Students have more online learning options than ever before. . . ." The report documents the rapid rise in the use of online education across America, but it also reports on one of the many problems that are related to this phenomenon, namely lack of inclusiveness. This issue can be seen in the dramatic geographic disparity; depending on where they live, students in some districts do not have any opportunities to enroll in online education, and yet students in other districts have no adequate option for traditional schooling. As is well documented in "Keeping Pace with K–12 Digital Learning," ". . . wide gaps remain in how these options are distributed among schools." Online learning will not truly serve students well until all students have the same opportunities.

The other disturbing problem in online education is the lack of diversity in the student population. The executive summary of the National Education Policy Center (Source C) explicitly states that, "relative to national public school enrollment, virtual schools had substantially fewer minority students, fewer low-income students, fewer students with disabilities, and fewer students classified as English language learners." Thus, students enrolled in most online education programs lose the opportunity to interact with students who come from different backgrounds; they lose the opportunity to learn and grow and mature in important ways. Furthermore, another major downside of online education is that students lose the opportunity for daily personal contact with other students. This problem is mentioned in Source A that acknowledges elementary school online classes are "deliberately designed to exclude" collaboration with others. Elementary-age students particularly need social interaction; it is an age when kids learn how to work, play, and cooperate appropriately with others. Going even further, Source D reports, "Considering that a large part of a student's life revolves around this personal contact, removing this valuable part of students' lives would be a loss that not only the students themselves would feel, but the faculty as well." Clearly, the isolation that online students face, including few interactions with students of different backgrounds, is a serious issue that weakens the appeal of online education.

Other criticisms of the online education movement are serious enough to warrant questioning the movement's effectiveness for students and school districts. Complaints include the lack of accountability (Source A), the extremely high student-teacher ratio (Source C), the lack of separation of church and state (Source E), and huge percentage of online schools' budgets that is spent on for-profit curriculum materials (Source E). However, of all the criticisms of online education, perhaps most damning of all is that they simply do not do a very good job of educating their students; their students' test performance is sub-par and their graduation rates are dismal. As is evident from the data in Source C, the performance of students in ". . . full-time virtual schools continued to lag significantly behind traditional brick-and-mortar schools." Also, the statistics in Source F show a clear difference in students' outcomes; the average graduation rate for traditional high schools is 85%, but for virtual schools, the average graduation rate is a miserable 40%. Collectively, the data show that online education, especially in full-time virtual schools, needs dramatic improvement before it can be considered beneficial.

While it is certainly true that there are a host of potential benefits that could be gleaned from properly run online education programs, benefits for both the students and for the school districts, this opportunity is unfortunately being squandered. The education establishment in this country must rise to the occasion; they must somehow help the nascent online education industry to overcome these deleterious effects, and thus, begin to use online education as an effective tool to benefit students and districts everywhere in America.

(793 words)

Analysis of the High-Scoring Essay

This student's essay begins with an enticing hint of praise for online education, acknowledging the intense growth in the field. However, the student then takes a turn and strongly states that online education is detrimental overall, given its current flawed implementation. This introduction is engaging and well developed, and it provides a concise thesis. The AP Reader has no doubt which side of the argument this student's essay will develop, and it earns a point for Row A.

The first body paragraph, similar to the opening of the introduction, presents specific evidence of the tremendous growth in online education, citing Source A. Then, also akin to the introduction, the student transitions into some of the "many problems" that online education faces. The student discusses the issues of lack of inclusiveness and geographic disparity in online schools and then concludes the paragraph well with the criticism that students will not be served well until they all have the same online opportunities. This paragraph only includes one source, but it explores the ideas from that source quite well, and it provides ample analysis of that source.

The second body paragraph examines a different objection to online education: the lack of diversity in the student population. The student articulates strong objections to this disparity of representation, acknowledging that without adequate interaction with low-income students, minority students, disabled students, and English language learners, these online participants lose many opportunities "to learn and grow and mature in important ways." This paragraph expands this theme and examines how isolated some online students can become. Particularly troubling to the student is the notion that elementary students' online learning experiences are "'deliberately designed to exclude'" collaboration. The student expresses a valid point about the need for elementary-age students to interact socially with others, to "learn how to work, play, and cooperate appropriately with others"; this is a point that Readers will appreciate. The paragraph continues to expand on this point by including another source, one that laments the lack of personal contact in online education and acknowledges that this isolation is a "serious issue" for the overall effectiveness of online education. This paragraph is very impressive in its development, synthesizing three sources effectively and adding ample analysis of the information in those sources. This student does much more than merely restate what the sources have to say, and it is refreshing for an AP Reader to watch a student process ideas so effectively, as he or she writes under time constraints.

Next, the essay presents another well-developed body paragraph that focuses on other serious criticisms of the online education movement. Masterfully condensing four sources into one sentence, the student outlines pressing concerns about accountability, student-teacher ratio, separation of church and state, and questionable spending of for-profit organizations that make money from buying curriculum materials that they write. If this student had much more time, a Reader can easily imagine what further insightful analysis the student would present regarding these problems. However, the items on this list all effectively and collectively add to the pool of difficulties facing online education. The student continues the paragraph with stronger outcry about the "sub-par" test performance and "dismal" graduation rates in virtual schools. The citation of two sources to back up the student's opinion convinces the Reader that the student is on solid ground. The body paragraphs earn 4 points in Row B.

The conclusion begins by circling back to an idea in the opening paragraph: acknowledging the potential of online education, if only it were properly run. Then, instead of merely restating what has been discussed in the essay, the student looks to the future and explains what education must do: rise to the occasion and begin to use online education to benefit all students and all districts.

The student earns praise for clearly addressing the topic throughout the essay and exploring a serious issue with integrity. The essay's organization is clear and logical, with each paragraph focusing on a strong criticism of online education. The development of ideas is stellar throughout, successfully integrating the source material with the student's own observations and commentary. The student manages to appropriately incorporate five of the seven sources, which is highly admirable. Finally, the student demonstrates a command of language and a style of composition that is pleasing and free of error. The student's writing and thoughts are significant and complex enough to earn a point for sophistication in Row C, for a total score of 6 points, the maximum possible.

Low-Scoring Essay

One of the fastest-growing segments of Education today is the growth of Online Education (OE), which is out-pacing the growth of traditional Education. OE is obviously beneficial to both the students and to their school districts, otherwise, why would it be growing so fast?

A typical example of the benefits of OE is in the reference to the Howard-Winn Community School District in Iowa, Source B. In this case, just one man, Superintendent John Carver, saved an entire school district from inevitable decline. The district faced declining enrollment, they couldn't meet the standards of the No Child Left Behind Act, and half the students were so poor that they qualified for a subsidized school lunch program. Plus, they had a lack of funding and no community support. But John Carver, all by himself, instituted a technology revolution, with 1,300 laptop computers and lots of OE opportunities. The District's statistics went through the roof after everyone realized that OE could save the District.

Another good example of the benefits of OE is found in Source A. The new report is extensive, at 176 pages, and it comes to the conclusion that "Online schools and courses are meeting needs for students in those cases where students do not have access to adequate physical school and course options." This is clear proof that OE is beneficial.

Finally, the writer in Source E, who has been teaching in an online environment for many years says, "This is good news, it means that online learning is "working."

Obviously, all of this evidence points in the same direction, that the growth of Online Education is good, it is beneficial for all students and all districts.

(279 words)

Analysis of the Low-Scoring Essay

AP Readers are instructed to reward the students for what they do well, and upon reading this essay, one can see the student's attempt to discuss the topic and organize paragraphs with some degree of cohesion. However, this essay lacks sufficient development of logical ideas, misreads the sources, and includes some sloppy language and distracting grammatical errors.

The introduction begins poorly, combining weak language with faulty logic. It is far from impressive to read "the fastest-growing segments of Education today is the growth of Online Education (OE), which is out-pacing the growth . . ." with its repetition and circular logic. The student continues to demonstrate fallacious logic by essentially claiming that if something is growing quickly, it must be advantageous. The student appears to have latched onto the idea that online education is beneficial without thinking about it very much. However, the student does present a defendable thesis, and it earns a point in Row A.

The first body paragraph suffers from a fairly significant misread of the passage. The student claims that Superintendent John Carver individually saved the Howard-Winn Community School District in Iowa, but Source B clearly states that Carver worked together with teachers, the school board, and the district. It is also a stretch to say that he "instituted a technology revolution" or that he provided "lots of OE opportunities." While the student is accurate as to the number of computers provided, 1,300, the passage does not address specific online opportunities. The student then engages in hyperbole by claiming that the "District's statistics went through the roof after everyone realized that OE could save the District," which is another factually erroneous claim. Source B states that "The district also has seen a 17 percent increase in students meeting and exceeding summative assessment benchmarks," but the report fails to identify which subjects saw such growth, and this gain, while indeed admirable, can hardly be described as "going through the roof." The student needs to slow down and read the passage more carefully before building a paragraph around such sloppy reading.

In the next paragraph, the student is again reaching for any phrase that will support his or her essay's thesis, regardless of its accuracy. The student bases a global claim of "clear proof that OE is beneficial" on one sentence that is cherry-picked from a lengthy report. Once again, the student is ignoring qualifying evidence in the source and jumping to predetermined conclusions. In addition, this paragraph, only three sentences long, is quite undeveloped.

The final body paragraph, just one single sentence, is anorexic in its development, and, like the two preceding paragraphs, suffers from ignoring much of the original source. The student extracts one quote from Source E that fits the thesis; however, the student fails to acknowledge that the rest of the source presents some serious questions about online education, especially in its funding. The student should not ignore evidence that qualifies his or her point. However, the student does reference three of the sources and so earns 2 of the 4 possible points in Row B.

The conclusion is a run-on, one-sentence summary, which merely repeats what has been said before. By this point in the essay, the Reader is neither convinced nor impressed.

Overall, this student needs to pay closer attention to details while reading the sources and make sure that they do indeed support what the student is presenting. This student does include the required minimum of three sources; however, the presentation is so rife with erroneous arguments and inaccuracies, in addition to being undeveloped and peppered with grammatical errors, that it definitely deserves a very low score. This essay does not earn a point in Row C, and it receives a total of 3 points out of the possible 6.

The Rhetorical Analysis Essay

In your rhetorical strategies essay, be sure to accurately identify rhetorical choices and figurative language the author uses and then examine *how* they create effects and help build the author's point. In your AP English classes, you will likely be introduced to terminology appropriate to rhetorical analysis; this book also offers a glossary of terms you can use (see Appendix A). However, high-scoring essays never merely provide a list of the devices an author uses. Instead, an intelligent analysis must explore the author's ideas in depth and describe how the author's presentation enhances those ideas. Dive into the depths of the author's thoughts and enjoy exploring how such good writing enhances interesting ideas.

You'll want to use the text liberally, both implicitly and explicitly. Sophisticated writers embed phrases from the text into their own sentences during discussion. Avoid copying complete sentences from the text. Rather, you should quote only the exact word or phrase that suits your purpose and analyze it within your own sentences. You do not need to cite or refer to any line numbers provided in the margin of the text.

The directions for this essay will begin by giving you any background information you need regarding the author and the passage. Then you will be told to "write an essay that analyzes the rhetorical choices [*the author*] makes to develop/achieve/convey [*the author's*] argument/purpose/message. Following this paragraph, you will find a bulleted list of what you should do in your essay. You will be instructed to respond to the prompt with a thesis that analyzes the author's rhetorical choices, to select and use evidence to support your reasoning, to explain how your evidence supports your reasoning, to demonstrate an understanding of the rhetorical situation, and to use appropriate grammar and punctuation in your argument.

Here are some specific strategies for writing the rhetorical strategies essay.

- Consider the implications of any information you may be given before the passage's text about the author: the time period in which the passage was written, the author's purpose, the intended audience, and what form of writing the passage presents (letter, speech, book excerpt, and so forth).
- Know what the passage is about and understand its overall message.
- Be sure you understand the author's rhetorical purpose. Is it to persuade? To satirize some fault in society? To express ideas?
- Be familiar with common rhetorical strategies authors use to develop their ideas: description, comparison/contrast, argumentation, exemplification, narration, cause and effect, and so forth.
- Always analyze *how* your examples help create the author's intended effect.
- Use transitions effectively to help your analysis. To introduce examples, use phrases such as "for instance," "for example," or "additionally." Then use appropriate transitions to move your discussion into analysis, such as "consequently," "resulting in," or "accordingly."
- Use verbs that lead you into analysis, such as "the author suggests," "implies," "reveals," "reflects," or "emphasizes." Avoid using verbs that lead you into paraphrasing, such as "the author says," "claims," "mentions," "states," "tells," or "writes."

A Few Words about Satire

Recent language and literature exams have sometimes included prompts that are from satiric and/or comedic works. Students who are not practiced in writing about satire and recognizing the devices of the satirist may be at a disadvantage compared with those who are comfortable with such tools. The subtleties and nuances of satire can sometimes go unnoticed. Some students may find it hard to know how to analyze the rhetorical strategies that satirists use. Although, of course, satirists can employ all of the devices of rhetoric, quite often they make use of caricature, hyperbole, understatement, irony, wit, sarcasm, allusion, and juxtaposition. (These terms are defined in "Terms for the Multiple-Choice and Free-Response Sections" in Appendix A.)

Frequently, satire is characterized as one of two types:

- *Horatian satire* is gentle, urbane, smiling; it aims to correct with broadly sympathetic laughter. Based on the works of the Roman lyrical poet Horace, its purpose may be "to hold up a mirror" so readers can see themselves and their world honestly. The vices and follies satirized are not destructive. However, they reflect the foolishness of people, the superficiality and meaninglessness of their lives, and the barrenness of their values. Alexander Pope's mock-epic poem "The Rape of the Lock" is a prime example of Horatian satire.
- *Juvenalian satire* is biting, bitter, and angry; it points out the corruption of human beings and institutions with contempt, using *saeva indignatio,* a savage outrage based on the style of the Roman poet Juvenal. Sometimes perceived as enraged, Juvenalian satire sees the vices and follies in the world as intolerable. Juvenalian satirists use large doses of sarcasm and irony. Jonathan Swift's famous essay "A Modest Proposal" is an example of Juvenalian satire.

If you do receive a piece of satire to discuss in your essay prompt, be aware of the rhetorical devices of the satirist and use them to your advantage.

A sample rhetorical analysis essay prompt follows, along with planning details, the scoring rubric, sample essay responses, and analysis of these responses.

Sample Rhetorical Analysis Prompt

William Hazlitt was a 19th-century British author, noted for being a literary critic, essayist, philosopher, and painter. The following excerpt comes from his *Lectures on the English Comic Writers,* which was delivered at the Surrey Institution in 1819.

Read the passage carefully, and then write an essay that analyzes the rhetorical choices Hazlitt makes to develop his point about people's sense of humor.

In your response you should do the following:

- Respond to the prompt with a thesis that analyzes the writer's rhetorical choices.
- Select and use evidence to support your line of reasoning.
- Explain how the evidence supports your line of reasoning.
- Demonstrate an understanding of the rhetorical situation.
- Use appropriate grammar and punctuation in communicating your argument.

     Man is the only animal that laughs and weeps; for he is the only animal that is struck with the difference between what things are, and what they ought to be. We weep at what thwarts or exceeds our desires in serious matters: we laugh at what only disappoints our expectations in trifles. We shed tears from sympathy with real and necessary distress; as we burst into laughter from want of sympathy with that which is

(5)   unreasonable and unnecessary, the absurdity of which provokes our spleen or mirth, rather than any serious reflections on it.

     To explain the nature of laughter and tears, is to account for the condition of human life; for it is in a manner compounded of these two! It is a tragedy or a comedy—sad or merry, as it happens. The crimes and misfortunes that are inseparable from it, shock and wound the mind when they once seize upon it, and when

(10) the pressure can no longer be borne, seek relief in tears: the follies and absurdities that men commit, or the odd accidents that befall them, afford us amusement from the very rejection of these false claims upon our sympathy, and end in laughter. If every thing that went wrong, if every vanity or weakness in another gave us a sensible pang, it would be hard indeed: but as long as the disagreeableness of the consequences of a sudden disaster is kept out of sight by the immediate oddity of the circumstances, and the absurdity or

(15) unaccountableness of a foolish action is the most striking thing in it, the ludicrous prevails over the pathetic, and we receive pleasure instead of pain from the farce of life which is played before us, and which discomposes our gravity as often as it fails to move our anger or our pity!

Planning Your Response

Now let's explore both the prompt and the passage, using the specific strategies suggested and jotting down a few of the ideas that are asked for in the prompt.

- **What information can you use from the introductory material?** Hazlitt wrote criticism, essays, and philosophy; the passage is a lecture from 1819. Therefore, it sounds "old and formal." The passage is philosophical, exploring the things that make people laugh and cry.
- **What is the passage about? What is Hazlitt's point? His purpose?** It points out how our ability to cry and laugh at disaster and absurdity in life helps us make sense of the world and keep our balance. Hazlitt wants us to understand why we react to extreme events the way we do, why we cry at tragedy and laugh at ridiculousness.
- **What rhetorical strategies does Hazlitt use?** Comparison/contrast, description, philosophical discussion, and persuasion all appear in this passage.
- **What rhetorical devices can help in analyzing the passage?** "Tone" = animated (exclamation points), reflective, instructive. "Point of view" = mankind needs both tears and laughter. "Stylistic devices" = varied syntax with lots of colons and semicolons, juxtaposition, parallel construction.

Now let's review some key portions of the passage, noting some observations a student might make while reading.

- The first sentence of paragraph one shows how man is different from animals. "Struck" is a strong word.
- The second and third sentences of paragraph one have parallel construction that creates a fast pace ("we" + verb, followed by a prepositional phrase).
- The first sentence of paragraph two expresses a universal idea, and the exclamation point adds emphasis. The short second sentence reinforces this idea. The third and fourth sentences of paragraph two are long, exploring the idea in depth.
- The long last sentence compounds negative ideas ("vanity," "weakness," "pang," "hard") but then ends with philosophical balance: When the "sudden disasters" of life are seen in light of their oddity and absurdity, "we receive pleasure instead of pain." The exclamation point is surprising because one does not expect such an exaggerated punctuation mark.
- The phrase "the ludicrous prevails over the pathetic" is memorable.

Scoring

Row A: Thesis (0–1 point)	
Scoring Criteria	
0 points for any of the following:	**1 point for**
• Having no defendable thesis. • Only restating the prompt in the thesis. • Only summarizing the issue with no apparent or coherent claim in the thesis. • Presenting a thesis that does not address the prompt.	• Addressing the prompt with a defendable thesis that analyzes the writer's rhetorical choices.
Decision Rules and Scoring Notes	
Theses that do not earn this point	**Theses that do earn this point**
• Only restate the prompt. • Neglect to address the writer's rhetorical choices. • Simply describe or repeat the text rather than making a defensible claim.	• Respond to the prompt (rather than restating it) and clearly articulate a defendable thesis exploring how Hazlitt's rhetorical choices affect the passage and create his attitude about people's sense of humor.
Additional Notes	
• The thesis may be one or more sentences that are in close proximity to each other anywhere in the essay. • A thesis that meets the criteria can be awarded the point whether or not the rest of the response successfully conveys that line of reasoning. • For a thesis to be defendable, the passage must have at least minimal evidence that could be used as support. • A thesis may present a line of reasoning, but it is not required to earn a point.	

Row B: Evidence AND Commentary (0–4 points)

Scoring Criteria

0 points for	1 point for	2 points for	3 points for	4 points for
• Simply repeating the thesis (if present). • **OR** restating provided information. • **OR** providing mostly irrelevant and/or incoherent evidence.	• Summarizing the passage without reference or connection to the thesis. • **OR** providing mostly general evidence. • **AND** providing little or no explanation or commentary.	• Providing some specific evidence that is relevant to the thesis. • **AND** explaining how some of the evidence relates to the thesis, but the line of reasoning may be nonexistent or faulty.	• Providing specific evidence to support all claims in the line of reasoning. • **AND** explaining how some of the evidence relates to the thesis and supports the line of reasoning. • **AND** explaining how at least one rhetorical choice in the passage contributes to the writer's thesis.	• Providing specific evidence to support all claims in the line of reasoning. • **AND** providing well-developed commentary that consistently and explicitly explains the relationship between the evidence and the thesis. • **AND** explaining how multiple rhetorical choices in the passage contribute to the writer's thesis.

Decision Rules and Scoring Notes

Typical responses that earn 0 points:	Typical responses that earn 1 point:	Typical responses that earn 2 points:	Typical responses that earn 3 points:	Typical responses that earn 4 points:
• Are unclear or fail to address the prompt. • May present mere opinion with little or no evidence.	• Only summarize or restate ideas from the passage without any analysis. • May mention rhetorical devices with little or no explanation or analysis.	• Mix specific details with broad generalities. • May contain simplistic, inaccurate, or repetitive explanations that do not strengthen the argument. • Fail to explain the connections between claims and establish a clear line of reasoning. • May make one point well but fail to adequately support any other claims.	• Consistently offer evidence to support all claims. • Focus on the importance of specific words and details from the passage to build an argument. • Use multiple supporting claims to organize an argument and line of reasoning. • May not integrate some evidence or support a key claim in the commentary.	• Consistently offer evidence to support all claims. • Focus on the importance of specific words and details from the passage to build an argument. • Use multiple supporting claims with adequate evidence and explanation to organize an argument and line of reasoning. • Explain how the writer's use of rhetorical devices contributes to the student's analysis of the passage.

Additional Notes

• Writing that suffers from grammatical and/or mechanical errors that interfere with communication cannot earn the fourth point in this row.

Row C: Sophistication (0–1 point)	
Scoring Criteria	
0 points for	**1 point for**
• Not meeting the criteria for 1 point.	• Exhibiting sophistication of thought and/or advancing a complex understanding of the rhetorical situation.
Decision Rules and Scoring Notes	
Responses that do not earn this point:	**Responses that earn this point demonstrate one (or more) of the following:**
• Try to contextualize the text, but make predominantly sweeping generalizations (*"Throughout all history . . ."* OR *"Everyone believes . . ."*). • Only hint at other possible arguments (*"Some may think . . ."*). • Examine individual rhetorical choices but fail to examine the relationship among varying choices throughout the passage. • Oversimplify textual complexities. • Present complicated or complex sentences or language that is ineffective and detracts from the argument.	• Explain the purpose or function of complexities or tension in the passage. • Explain the significance of the writer's rhetorical choices for the given rhetorical situation. • Develop a prose style that is especially vivid, persuasive, resounding, or appropriate to the student's argument.
Additional Notes	
• This point should be awarded only if the demonstration of sophistication or complex understanding is part of the argument, not merely a phrase or brief reference.	

Sample Responses

Note: The following sample essays were not written by the student who brainstormed the above ideas.

Medium-Scoring Essay

Two masks symbolize the theater, the one merry and joyful, the other weeping and forlorn. In its turn, the theater acts as a microcosm of life, its twin emblems representative of life's paramount elements: comedy coupled with tragedy.

William Hazlitt explores the relationship of comedy and tragedy, tears and laughter, in <u>Lectures on the English Comic Writers</u>. Hazlitt proposes that, like love and hate, mirth and sadness are not really the opposites that some assume them to be. Apathy is perhaps the true opposite of all four emotions. Both comedy and tragedy are intensely concerned with the human condition. Responses to comedy and tragedy are perhaps our most profound reflexive reactions to the world around us, so it is instructive to examine, as Hazlitt does, the similar foundations of the two.

Hazlitt's enthusiastic tone fits his purpose of persuasion. He writes as if he has just made an amazing discovery and cannot wait to tell readers about his find. The <u>eureka</u> tone of amazed discovery is in part achieved by a liberal smattering of exclamation points throughout the essay, such as "it is in a manner compounded of these two!" and "it fails to move our anger or our pity!" which emphasizes this glee. Exploring the nature of the two responses, comedy and tragedy, to the world, Hazlitt writes that both are spurred by man's perception of possibilities, and disappointment or joy results when these are not met, depending on the gravity or ludicrousness of the situation. The more reflective tone at this point serves Hazlitt's purpose well. Indeed, comedy often issues from the wellsprings of tragedy and hurt. Laughter can be a defense mechanism, a protective response to the realities of the world and an opportunity to mock the frightening rather than cower before it.

Hazlitt's point of view has arguably become a part of the conventional wisdom these days. Comedy and tragedy are two sides of the same coin, he asserts. Comedy is made up of trifling tragedies. Not serious enough to wound, they instead inspire ridicule and heckling. Confusion can exist between the emotions: People often cry tears of joy on happy occasions or laugh inappropriately in the face of despair. Hazlitt successfully persuades readers of the inexorable relationship between the emotions.

Hazlitt's prose is brisk, almost breathless. Even though compounded with prepositional phrases and the like, the first paragraph of his essay speeds along with emphasized repetition: "We weep . . . we laugh . . . we shed tears . . . we burst into laughter." Hazlitt keeps the reader to a relentless pace with a series of phrases and clauses separated by commas and semicolons, filling long complex sentences. His last sentence in the essay effectively uses technique as it builds to a crescendo. It piles many negative ideas on top of one another before leaving us with the pleasing idea that we need laughter to give us "pleasure instead of pain from the farce of life." This technique of building negativity and then balancing it helps persuade the reader that Hazlitt's conclusions are valid.

Hazlitt's skillful, rhythmic writing seems capable of lulling readers into believing anything he asserts. He accomplishes his purpose with an enthusiastic passage that clearly demonstrates the inseparable connection between laughter and tears. Understand that, and we are well on our way to understanding life.

(555 words)

Analysis of the Medium-Scoring Essay

This well-written essay begins with two paragraphs that immediately spark the AP Exam Reader's interest, mentioning the comic and tragic masks of the theater and then effectively relating the theater, as a "microcosm of life," to the essay's content and to the topic question. The introduction has no thesis statement, but that isn't an absolute requirement in the introduction. Because the student's thesis is found in "one or more sentences throughout the essay," it earns a point in Row A. This student is definitely on the right track, addressing the issue of Hazlitt's purpose and his means of achieving it.

The next two paragraphs explore Hazlitt's point of view, his success in achieving his purpose, and his perception of comedy and tragedy, relating that perception to contemporary society's ideas. Some textual evidence is presented in the paragraph that discusses tone—for example, noting that Hazlitt's use of exclamation points produces a "tone of amazed discovery." However, no specific examples are used in the brief point-of-view paragraph. In any case, both of these paragraphs serve the student's purpose well; they clearly analyze Hazlitt's ideas.

The fifth paragraph presents an analysis of Hazlitt's technique and style, noting the use of repetition and aptly describing the essay's pace as "breathless . . . relentless." This student demonstrates an accurate understanding of how a writer's technique can produce a specific effect on the reader, especially in the analysis of Hazlitt's last sentence, which the student aptly notes "builds to a crescendo." The body paragraphs are sufficient to earn 3 points out of 4 in Row B.

The concluding paragraph reiterates the relationship of Hazlitt's "rhythmic writing" to his purpose but doesn't stop at mere summary. It points to the essay's wider implication—that through understanding laughter and tears, we can broaden our understanding of life. This student, like Hazlitt, demonstrates both lively style and discriminating diction, but not enough to earn a point in Row C. The essay would receive a total score of 4; it is not as thorough as a top-scoring essay.

Medium-Low-Scoring Essay

William Hazlitt begins by describing the differences between humans and animals. He writes that man has the emotions of humor and sadness that animals don't because men see that things aren't always as good as they could be.

Sometimes people laugh, and sometimes people cry about life, depending on the situation. Through Hazlitt's use of tone and stylistic devices he achieves his purpose to convince the reader that comedy and tragedy spring from the same well of emotion and essentially help mankind to cope with the vicissitudes of life. People just react to life in different ways.

Depending on people and situations, this can be true. "It is a tragedy or a comedy—sad or merry, as it happens," Hazlitt wrote, showing that people can and do react in a different way to the same event. One of Hazlitt's reasons for writing is to prove that mankind needs different reactions; it is part of man's defense mechanism.

Hazlitt's tone tries to educate people about laughing and crying. Perhaps this is so people can feel less self conscious and work together better in the future without worrying whether their response is right or not, since there isn't a lot of difference between comedy and tragedy. So where one person might see one thing as tragic, the other person may not.

Hazlitt uses many literary devices so readers can picture the differing details of comedy and sadness he discusses. He says tragedy can "shock and wound the mind." He describes tears of relief about comedy or happy times without tragedy. He also uses repetition and exclamation to achieve his purpose. Readers now understand the relationship of comedy and tragedy, and agree with his conclusions.

(282 words)

Analysis of the Medium-Low-Scoring Essay

This essay clearly demonstrates areas in which a student writing under time pressure can make mistakes. This paper has a variety of problems in coherence, organization, diction, and proof.

The first paragraph fails to elicit much excitement. A good AP essay doesn't necessarily have to grab attention, but this one is particularly uninteresting, merely paraphrasing Hazlitt's opening comment on humans and animals. The second paragraph improves somewhat. The student attempts to identify Hazlitt's purpose. But while the statement is well worded, it does not yet deal with one of the assigned tasks, a discussion of Hazlitt's technique. The student eventually produces a defendable thesis, earning a point in Row A.

The third and fourth paragraphs discuss Hazlitt's contentions, but perfunctorily and without great insight. Although Hazlitt's tone is mentioned at the beginning of the fourth paragraph, no analysis or examples follow. Weaknesses of this sort usually arise from inadequacies in planning and organization.

The last paragraph finally addresses literary devices and lists "repetition and exclamation," but once again, no evidence follows proving the connection between literary devices and purpose. Here, the student seems to be grasping for ideas and unsure of his or her point. The body paragraphs deserve 2 points out of 4 in Row B.

While this essay shows some understanding of Hazlitt's purpose, which is to be commended, attempts at proof, analysis, and discussion produce confused sentences with murky ideas. In addition, the student's language, while occasionally sophisticated, is more often than not simplistic. It cannot earn a point in Row C. Overall, the essay fails to convince the AP Exam Reader. It deserves a score of 3.

The Argument Essay

Keep in mind that the argument and the synthesis essays are similar in intent; they both give you the opportunity to present your position on an issue. In this section, we'll exclusively examine the argument essay.

The argument essay will be based on one brief passage or statement from an author. Occasionally, you may be presented with opposing statements from two authors, or even a brief summary of ideas from three authors. You will usually be given some information about the author(s), the passage source(s), the audience, or other relevant material. The passage itself may be a short paragraph, a single quotation, an anecdote, or some other brief work. In that regard, this will be the fastest of the three topics to read, but it provides you with the least material to support your essay. You therefore have to garner examples from your own reading, observation, and experience.

Your task is to evaluate the argument's point(s) and then take a position that either defends, challenges, or qualifies that point, using concrete examples and clear logic to make your case. In this essay, demonstrate your awareness of culture, history, philosophy, and politics. Establish that you are in touch with your own society and with the larger world around you. These topics give you the opportunity to intelligently discuss issues; seize that opportunity and make the most of it.

The directions for the argument prompt will begin with pertinent background information, followed by a short quotation. In the following paragraph, you will be directed to write an essay that argues your position on the author's claim. You will then see a bulleted list of what you should do in your essay. You will be reminded to respond to the prompt with a defendable thesis, to provide evidence to support your line of reasoning, to explain how the evidence supports your reasoning, and to use appropriate grammar and punctuation.

Here are some specific strategies for writing the argument essay.

- Read carefully the introductory information about the author, the passage's source, and so forth. Note items that you can use to your advantage in your essay.
- Clarify precisely what the issue is and what the author's position is.
- Articulate clearly your position on the issue. Of course, it's acceptable to agree with an issue in some circumstances and disagree in others, but do not be wishy-washy. Take your position and make it clear.
- Use concrete examples from your own readings, observations, and experiences. You can select examples from world history to current events; you can draw from everything you have ever read, known of, or experienced. Organize your thoughts coherently and integrate your examples with style.
- Demonstrate your logical reasoning skills. Avoid logical fallacies, such as circular reasoning, non sequitur arguments, or begging the question.
- Be fair in your essay. Use undistorted language and avoid hyperbole. Avoid using absolute words that may be inaccurate, such as "never," "only," "all," "must," "will," or "everyone." Instead, use more general qualifying terms that are likely to be more accurate, such as "some," "often," "frequently," "might," "occasionally," or "likely."
- Be sincere. Show that you find the topic interesting and worthy of intelligent discussion.
- Know your audience. All AP Readers are high school English teachers or college professors.

A sample argument essay prompt follows, along with planning details, the scoring rubric, sample essay responses, and analysis of these responses.

Sample Argument Prompt

The British author Fanny Burney (1752–1840) was noted for being a novelist, diarist, and playwright. She became Mme d'Arblay upon her marriage to a French exile in 1793. Known for her social commentary, she wrote in her novel *Camilla* (1796), "there is nothing upon the face of the earth so insipid as a medium. Give me love or hate! a friend that will go to jail for me, or an enemy that will run me through the body!"

Write an essay that argues your position on Burney's assertion about extremes. In your response you should do the following:

- Respond to the prompt with a thesis that presents a defensible position.
- Provide evidence to support your line of reasoning.
- Explain how the evidence supports your line of reasoning.
- Use appropriate grammar and punctuation in communicating your argument.

Planning Your Response

Now let's explore the prompt and Burney's quotation, using the first four specific strategies listed above, and jot down a few ideas. (The remaining four strategies will help more with writing the essay, not with the brainstorming portion of your planning.)

- **How can the introductory material help guide your ideas?** Fanny Burney was known for social commentary. Although the quotation is more than 200 years old, it is still relevant today.
- **What is the issue in the prompt?** The author dislikes things that are middle-of-the-road, calling them "insipid." She prefers people who show extremes, such as love and hate. It is likely that she is referring to people being honest with others and to the way people are drawn to things at the far end of any spectrum.

- **What is your stance on the issue?** I agree that people are attracted by extremes.
- **What concrete examples can you use?** Now's the time to brainstorm from your observations, readings, and/or experiences.
    1. Extreme personalities get publicity: Lord Byron, Charles Manson, Kanye West, Lady Gaga.
    2. Extreme events are remembered: French and American revolutions, Japanese earthquake and tsunami, Hurricane Harvey.
    3. Extreme acts are remembered: Kirk Gibson's improbable home run in the 1988 World Series, a student protester stands up to tanks in Tiananmen Square, the attacks of 9/11. Maybe use the quote, "It was the best of times, it was the worst of times. . . ."
    4. Humanity is "attracted" to extreme things: car crashes or fights, "extreme" TV shows like *Deadliest Catch,* big weddings like Meghan Markle and Prince Harry's.
    5. I'm a teenager! We're known for extremes in clothing, emotions, language, music. We like to be thought of as "out there."
- **How is it best to organize?** I like my five categories, but I can't write it all in a timed essay. I'll use the ideas from (1), (3), and (4), in that order.

Scoring

Row A: Thesis (0–1 point)	
Scoring Criteria	
0 points for any of the following:	**1 point for**
• Having no defendable thesis. • Only restating the prompt in the thesis. • Only summarizing the issue with no apparent or coherent claim in the thesis. • Presenting a thesis that does not address the prompt.	• Addressing the prompt with a defendable thesis.
Decision Rules and Scoring Notes	
Theses that do not earn this point	**Theses that do earn this point**
• Only restate the prompt. • Are vague or do not take a position. • Simply state obvious facts rather than making a defendable claim.	• Respond to the prompt (rather than restating it) and clearly evaluate the validity of Burney's assertion about extremes instead of simply stating pros and cons.
Additional Notes	
• The thesis may be one or more sentences that are in close proximity to each other anywhere in the essay. • A thesis that meets the criteria can be awarded the point whether or not the rest of the response successfully conveys that line of reasoning. • A thesis may present a line of reasoning, but it is not required to earn a point.	

Row B: Evidence AND Commentary (0–4 points)

Scoring Criteria

0 points for	1 point for	2 points for	3 points for	4 points for
• Simply repeating the thesis (if present). • **OR** restating provided information. • **OR** providing mostly irrelevant and/or incoherent examples.	• Summarizing the passage without reference or connection to the thesis. • **OR** providing mostly general evidence. • **AND** providing little or no explanation or commentary.	• Providing some specific evidence that is relevant to the thesis. • **AND** explaining how some of the evidence relates to the thesis, but the line of reasoning may be nonexistent or faulty.	• Providing specific evidence to support all claims in the line of reasoning. • **AND** explaining how some of the evidence relates to the thesis and supports the line of reasoning.	• Providing specific evidence to support all claims in the line of reasoning. • **AND** providing well-developed commentary that consistently and explicitly explains the relationship between the evidence and the thesis.

Decision Rules and Scoring Notes

Typical responses that earn 0 points:	Typical responses that earn 1 point:	Typical responses that earn 2 points:	Typical responses that earn 3 points:	Typical responses that earn 4 points:
• Are unclear or fail to address the prompt. • May present mere opinion with little or no relevant evidence.	• Only summarize or restate ideas from the passage without any analysis.	• Mix specific details with broad generalities. • May contain simplistic, inaccurate, or repetitive explanations that do not strengthen the argument. • Fail to explain the connections between claims and to establish a clear line of reasoning. • May make one point well but fail to adequately support any other claims.	• Consistently offer evidence to support all claims. • Focus on the importance of specific words and details to build an argument. • Use multiple supporting claims to organize an argument and line of reasoning. • May not integrate some evidence or support a key claim in the commentary.	• Engage specific evidence to draw conclusions. • Focus on the importance of specific details to build an argument. • Use multiple supporting claims with adequate evidence and explanation to organize an argument and line of reasoning.

Additional Notes

• Writing that suffers from grammatical and/or mechanical errors that interfere with communication cannot earn the fourth point in this row.

Row C: Sophistication (0–1 point)	
Scoring Criteria	
0 points for	**1 point for**
• Not meeting the criteria for 1 point.	• Exhibiting sophistication of thought and/or advancing a complex understanding of the rhetorical situation.
Decision Rules and Scoring Notes	
Responses that do not earn this point:	**Responses that earn this point demonstrate one (or more) of the following:**
• Try to contextualize their argument, but make predominantly sweeping generalizations (*"Throughout all history . . ."* OR *"Everyone believes . . ."*). • Only hint at other possible arguments (*"Some may think . . ."*). • Present complicated or complex sentences or language that is ineffective and detracts from the argument.	• Present a nuanced argument that consistently identifies and examines complexities or tension across the sources. • Illuminate the significance or implications of the argument (either the student's argument or the arguments within the sources) within a broader context. • Make effective rhetorical choices that consistently strengthen the force and impact of the student's argument. • Develop a prose style that is especially vivid, persuasive, resounding, or appropriate to the student's argument.

Additional Notes

• This point should be awarded only if the demonstration of sophistication or complex understanding is part of the argument, not merely a phrase or brief reference.

Sample Responses

Note: The following sample essays were not written by the student who brainstormed the above ideas.

High-Scoring Essay

Our fascination with extremes is a phenomenon that is unexplainable by any biological method—we have no genuine need for it, and yet Fanny Burney is accurate; this purely human condition is prevalent in nearly all of us. Burney implies a psychological explanation, simple yet multifaceted. In essence, we simply find the extreme to be more interesting. We cannot rely on any scientific techniques to measure such an abstract concept. But perhaps the most effective way to relate Burney's assertion to current public opinion is to look at the press's choices in content. When considering the stories covered by the press, while we are actually looking at events or people which an editorial staff deems newsworthy, in the interest of sales and advertising profits, we can assume that the media caters to the public's interests. Clearly, news about the best or the worst in our world sells. Clearly, the major headlines generating the most interest have all been the result of some sort of extreme. Plane crashes involving hundreds of lives lost, baseball players booming baseballs farther and more frequently, stock market jumps that affect everyone—these are the most readable, most interesting stories. Not the car crash that injured a twenty-five-year-old man (though it may be just as heart-wrenching); not the consistent .330 batting average of a seasoned baseball veteran (though it may be just as difficult to achieve); and certainly not the steady conglomerate (though it may be just as profitable). Certainly, our hearts and minds gravitate to stories and people that pique our interest.

Hollywood, especially, gears its entertainment to fulfilling this interest. We love to watch the over-the-top, clever, and cruel arch-villains who plot to take over the universe, and the overly saccharine brave young heroes who valiantly stop their plans (and win the damsel in distress while they're at it). Even ordinary Clark Kent became the strong Superman, perhaps convincing us that we too, would be able to fly, have x-ray vision, and save the world from any evil nemesis. It appears we want movies to represent extremes of good and evil, not just some "insipid" everyman. And certainly, this interest in the extreme is not a recent phenomenon. If we go back to Shakespeare's work, considered by many to be the archetypal settings and characters for so many stories to come, we see that Burney's comment holds no less truth. For instance, in *Hamlet,* we have Horatio, "a friend that will go to jail for me" and Polonius, "an enemy that will run me through the body," occupying different extremes. There can be no medium in effective drama, for our imaginations and emotions feed off characters and conflicts that are more grandiose than our daily lives. It's what the audience wants; it's what the playwright delivers.

Our insistent need for the extreme serves no harmful purpose. Indeed, it has shaped our modern conceptions of drama, comedy, and news, helping us define our psychological boundaries and sparking the imaginations of generations to come.

(498 words)

Analysis of the High-Scoring Essay

The student who wrote this high-scoring essay has a firm grasp of the topic and a clear view of the world. He or she appropriately uses examples from the news media, Hollywood cinema, and Shakespearean drama to prove that Fanny Burney's quotation is an accurate perception of humanity; we do relish extremes over the mediocre. Its defendable thesis earns a point in Row A.

The first paragraph blends the introductory material and its effective thesis into a body paragraph that explores the current state of print journalism. Although the student does not use specific existing headlines or news stories as examples, he or she does not need to—the universal point here is that the news media depicts the extremes in life, and the "generic" examples that are presented here work very well. Plane crashes, unthinkable baseball achievements, and the excessive ups and downs of the stock market are all examples that the AP Exam Reader can relate to and easily connect to the student's point. The student also slips in a legitimate business rationale for these types of stories: Not only does the public crave them, but the paper also profits by them. This paragraph, nicely on topic, focuses on observations of our modern life and convinces the Reader that the media does present extremes in the news, which in turn reflects humanity's desire for such sensationalism.

The next paragraph explores Hollywood movies and Shakespearean drama, again effectively using both to prove that humanity craves extremes in fictional characters. Everyone knows so well the "cruel arch-villain" and the "brave young hero" that Hollywood exaggerates. The student's declaration that we would all like to become a Superman and "save the world from any evil nemesis" both rings true and helps prove Burney's assertion. Middle-of-the-road personalities do not save the world; extreme ones do.

The student's use of *Hamlet* gives the essay a sophisticated and cultured flair, not merely because it is an accurate Shakespearean reference but because it also proves the student is well read and well rounded. It helps balance the previous contemporary examples in the essay. Perhaps the *Hamlet* discussion could be developed more, explaining how Horatio and Polonius exemplify these extremes in character, but an essay that is written under timed pressure cannot always elaborate as much as an untimed one. Remember that the Reader will reward the student for what he or she does well, and this student proves his or her point admirably. The quality of the body paragraphs earns the maximum of 4 points in Row B.

This essay earns its high score through the development of its clear and relevant ideas as well as its abundant examples, strong organization, and commendable control of written English. The sense of rhythm found in parallel construction that is so pleasing to the ear can be observed in such areas as the repetition of the word "clearly" to begin two sentences, the parenthetical "though it may be . . ." phrasing in the first paragraph, and in the sentence, "It's what the audience wants; it's what the playwright delivers" in the second paragraph. Although parallelism is never a specific requirement, any student who effectively uses such sophisticated devices will demonstrate a sense of style that shines through to the Reader. The essay's strong style deserves a point in Row C, and the total score of 6 is warranted.

Low-Scoring Essay

We can't help but be interested by extremes. They represent both the bad and the good of life and are interesting simply because they differ from the typical person. Like scientists who also are interested in differences from the standard, we classify and thus notice these differences. For example, the world records in running have, time and time again, deserved media coverage while the average speed of a typical healthy males may perhaps be an obscure fact. Our societies focus on the individual inevitably results in the few strongest, smartest, quickest being not only isolated but at times revered. The opposite side of the spectrum is similarly true. The publics fascination with, for example, a cereal killer, is only rivaled by its fascination with the fireman who saved twenty lives. Everything in between (with varying degrees), is ordinary and, as Fanny Burney wrote, "insipid."

Perhaps our dedication to seeking out the extremes in life represents our own struggle to find who we are. Extremes provide a watermark to our own situation. Are we that "friend that will go to jail for me" or the "enemy that will run me through the body?" We are most likely in between. But are fascination with this scale is a symbol of our dreams. We certainly cannot achieve such heights (or such lows) but we can often live vicariously through these extreme individuals.

(229 words)

Analysis of the Low-Scoring Essay

This essay attempts to agree with Burney's assertion. However, it does not make a strong point in doing so, nor does it actually convince the AP Exam Reader. Simply stated, because of its brevity, the essay is not fulfilling. The example with which the student begins, that of track-and-field world records, does not work particularly well; it appears that the student has not thought it through. After all, it *does* make sense that a new world record would "deserve media coverage," while at the same time the "average speed of a typical, healthy male" would not. This average statistical information can be obtained, but it is not particularly newsworthy, so the example does not make much sense to the Reader. The later example of the public's fascination with murderers and heroes is more logically sound, but it is not enough to save the entire paragraph from mediocrity. The semblance of a thesis earns a point in Row A.

The second paragraph appears to be a hastily drawn conclusion; it certainly offers no new examples or ideas to support the student's thesis. Although it may be philosophically interesting to ponder how "seeking out the extremes in life represents our own struggle to find who we are," it does not persuade the Reader of the validity of Burney's assertion and therefore falls flat. This paragraph does not meet the requirement in the directions—namely, using "appropriate evidence" to support ideas. It needs stronger organization and development. It earns just 1 point in Row B.

The large number of diction and grammatical mistakes also hurts this essay's score. Although the Readers want to reward the student for what he or she does well, they simply cannot ignore so many errors. Notice the first two sentences. The student claims we are interested "*by*" extremes (an unidiomatic expression to start), then claims "they differ from the typical person," which is not possible. One cannot logically compare "extremes" to "people." Notice also the number agreement problem in the phrase "speed of *a* typically healthy *males*."

The student also has many diction and/or punctuation mistakes, such as "societies" instead of "society's," "publics" without its apostrophe, and "cereal" instead of "serial." The homophone confusion of using "are" instead of "our" strikes the Reader as yet another careless error. Although a Reader can disregard minor mistakes here and there, this essay is riddled with far too many errors to disregard without affecting the score. It clearly fails to earn a point in Row C.

The essay earns a low total score of 2 because of its combination of being barely on topic, having weak development, displaying ineffectual organization, and exhibiting numerous mechanical errors.

Diagnostic Mini-Test

Answer Sheet

Section I: Multiple-Choice Questions

1 Ⓐ Ⓑ Ⓒ Ⓓ Ⓔ
2 Ⓐ Ⓑ Ⓒ Ⓓ Ⓔ
3 Ⓐ Ⓑ Ⓒ Ⓓ Ⓔ
4 Ⓐ Ⓑ Ⓒ Ⓓ Ⓔ
5 Ⓐ Ⓑ Ⓒ Ⓓ Ⓔ

6 Ⓐ Ⓑ Ⓒ Ⓓ Ⓔ
7 Ⓐ Ⓑ Ⓒ Ⓓ Ⓔ
8 Ⓐ Ⓑ Ⓒ Ⓓ Ⓔ
9 Ⓐ Ⓑ Ⓒ Ⓓ Ⓔ
10 Ⓐ Ⓑ Ⓒ Ⓓ Ⓔ

11 Ⓐ Ⓑ Ⓒ Ⓓ Ⓔ
12 Ⓐ Ⓑ Ⓒ Ⓓ Ⓔ
13 Ⓐ Ⓑ Ⓒ Ⓓ Ⓔ
14 Ⓐ Ⓑ Ⓒ Ⓓ Ⓔ
15 Ⓐ Ⓑ Ⓒ Ⓓ Ⓔ

16 Ⓐ Ⓑ Ⓒ Ⓓ Ⓔ
17 Ⓐ Ⓑ Ⓒ Ⓓ Ⓔ

CUT HERE

Section II: Free-Response Question

_____
_____
_____
_____
_____
_____
_____
_____
_____
_____
_____
_____
_____
_____
_____
_____
_____
_____
_____
_____
_____
_____
_____
_____
_____
_____
_____
_____
_____

CUT HERE

CUT HERE

CUT HERE

CUT HERE

CUT HERE

Questions

Section I: Multiple-Choice Questions

Time: 15 minutes

17 questions

Directions: This section contains a selection from a prose work with questions about its content, style, and form, plus a draft passage with questions about improving its content and clarity. Read each section carefully. For each question, choose the best answer of the five choices.

This excerpt for questions 1–10 is taken from a 1981 book that explores specific American communities.

On Route 301 south of Tampa, billboards advertising Sun City Center crop up every few miles, with pictures of Cesar Romero and slogans that read FLORIDA'S RETIREMENT
(5) COMMUNITY OF THE YEAR, 87 HOLES OF GOLF, THE TOWN TOO BUSY TO RETIRE. According to a real-estate brochure, the town is "sensibly located . . . comfortably removed from the crowded downtown areas, the
(10) highway clutter, the tourists, and the traffic." It is 25 miles from Sarasota, and 11 miles from the nearest beach on the Gulf Coast. Route 301, an inland route—to be taken in preference to the coast road, with its lines of trucks from the
(15) phosphate plants—passes through a lot of swampland, some scraggly pinewoods, and acre upon acre of strawberry beds covered with sheets of black plastic. There are fields where hairy, tough-looking cattle snatch at the grass between
(20) the palmettos. There are aluminum warehouses, cinder-block stores, and trailer homes in patches of dirt with laundry sailing out behind. There are Pentecostal churches and run-down cafes and bars with rows of pickup trucks parked out front.
(25) Turn right with the billboards onto Route 674, and there is a green-and-white, suburban-looking resort town. Off the main road, white asphalt boulevards with avenues of palm trees give onto streets that curve pleasingly around
(30) golf courses and small lakes. White, ranch-style houses sit back from the streets on small, impeccably manicured lawns. A glossy, four-color map of the town put out by a real-estate company shows cartoon figures of golfers on the
(35) fairways and boats on the lakes, along with drawings of churches, clubhouses, and curly green trees. The map is a necessity for the visitor, since the streets curve around in a maze fashion, ending in culs-de-sac or doubling back on

(40) themselves. There is no way in or out of Sun City Center except by the main road bisecting the town. The map, which looks like a child's board game (Snakes and Ladders or Uncle Wiggily), shows a vague area—a kind of no-man's-land—
(45) surrounding the town. As the map suggests, there is nothing natural about Sun City Center. The lakes are artificial, and there is hardly a tree or shrub or blade of grass that has any correspondence in the world just beyond it. At
(50) the edges of the development, there are houses under construction, with the seams still showing in the transplanted lawns. From there, you can look out at a flat, brown plain that used to be a cattle ranch. The developer simply scraped the
(55) surface off the land and started over again.
Sun City Center is an unincorporated town of about 8,500 people, almost all of whom are over the age of 60. It is a self-contained community, with stores, banks, restaurants, and doctors'
(60) offices. It has the advertised 87 holes of golf; it also has tennis courts, shuffleboard courts, swimming pools, and lawn-bowling greens. In addition to the regular housing, it has a "life-care facility"—a six-story apartment building
(65) with a nursing home in one wing. "It's a strange town," a clinical psychologist at the University of South Florida, in Tampa, told me before I went. "It's out there in the middle of nowhere. It has a section of private houses, where people go
(70) when they retire. Then it has a section of condos and apartments, where people go when they can't keep up their houses. Then it has a nursing home. Then it has a cemetery." In fact, there is no cemetery in Sun City Center, but the doctor was
(75) otherwise correct.
Sun City Center has become a world unto itself. Over the years, the town attracted a supermarket and all the stores and services necessary to the maintenance of daily life. Now,
(80) in addition, it has a golf-cart dealer, two banks, three savings and loan associations, four

restaurants, and a brokerage firm. For visitors, there is the Sun City Center Inn. The town has a post office. Five churches have been built by the
(85) residents and a sixth is under construction. A number of doctors have set up offices in the town, and a Bradenton hospital recently opened a satellite hospital with 112 beds. There is no school, of course. The commercial establishments
(90) all front on the state road running through the center of town, but, because most of them are more expensive than those in the neighboring towns, the people from the surrounding area patronize only the supermarket, the Laundromat,
(95) and one or two others. The local farmers and the migrant workers they employ, many of whom are Mexican, have little relationship to golf courses or to dinner dances with organ music. Conversely, Sun Citians are not the sort of people who would
(100) go to bean suppers in the Pentecostal churches or hang out at raunchy bars where gravel-voiced women sing "Satin Sheets and Satin Pillows." The result is that Sun Citians see very little of their Florida neighbors. They take trips to
(105) Tampa, Bradenton, and Sarasota, but otherwise they rarely leave the green-and-white developments, with their palm-lined avenues and artificial lakes. In the normal course of a week, they rarely see anyone under sixty.

1. In the first paragraph, the author refers to the "fields where hairy, tough-looking cattle snatch at the grass between the palmettos" (lines 18–20) in order to

   A. deny the area any pastoral attractiveness
   B. underscore the loss when farmland is subdivided for retirement homes
   C. suggest the savagery of the natural world that can be ordered and made beautiful by human projects
   D. juxtapose the image of the cattle with that of swampland and scrawny pinewoods
   E. compare the cattle to those who live in the trailer homes that are surrounded by dirt

2. In the last three sentences of the first paragraph ("There are fields . . . parked out front"; lines 18–24), the author uses all of the following EXCEPT

   A. parallel structure
   B. periodic sentences
   C. specific details
   D. direct statements
   E. subject-verb inversions

3. In the University of South Florida clinical psychologist's quotation at the end of the third paragraph (lines 68–73), the use of two sentences with "where" clauses and three sentences beginning with "then" has which of the following effects?

   A. It requires the reader to supply the "where" clauses for the last two sentences that begin with "then."
   B. It provides a rhetorical parallelism for an unspoken chronological progression.
   C. It includes a series of transitions that direct the reader's attention to the speaker.
   D. It implies the psychologist has studied the Sun City Center residents closely.
   E. It emphasizes why retirees would be attracted to Sun City Center.

4. In the last paragraph, the list of services available in Sun City Center itemized in the sentence in lines 79–82 ("Now, in addition . . . brokerage firm") primarily suggests the residents' concern with

   A. avoiding the idea of death
   B. physical comforts
   C. impressing one another
   D. relaxation
   E. money

5. Which of the following does NOT accurately describe this sentence from the fourth paragraph: "Conversely, Sun Citians are not the sort of people who would go to bean suppers in the Pentecostal churches or hang out at raunchy bars where gravel-voiced women sing 'Satin Sheets and Satin Pillows'" (lines 98–102)?

   A. It reinforces the idea of the preceding sentence.
   B. It effectively contrasts Sun City Center residents and their neighbors.
   C. It recalls details of the description at the end of the first paragraph.
   D. It attacks the values of the people who live in the area near Sun City Center.
   E. It presents an image that is amusing in its incongruity.

6. The overall effect of the last paragraph of the passage is to call attention to the

   A. age of Sun City Center's residents
   B. convenience of life in Sun City Center
   C. political indifference of Sun City Center's residents
   D. isolation of Sun City Center's residents
   E. wealth of Sun City Center's residents

7. Which of the following best describes the diction of the passage?

   A. formal and austere
   B. informal and documentary
   C. abstract
   D. artless and colloquial
   E. highly metaphorical

8. Which of the following quotations from the passage best sums up the author's main point about Sun City Center?

   A. "As the map suggests, there is nothing natural about Sun City Center." (lines 45–46)
   B. "The developer simply scraped the surface off the land and started over again." (lines 54–55)
   C. "Sun City Center is an unincorporated town of about 8,500 people, almost all of whom are over the age of 60." (lines 56–58)
   D. "In fact, there is no cemetery in Sun City Center, but the doctor was otherwise correct." (lines 73–75)
   E. "The result is that Sun Citians see very little of their Florida neighbors." (lines 103–104)

9. A principal rhetorical strategy of the passage as a whole is to

   A. depict a small city by presenting information in a chronological narrative
   B. portray a place by comparison and contrast
   C. raise and then answer questions about the nature of a place
   D. progressively narrow the focus from a larger area to a smaller one and its residents
   E. develop a discussion of a unique location by using multiple points of view

10. All of the following are characteristics of the style of this passage EXCEPT

   A. variety in the length of its sentences
   B. infrequent use of the first person
   C. infrequent use of adjectives
   D. infrequent use of simile
   E. frequent use of specific details

Questions 11–17 refer to the following draft.

(1) When confronting the world's political and social problems, it may be easy to write off theatrical artistic pursuits as merely a distraction, something to watch while the world outside burns. (2) However, this is not—nor has it ever been—the case. (3) Art is not just an escape, but a vehicle to express discontent, anger, and sadness, along with the hope, perseverance, and strength we know we are capable of. (4) Theatrical art makes us resilient.

(5) In 1937, composer Marc Blitzstein wrote the musical *The Cradle Will Rock*. (6) Highly allegorical, the plot follows an attempt to unionize workers and fight against the corrupt factory owner. (7) The production was shut down for being "too radical" just before its Broadway opening. (8) But bravely, Blitzstein, along with the director Orson Welles, the cast, and 600 audience members, walked 21 blocks across Manhattan to the Venice Theatre, making *The Cradle Will Rock* about the determination of artists and communities to access and perform art.

(9) The 1960s marked another decidedly challenging time in American politics, especially with protest against the Vietnam War. (10) Unexpectedly, a gentle musical tale of peace, love, and understanding captured the innocent, naïve joy of the hippie movement. (11) *Hair* helped mainstream audiences understand and empathize with young counter-culture protesters.

(12) Three decades later, the country was faced with a new crisis: AIDS and the social stigma it presented. (13) Then, in 1993, the musical *Rent* appeared off-Broadway. (14) Focused on the lives of young artists at the height of the AIDS crisis, the piece sympathized with them. (15) Additionally, the play *Angels in America* opened that same year, focusing on AIDS as a health crisis and humanizing the individuals who suffered from the disease.

(16) The dialectical nature of theater helps to address both sides of an issue rather than avoiding conflict. (17) Art is a reflection of who we are, where we come from, and where we are going. (18) It can both critique and provide understanding of current events

in a way that news clips and status updates can't. (19) Art may be a way to both process and examine where we stand and provide a formidable platform. (20) After all, as a lyric asserts in *Rent,* "The opposite of war isn't peace. It's creation!"

11. The writer is considering adding the following sentence to the first paragraph (sentences 1–4) to further develop the introductory remarks.

From ancient time to the present, theater from all cultures has presented works that not only entertain but also force the audience to think, to ponder, and to confront controversial issues.

If the writer makes this addition, where would the sentence best be placed?

   A.   before sentence 1
   B.   after sentence 1
   C.   after sentence 2
   D.   after sentence 3
   E.   after sentence 4

12. The writer is considering incorporating additional information about other plays to bolster the passage's point. Which of the following plays would NOT make a relevant addition?

   A.   *Lysistrata,* the Aristophanes 411 B.C. comedy in which the title character convinces the women of Greece to withhold sexual privileges from their husbands as a means of forcing the men to negotiate a peace to the Peloponnesian War

   B.   *Six Characters in Search of an Author,* the Luigi Pirandello 1921 absurdist play that has six strangers burst into a theater, interrupt a rehearsal, and demand that the show's director complete the unfinished story of their lives

   C.   *Macbeth,* Shakespeare's 17th-century exploration of the corrupting power of political ambition, as the title character murders others for his own personal gain

   D.   *An Enemy of the People,* the 1882 Henrik Ibsen political drama about a scientist who tries to save his town from water pollution and expose vice in officials

   E.   *Judgment at Nuremburg,* Abby Mann's historical 1959 play about the trial of German officers accused of crimes against humanity for their involvement in atrocities committed under the Nazi regime

13. The writer is considering further development of the second paragraph by adding the following:

The political message of The Cradle Will Rock *maintains its relevance and reflects on contemporary society today; conflicts between freedom and security, corruption and innocence, and power and integrity still exist today, and the continuing impact of* The Cradle Will Rock *can be found in its ability to speak plainly to these issues.*

Should the writer make this addition?

   A.   No, because the paragraph already makes the same point; the addition is redundant.

   B.   No, because the ideas presented stray too far from the point of the passage.

   C.   Yes, because the commentary is germane to the passage as a whole.

   D.   Yes, because it clarifies why the play was so politically charged.

   E.   Yes, because readers need to be reminded of the importance of political theater.

14. Which of the following would best refute the point of the third paragraph (sentences 9–11)?

   A.   The closing number, "Let the Sunshine In," leaves audiences with an upbeat message.

   B.   When *Hair* opened in April 1968, Martin Luther King Jr. had just been assassinated, Robert Kennedy would meet the same fate months later, and society was unsure of how to react to this upheaval.

   C.   *Hair* was noted for crass language, sexual politics, drug use, and lack of reverence for the American flag.

   D.   *Hair* defined the new genre of rock musical and introduced a racially integrated cast.

   E.   *Hair* is sometimes criticized for its misogynistic depiction of women.

15. The writer wants to further develop the fourth paragraph (sentences 12–15) by adding the following sentence:

Over 18,000 deaths from AIDS occurred in the United States in 1990 alone, and those who contracted the disease were stigmatized and ostracized.

Should the writer include this addition?

A. Yes, because it reinforces the extent of the AIDS crisis discussed in the paragraph.

B. Yes, because readers without such knowledge will find it surprising.

C. Yes, because both plays mentioned in the paragraph deal with the subject of AIDS.

D. No, because it is irrelevant to the main point of the fourth paragraph.

E. No, because the number of AIDS victims has decreased substantially since the 1990s.

16. The writer is considering deleting the final sentence of the passage (reprinted below).

After all, as a lyric asserts in Rent, *"The opposite of war isn't peace. It's creation!"*

Should the writer delete the sentence?

A. Yes, because it does not relate to the ideas presented in the last paragraph.

B. Yes, because the quotation contradicts the earlier statements about the play.

C. No, because it draws a distinction between peace and creation.

D. No, because the word "creation" clearly relates to and encapsulates the act of playwriting.

E. No, because it reminds the reader of the main idea presented in *Rent*.

17. Which of the following would provide the strongest criticism of the argument in the passage?

A. Some theater patrons only want theater to entertain, not to provoke them with political content.

B. All of the plays mentioned in the passage were met with intense disapproval by some critics.

C. Mainstream theatergoers are traditionally skeptical of plays that present strong political statements.

D. Not all political theater makes a society more resilient.

E. Theater does not change a society's zeitgeist because it only reflects a portion of society.

IF YOU FINISH BEFORE TIME IS CALLED, CHECK YOUR WORK ON THIS SECTION ONLY. DO NOT WORK ON ANY OTHER SECTION IN THE TEST.

Section II: Free-Response Question

Time: 40 minutes

1 question

The following passage comes from J. Hector St. John de Crèvecoeur's *Letters from an American Farmer* (1782).

Directions: Read the selection carefully, and then write an essay that analyzes the rhetorical choices Crèvecoeur makes to develop his attitude toward Europeans and Americans.

In your response you should do the following:

- Respond to the prompt with a thesis that analyzes the writer's rhetorical choices.
- Select and use evidence to support your line of reasoning.
- Explain how the evidence supports your line of reasoning.
- Demonstrate an understanding of the rhetorical situation.
- Use appropriate grammar and punctuation in communicating your argument.

In this great American asylum, the poor of Europe have by some means met together, and in consequence of various causes; to what purpose should they ask one another what countrymen they are? Alas, two thirds of them had no country. Can a wretch who wanders about, who works and starves, whose life is a continual scene of sore affliction or pinching penury; can that man call England or any other kingdom his country? A
(5)　country that had no bread for him, whose fields procured him no harvest, who met with nothing but the frowns of the rich, the severity of the laws, with jails and punishments; who owned not a single foot of extensive surface of this planet? No! Urged by a variety of motives, here they came. Everything has tended to regenerate them; new laws, a new mode of living, a new social system; here they are become men: in Europe they were as so many useless plants, wanting vegetative mold and refreshing showers; they withered, and were
(10)　mowed down by want, hunger, and war; but now by the power of transplantation, like all other plants they have taken root and flourished! Formerly they were not numbered in any civil lists of their country, except in those of the poor; here they rank as citizens. By what invisible power has this surprising metamorphosis been performed? By that of the laws and that of their industry. . . .

What then is the American, this new man? He is either a European, or the descendant of a European,
(15)　hence that strange mixture of blood, which you will find in no other country. I could point out to you a family whose grandfather was an Englishman, whose wife was Dutch, whose son married a French woman, and whose present four sons have now four wives of different nations. *He* is an American, who leaving behind him all his ancient prejudices and manners, receives new ones from the new mode of life he has embraced, the new government he obeys, and the new rank he holds. He becomes an American by being received in the
(20)　broad lap of our great *Alma Mater.* Here individuals of all nations are melted into a new race of men, whose labors and posterity will one day cause great changes in the world. Americans are the western pilgrims, who are carrying only with them that great mass of arts, sciences, vigor, and industry which began long since in the east; they will finish the great circle.

IF YOU FINISH BEFORE TIME IS CALLED, CHECK YOUR WORK ON THIS SECTION ONLY. DO NOT WORK ON ANY OTHER SECTION IN THE TEST.

Answer Key

Section I: Multiple-Choice Questions

1. A	**6.** D	**11.** C	**16.** D
2. B	**7.** B	**12.** B	**17.** A
3. B	**8.** A	**13.** C	
4. E	**9.** D	**14.** E	
5. D	**10.** C	**15.** A	

Section II: Free-Response Question

An essay scoring rubric, student essays, and analysis appear beginning on p. 84.

Answer Explanations

Section I: Multiple-Choice Questions

The passage referred to in questions 1–10 is from Cities on a Hill *(1981) by Frances Fitzgerald.*

1. **A.** The passage presents the area around Sun City Center as ugly: "scraggly pinewoods" and "a lot of swampland." Although the land is used for cattle ranching, the prose denies it any charm or beauty, choice A. The passage has no concern with making a case for the subdivision as ecologically bad (B) or good (C). In the passage, ecology is not an issue. The description in the first paragraph contains a series of images, but nothing suggests the cattle image is supposed to juxtapose against any other image (D). Rather, all of the images combine to create a unified effect. Similarly, the cattle are never compared to those who live in the trailer homes (E); both are just separate images.

2. **B.** These are all loose sentences, not periodic sentences, choice B. Each of the sentences could end after just three or four words, whereas a periodic sentence makes its point in a main clause at the end. Parallel structure (A) exists in the repeated sentence beginnings, "There are." The sentences are direct statements (D) chiefly made up of specific details (C). All three sentences place the verbs ("are") before the subjects ("fields," "warehouses," "churches") (E).

3. **B.** The repetition of "it has" and "then it has" is an example of parallel structure, and the chronology progresses from the time when the people first move to Sun City Center to a later time when their health begins to fail, to a time of greater weakness, to death, choice B. Although the two "where" clauses invite us to add two more "where" clauses into the last two sentences, thus mentally completing the implied parallel construction, the reader is not required to do so (A). The series does not call attention to the speaker (C). The passage offers no evidence that the psychologist has studied the residents closely (D). The psychologist's quotation hardly makes Sun City Center attractive (E); in fact, the doctor calls it a "strange town."

4. **E.** There are five services listed, and three of the five (banks, savings and loan associations, and a brokerage firm) are specifically related to money, choice E. A fourth, the golf-cart dealer, is at least tangentially related to affluence. Choice A is not related to the list of services. Choices B, C, and D are plausible, but choice E, although it may seem obvious, is the best choice.

5. **D.** The passage is not satiric. Its point is not that Sun Citians or their neighbors are flawed, choice D, but that they have nothing in common. The sentence reinforces the idea of the sentence before—the alienation

of the Sun Citians from their neighbors (A and B). The bars and Pentecostal churches are mentioned in the last sentence of the first paragraph (C). The notion of a group of middle-class senior citizens sitting in a run-down café listening to country-western music is amusing in its incongruity (E).

6. D. Although the paragraph begins with an account of the stores and services of Sun City Center, even the first sentence insists on this development as "a world unto itself." And the last two-thirds of the paragraph (beginning with "There is no school, of course") supports the notion of the residents' isolation from the rest of the world, choice D. The age of the residents (A) and their wealth (E), along with the convenience of life in Sun City Center (B), are all mentioned in the passage, but these are not the thrust of the final paragraph. The residents' political indifference (C) is never mentioned or hinted at in the passage.

7. B. Although other words may also describe the passage, choice B is the best of the five choices here; the diction is informal (relaxed and casual) and documentary (factual). The passage is not formal and austere (A), not abstract (C), not artless (although a few phrases could be called colloquial) (D), and not at all metaphorical (E).

8. A. Choices B, C, and D don't really sum up a central idea of the passage. Both choices A and E are good answers, but choice A can include the idea of choice E, while choice E is more narrow and not the focus of the whole passage. The whole passage is about the unnaturalness of Sun City Center, its oddness in this geographical area, and the segregation of its residents from their neighbors and from a world where many people are still under 60.

9. D. The best choice here is choice D. The passage begins with the geography of the central west coast of Florida but narrows to Sun City Center ("Turn right with the billboards onto Route 674"). The second paragraph maps out the town, while the third and fourth paragraphs describe its residents. The passage is not a chronological narrative (A). It uses contrast only in the last paragraph (B), asks no questions (C), and has only one point of view and one additional quoted comment (E).

10. C. The passage varies its sentence length (A), uses the first person only once in paragraph three (B), contains only one simile (D), and uses a large number of specific details (E). It is very dependent on adjectives, making choice C correct. Without its adjectives, the passage would be barren and would lose its purpose.

The draft referred to in questions 11–17 discusses theater as a vehicle for social commentary.

11. C. It would be best to place the new sentence after sentence 2, choice C. To understand why, examine the progression of ideas in the first two sentences. The first sentence suggests that theater serves as a distraction from the world's social and political problems. The new addition would not begin the paragraph nearly as well (A), nor would it be effective in following that first sentence effectively (B). Notice that sentence 2 counters the first sentence by claiming that theater is not and has never been a mere distraction. The additional sentence, when placed after sentence 2 (as in C), would continue this logic by reinforcing the idea that, historically, theater has always presented controversial issues. Sentence 3 continues the discussion and flow of the paragraph by stating that art is a vehicle to express our emotions; the new sentence would be a disruption if placed after this idea (D). Sentence 4 serves as a logical conclusion to the opening paragraph by asserting that "art makes us resilient," and adding the new sentence after it would be jarring (E). As it is, sentence 4 provides an appropriate ending to the paragraph.

12. B. The Pirandello absurdist play, *Six Characters in Search of an Author,* while interesting in itself, does not fit the passage's overall message, which encompasses plays with political and social messages; thus, this play would not make an appropriate addition to the development of the passage because it has no such message, choice B. On the other hand, *Lysistrata* (A) would make a very good inclusion because it reinforces the passage's main idea about the timelessness of controversial theater by noting that even ancient Greek theater presented politically provocative plays. *Macbeth* (C) would also be entirely appropriate because Shakespeare's famous exploration of the downfall of a politically ambitious man precisely fits the overall message of the passage. *An Enemy of the People* (D) would also make a fitting addition because it explores the idea of corruption and vice in local town officials. *Judgment at Nuremburg* (E) clearly provides a fitting addition with its dark political and historical themes.

13. **C.** The development of the second paragraph would indeed benefit from the addition of the new sentence in this question. The new sentence provides further pertinent commentary about the political message of *The Cradle Will Rock,* and it affirms its relevance to today's society, which makes this new sentence directly germane to the passage as a whole, choice C. Choice A incorrectly claims the sentence should not be added, and its reasoning is completely wrong in stating that the information in the new sentence is redundant; the paragraph has not already made the same point. Choice B also fails to appreciate the importance of the new sentence, erroneously stating that it strays too far from the passage; instead, the new sentence is right in line with the passage's point. Choice D correctly wants to include the addition, but for a weak reason; merely stating that it shows why the play was politically charged is not necessary because that idea is indeed in the passage already, so this would actually be redundant. Choice E also votes in favor of adding the new sentence; however, its reasoning is also weak, simply restating that readers need to be reminded of the importance of political theater. Therefore, choice C presents a much more relevant reason for adding the sentence, one that relates to the whole passage.

14. **E.** To answer this question, you need to clearly understand the overall point of the third paragraph, which introduces the 1960s as a "decidedly challenging time in American politics" before discussing how the "gentle musical" *Hair* "unexpectedly" encapsulated the innocent joy of the hippie movement with the ideals of "peace, love, and understanding." Choice E provides the best refutation of these ideas by pointing out that the play is sometimes criticized for its misogynistic depiction of women, an idea that hardly fits with gentle and peaceful ideals. Choice A does not refute the idea in the paragraph; rather, it complements the message of understanding by pointing out that the final number leaves everyone upbeat. Choice B ties into the turbulent times of the 1960s that are brought up in the first sentence of the paragraph by mentioning the assassinations of Martin Luther King Jr. and Robert Kennedy months apart; this idea fits in with the paragraph and does not counter its message. Choice C serves as an attractive distractor; it is in the right direction, but it is not the *best* answer because the negative ideas in choice C reinforce the concept of the "decidedly challenging time in American politics." Because the 1960s were quite turbulent and divisive, exposing mainstream audiences to such crass language and other negative ideas helps make their eventual understanding of and empathy for the "young counter-culture protesters" even more potent. Choice D does not refute ideas in the paragraph at all; while it may be true that *Hair* introduced the new genre of the rock musical and it certainly had a racially integrated cast, those points do not contest anything in the paragraph.

15. **A.** The fourth paragraph brings up the overwhelming urgency of the AIDS crisis in the 1990s, and the addition of this new sentence, affirming the staggering number of 18,000 deaths, would substantially reinforce the extent of the crisis, choice A. Thus, this sentence would make a significant addition to the paragraph. Choice B correctly votes for including the additional sentence, but for a weak reason; simply stating that readers without this knowledge will find it surprising is not a very strong reason for including it. The writer should have a better rationale if he or she is going to add the sentence. Choice C also votes for the addition, but again, it has a weak rationale; the mere fact that both plays mentioned in the paragraph deal with AIDS does not provide sufficient justification for adding the new sentence. Choice D incorrectly fails to include the new sentence and also erroneously states that it is not relevant to the paragraph, when indeed it is very much so. Choice E also votes against its addition, and it brings up the irrelevant point that the number of AIDS victims has decreased substantially; while that fact is encouraging, it does not diminish the importance of the enormous number of deaths in 1990.

16. **D.** Finishing the passage with the idea of "creation" is very appropriate because playwrights create when they give their characters a voice, and those voices in turn help audiences ponder and understand the world, an idea that encapsulates the passage's main point. Thus, the last sentence should not be deleted, choice D. Choice A incorrectly votes to remove the sentence, and it states a poor rationale, that the sentence does not relate, when indeed it does. Choice B also wants to remove the last sentence, and it provides yet another faulty reason; the last sentence clearly does not contradict earlier information about the play *Rent.* Choice C rightfully wants to retain the sentence, but its logic is flawed; the sentence does not draw any distinction between peace and creation. Choice E is clearly wrong; although the quotation in the last sentence does come from the play *Rent,* it is not a specific reminder of the play's main idea, which deals with the inclusion of marginalized and ostracized members of society.

17. A. The fact that some theatergoers simply want the theater to entertain them and not provoke them with political content, choice A, would make a strong criticism of the passage, which advocates for controversial theater as "a way to both process and examine where we stand." Choice B is not a criticism, so it irrelevant; it does not matter that all of the plays mentioned received some critical reviews and provoked some intense disapproval; whether or not critics like a play is not meaningful to the theatergoers who see a new play and are moved by it. Choice C is a possible second-best answer, a so-called distractor, but the term "mainstream theatergoers" implies conventional patrons who would not necessarily want controversial theater in the first place; therefore, the point that they might be skeptical of strongly political plays does not provide a criticism of the passage's point. Choice D merely focuses on negating one sentence of the passage, sentence 4 that claims "theatrical art makes us resilient," but it does not provide a criticism of the passage as a whole. Choice E makes a reasonable point; while it is probably true that theater alone cannot change a society's overall outlook, spirit, or zeitgeist, that does not provide an adequate criticism of the passage as a whole; the passage does not imply that theater alone can change a society's entire outlook, only that theater can help people come to terms with the serious issues they face.

Section II: Free-Response Question

Row A: Thesis (0–1 point)	
Scoring Criteria	
0 points for any of the following:	**1 point for**
• Having no defendable thesis. • Only restating the prompt in the thesis. • Only summarizing the issue with no apparent or coherent claim in the thesis. • Presenting a thesis that does not address the prompt.	• Addressing the prompt with a defendable thesis that analyzes the writer's rhetorical choices.
Decision Rules and Scoring Notes	
Theses that do not earn this point	**Theses that do earn this point**
• Only restate the prompt. • Neglect to address the writer's rhetorical choices. • Simply describe or repeat the text rather than making a defendable claim.	• Respond to the prompt (rather than restating it) <u>and</u> clearly articulate a defendable thesis about how Crèvecoeur's rhetorical strategies reflect his attitude toward Europeans and Americans.
Additional Notes	
• The thesis may be one or more sentences that are in close proximity to each other anywhere in the essay. • A thesis that meets the criteria can be awarded the point whether or not the rest of the response successfully conveys that line of reasoning. • For a thesis to be defendable, the passage must have at least minimal evidence that could be used as support. • A thesis may present a line of reasoning, but it is not required to earn a point.	

Row B: Evidence AND Commentary (0–4 points)				
Scoring Criteria				
0 points for	**1 point for**	**2 points for**	**3 points for**	**4 points for**
• Simply repeating the thesis (if present). • **OR** restating provided information. • **OR** providing mostly irrelevant and/or incoherent evidence.	• Summarizing the passage without reference or connection to the thesis. • **OR** providing mostly general evidence. • **AND** providing little or no explanation or commentary.	• Providing some specific evidence that is relevant to the thesis. • **AND** explaining how some of the evidence relates to the thesis, but the line of reasoning may be nonexistent or faulty.	• Providing specific evidence to support all claims in the line of reasoning. • **AND** explaining how some of the evidence relates to the thesis and supports the line of reasoning. • **AND** explaining how at least one rhetorical choice in the passage contributes to the writer's thesis.	• Providing specific evidence to support all claims in the line of reasoning. • **AND** providing well-developed commentary that consistently and explicitly explains the relationship between the evidence and the thesis. • **AND** explaining how multiple rhetorical choices in the passage contribute to the writer's thesis.
Decision Rules and Scoring Notes				
Typical responses that earn 0 points:	**Typical responses that earn 1 point:**	**Typical responses that earn 2 points:**	**Typical responses that earn 3 points:**	**Typical responses that earn 4 points:**
• Are unclear or fail to address the prompt. • May present mere opinion with little or no evidence.	• Only summarize or restate ideas from the passage without any analysis. • May mention rhetorical devices with little or no explanation or analysis.	• Mix specific details with broad generalities. • May contain simplistic, inaccurate, or repetitive explanations that do not strengthen the argument. • Fail to explain the connections between claims and establish a clear line of reasoning. • May make one point well but fail to adequately support any other claims.	• Consistently offer evidence to support all claims. • Focus on the importance of specific words and details from the passage to build an argument. • Use multiple supporting claims to organize an argument and line of reasoning. • May not integrate some evidence or support a key claim in the commentary.	• Consistently offer evidence to support all claims. • Focus on the importance of specific words and details from the passage to build an argument. • Use multiple supporting claims with adequate evidence and explanation to organize an argument and line of reasoning. • Explain how the writer's use of rhetorical devices contributes to the student's analysis of the passage.

Additional Notes

• Writing that suffers from grammatical and/or mechanical errors that interfere with communication cannot earn the fourth point in this row.

Row C: Sophistication (0–1 point)	
Scoring Criteria	
0 points for	**1 point for**
• Not meeting the criteria for 1 point.	• Exhibiting sophistication of thought and/or advancing a complex understanding of the rhetorical situation.
Decision Rules and Scoring Notes	
Responses that do not earn this point:	**Responses that earn this point demonstrate one (or more) of the following:**
• Try to contextualize the text, but make predominantly sweeping generalizations (*"Throughout all history . . ."* OR *"Everyone believes . . ."*). • Only hint at other possible arguments (*"Some may think . . ."*). • Examine individual rhetorical choices but fail to examine the relationship among varying choices throughout the passage. • Oversimplify textual complexities. • Present complicated or complex sentences or language that is ineffective and detracts from the argument.	• Explain the purpose or function of complexities or tension in the passage. • Explain the significance of the writer's rhetorical choices for the given rhetorical situation. • Develop a prose style that is especially vivid, persuasive, resounding, or appropriate to the student's argument.
Additional Notes	
• This point should be awarded only if the demonstration of sophistication or complex understanding is part of the argument, not merely a phrase or brief reference.	

High-Scoring Essay

Many foreigners came to America during the republic's formative years to explore life in the new nation. The writings of de Tocqueville and Charles Dickens commented on the new American character and government in the nineteenth century. J. Hector St. John de Crèvecoeur, who wrote <u>Letters from an American Farmer</u> in 1782, was not alone in his endeavor, though he was one of the first to visit the new United States. His writing generally reflects a positive image of Americans. While taking note of their humble origins and lack of cultural refinement, he praises the resilience of American citizens. Crèvecoeur's diction, and the positive connotations of the words he uses to describe Americans, clearly present his positive, though occasionally paternal and superior, attitude toward Americans.

Americans are defined by Crèvecoeur largely in terms of the land they left. Their new nation is a haven from a Europe of severe laws, "with jails and punishments." The common folk in England are faced by the "frowns of the rich." The new Americans have left the "refinement" of Europe behind, along with the class system and much else which had restricted them. These images tell as much about Crèvecoeur's attitude toward Europeans as it does toward Americans. The negativity attached to Americans' backgrounds perhaps emphasizes their ultimate determination and drive once they arrived on new soil. Crèvecoeur deliberately uses negative phrases in describing Americans' pasts so that their change in the new country will be even more dramatic.

Crèvecoeur emphasizes the newness of the United States, thus implying a positive impression of the land. While he may look down somewhat on the breeding and manners of the Americans, noting that they come from the lower rungs of European social hierarchy, he certainly believes the new land is good for them. America is a place of regenerative powers, with "new laws, a new mode of living, a new social system." Crèvecoeur credits America with encouraging the flourishing of the world's poor and unwanted. Might he then be looking down on America, as the "asylum" he describes in the opening sentence, a refuge suitable only for the wretches of sophisticated European life? Perhaps. But he leaves no doubt about the successful attainment of such a goal, lauding it by writing that the "surprising metamorphosis" from wretches to citizens is thanks to American "laws and . . . industry."

Although Crèvecoeur generally presents Americans in laudable terms, a trace of condescension appears in some phrases. America was made up of "wretches" who had previously wandered about. They had endured lives of "sore affliction or pinching penury." But despite the seeming elitism of Crèvecoeur's description, his word choices elicit sympathy rather than scorn in the attentive reader because he is referring to the Americans' previous lives in Europe. Crèvecoeur makes a careful point of the work ethic of these derelict new countrymen, essentially homeless among the world's nations. Such attention clearly shows that Crèvecoeur is sensitive to the plight of the new Americans.

Crèvecoeur writes as if America has surpassed his expectations as a melting pot of undesirables. He has an optimistic view of the country's role in the future. Compared to crusaders, the Americans he praises are the "western pilgrims" full of the "great mass of arts, sciences, vigor, and industry" that once issued from the east. It is important to note that Crèvecoeur ends his essay on a positive tone, with phrasing that emphasizes greatness. Here, in his conclusion, Crèvecoeur's attitude toward Americans really shines with enthusiasm. They are the nation of the future, he believes, and they will deeply influence the future of the world with their newborn splendor.

(605 words)

Analysis of the High-Scoring Essay

This thorough and well-written essay succeeds both in covering the topic and in convincing the AP Exam Reader. The student demonstrates a clear comprehension of the passage and does not merely present a one-sided view of Crèvecoeur. The first paragraph introduces and relates other foreign authors who also addressed the personality of the new Americans. Ultimately, it presents a thoughtful thesis that shows a full understanding of Crèvecoeur's attitude while also mentioning his rhetorical strategies, especially diction and connotation. It deserves a point in Row A.

In the second paragraph, the student addresses Crèvecoeur's negative statements about the Americans' background in Europe and does a nice job of placing this negativity in context by pointing out that it will be balanced with the "dramatic" changes that take place once the new citizens have become Americans. This paragraph, like those that follow, is thoughtful and articulate, presenting an ample number of specific examples for the student's points and providing a connection to the thesis.

The next paragraph addresses the transformation that took place in the Americans after they arrived in the new country. This unified paragraph uses quotations from the passage well and presents interesting ideas from the student. This student shows the ability to think about and interpret Crèvecoeur's ideas, not simply to present them.

The fourth paragraph describes the "condescension" in some of Crèvecoeur's phrasing; again, the student does an admirable job of presenting Crèvecoeur's attitude while remembering that the topic asks for an analysis of rhetorical strategies. The student clearly sees that, although Crèvecoeur presents many negative ideas about the Americans' background, essentially, he praises Americans. The quality of the body paragraphs earns 4 points in Row B.

The essay ends positively, just as Crèvecoeur's does. The student's wording, like Crèvecoeur's, shows optimism and provides a clean ending to a fairly long essay. Influencing the future with "newborn splendor" sums up both Crèvecoeur's attitude and the student's ideas very nicely. Overall, the essay uses sophisticated wording and contains many intelligent ideas. It reads well because it's clear that the student has ideas of his or her own and is not merely listing Crèvecoeur's. It deserves to be rewarded with a point in Row C and an overall score of 6.

Low-Scoring Essay

Crèvecoeur was a French writer who wrote about life in the rural parts of America. He has a partly negative attitude about America, and cuts down the Americans many times in his essay. He also gives them some praise for starting over and doing something new. He also praises them for succeeding at something new.

He uses diction to obtain these results. A careful use of diction shows readers that he sometimes doesn't think much of the American people as a whole. He points out that they were "the poor of Europe" who, as wretches, lived a life of "sore affliction." He also says that "two thirds of them had no country." This hardly sounds like Crèvecoeur admires the Americans background. He stereotypes Americans to all be like this.

Crèvecoeur continues his diatribe against Americans as he calls them "useless plants" in Europe. But finally, he has something more generous to say about Americans as he claims these plants have "taken root and flourished" here in American soil. So, although these Americans were low-life Europeans, once they became Americans they became "new." They became "citizens." Crèvecoeur also notices that Americans work hard and have good laws. I find it interesting that even though he has some good things to say about Americans, he still claims negative things; he believes that once the new Americans arrived, they left behind them all their "ancient prejudices . . . receiving new ones. . . ." We in America today like to believe that we hold no prejudices; at least that's one of the principles that our country was founded on.

Thus it can be seen that Crèvecoeur seemed to have some good thoughts about Americans, but that he was by no means entirely impressed by them. He uses his diction to present his opinions, and very strong diction at that. His wording is surprisingly harsh at times, considering that he seems to want to praise Americans for what they have accomplished, yet he spends so much time degrading their background. His attitude toward Americans is best described as guarded; he certainly does not show Americans in nothing but glowing terms.

(357 words)

Analysis of the Low-Scoring Essay

This essay, although well organized, clearly shows the student's problems in both reading and writing skills. It begins by attempting to address the topic, but it does so with such a vague thesis that all it essentially sets forth is the simplistic idea that Crèvecoeur is both positive and negative about Americans. How Crèvecoeur's rhetorical strategies establish that attitude is not yet addressed. The student never presents a defendable thesis; instead, he or she merely reports what Crèvecoeur says. The essay will not earn a point in Row A.

The student then devotes a paragraph to proving how negatively Crèvecoeur viewed the Americans' backgrounds by supplying a fair amount of evidence from Crèvecoeur's text. The student cites several examples of negative wording but also makes mistakes. First, the student borders on a misreading of the passage. In explaining the despair that Americans felt before coming to this country, Crèvecoeur's purpose seems to be to show how much the Americans had to overcome, thus emphasizing their strength. However, this student concentrates on only the negative European experience and transfers that negativity to the Americans *after* they became Americans. The student's second mistake is failing to address the topic clearly, failing to comment on exactly *how* Crèvecoeur's attitude is presented through his diction. This student simply gives the evidence and leaves it to the AP Exam Reader to make the connection.

The next paragraph tries to establish Crèvecoeur's positive attitude toward Americans, but the evidence presented is weak; the student offers little more than that the country is "new" and that people are now "citizens." The student turns again to a negative reading of the text, focusing on Crèvecoeur's claim that Americans have prejudices. Because of this change in direction, the paragraph lacks unity. The body paragraphs deserve 2 points out of 4 in Row B.

The concluding paragraph finally mentions diction again, but again it makes no connection between Crèvecoeur's word choice and the attitude it reflects. Unfortunately, this paragraph is merely summary. Overall, the essay's weaknesses stem from a cursory reading of the passage, weak presentation of evidence, and a lack of attention to the topic of the thesis. Simplistic thinking and simplistic diction combine here to produce a bland essay that fails to convince the Reader. It does not earn a point in Row C, getting a total of 2 points out of 6.

Chapter 4

Practice Exam 1

Answer Sheet

Section I: Multiple-Choice Questions

1 Ⓐ Ⓑ Ⓒ Ⓓ Ⓔ	21 Ⓐ Ⓑ Ⓒ Ⓓ Ⓔ	41 Ⓐ Ⓑ Ⓒ Ⓓ Ⓔ
2 Ⓐ Ⓑ Ⓒ Ⓓ Ⓔ	22 Ⓐ Ⓑ Ⓒ Ⓓ Ⓔ	42 Ⓐ Ⓑ Ⓒ Ⓓ Ⓔ
3 Ⓐ Ⓑ Ⓒ Ⓓ Ⓔ	23 Ⓐ Ⓑ Ⓒ Ⓓ Ⓔ	43 Ⓐ Ⓑ Ⓒ Ⓓ Ⓔ
4 Ⓐ Ⓑ Ⓒ Ⓓ Ⓔ	24 Ⓐ Ⓑ Ⓒ Ⓓ Ⓔ	44 Ⓐ Ⓑ Ⓒ Ⓓ Ⓔ
5 Ⓐ Ⓑ Ⓒ Ⓓ Ⓔ	25 Ⓐ Ⓑ Ⓒ Ⓓ Ⓔ	45 Ⓐ Ⓑ Ⓒ Ⓓ Ⓔ
6 Ⓐ Ⓑ Ⓒ Ⓓ Ⓔ	26 Ⓐ Ⓑ Ⓒ Ⓓ Ⓔ	
7 Ⓐ Ⓑ Ⓒ Ⓓ Ⓔ	27 Ⓐ Ⓑ Ⓒ Ⓓ Ⓔ	
8 Ⓐ Ⓑ Ⓒ Ⓓ Ⓔ	28 Ⓐ Ⓑ Ⓒ Ⓓ Ⓔ	
9 Ⓐ Ⓑ Ⓒ Ⓓ Ⓔ	29 Ⓐ Ⓑ Ⓒ Ⓓ Ⓔ	
10 Ⓐ Ⓑ Ⓒ Ⓓ Ⓔ	30 Ⓐ Ⓑ Ⓒ Ⓓ Ⓔ	
11 Ⓐ Ⓑ Ⓒ Ⓓ Ⓔ	31 Ⓐ Ⓑ Ⓒ Ⓓ Ⓔ	
12 Ⓐ Ⓑ Ⓒ Ⓓ Ⓔ	32 Ⓐ Ⓑ Ⓒ Ⓓ Ⓔ	
13 Ⓐ Ⓑ Ⓒ Ⓓ Ⓔ	33 Ⓐ Ⓑ Ⓒ Ⓓ Ⓔ	
14 Ⓐ Ⓑ Ⓒ Ⓓ Ⓔ	34 Ⓐ Ⓑ Ⓒ Ⓓ Ⓔ	
15 Ⓐ Ⓑ Ⓒ Ⓓ Ⓔ	35 Ⓐ Ⓑ Ⓒ Ⓓ Ⓔ	
16 Ⓐ Ⓑ Ⓒ Ⓓ Ⓔ	36 Ⓐ Ⓑ Ⓒ Ⓓ Ⓔ	
17 Ⓐ Ⓑ Ⓒ Ⓓ Ⓔ	37 Ⓐ Ⓑ Ⓒ Ⓓ Ⓔ	
18 Ⓐ Ⓑ Ⓒ Ⓓ Ⓔ	38 Ⓐ Ⓑ Ⓒ Ⓓ Ⓔ	
19 Ⓐ Ⓑ Ⓒ Ⓓ Ⓔ	39 Ⓐ Ⓑ Ⓒ Ⓓ Ⓔ	
20 Ⓐ Ⓑ Ⓒ Ⓓ Ⓔ	40 Ⓐ Ⓑ Ⓒ Ⓓ Ⓔ	

CUT HERE

Section II: Free-Response Questions

Question 1

ISRR's main Job is to educate and ehance poblic saftey. The media's coverage of natural disasters are only a accurate discription of what happened. America itself has a effective risk of communication.

American mainstream media has become more critical of power as said in Document F "poor response of authorities." Many Americans think declining trust in the government and in each other makes it harder to slove key problems. They have a wealth of ideas about whats wrong and how to move forward and fix it. Trust and power are essenetial for public life and neibourly relations. The federal government provides short-term and long term help for victims of natural disasters, these desasters relief agencies like FEMA provide food, shelter, water, money, and healthcare affected after natural elesasters.

In a disaster, you face the danger of death or physical injury. You also may lose your home, possession and community. Media coverage of natural disasters is only a broken, watered down discription of what happened as stated in Surce B "Is accepted as an aqurate discription of what happened." Media helps during natural desasters by providing review, update, or establish emergency response plans in local areas. also as a tool by providing information and instructions with real time alerts and warnings.

For disasters, government practices calmness and coordination between government and communities to reduse disaster risk and impacts. Social media adds another channel for the flow of information

CUT HERE

During emergences, it speeds up news delivery and enhances joint efforts for immediate relief.

CUT HERE

CUT HERE

Question 2

CUT HERE

Question 3

CUT HERE

CUT HERE

CUT HERE

CUT HERE

Section I: Multiple-Choice Questions

Time: 1 hour

45 questions

Directions: This section consists of selections from prose works with questions about their content, style, and form, plus draft passages with questions about improving their content and clarity. Read each selection carefully. For each question, choose the best answer of the five choices.

Questions 1–13 refer to the following passage from a 1848 speech.

We have met here today to discuss our rights and wrongs, civil and political, and not, as some have supposed, to go into the detail of social life alone. We do not propose to petition the
(5) legislature to make our husbands just, generous, and courteous, to seat every man at the head of a cradle, and to clothe every woman in male attire. None of these points, however important they may be considered by leading men, will be
(10) touched in this convention. As to their costume, the gentlemen need feel no fear of our imitating that, for we think it in violation of every principle of taste, beauty, and dignity; notwithstanding all the contempt cast upon our loose, flowing
(15) garments, we still admire the graceful folds and consider our costume far more artistic than theirs. Many of the nobler sex seem to agree with us in this opinion, for the bishops, priests, judges, barristers, and lord mayors of the first nation on
(20) the globe, and the Pope of Rome, with his cardinals, too, all wear the loose flowing robes, thus tacitly acknowledging that the male attire is neither dignified nor imposing. No, we shall not molest you in your philosophical experiments
(25) with stocks[1], pants, high-heeled boots, and Russian belts. Yours be the glory to discover, by personal experience, how long the kneepan can resist the terrible strapping down which you impose, in how short time the well-developed
(30) muscles of the throat can be reduced to mere threads by the constant pressure of the stock[2], how high the heel of a boot must be to make a short man tall, and how tight the Russian belt may be drawn and yet have wind enough left to
(35) sustain life.

But we are assembled to protest against a form of government existing without the consent of the governed—to declare our right to be free

as man is free, to be represented in the government
(40) which we are taxed to support, to have such disgraceful laws as give man the power to chastise and imprison his wife, to take the wages which she earns, the property which she inherits, and, in case of separation, the children of her love; laws
(45) which make her the mere dependent on his bounty. It is to protest against such unjust laws as these that we are assembled today, and to have them, if possible, forever erased from our statute books, deeming them a shame and a disgrace to
(50) a Christian republic in the nineteenth century. We have met to uplift woman's fallen divinity upon an even pedestal with man's.

And strange as it may seem to many, we now demand our right to vote according to the
(55) declaration of the government under which we live. This right no one pretends to deny. We need not prove ourselves equal to Daniel Webster to enjoy this privilege, for the ignorant Irishman in the ditch has all the civil rights he has. We need
(60) not prove our muscular power equal to this same Irishman to enjoy this privilege, for the most tiny, weak, ill-shaped stripling of twenty-one has all the civil rights of the Irishman. We have no objections to discuss the question of equality, for
(65) we feel that the weight of argument lies wholly with us, but we wish the question of equality kept distinct from the question of rights, for the proof of the one does not determine the truth of the other. All white men in this country have the
(70) same rights, however they may differ in mind, body, or estate.

---

[1] stocks, line 25;

[2] stock, line 31: a stock is a wide, stiff, necktie worn by men in the mid-nineteenth century.

1. Which of the following words is used with two meanings?

   A. "rights" (line 1)
   B. "wrongs" (line 2)
   C. "seat" (line 6)
   D. "head" (line 6)
   E. "attire" (line 7)

2. The details of lines 6–7 ("to seat every man at the head of a cradle, and to clothe every woman in male attire") probably derive from the

A. agenda of feminists seeking the franchise
B. attacks by men on women agitating for the vote
C. creative imagination of the speaker
D. historically observed results of granting women the vote
E. classical ideal of society in which men and women are equal

3. "Many of the nobler sex . . . neither dignified nor imposing," (lines 17–23) advances the argument that

A. the sexes achieve greater dignity by cross-dressing
B. judges and clergymen wear flowing robes because this form of dress is traditional
C. American lawyers and clergymen, as well as members of the Roman Catholic hierarchy, regard women's dress as dignified
D. human value should not be judged by manner of dress
E. women's clothing is more distinguished than men's

4. In the first paragraph, which of the following phrases is used ironically?

A. "social life" (line 3)
B. "male attire" (line 7)
C. "every principle of taste, beauty, and dignity" (lines 12–13)
D. "nobler sex" (line 17)
E. "neither dignified nor imposing" (line 23)

5. In which of the following phrases in the first paragraph does the speaker use mock-serious diction for satiric effect?

A. "with his cardinals, too" (lines 20–21)
B. "thus tacitly acknowledging" (line 22)
C. "philosophical experiments" (line 24)
D. "well-developed muscles of the throat" (lines 29–30)
E. "the constant pressure of the stock" (line 31)

6. In lines 32–35, part of the comedy in the references to the "heel of a boot" and "the Russian belt" is due to the fact that

A. they are worn by men to appear taller and thinner
B. both men and women wear boots and belts
C. women are more likely to dress to impress other women than to impress men
D. men's clothes are, in fact, more comfortable to wear than women's
E. the heels of women's shoes are usually higher than those of men's

7. The rhetorical purpose of the first paragraph of the speech is to

A. develop examples of the issues that will be discussed in the second paragraph
B. lightly introduce issues that will be seriously developed in the second paragraph
C. comically present issues with which the serious second paragraph will not be concerned
D. raise questions to which the second paragraph will give answers
E. grant concessions to the opponents that the second paragraph will retract

8. The tone of the second paragraph can best be described as

A. reasonable and disinterested
B. soft-spoken and confident
C. dry and ironical
D. angry and authoritative
E. tactful and firm

9. Which of the following best describes the relationship between the first paragraph and the second paragraph?

A. The second paragraph intensifies the irony of the first paragraph.
B. The second paragraph marks an important shift in the tone of the passage.
C. The first paragraph has a prose style that is more dependent on concrete details.
D. The second paragraph echoes the tone of the first paragraph but with greater restraint.
E. The first paragraph is less personal than the second paragraph.

10. In the third paragraph, the author refers to Daniel Webster as

    A.   a representative of American patriotism

    B.   an example of a great orator

    C.   a representative of the injustice of the American voting system

    D.   an example of the male's superiority to the female

    E.   a representative of intelligence

11. Together with lines 56–59 ("We need not prove ourselves . . ."), the argument in lines 59–63 ("We need not prove our . . .")

    A.   repeats the idea of the sentence that precedes it

    B.   raises possible objections to the idea of the sentence that precedes it

    C.   appears to concede a point, but, in fact, does not

    D.   demonstrates that the weak as well as the ignorant may vote

    E.   is concerned with the question of rights rather than with the question of equality

12. The speaker wishes to keep "the question of equality . . . distinct from the question of rights" (lines 66–67) because

    A.   women cannot be equal to men until their rights are equal to men's

    B.   though their equality may be doubted, there can be no doubt about women being denied their rights

    C.   the question of the equality of men and women must determine whether or not their civil rights should be the same

    D.   she believes the question of equality has already been settled, but the question of rights has not

    E.   she can see no real distinction between the two

13. The primary rhetorical purpose of the speaker of the passage is to

    A.   reveal the injustice to women in the present laws

    B.   report events as objectively as possible

    C.   obscure a complex issue

    D.   discuss the common humanity of both men and women

    E.   appeal to the gender prejudices of the audience

Questions 14–25 refer to the following passage from an 18th-century political pamphlet.

These are the times that try men's souls. The summer soldier and the sunshine patriot will, in this crisis, shrink from the service of their country; but he that stands it now deserves the
(5) love and thanks of man and woman. Tyranny, like hell, is not easily conquered; yet we have this consolation with us, that the harder the conflict, the more glorious the triumph. What we obtain too cheap, we esteem too lightly: it is dearness
(10) only that gives everything its value. Heaven knows how to put a proper price upon its goods; and it would be strange indeed if so celestial an article as freedom should not be highly rated. Britain, with an army to enforce her tyranny, has
(15) declared that she has a right not only to tax, but "to bind us in all cases whatsoever," and if being bound in that manner is not slavery, then is there not such a thing as slavery upon earth. Even the expression is impious; for so unlimited a power
(20) can belong only to God. . . .

I have as little superstition in me as any man living, but my secret opinion has ever been, and still is, that God Almighty will not give up a people to military destruction, or leave them
(25) unsupportedly to perish, who have so earnestly and so repeatedly sought to avoid the calamities of war, by every decent method which wisdom could invent. Neither have I so much of the infidel in me as to suppose that He has
(30) relinquished the government of the world, and given us up to the care of devils; and as I do not, I cannot see on what grounds the King of Britain can look up to heaven for help against us: a common murderer, a highwayman, or a
(35) housebreaker has as good a pretense as he. . . .

I once felt all that kind of anger, which a man ought to feel, against the mean principles that are held by the Tories: a noted one, who kept a tavern at Amboy, was standing at his door, with
(40) as pretty a child in his hand, about eight or nine years old, as I ever saw, and after speaking his mind as freely as he thought was prudent, finished with this unfatherly expression, "Well! Give me peace in my day." Not a man lives on the
(45) continent but fully believes that a separation must some time or other finally take place, and a generous parent should have said, "If there must be trouble, let it be in my day, that my children may have peace"; and this single reflection, well
(50) applied, is sufficient to awaken every man to duty. Not a place upon earth might be so happy as America. Her situation is remote from all the

wrangling world, and she has nothing to do but
to trade with them. A man can distinguish
(55) himself between temper and principle, and I am
as confident, as I am that God governs the world,
that America will never be happy till she gets
clear of foreign dominion. Wars, without ceasing,
will break out till that period arrives, and the
(60) continent must in the end be conqueror; for
though the flame of liberty may sometimes cease
to shine, the coal can never expire. . . .

The heart that feels not now is dead: the blood
of his children will curse his cowardice who
(65) shrinks back at a time when a little might have
saved the whole, and made them happy. I love the
man that can smile in trouble, that can gather
strength from distress, and grow brave by
reflection. 'Tis the business of little minds to
(70) shrink; but he whose heart is firm, and whose
conscience approves his conduct, will pursue his
principles unto death. My own line of reasoning
is to myself as straight and clear as a ray of light.
Not all the treasures of the world so far as I
(75) believe, could have induced me to support an
offensive war, for I think it murder; but if a thief
breaks into my house, burns and destroys my
property, and kills or threatens to kill me, or
those that are in it, and to "bind me in all cases
(80) whatsoever" to his absolute will, am I to suffer it?
What signifies it to me, whether he who does it is
a king or a common man; my countryman or not
my countryman; whether it be done by an
individual villain, or an army of them? If we
(85) reason to the root of things we shall find no
difference; neither can any just cause be assigned
why we should punish in the one case and pardon
in the other.

14. When the author addresses the "summer soldier
and the sunshine patriot" (line 2), he is most
likely referring to

 A. the American army's reserve soldiers
 B. those citizens who are infidels
 C. the British soldiers stationed in America
 D. those who support the Revolution only
  when convenient
 E. the government's specialized forces

15. The author's style relies on heavy use of

 A. allegory and didactic rhetoric
 B. aphorism and emotional appeal
 C. symbolism and biblical allusion
 D. paradox and invective
 E. historical background and illustration

16. Which of the following does the author NOT
group with the others?

 A. common murderer
 B. highwayman
 C. housebreaker
 D. king
 E. coward

17. The "God" that the author refers to can be
characterized as

 A. principled
 B. vexed
 C. indifferent
 D. contemplative
 E. pernicious

18. According to the author, freedom should be
considered

 A. that which will vanquish cowards
 B. one of the most valuable commodities in
  heaven
 C. that which can be achieved quickly
 D. desirable but never attainable
 E. an issue only governments should negotiate

19. The author's purpose in using the phrase "with
as pretty a child in his hand . . . as I ever saw"
(lines 39–41) is most likely to

 A. prove that the tavern owner has a family
 B. display his anger
 C. add emotional appeal to his argument
 D. symbolically increase the tavern owner's
  evil
 E. dismiss traditional values

20. Which of the following would NOT be
considered an aphorism?

 A. "Tyranny, like hell, is not easily
  conquered . . ." (lines 5–6)
 B. ". . . the harder the conflict, the more
  glorious the triumph" (lines 7–8)
 C. "What we obtain too cheap, we esteem too
  lightly . . ." (lines 8–9)
 D. "Not a place upon earth might be so happy
  as America" (lines 51–52)
 E. ". . . though the flame of liberty may
  sometimes cease to shine, the coal can
  never expire . . ." (lines 61–62)

21. As seen in lines 51–62, the author feels that, in an ideal world, America's role in relation to the rest of the world would be

    A. only one of commerce
    B. one of aggressive self-assertion
    C. more exalted than Britain's
    D. sanctified by God
    E. one of complete isolationism

22. The rhetorical mode that the author uses can best be classified as

    A. explanation
    B. description
    C. narration
    D. illustration
    E. persuasion

23. Which of the following best describes the rhetorical purpose in the sentence "The heart that feels . . . made them happy" (lines 63–66)?

    A. It suggests that children should also join the Revolution.
    B. It plants fear in people's hearts.
    C. It pleads to the king once again for liberty.
    D. It encourages retreat in the face of superior force.
    E. It encourages support by an emotional appeal to all American patriots.

24. All of the following rhetorical devices are particularly effective in the last paragraph of the passage EXCEPT

    A. aphorism
    B. simile
    C. deliberate ambivalence
    D. parallel construction
    E. analogy

25. The main rhetorical purpose in the passage can best be described as

    A. a summons for peace and rational thinking
    B. overemotional preaching for equality
    C. a series of unwarranted conclusions
    D. a patriotic call to duty and action
    E. a demand for immediate liberty

Questions 26–34 refer to the following draft.

(1) A major shift in European philosophical thinking occurred over time as the Middle Ages transformed into the Renaissance, which, later, morphed into the Age of Enlightenment. (2) It was common during the Middle Ages and the Renaissance for Europeans to view God at the center of the universe, dictating events on Earth. (3) This philosophy was represented by superstition and dependence on an angry God to whom people owed absolute submission to authority. (4) Consequently, most people generally believed that God played a direct role in their own lives. (5) When the plague hit a village particularly hard, it was obviously a punishment for those villagers' many faults; when a family's home was destroyed in a fire, it was obviously a sign that the family had sinned and thus they deserved it; when a comet streaked across the sky, it was obviously a foreboding that evil was to come. (6) During the Renaissance, man's dominant question regarding natural events such as these was invariably "why did that happen to us?"

(7) However, as the ideals of the new Age of Enlightenment become more prevalent, humanity's essential question evolved into "how did that happen?" (8) Instead of simply accepting that all bad events were sent by an angry God, some people looked for scientific and natural explanations; they now pondered *how* things worked. (9) How is it that dirty water might trigger disease; what causes earthquakes; when should one expect the next comet?

(10) The effect of this shift in humanity's thinking cannot be underestimated. (11) It marked a significant change in outlook, making humankind central and placing them at the helm of a smoothly running ship that they can control. (12) The still-powerful God was left to his heavens, smiling beatifically as he watched his creations working through their own problems, coming up with their own solutions.

26. Which of the following sentences, if placed before sentence 1, would help capture the audience's interest and also provide the most effective introduction to the main topic of the passage as a whole?

    A. A darkness had lain over all of Europe for centuries; it was not called "the Dark Ages" for nothing.

    B. A black darkness had entombed Europe for centuries; with no education, no sanitation, and no medication, it was a sad time for humanity.

    C. A cloud of disease, despair, and ignorance had clung to Europe for centuries; people desperately prayed to God for relief, but it seemed that God had abandoned them, and they began to look elsewhere for answers.

    D. It is fascinating to compare the philosophical shift between the Renaissance and the Enlightenment.

    E. The coming Enlightenment era would come none-too-soon for the poor, beleaguered Europeans.

27. The writer wants to add information to the first paragraph to support the first sentence of the paragraph (reprinted below).

A major shift in European philosophical thinking occurred over time as the Middle Ages transformed into the Renaissance, which, later, morphed into the Age of Enlightenment.

Which of the following information, if added to the first paragraph, would best accomplish this goal?

    A. names of philosophers in each time period

    B. specific dates of the different time periods

    C. evidence of viewing God as the center of the universe

    D. examples of the changes in thinking

    E. clarification of the phrase "A major shift in European philosophical thinking"

28. The writer wants sentence 5 (reprinted below) to serve as evidence that reinforces the argument of the first paragraph.

When the plague hit a village particularly hard, it was obviously a punishment for those villagers' many faults; when a family's home was destroyed in a fire, it was obviously a sign that the family had sinned and thus they deserved it; when a comet streaked across the sky, it was obviously a foreboding that evil was to come.

Which of the following versions best accomplishes that goal?

    A. (as it is now)

    B. Some examples: (1) when the plague hit a village particularly hard, it was obviously a punishment for those villagers' many faults; (2) when a family's home was destroyed in a fire, it was obviously because that family had sinned and thus they deserved it; or (3) when a comet streaked across the sky, it was obviously a foreboding that evil was to come.

    C. One example is when the plague hits a village particularly hard, it was obviously a punishment for those villagers' many faults. Another example is when a family's home is destroyed in a fire, it was obviously because that family had sinned and thus they deserved it. A final example is when a comet streaked across the sky, it was obviously a foreboding that evil was to come.

    D. For example, plagues punish villages for their many faults, families' homes are burned down because they are sinners, and a comet promises imminent doom.

    E. A plague outbreak in a sinful village is one example, another is a fire burning down a sinning family's house, and another is that evil is always foretold by a comet.

29. At the beginning of sentence 5 (reprinted below), the writer wants to add a phrase, adjusting the capitalization as needed, to better introduce the sentence's purpose.

When the plague hit a village particularly hard, it was obviously a punishment for those villagers' many faults; when a family's home was destroyed in a fire, it was obviously a sign that the family had sinned and thus they deserved it; when a comet streaked across the sky, it was obviously a foreboding that evil was to come.

Which of the following best accomplishes this goal?

A. As an example,
B. For example,
C. Hence,
D. Obviously,
E. In this situation,

30. Within the context of the passage as a whole, which of the following best describes the purpose of the second paragraph?

A. It diverges from the first paragraph by exploring new questions.
B. It clarifies the different philosophical outlook that occurred during the Age of Enlightenment.
C. It magnifies the philosophical problems faced during the Renaissance.
D. It increases the audience's appreciation of the new age by explaining humanity's changed perspective.
E. It simplifies a philosophy that is otherwise awkward to understand.

31. In sentence 8 (reprinted below), the writer wants to provide a more convincing explanation.

Instead of simply accepting that all bad events were sent by an angry God, <u>some people looked for scientific and natural explanations;</u> they now pondered how things worked.

Which of the following revisions of the underlined portion best serves that goal?

A. some people looked elsewhere for explanations;
B. some people now looked to the heavens, hoping God would explain natural catastrophes;
C. some people were satisfied with traditional explanations and felt no need to explore alternatives;
D. some enlightened people applied scientific knowledge and rational explanation to understand underlying mechanisms of natural phenomena;
E. some people continued to accept no personal responsibility for bad events; rather,

32. The writer wants to add more information to the second paragraph (sentences 7–9) to support the main argument in that paragraph. All of the following pieces of accurate evidence help achieve this purpose EXCEPT

A. Sir Isaac Newton's laws of gravity and motion depicted the natural world in terms of natural laws beyond any spiritual force.
B. People began to doubt a God who could predestine human beings to eternal damnation while empowering a tyrannical king.
C. John Locke asserted that people had the right to change government that did not protect natural rights of life, liberty, and property.
D. People devoutly believed that monarchs were the direct descendants of God and ruled supremely with divine approval.
E. During the Enlightenment, people realized that science and reason could bring a degree of understanding.

33. In the third paragraph, the writer is considering placing the following sentence before sentence 10 to further develop the paragraph's ideas.

The Enlightenment world view continued the Renaissance world view except for the difference in focus; this world view was more focused on science, reason, and logic instead of the arts.

Should the writer make this addition?

A. Yes, because it enhances the purpose of the writer's argument as a whole.

B. Yes, because it clarifies the differences between the two time periods.

C. Yes, because it adds information that more readers can relate to.

D. No, because the passage does not need more distinction.

E. No, because any similarities between the ages is not a part of the main argument.

34. The writer is considering adding the following sentence to the third paragraph (sentences 10–12) to provide additional explication.

This new way of thinking also allowed for the concept of a balance; the celestial domain would continue to be controlled by God, but the physical elements of the Earth might be understood and potentially controlled by mankind.

Where would the sentence best be placed?

A. before sentence 10

B. after sentence 10

C. after sentence 11

D. after sentence 12

E. it should not be added to the paragraph

Questions 35–41 refer to the following draft.

(1) Many environmental factors must be evaluated before the construction of roads and highways can receive federal approval. (2) One of the many factors that must be measured and scrutinized when considering where to build highways is traffic noise, which is generally defined as unwanted or objectionable sound. (3) The unit of measurement used to describe a noise level is the decibel (dB). (4) Decibels are measured on a logarithmic scale that quantifies sound intensity in a manner similar to the Richter scale used for earthquake magnitudes. (5) Thus, a doubling of the energy of a noise source, such as doubling of traffic volume, would increase the noise level by 3 dB; a halving of the energy would result in a 3 dB decrease. (6) The human ear is not equally sensitive to all frequencies within the sound spectrum.

(7) Noise-sensitive receptors are generally considered as those locations or areas where housing units or other fixed, developed sites where frequent human use currently occurs, or where it is expected to occur as development expands. (8) They are usually within 1,000 feet of the highway right-of-way line and represent the area where humans are engaged in activities that may be subject to the stress of significant interference from noise. (9) Activities usually associated with sensitive receptors include, but are not limited to, talking, reading, and sleeping. (10) Land uses often associated with sensitive receptors include residential dwellings, mobile homes, hotels, motels, hospitals, nursing homes, education facilities, and libraries.

(11) Federal rules limiting the allowable decibel level in noise-sensitive receptors are an attempt to create a balance between that which is desirable and that which is achievable. (12) Numerous approaches have been considered in establishing these decibel levels; however, speech interference is the key factor applied to the problem of highway traffic noise. (13) Thus, it should be remembered that noise-abatement rules are based on noise levels associated with the interference of speech.

35. The writer wants to revise sentence 1 (reprinted below) to increase the reader's interest and add relevant information.

Many environmental factors must be evaluated before the construction of roads and highways can receive federal approval.

Which of the following revisions best accomplishes the writer's goal?

A. In addition to everything else, many environmental factors must be evaluated before the construction of roads and highways can receive federal approval.

B. Many environmental factors must be carefully weighed and evaluated before the construction of roads and highways can receive federal approval.

C. In addition to the financial cost of building the highway, many environmental factors must be evaluated before the construction of roads and highways can receive federal approval.

D. Specialists and experts must be hired because many environmental factors must be evaluated before the construction of roads and highways can receive federal approval.

E. Population growth and increased demand drive the ever-urgent plans of highway engineers, but many environmental factors must be evaluated before the construction of roads and highways can receive federal approval.

36. The writer wants to add more information to the first paragraph (sentences 1–6) so that readers can better relate to the information about the decibel.

All of the following ideas help achieve that goal EXCEPT

A. The decibel (dB) was first invented and named at the Bell Laboratories in 1924.

B. The decibel is used in acoustics, the study of the physical properties of sound, to measure sound pressure levels.

C. The decibel level of a normal spoken conversation is about 60 dB.

D. The decibel level of an average vacuum cleaner is about 75 dB.

E. The decibel level of a rock concert is about 110 dB.

37. To add additional evidence and make it more convincing, the writer wants to revise sentence 6 (reprinted below).

The human ear is not equally sensitive to all frequencies within the sound spectrum.

Which of the following revisions best accomplishes that goal?

A. The human ear is not equally sensitive to all frequencies within the sound spectrum, and, in addition, there are large differences among different people.

B. The human ear is not equally sensitive to all frequencies within the sound spectrum, and this sensitivity changes as people age; in general, younger people have better hearing, and older people do not.

C. The human ear is not equally sensitive to all frequencies within the sound spectrum; some frequencies affect people more than others, and this has profound implications for noise-limitation strategies.

D. Due to specific adaptation within its structure, the human ear is not equally sensitive to all frequencies within the sound spectrum, thus leading to wide variances among people.

E. It is a complex mystery of human anatomy, but the human ear is not equally sensitive to all frequencies within the sound spectrum; no one, neither layman nor scientist, seems to know exactly why.

38. The writer is considering adding the following sentence after sentence 7.

Non-sensitive receptors include multi-story car parks or shopping centers, markets, and sports complexes.

Should the writer make this addition?

A. No, because readers will find it confusing to distinguish between sensitive and non-sensitive receptors.

B. No, because it is irrelevant to the overall passage and interrupts the logical flow of the paragraph.

C. No, because the information is already understood, making it a redundant addition.

D. Yes, because it is important to understand the difference between noise-sensitive receptors and non-sensitive receptors.

E. Yes, because all city dwellers are familiar with shopping centers and markets.

39. In the second paragraph (sentences 7–10), the writer wishes to add the following sentence to provide a better transition within the paragraph.

Consideration of the impact of problematic noise on sensitive receptors generally centers on two divergent categories, activities and land uses.

Where is the best location to insert this sentence?

A. before sentence 7
B. after sentence 7
C. after sentence 8
D. after sentence 9
E. after sentence 10

40. The writer wants to add emphasis to the point made in sentence 12 (reprinted below).

Numerous approaches have been considered in establishing these decibel levels; however, speech interference is the key factor applied to the problem of highway traffic noise.

All of the following revisions would add emphasis EXCEPT

A. Numerous approaches have been considered in establishing these many decibel levels, but being able to speak normally over traffic noise is one key factor.

B. Numerous approaches have been considered in establishing these decibel levels, but, by far most important, interference with normal speech is the key criterion for the problem of highway traffic noise.

C. Numerous approaches have been considered in establishing these decibel levels, but of these, one has proven to be the most appropriate: Speech interference is the key factor applied to the problem of highway traffic noise.

D. Noise remediation specialists have investigated numerous approaches in establishing rules on decibel levels; most notably, speech interference is the key factor applied to the problem of highway traffic noise.

E. Numerous approaches have been considered by noise experts in establishing these detailed decibel levels; the consensus is that speech interference is the key factor applied to the problem of highway traffic noise.

41. The writer wants to add a new concluding sentence at the end of the passage. Which of the following would provide the best summary of the passage?

A. Federal regulators who determine acceptable noise levels walk a tightrope that is strung between two opposing goals, protecting citizens' interests and helping expand the Interstate Highway System.

B. Federal regulations about acceptable noise levels are based entirely on their interference with spoken language in areas with noise-sensitive receptors.

C. Many environmental factors must be considered when planning a highway; the most important of these is noise abatement for noise-sensitive receptors, such as residential areas and business parks.

D. Noise abatement is an important environmental factor in planning highway construction, and because noise-sensitive receptors must be taken into account, federal regulations attempt to keep noise from interfering with normal conversations.

E. Unpleasant sound is called noise, and noise affects noise-sensitive receptors, and federal regulations are trying to protect citizens' rights to be able to talk in a normal conversation in their homes and businesses.

Questions 42–45 refer to the following draft.

(1) Lawrence of Arabia was the most visible military figure, and certainly the most dashing, to emerge from World War I. (2) Lawrence's daring exploits on desert battlefields of the Eastern Front, plus his leading the local Arab tribes to a surprise victory over the Ottoman Turks, helped turn the tide of the war and earned him the respect and admiration of his peers and commanding officers. (3) Lawrence was trumpeted in the popular press of the day, always photographed in the dashing robes of a desert prince, and he received the overwhelming adulation of a battered public that was all-too-eager to embrace a wartime hero, a solace that had been denied them by the war's dearth of publicly celebrated individuals.

(4) Lawrence was also famous as a prolific writer, and his books tended to glamorize his wartime exploits. (5) In *The Seven Pillars of Wisdom*, Lawrence related tales of military strategy in WWI, as well as Arabic culture, geography, and a variety of other topics. (6) His later *Revolt in the Desert* was an abridged version of *The Seven Pillars*, and it went on to become a huge best-seller; this was due not only to Lawrence's fame and popularity, but also to a shrewd marketing campaign by the publisher. (7) Additional Lawrence books were published posthumously, including *The Mint* and *The Odyssey of Homer*.

(8) After the war, Lawrence experienced a series of triumphs and setbacks. (9) He returned from the war with the rank of Full Colonel in the Royal Army, and yet he was rejected when he first applied to join the Royal Air Force. (10) He attended the Paris Peace Conference from January–May 1919 as an official member of King Faisal's delegation, and yet he was despised by the French for taking the side of the Syrians in their revolt against French colonial rule.

(11) Perhaps the event that most clearly exemplifies the highs and lows of Lawrence's life was his tragic and meaningless death. (12) In May 1935, Lawrence was riding his prized motorcycle that he called "George V" near his home cottage outside London. (13) He suddenly came upon two boys on bicycles directly in his path; by swerving to avoid the boys, Lawrence traded his life for theirs. (14) Thus, the world lost a great military leader and statesman, a great writer, and a great "man of the people." (15) He was all of 46 years old.

42. The writer is considering revising sentence 1 (reprinted below) to provide an informative and attention-getting opening line.

Lawrence of Arabia was the most visible military figure, and certainly the most dashing, to emerge from World War I.

Which of the following best accomplishes that goal?

A. (as it is now)
B. Thomas Edward Lawrence, aka Lawrence of Arabia, was the most dashing romantic hero to emerge from World War I.
C. Thomas Edward Lawrence was the most visible military figure, and certainly the most dashing romantic hero, to emerge from the ashes of World War I.
D. Thomas Edward Lawrence, the world-famous Lawrence of Arabia, was a starring British military figure and a dashing romantic hero who emerged from World War I.
E. Thomas Edward Lawrence, the British soldier who rose to world-wide fame as Lawrence of Arabia, was the most visible military figure, and certainly the most dashing romantic hero, to emerge from the fire and chaos of World War I.

43. The writer is considering deleting the underlined portion of sentence 6 (reprinted below) and adjusting the punctuation as necessary.

His later Revolt in the Desert *was an abridged version of* The Seven Pillars, *and it went on to become a huge best-seller; this was due not only to Lawrence's fame and popularity, but also to a shrewd marketing campaign by the publisher*.

Should the writer keep or delete the underlined text?

A. Yes, it should be deleted because the sentence is more succinct without it.
B. Yes, it should be deleted because that portion adds no new information to the sentence.
C. Yes, it should be deleted because the phrase does not provide relevant information to the passage.
D. No, it should not be deleted because the phrase adds information that readers will not know.
E. No, it should not be deleted because it helps expand the passage.

44. The writer wants to add a phrase to the beginning of sentence 4 (reprinted below) to emphasize the transition from the main point of first paragraph.

Lawrence was also famous as a prolific writer, and his books tended to glamorize his wartime exploits.

Which of the following best fulfills that goal?

A. In contrast to his feats in war,
B. Lawrence was always larger-than-life, and
C. While being famous for his wartime achievements in the British Royal Army,
D. Lawrence became well-known for many triumphs, and
E. Not only renowned for his battleground achievements,

45. Which of the following sentences summarizes the main point of the last paragraph?

A. sentence 11
B. sentence 12
C. sentence 13
D. sentence 14
E. sentence 15

IF YOU FINISH BEFORE TIME IS CALLED, CHECK YOUR WORK ON THIS SECTION ONLY. DO NOT WORK ON ANY OTHER SECTION IN THE TEST.

Section II: Free-Response Questions

Time: 2 hours, 15 minutes

3 questions

Question 1

(Suggested writing time—40 minutes. This question counts for one-third of the total free-response section score.)

The media has been influential in the world's reaction to natural disasters, terrorist attacks, and school shootings since the advent of radio and television. What exactly has this influence been, and how has it affected the number of people who help or care for the victims of these disasters? Has it encouraged people to help, or has it merely shown them that they are the lucky ones who were not involved in each particular disaster?

Considering the influence of the media during disasters, read the following seven sources (including any introductory information) carefully. Then, write an essay that synthesizes material from at least three of the sources and develops your position on the notion that the media has had a positive influence on the effects of disasters.

> Source A (ISDR)
>
> Source B (Cockburn)
>
> Source C (Floroiu)
>
> Source D (Maron)
>
> Source E (Pujol)
>
> Source F (Shah)
>
> Source G (photo)

In your response, you should do the following:

- Respond to the prompt with a thesis that presents a defensible position.
- Select and use evidence from at least three of the provided sources to support your line of reasoning. Indicate clearly the sources used through direct quotation, paraphrase, or summary. Sources may be cited as Source A, Source B, etc., or by using the description in parentheses.
- Explain how the evidence supports your line of reasoning.
- Use appropriate grammar and punctuation in communicating your argument.

Body paragraph #1 → Sources A, F/C → +

Body paragraph #2 → Source G/B → −

Source A

"ISDR Joins Asia-Pacific Broadcasting Union to boost information, education on disasters." *UNESCAP News Services*. 10 June 2005. Web. 25 Sept. 2005.

The following excerpt is from an online article that introduces new radio and television programs that will educate and prepare people for natural disasters in the Asia-Pacific countries.

ISDR (International Strategy for Disaster Reduction) considers media an essential partner to enhance public safety and adverse impacts of natural disasters. "Media are not only part of the early warning chain; they are the best channel to prepare communities for disasters. They can help educate people on the need to reduce risk by regularly informing on the hazards and social vulnerabilities that may lead to disasters. Media also play an important role in convincing Governments and citizens to invest in disaster reduction," says Salvano Briceño, Director of the ISDR secretariat.

"It is just the beginning of a new collaboration. We are planning to promote educational programmes like the ones we are already developing in Africa, in Latin America and the Caribbean, and incite broadcasters to invest more in disaster reduction. Education and preparedness are the key to reduce the number of affected people by natural hazards every year. If people know what to do, they can save their own life. Education on disasters should be part of the school's curriculum like it is in Japan and Cuba, for instance. The more people are aware of the risks they face, the better chance they have to save their lives when hazards strike," says Mr. Briceño.

"Broadcasters have a responsibility to educate people and raise their awareness of the dangers of natural disasters. They can do this by airing public service announcements, producing special programmes to mark the anniversaries of previous disasters and creating other content," says David Astley, Secretary-General of the ABU. "The ABU is well positioned to both coordinate the improvement of emergency warning systems through television and radio among broadcasters across the Pacific region and to assist in the development of content designed to educate audiences in advance on how to respond in the event of emergencies and natural disasters."

Source B

Cockburn, Patrick. "Catastrophe on camera: Why media coverage of natural disasters is flawed." *The Independent*. 20 Jan. 2011. Web. 29 Nov. 2017.

The following is an excerpted online article discussing the accuracy and impact of media coverage of disasters.

Media coverage of natural disasters—floods, blizzards, hurricanes, earthquakes and volcanoes—is largely accepted as an accurate reflection of what really happened. But in my experience, the opposite is true: the reporting of cataclysms or lesser disasters is often wildly misleading. Stereotyping is common: whichever the country involved, there are similar images of wrecked bridges, half-submerged houses and last-minute rescues.

The scale of the disaster is difficult to assess from news coverage: are we seeing or reading about the worst examples of devastation, or are these the norm? Are victims in the hundreds or the millions? Most usually the extent of the damage and the number of casualties are exaggerated, particularly in the developed world. I remember covering floods on the Mississippi in the 1990s and watching as a wall of cameras and cameramen focused on a well-built house in a St Louis suburb which was slowly disappearing under the water. But just a few hundred yards away, ignored by all the cameramen, a long line of gamblers was walking unconcernedly along wooden walkways to board a river boat casino.

The reporting of natural disasters appears easy, but it is difficult to do convincingly. Over the past year, a series of calamities or, at the least, surprisingly severe weather, has dominated the news for weeks at a time. [In 2010], Haiti had its worst earthquake in 200 years, which killed more than 250,000 people. In [2010], exceptionally heavy monsoon rain turned the Indus river into a vast dangerous lake, forcing millions of Pakistani farmers to flee their homes and take refuge on the embankments. Less devastating was unexpectedly heavy snow in Britain in December and the severe blizzard which struck New York at Christmas. In the first half of January [2011], the news was once again being led by climatic disasters: the floods in Queensland and the mudslides in Brazil.

All these events are dramatic and should be interesting, but the reporting of them is frequently repetitious and dull. This may be partly because news coverage of all disasters, actual or forecast, is delivered in similarly apocalyptic tones. Particularly in the US, weather dramas are so frequently predicted that dire warnings have long lost their impact. This helps to explain why so many people are caught by surprise when there is a real catastrophe, such as Hurricane Katrina breaking the levees protecting New Orleans in 2005 and flooding the city. US television news never admits the role it plays in ensuring that nobody takes warnings of floods and hurricanes too seriously because they have heard it all before.

Once the initial drama of a disaster is over, coverage frequently dribbles away because nothing new is happening. I remember how bizarre the foreign editor of the newspaper I was then working for found it that I should want to go back to Florida a month after Hurricane Andrew to see what had happened to the victims. "I am not sure that is still a story," he responded sourly to what he evidently considered a highly eccentric request.

[handwritten] media coverage of natural disasters is only a accurate discription of what happened.

Source C

Floroiu, Ruxandra. "Alerting America: Effective Risk Communication." Washington, D.C.: The National Academic Press, 2002. Print.

The following excerpt is from a book discussing communications to the public about the risk associated with various kinds of hazards and disasters.

The sixth Natural Disasters Roundtable (NDR) forum, "Alerting America: Effective Risk Communication," was held on October 31, 2002, at the National Academies in Washington, D.C. Approximately 140 participants from government, academia, business, industry and civil society attended the one-day forum. The objective of the forum was to provide the opportunity for researchers, decision-makers, practitioners and other stakeholders to exchange views and perspectives on communicating risk information to the public about various kinds of hazards and disasters.

Effective and consistent risk communication is vital to disaster reduction and response. Formal and informal groups and the media are important channels for risk communication. And technology is playing an increasingly crucial role, making it possible to track potential disaster agents, alert authorities, and educate and warn the public in a more timely manner. However, underlying the public response to risk communication are other factors such as social structure, norms, resources and risk perception, which are embedded in past experience and group interaction.

Alearting America has a effective Risk of communication

Source D

Maron, Dina Fine. "How Social Media Is Changing Disaster Response." *Scientific American*. 7 June 2017. Web. 12 Sept. 2017.

The following excerpt examines the degree to which social media has helped improve disaster response and offers suggestions for improvement.

The Federal Emergency Management Agency (FEMA) wrote in its 2013 National Preparedness report that during and immediately following Hurricane Sandy, "users sent more than 20 million Sandy-related Twitter posts despite the loss of cell phone service during the peak of the storm." New Jersey's largest utility company, PSE&G, said at the subcommittee hearing that during Sandy they staffed up their Twitter feeds and used them to send word about the daily locations of their giant tents and generators. "At one point during the storm, we sent so many tweets to alert customers, we exceeded the [number] of tweets allowed per day," PSE&G'S Jorge Cardenas, vice president of asset management and centralized services, told the subcommittee.

Following the Boston Marathon bombings, one quarter of Americans reportedly looked to Facebook, Twitter and other social networking sites for information, according to The Pew Research Center. The sites also formed a key part of the information cycle: when the Boston Police Department posted its final "CAPTURED!!!" tweet of the manhunt, more than 140,000 people retweeted it. Community members via a simple Google document offered strangers lodging, food or a hot shower when roads and hotels were closed.

Each disaster sparks its own complex web of fast-paced information exchange. That's a good thing, says Mark Keim, associate director for science in the Office of Environmental Health Emergencies; it can both improve disaster response and allow affected populations to take control of their situation as well as feel empowered.

Drawing up an effective social media strategy and tweaking it to fit an emergency, however, is a crucial part of preparedness planning, says disaster sociologist Jeannette Sutton, a senior research scientist at the University of Colorado at Colorado Springs who studies social media in crises and disaster. For the Boston Marathon incident, she found no consistent hashtag on Twitter, which can make tracking relevant information difficult. Even searching for the word "Boston" may fall short, she says, because it could lead to unrelated matter like Boston tourism or fail to capture relevant tweets that did not include the word Boston.

As part of disaster preparedness, she says, it would be useful to teach the public how to use social media effectively, how to get information from the Web and also how to put out useful information. "Tweets flow so quickly it's like a fire hose where you're trying to extract bits of information that are relevant."

The Federal emergency Management reported

Source E

Pujol, Frances. "Fukushima as a Chernobyl Nuclear Disaster: Media References by Countries." *Reputation-Metrics*. Newsreputation.com. 16 March 2011. Web. 16 Sept. 2017.

The Fukushima Daiichi Nuclear Power Plant disaster was an energy accident that was primarily initiated by the tsunami following the Tōhoku earthquake on March 11, 2011. The following charts present how much of the news coverage about the Fukushima disaster referred to the previous nuclear disaster at Chernobyl, which had occurred in 1986 in the Ukrainian Soviet Socialist Republic of the Soviet Union (USSR). Each chart explores individual countries in different locations of the world.

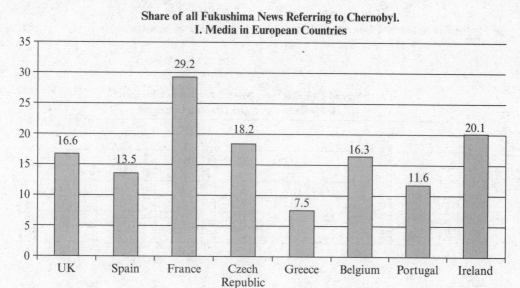

Share of all Fukushima News Referring to Chernobyl.
I. Media in European Countries

Media, Reputation and Intangibles Center, MRI Universidad de Navarra

[handwritten] Nuclear Power Plant disaster was an emergency accident.

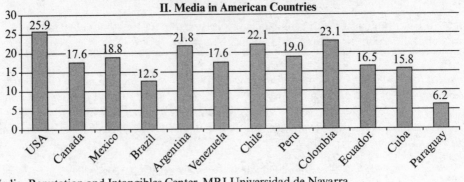

Share of all Fukushima News Referring to Chernobyl.
II. Media in American Countries

Media, Reputation and Intangibles Center, MRI Universidad de Navarra

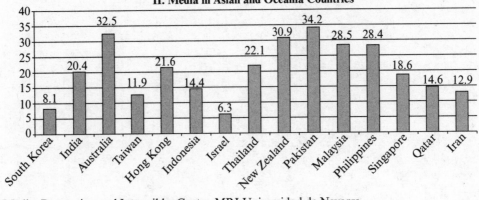

Share of all Fukushima News Referring to Chernobyl.
II. Media in Asian and Oceania Countries

Media, Reputation and Intangibles Center, MRI Universidad de Navarra

Source F

Shah, Anup. "Hurricane Katrina—Rejuvenating the Mainstream Media?" *Global Issues*. 9 Sept. 2005. Web. 12 Dec. 2005.

The following is an online article about the effects of Hurricane Katrina on the media.

It has not gone unnoticed by many that the American mainstream media has become more critical of power in the wake of Hurricane Katrina and the poor response of authorities and George Bush in its aftermath. Many have wondered if this finally means the mainstream media will do what it is supposed to: provide a quality service, critiquing claims rather than simply reporting them, and fundamentally, allowing people to make informed decisions.

Media watchdog *FAIR* is guarded in its optimism, noting that not all reporting has been that good. In addition:

In the aftermath of Hurricane Katrina, a more aggressive press corps seems to have caught the White House public relations team off-balance—a situation the White House has not had to face very often in the last five years. Many might wonder why it took reporters so long; as Eric Boehlert wrote in Salon.com (9/7/05):

"It's hard to decide which is more troubling: that it took the national press corps five years to summon up enough courage to report, without apology, that what the Bush administration says and does are often two different things, or that it took the sight of bodies floating facedown in the streets of New Orleans to trigger a change in the press's behavior."

American mainstream media has become more critical of power.

121

Source G

Wikipedia Commons. 7 Aug. 2016. Web. 1 Nov. 2019.

The following photo, taken by a U.S. Navy photographer, depicts the German zeppelin airship Hindenburg shortly *after catching fire on May 6, 1937, at Lakehurst Air Station in New Jersey. The Hindenburg, which had recently arrived from Germany, was attempting to dock with its mooring mast when it burst into flames, killing 36. Shattering public confidence in airship safety, the disaster abruptly ended the era of airship travel.*

the disaster aburptty ended
the era of airship travel.

Question 2

(Suggested writing time—40 minutes. This question counts for one-third of the total free-response section score.)

In the following two passages, Virginia Woolf describes two different meals she was served during a university visit. The first meal was served at the men's college, while the second meal was served at the women's college.

Read the two passages carefully, then write an essay in which you analyze the rhetorical choices Woolf makes to convey her underlying attitude toward women's place in society as she describes the two meals.

In your response, you should do the following:

- Respond to the prompt with a thesis that analyzes the writer's rhetorical choices.
- Select and use evidence to support your line of reasoning.
- Explain how the evidence supports your line of reasoning.
- Demonstrate an understanding of the rhetorical situation.
- Use appropriate grammar and punctuation in communicating your argument.

Passage 1

It is a curious fact that novelists have a way of making us believe that luncheon parties are invariably memorable for something very witty that was said, or for something very wise that was done. But they seldom spare a word for what was eaten. It is part of the novelist's convention not to mention soup and salmon and ducklings, as if soup and a salmon and ducklings were of no importance whatsoever, as if nobody ever
(5) smoked a cigar or drank a glass of wine. Here, however, I shall take the liberty to defy that convention and to tell you that the lunch on this occasion began with soles, sunk in a deep dish, over which the college cook had spread a counterpane of the whitest cream, save that it was branded here and there with brown spots like the spots on the flanks of a doe. After that, came the partridges, but if this suggests a couple of bald, brown birds on a plate you are mistaken. The partridges, many and various, came with all their retinue of sauces and
(10) salads, the sharp and the sweet, each in its order; their potatoes, thin as coins but not so hard; their sprouts, foliated as rosebuds but more succulent. And no sooner had the roast and its retinue been done with than the silent serving-man, the Beadle himself perhaps in a milder manifestation, set before us, wreathed in napkins, a confection which rose all sugar from the waves. To call it pudding and so relate it to rice and tapioca would be an insult. Meanwhile the wineglasses had flushed yellow and flushed crimson; had been emptied; had been
(15) filled. And thus by degrees was lit, halfway down the spine, which is the seat of the soul, not that hard little electric light which we call brilliance, as it pops in and out upon our lips, but the more profound, subtle and subterranean glow, which is the rich yellow flame of rational intercourse. No need to hurry. No need to sparkle. No need to be anybody but oneself. We are all going to heaven . . . in other words, how good life seemed, how sweet its rewards, how trivial this grudge or that grievance, how admirable friendship and the
(20) society of one's kind, as, lighting a good cigarette, one sunk among the cushions in the window-seat.

Passage 2

Here was my soup. Dinner was being served in the great dining-hall. Far from being spring it was in fact an evening in October. Everybody was assembled in the big dining-room. Dinner was ready. Here was the soup. It was a plain gravy soup. There was nothing to stir the fancy in that. One could have seen through the transparent liquid any pattern that there might have been on the plate itself. But there was no pattern. The plate was plain.
(25) Next came beef with its attendant greens and potatoes—a homely trinity, suggesting the rumps of cattle in a muddy market, and sprouts curled and yellowed at the edge, and bargaining and cheapening, and women with string bags on Monday morning. There was no reason to complain of human nature's daily food, seeing that the supply was sufficient and coal-miners doubtless were sitting down to less. Prunes and custard followed. And if any one complains that prunes, even when mitigated by custard, are an uncharitable vegetable (fruit
(30) they are not), stringy as a miser's heart and exuding a fluid such as might run in miser's veins who have denied themselves wine and warmth for eighty years and yet not given to the poor, he should reflect that there are people whose charity embraces even the prune. Biscuits and cheese came next, and here the water-jug was liberally passed round, for it is the nature of biscuits to be dry, and these were biscuits to the core. That was all. The meal was over. Everybody scraped their chairs back; the swing-doors swung violently to and fro; soon the
(35) hall was emptied of every sign of food and made ready no doubt for breakfast next morning.

123

Question 3

(Suggested writing time—40 minutes. This question counts for one-third of the total free-response section score.)

Read the following excerpt from Ralph Waldo Emerson's speech, "The American Scholar," which was delivered at Cambridge on August 31, 1837. Then write an essay that argues your position regarding Emerson's ideas about books and their usefulness.

In your response, you should do the following:

- Respond to the prompt with a thesis that presents a defensible position.
- Provide evidence to support your line of reasoning.
- Explain how the evidence supports your line of reasoning.
- Use appropriate grammar and punctuation in communicating your argument.

The theory of books is noble. The scholar of the first age received into him the world around; brooded thereon; gave it the new arrangement of his own mind, and uttered it again. It came into him—life; it went out from him—truth. It came to him—short-lived actions; it went out from him—immortal thoughts. It came to him—business; it went from him—poetry. It was—dead fact; now, it is quick thought. It can stand, and it can go. It now endures, it now flies, it now inspires. Precisely in proportion to the depth of mind from which it issued, so high does it soar, so long does it sing.

Each age, it is found, must write its own books; or rather, each generation for the next succeeding. Yet hence arises a grave mischief. The sacredness which attaches to the act of creation—the act of thought—is instantly transferred to the record. The poet chanting was felt to be a divine man. Henceforth the chant is divine also. The writer was a just and wise spirit. Henceforth it is settled, the book is perfect; as love of the hero corrupts into worship of his statue. Instantly, the book becomes noxious. The guide is a tyrant. . . . Colleges are built on it. Books are written on it by thinkers, not by Man Thinking; by men of talent, that is, who start wrong, who set out from accepted dogmas, not from their own sight of principles. Meek young men grow up in libraries, believing it their duty to accept the views which Cicero, which Locke, which Bacon, have given, forgetful that Cicero, Locke, and Bacon were only young men in libraries when they wrote these books.

Hence, instead of Man Thinking, we have the book-worm. . . .

Books are the best of things, well used; abused, among the worst.

IF YOU FINISH BEFORE TIME IS CALLED, CHECK YOUR WORK ON THIS SECTION ONLY. DO NOT WORK ON ANY OTHER SECTION IN THE TEST.

Answer Key

Section I: Multiple-Choice Questions

1. A	**10.** E	**19.** C	**28.** A	**37.** C
2. B	**11.** D	**20.** D	**29.** B	**38.** B
3. E	**12.** B	**21.** A	**30.** B	**39.** C
4. D	**13.** A	**22.** E	**31.** D	**40.** A
5. C	**14.** D	**23.** E	**32.** D	**41.** D
6. A	**15.** B	**24.** C	**33.** E	**42.** E
7. C	**16.** E	**25.** D	**34.** C	**43.** C
8. D	**17.** A	**26.** C	**35.** E	**44.** E
9. B	**18.** B	**27.** E	**36.** A	**45.** D

Section II: Free-Response Questions

Essay scoring rubrics, student essays, and analyses appear beginning on p. 133.

Answer Explanations

Section I: Multiple-Choice Questions

The passage referred to in questions 1–13 is taken from an address delivered by Elizabeth Cady Stanton to the women's rights convention at Seneca Falls in 1848.

1. **A.** Used as it is in the phrase "rights and wrongs" (lines 1–2), the word "rights," choice A, means that which is morally good or proper. However, when modified by "civil and political," the word "rights" also means privileges. All other answer choices have only one meaning. "Wrongs" (B) refers to the injustices that women have historically faced. "Seat" (C) refers to a sitting position, in this case at the head of a baby's cradle. "Head" (D) refers to the top of a cradle where the baby's head is placed. "Attire" (E) refers to clothing.

2. **B.** Stanton here is almost certainly taking up the points repeatedly made by the opponents of women's suffrage and using them to provide a comic opening for her address, choice B. Choice A is incorrect because the speech offers no evidence that feminists desire to wear men's clothing or have men taking care of babies in their cradles. Choice C, thinking that Stanton's details derive from her creative imagination, contradicts her purpose; she is not imagining these details but instead stating that women do *not* propose them. Choice D is unreasonable and historically inaccurate; when women have been given the ability to vote, men have not been forced to raise babies, nor have women taken to wearing men's attire. Choice E is also historically inaccurate; no such classical ideal of men and women in an equal society exists.

3. **E.** Stanton states that clergymen and men in the legal profession in England ("the first nation on the globe") as well as the Pope and his cardinals wear flowing robes, and so they must tacitly agree with women that this attire is more dignified and imposing than men's clothing, choice E. Choice A is unreasonable; Stanton hardly suggests that cross-dressing creates greater dignity, and it is erroneous to consider clergy and

British legal attire as cross-dressing in the first place. Choice B is true in that judges and clergymen do traditionally wear flowing robes, but this is not the argument that Stanton is advancing. Choice C has no evidence in the speech, which simply does not address American lawyers and clergymen, let alone what they may think of women's clothing. Choice D, that human value should not be judged by clothing, is a nice sentiment, but it is not the argument that Stanton advances.

4. **D.** The words and phrases in choices A, B, C, and E are literal and mean what they say, but the phrase "nobler sex," used in the speech to refer to men, is ironic. The passage makes clear that Stanton does not believe men are "nobler" than women.

5. **C.** The question asks about the use of mock-serious diction for satiric effect, and choice C grants pompous dignity to men's fashions by calling them "philosophical experiments." Choice A is literal, referring to the Pope's cardinals, and it is not satirical or mocking. Choice B does not mock, and it is not satirical to claim that the flowing robes of some professions subtly acknowledge the undignified appearance of men's clothing. Choices D and E are satiric, but the language is not inflated or mock-serious; the descriptions are too literal for that description.

6. **A.** An audience (then or now) accustomed to hearing of women overconcerned for their clothes and appearance should be amused by this pointing of the finger at men engaging in the same behavior. Modern readers may be surprised to learn of elevator shoes in the mid-19th century, or the Russian belt that, like a corset, would make the waist appear smaller, choice A. Choice B, that both men and women wear boots and belts, is simply a fact and not comical. Choice C may or may not be true; whether or not women dress to impress other women more than men does not create comedy in the speech. Choice D, stating that men's clothing is more comfortable than women's, contradicts the description of uncomfortable high-heeled boots and the constraint of Russian belts. Choice E is irrelevant; whether or not women's shoes are usually higher than men's does not play a part in the comedy.

7. **C.** The first paragraph has a comic point about clothing, but it does not introduce the real issues of the address. In fact, the whole paragraph is a good example of the rhetorical technique in which the speaker, by saying she will not talk about something, does indeed talk about it, and we cannot help but chuckle at the teasing tone. As choice C states, the second paragraph has a serious tone and is not concerned with the comedic issues discussed in the first paragraph. Choice A is not true to the speech's organization; the first paragraph does not develop examples of the issues that are discussed in the second paragraph. Instead, it engages the audience's attention with comical banter about clothing. Choice B erroneously claims the issues of the first paragraph are seriously developed in the second; they are not. Choice D is wrong because the first paragraph does not raise any questions at all, nor does the second paragraph answer them. It is a misreading of the speech to think so. Choice E is flat-out wrong; the first paragraph grants no concessions; therefore, the second cannot retract something that does not exist.

8. **D.** Stanton's tone in the second paragraph is indeed irritated and authoritative; her use of words and phrases like "disgraceful," "chastise and imprison his wife," "unjust," and "a shame and a disgrace" support choice D. In all of the incorrect choices, you can eliminate at least one of adjectives. Stanton is not "disinterested" (A), not "soft-spoken" (B), not "dry and ironical" (C), and not "tactful" (E).

9. **B.** The tenor of the second paragraph is totally unlike that of the first. The first paragraph is witty and ironic; the second is somber and serious. Thus, the second paragraph marks an important shift in the passage, choice B. Choice A is inaccurate because the second paragraph does not intensify the irony of the first; instead, it changes the tone and thrust entirely. Both paragraphs use concrete details (C), and the first is not *more dependent* on them. Regarding choice D, the exact opposite is true; the second paragraph changes, not echoes, the tone and has less restraint and more anger than the first. Choice E incorrectly claims the first paragraph is less personal than the second; both paragraphs present the author's point of view and are equally personal.

10. **E.** Stanton refers to Daniel Webster to show that males may vote regardless of their education or intelligence. As males, both Daniel Webster (a representative of intelligence) and the ignorant ditch-digger have the right to vote, choice E. Choices A and B are both historically accurate; Daniel Webster was an American patriot and a great orator, but neither answer choice addresses why Stanton refers to him. Choice C contradicts the speech, Stanton's purpose, and history; Daniel Webster does not represent the injustice of

the American voting system. Choice D is wrong because Stanton does not believe men are superior to women, and she does not use Webster to exemplify any such idea.

11. D. The two parallel sentences make the argument that males may vote regardless of their education and regardless of their strength. The vote is not given to males because they are physically stronger than females, because gender alone, not physical strength, determines who may vote. Therefore, choice D is correct. Choice A wrongly states that the second sentence repeats the idea of the first; instead, the first discusses intellectual ability, while the second discusses physical ability. Choice B erroneously claims the second sentence raises objections to the first sentence; this is simply not true. Choice C also represents a misread of the speech; the second sentence does not concede anything. Choice E contradicts the speech; the two sentences are indeed concerned with equality, not rights.

12. B. Stanton wants the question of women's rights kept separate from the question of their equality. In context, "the question of equality" in this portion of the speech refers to the fact that no citizen has to be equal in mental and physical abilities to be granted Constitutional rights, while "the question of rights" refers directly to women being denied rights that the Constitution guarantees. Therefore, the proof of women's denied rights does not determine the truth that all people do not have the same mental or physical abilities, choice B. Choice A demonstrates a misread of the quotation in question; in this part of the passage, Stanton is merely pointing out that women deserve the same Constitutional rights as men, not that they will be equal to men. Choice C contradicts her point; the equality of men and women *cannot* determine whether they have equal civil rights. Choice D is wrong because she believes the question of equality, as defined in the speech, is irrelevant to the question of civil rights. Choice E presents another misread; she certainly sees a distinction between equality and rights.

13. A. Choice A pinpoints Stanton's rhetorical purpose; by the end of the third paragraph she has outlined the injustices done to women with present laws; specifically, she mentions man's ability to "chastise and imprison" his wife; take her wages, property, and children; and deny her the right to vote. Choice B misreads her tone; she is subjective and personal, not objective. Choice C incorrectly states that she obscures a complex issue; instead, she clarifies it. Choice D makes no sense; it is unreasonable to think that her purpose is to discuss the common humanity of men and women when she points out the inequalities between them. Choice E is off-base; her *purpose* is not to appeal to gender prejudices of the audience; it is to inform them of injustice to women.

The passage referred to in questions 14–25 is from The American Crisis *(1776) by Thomas Paine.*

14. D. The "summer soldier" and the "sunshine patriot" serve their country only when conditions are favorable to themselves, a behavior akin to that of the proverbial "fair-weather friend." These conditionally patriotic citizens, who want to get involved only on their own terms, are the target of the author's criticism in this sentence, choice D. Choices A and E are unreasonable; neither army reserves (A) nor specialized forces (E) existed at this time. Choice B also makes no sense; while the word "infidel" is used in the second paragraph, it has nothing to do with the quotation given. Choice C is contradictory to the meaning of the quotation given; if the professional British soldiers were instead "summer soldiers," the Revolution would be easier to accomplish.

15. B. The essay is filled with aphorisms—brief, witty sayings—and emotional appeals, choice B. Examples of aphorisms here are "the harder the conflict, the more glorious the triumph" (lines 7–8) and "What we obtain too cheap, we esteem too lightly" (lines 8–9). The author appeals to emotions in his claim that a man's children will curse his cowardice if he fails to act now. Choice A is inaccurate because, although it can be argued that parts of the essay are allegorical, it does not use didactic rhetoric. The author's purpose is clearly to persuade, not to teach, and the rhetoric is too highly charged with emotion to be described as didactic. Choice C is only partially correct. An argument can be made that the essay uses symbolism; for example, the man who runs the tavern at Amboy may be a symbol for all that the author considers to be wrong with American citizens. But this lone example does not constitute "heavy use." Although God is mentioned in three of the four paragraphs, those references are not technically biblical allusion. The author does not use paradox and invective (highly critical language), as in choice D, or historical background and illustration (E).

16. E. The author groups the king (D) of Britain with murderers (A), highwaymen (B), and housebreakers (C) (lines 32–35), but not with cowards, choice E. The line "the blood of his children will curse his cowardice" (lines 6? 4) refers to Americans who fail to sup?t the Revolution, not to the king.

17. A. God, as characterized here, is a just and principled deity, choice A, who will not let a people perish through military destruction because they have "so earnestly and so repeatedly sought to avoid the calamities of war" (lines 25–27). Nor, the author suggests, will this God abandon humans, giving them up "to the care of devils" (line 31). None of the references to God are negative, so choice B, "vexed" (angry), choice C, "indifferent," and choice E, "pernicious" (extremely destructive), are inappropriate answers. Choice D ("contemplative") implies merely that God meditates, but the author suggests a more active God.

18. B. In lines 10–13, the author claims, "Heaven knows how to put a proper price upon its goods; and it would be strange indeed if so celestial an article as freedom should not be highly rated," choice B. Choice A is inaccurate because the author never addresses the relationship between freedom and cowardice. Choice C contradicts the passage; the author states strongly that freedom does not come easily. Choice D also contradicts the passage; the author hopes that one day Americans will know true freedom. Choice E is not addressed in the passage.

19. C. The image of the tavern owner holding the hand of his child is likely designed to increase the emotional appeal of this essay, choice C, appealing to every man's desire to protect his family, even if he has to fight to save it. As the author says, it is "sufficient to awaken every man to duty." Choice A is too simplistic. True, the mention of the child shows that this man has a family, but introducing that fact is not the purpose of the reference. Choice B is incorrect because it isn't the image of the child that provokes the author's anger, but the image of the child's complacent father. The author may feel that the tavern owner is "evil," but the child's image doesn't symbolically increase the evil (D). Choice E contradicts the passage. The author appeals to the traditional values of family and freedom; he does not dismiss them.

20. D. Because aphorisms are short, proverbial sayings of general truth, choice D doesn't fit the definition but rather may be more accurately considered a cliché.

21. A. The author states that America's "situation is remote from all the wrangling world, and she has nothing to do but to trade with them" (lines 52–54), choice A. The author does picture America as the "conqueror" but only with regard to winning its freedom from Britain, which makes choice B too strong a statement to be correct. The author never implies that America should be greater than Britain (C) or sanctified by God (D). Choice E contradicts the passage; if a country conducts trade, its stance is not one of "complete isolationism."

22. E. The author hopes to encourage his readers to take action, and he writes persuasively to achieve that aim. In order to achieve that overall goal, the author employs many modes, but his overriding rhetorical mode is persuasion, choice E. Remember that the question asks for the "best" classification of the passage's mode, and the incorrect responses do not identify the author's main purpose.

23. E. There is a strong emotional appeal, choice E, as the author warns American men that their children will think them cowards and, as he claims, that the heart of a reader who does not feel as he does is "dead." Choice A, that children should also join the Revolution, has no support in the essay. Choice B isn't his purpose, the outcome he desires. He wants men to join the Revolution, to take action, not simply to be afraid. Choice C is inaccurate because the sentence quoted in this question is not directed to the king, but to American citizens. There is no mention of the superiority of either American or British forces and no mention of the advisability of retreat (D).

24. C. The author demonstrates no ambivalence in this paragraph, choice C. He takes a strong stand without vacillation. The paragraph does include the other devices listed: aphorism (A, "'Tis the business of little minds to shrink," lines 69–70), simile (B, "My own line of reasoning is . . . as straight and clear as a ray of light," lines 72–73), parallel construction (D, "What signifies it to me . . . an army of them?", lines 81–84), and analogy (E, the comparison of the king to common thieves, lines 81–88).

25. D. Clearly, this author hopes his readers will feel that it is their patriotic duty toward America to join in supporting the Revolution, choice D. While the author might value "peace and rational thinking" (A), he also clearly suggests that Revolution now is necessary to produce later peace. The negative "overemotional" (B) and "unwarranted" (C) should alert you to the fact that these are not likely answers. The passage contradicts choice E. The author suggests that "Tyranny, like hell, is not easily conquered"—that is, freedom will not come immediately. In addition, the essay's primary purpose is to persuade Americans to join in the struggle to win their liberty, not simply to demand that the British government grant it to them.

The draft referred to in questions 26–34 discusses philosophical changes during the Age of Enlightenment.

26. C. This question calls for a new opening line, to be inserted prior to sentence 1, that will capture the audience's interest as well as provide an introduction to the subject. Choice C offers the best and the most attention-getting introductory sentence for this opening paragraph. It includes sufficient detail ("disease, despair, and ignorance"), along with epic perspective ("for centuries"), and it includes philosophical aspects ("it seemed that God had abandoned them") before affirming that "they began to look elsewhere for answers." It alludes to all of the ideas in the passage, and thus it provides an effective introduction. Choice A seems to begin in the right direction, but its phrase "A darkness had lain over all of Europe" is vague and imprecise, and the phrase "Dark Ages" is pejorative; it is no longer in popular use, and it does not fit the overall time period discussed in the passage. Likewise, choice B tries to catch the reader's attention, but it limits itself to listing multiple examples, and it does not introduce the philosophical concepts that are central to the passage. Choice D offers nothing of substance; it may indeed be "fascinating to compare the philosophical shift" of the time periods, but this alone does not entice a reader's interest, nor does it introduce the passage's content. Choice E, with its idea that "poor, beleaguered Europeans" would welcome the coming Enlightenment, does not address the overall thrust of the passage.

27. E. The first sentence begins by introducing "a major shift in European philosophical thinking," but the paragraph never explains what exactly that shift was; therefore, the paragraph could be improved if some appropriate clarification of the shift were provided, choice E. The suggestion of adding names of philosophers in each time period (A) is irrelevant to the paragraph overall and to its opening sentence. Likewise, the paragraph would not benefit from the addition of the dates of the time periods (B) because the thrust of the paragraph deals with a philosophical shift in thought; in addition, the word "specific" makes choice B incorrect because the philosophical shift actually "morphed" over a long time period. The paragraph would not benefit from the inclusion of evidence that people viewed God as the center of the universe (C); rather, this is a statement of common knowledge about the time period. Choice D is incorrect because the first paragraph is not the best location for giving examples of the changes in thinking; indeed, those changes are addressed in the second paragraph.

28. A. This question asks for the version that best serves as evidence to reinforce the argument of the first paragraph, and the original sentence 5, choice A, is superior to all of the revisions in the other choices. The sentence as written is clear, it flows well with its use of the semicolon to separate ideas, and it succinctly presents three examples to support the writer's argument. Choice B presents a poor transition and sloppy use of a colon, and the unnecessary numbering of the three examples is both distracting and cumbersome. Breaking the ideas into three separate sentences (C) becomes excessively wordy with each sentence's repetitive opening phrase: "One example is when . . . ," "Another example is when . . . ," and "A final example is when. . . ." Choice D can be easily dismissed because it seems to eliminate the cause-and-effect intent of the original, and, in addition, it erroneously uses present tense. Choice E is far too brief, dropping the appropriate transition and bungling the sentence structure. Additionally, with the word "always," choice E turns the third example into an absolute, which changes the intent of the original.

29. B. Sentence 5 contains examples of the idea introduced in sentence 4, that people believed God directed people's lives. Therefore, the transitional phrase "for example" would best introduce sentence 5's purpose, choice B. Choice A, "as an example," is not accurate because it is worded in the singular, while sentence 5 has three examples. The word "hence" (C) makes no sense; it is the equivalent of saying "consequently," or "therefore," and does not fit in with the claims in sentence 5. Choice D, stating "obviously," is wrong for more than one reason; the ideas in sentence 5 are not obvious, and the word "obviously" is already used three times in the sentence, making it a very poor opening word. Choice E, "in this situation," is too vague to be a good transition; believing God played a direct role in people's lives is not a "situation."

30. B. The second paragraph exclusively discusses how the Age of Enlightenment differed philosophically from previous ages. Its purpose is to clarify these differences, and it does so by explicating how "humanity's essential question evolved." Choice B best articulates this purpose. Choice A, with its bland and vague wording, does not address the paragraph's purpose. The second paragraph does not "diverge" (or deviate) from the first; instead, it continues the train of thought as it explores philosophical questions. Choice C is a contradiction; the second paragraph does not magnify (or enlarge) the philosophical problems of the Renaissance; it explains how the ages differed. Choice D incorrectly anticipates what an audience might appreciate, which is impossible to predict. Additionally, an audience's appreciation is not remotely the purpose of the paragraph. Choice E incorrectly states that the philosophy is awkward to understand, and it is questionable whether the second paragraph simplifies it or not. In any case, choice E does not describe the purpose of the second paragraph.

31. D. This question calls for a revision that strengthens the explanation contained in sentence 8. Choice D provides the strongest explanatory statement by positing the idea that "some enlightened people applied scientific knowledge and rational explanation to understand underlying mechanisms of natural phenomena," thus providing a logically convincing introduction to the notion of "*how* things worked" in the second half of the sentence. Choice A, "some people looked elsewhere for explanations," neither amplifies the explanation nor clarifies the vague idea of looking elsewhere. Choice B conflates the two ideas; people had *previously* looked only to the heavens, they were not just beginning to do so. In addition, the passage does not support the idea in choice B that people hoped "God would *explain* natural catastrophes." Choice C misreads the passage; people had become increasingly *dissatisfied*, not satisfied, with traditional explanation, and they began to realize that God was *not responsible* for all bad events; therefore, they began to ask "*how* things worked." Additionally, the idea that they felt no need to explore alternatives contradicts the second half of the sentence. Choice E also displays an illogical contradiction; if people continued to not accept personal responsibility for bad events, it makes no sense that they would in turn ponder *how* things worked.

32. D. This question asks which information would NOT make a good addition to the second paragraph; in order to discern the correct response, you must understand exactly what the paragraph is about. In this case, all the points in the second paragraph explore how thinking changed during the Enlightenment, and it is choice D that instead deals with the antiquated thinking of prior ages; it does not fit in with this discussion of Enlightenment thinking. All of the other choices do support the main idea of this paragraph. Isaac Newton (A), who was the most prominent scientist and mathematician of the Age of Enlightenment, helped shift ideas toward finding natural cause-and-effect relationships rather than believing in divine intervention. The idea in choice B, that people during the Enlightenment began to doubt that God could predestine humans to eternal damnation while empowering tyrannical kings, is part of the overall shift in thinking that is detailed in the second paragraph and, therefore, would make an appropriate addition. Choice C, which explains John Locke's assertion that men had the power to change governments, would likewise be a very appropriate addition to the paragraph. Part of the thrust of the Enlightenment is that people began to place more trust in science and rational thinking, which would make choice E another appropriate addition.

33. E. This proposed additional sentence does not relate to the overall argument, so it should not be added. Choice E recognizes that the potential addition addresses similarities between the two ages that are irrelevant to the rest of the passage. The new sentence makes the inappropriate claim that "The Enlightenment world view continued the Renaissance world view," and it also adds the idea of the focus on the arts in the Renaissance, an idea that is not in the passage at all. Choice A votes for adding the sentence with the incorrect reason that it enhances the writer's argument, when, in fact, it gets too off track to augment the passage. Choice B also votes for the addition, erroneously claiming it clarifies the differences between the two time periods, but it actually notes similarities between them. Choice C also claims the addition is a valid one, stating that readers can relate to the new information; this bland and questionable idea does not relate to the theme of the passage as a whole. Choice D accurately dismisses the addition, but for the wrong reason, claiming the passage does not need more distinction; however, because the potential addition deals with similarities between the two ages, it does not actually add distinction at all.

34. C. When you are asked a question about where to place a new sentence within a paragraph, be sure to understand the organization of the paragraph as a whole. In this case, the opening sentence 10 explains that the shift in humanity's thinking cannot be underestimated; next, sentence 11 explains how this philosophical shift placed mankind in charge of a smooth-running ship; then sentence 12 explains the outcome of the shift, leaving God in the heavens and humanity solving their own problems on Earth. Notice that when placed after sentence 11, choice C, the new sentence is used to provide a transition to the idea of balance, whereby God can still rule the heavens, but humanity can come to understand events that fall under their control. Thus, the most logical location to place this new sentence is between sentence 11 and sentence 12 because it transitions from the idea in sentence 11 and introduces the idea in sentence 12. It is not logical to place this transition before sentence 10 (A), as it has no relation to the idea that the effect "cannot be underestimated." Nor does the new sentence fit between sentences 10 and 11 (B). The ideas in sentences 10 and 11 complement each other; they do not need an intermediary transition. Likewise, this sentence also does not fit after sentence 12 (D); that would make it the closing line of the essay, but the new sentence is a transition, so it must precede something else. Finally, choice E claims the sentence should not be added, but the paragraph as a whole is definitely stronger with the additional sentence when placed between sentences 11 and 12.

The draft referred to in questions 35–41 discusses environmental factors that must be considered in highway construction.

35. E. This question specifies that the goal of revising the opening sentence is to increase the reader's interest and add relevant information, so the correct answer must include something stimulating to make the reader want to continue. One means to meet this goal is to introduce a contradiction, something to pique the reader's curiosity and, thus, make readers want to read on. Choice E presents an interesting contradiction: Accelerating population growth and suburban sprawl increase the demand for highway-building, but increased environmental protections tend to curtail or limit highway construction. The other options all try to increase the impact of the opening sentence, but none is as effective as choice E. Choice A makes only a minimal change to the original, merely adding the insipid and vague phrase, "In addition to everything else." It adds nothing of interest or any relevant information. Choice B adds that environmental factors must be "carefully weighed," but this improvement is negligible and adds no degree of interest or relevance. Choice C addresses the financial costs associated with such projects, but the remainder of the passage does not address financial considerations, so this addition is irrelevant. Choice D introduces the concept of additional labor needs and the costs associated with hiring specialists and experts, but that too is irrelevant, and it is also worded poorly.

36. A. This question is fairly straightforward; try to find the right answer quickly and move on. Choice A is the correct exception; knowing that Bell Laboratories invented the decibel in 1924 does not help anyone better understand what the dB numbers actually mean. Choice B helps further define the decibel, explaining that decibels measure sound pressure levels, adding relevant information. Choices C, D, and E also help make the numbers more understandable; virtually everyone has an idea of the volume of spoken conversation (C), or a vacuum cleaner (D), or a rock concert (E). All of these examples help readers better appreciate and comprehend the dB numbers.

37. C. Choice C provides the most direct, on-topic, and convincing evidence for this sentence because it expands on the idea of some frequencies being more problematic than others, and it also ties this idea to the topic of the passage, the planning of noise-limitation strategies. Choice A merely mentions some vague differences between people and thus fails to add any convincing evidence. Choice B simply remarks that hearing changes as people age, but that information is not significant evidence; it does not make the sentence more convincing and does not relate to highway construction. Choice D brings up a "specific adaptation within . . . the human ear," but that small fact does not add much to our understanding of noise pollution as it relates to highways, the main topic of the passage. Choice E brings nothing to the argument, stating the forgettable phrase "It's a complex mystery. . . ." Instead of adding convincing evidence, it adds more confusion.

38. B. The suggested sentence would not be a good addition to the passage. The main argument deals with the need for considering noise abatement in highway construction, especially in locations with noise-sensitive receptors. Choice B accurately states that a simple list of non-sensitive noise receptors is irrelevant to the overall argument. Choice A agrees that the suggested sentence is not a good idea, but its reasoning is flawed; it is unreasonable to claim that readers cannot distinguish between the two kinds of receptors, especially because noise-sensitive receptors are clearly defined in the passage. Choice C likewise votes correctly for not including the sentence, but for the wrong reason. The information in the new sentence has not, in fact, been explained, and also it does not appear to be necessary or relevant to the rest of the passage. Choice D presents a poor rationale for adding the new sentence; within the scope of this particular argument, it is not important to further distinguish between sensitive and non-sensitive noise receptors. Choice E voices a completely unreasonable idea for the inclusion of the new sentence; it is irrelevant to the theme of this passage whether or not city dwellers are familiar with shopping centers and markets.

39. C. Whenever you are asked for the best location to insert a sentence into a paragraph, you need to understand the progression of ideas and the overall organization of the paragraph. In this case, sentence 7 introduces noise-sensitive receptors and explains their locations. Sentence 8 gives more detail of the location of the receptors. Sentence 9 jumps to describing activities associated with noise-sensitive receptors, and sentence 10 describes land use associated with the receptors. Because the new sentence introduces activities and land use, it logically belongs between sentence 8 and sentence 9; thus, choice C is correct. The purpose of the new sentence is to provide a transition between the ideas in sentences 7 and 8 versus the examples that are presented in sentences 9 and 10. The new sentence simply does not fit anywhere else in this paragraph. It cannot be the opening to the paragraph (A) because it does not introduce the whole paragraph. It cannot follow sentence 7 (B), which would interrupt the logical coherence between sentences 7 and 8. It cannot follow the activities described in sentence 9 (D), nor can it follow the land-use ideas of sentence 10 (E). It must precede sentences 9 and 10 because it introduces the idea of activities and land uses.

40. A. The key to this question is finding one option that does NOT increase the emphasis of the point in sentence 12, and choice A is the weakest option. The revision in choice A merely adds the word "many" to the first half of the sentence and then simply rephrases the second half; neither change adds emphasis. In fact, changing the original phrase "is the key factor" to "is one key factor" weakens the intent of the original sentence and changes the meaning by implying other factors are equally important. Notice that all of the other choices do, in fact, increase the emphasis of the point. Choice B does not change the first idea, but it effectively emphasizes the idea in the second part by claiming the idea is "by far most important." Likewise, choice C concentrates on expanding and emphasizing the later idea, calling it "most appropriate." Choice D effectively rewrites the first part of the sentence, adding the credence of "noise remediation specialists." Choice E adds emphasis by explaining how "the consensus is that speech interference is the key factor" as it relates to highway traffic noise.

41. D. In selecting a new concluding sentence, you should look for one that includes ideas from the whole essay, not just one that expounds on an individual aspect. Choice D does this job well by including a multitude of ideas from the essay, ranging from noise abatement, to highway planning, to noise-sensitive receptors, and finally to the need for "normal conversations." Choice A is not an appropriate conclusion because it includes only one idea, the conflict between citizens' rights and highway noise; additionally, it is questionable whether these are actually "opposing goals." Choice B makes a similar mistake, focusing entirely on one idea, namely that regulations are based entirely on protecting people's conversations; additionally, the absolute word "entirely" is inaccurate. Choice C does hint at "Many environmental factors," but it fails to enumerate them, and then it takes the argument in the essay to an extreme by claiming noise abatement is "the most important" factor in highway planning; the passage does not support that absolute idea. Choice E is far too simplistic; first it defines "noise" (which was already defined in the first paragraph), and then it makes a vague statement about protecting the right to be able to talk. This passage deserves a more appropriate and well-developed conclusion.

The draft referred to in questions 42–45 discusses the life of T. E. Lawrence.

42. E. Choice E is the most informative and attention-getting version of the opening sentence; it includes all of the information in the original, plus it adds the information that Lawrence was British, a fact some may not know. It also elaborates his accomplishments by claiming that he "rose to world-wide fame" and later emerged "from the fire and chaos of World War I." Choice A fails to identify who Lawrence of Arabia was and therefore is not sufficiently attention-getting to serve as the opening sentence. Choice B adds another fact, connecting T. E. Lawrence to his moniker, Lawrence of Arabia, but it otherwise falls flat as an opening sentence. Choice C, like choice A, fails to identify that T. E. Lawrence was later known as Lawrence of Arabia, and so it does not provide adequate information. Choice D identifies Lawrence as British but then simply states that he was a military figure and hero; it does not grab attention as choice E does.

43. C. In considering whether or not to delete the underlined portion, the writer should consider whether it actually adds anything important to the sentence. The underlined portion in sentence 6 does not meet this criterion, so it should be deleted, choice C. It is simply unnecessary to know that Lawrence's publisher operated a "shrewd marketing campaign" or that "Lawrence's fame and popularity" helped book sales. Choice A votes for deleting the portion, but its reasoning is flawed; it is irrelevant that deleting it makes the sentence "more succinct." The issue is not whether the sentence is more concise, but whether the information is necessary. Choice B also votes for deleting the portion, but it incorrectly claims it adds "no new information to the sentence." It does add information, but the information is not necessary. Choice D inaccurately suggests keeping the portion, and its reasoning is weak; it is likely true that readers will not know how Lawrence's publisher helped book sales, but that information is not necessary to the passage. Choice E also erroneously votes for keeping the portion and bases that suggestion on a very bland idea; bulking up the passage is not an issue, but adding relevant information should dictate whether or not to delete the portion.

44. E. The second paragraph discusses Lawrence's literary triumphs, but it does not have an adequate transition from the first paragraph, which centers on his military achievements. Choice E provides an excellent transition because it includes a reminder of the first paragraph with the phrase "renowned for his battleground achievements," and it also acknowledges that he was known for other feats with the opening phrase, "Not only. . . ." When this phrase is added, the reader learns Lawrence not only was known for his role in the war, but "was also famous as a prolific writer. . . ." Choice A uses the inaccurate phrase "In contrast." The second paragraph adds relevant information about Lawrence's literary accomplishments detailing his military life; it does not contrast with the first paragraph; rather, it supplements the first. Choice B does not provide a transition from the first paragraph because it merely mentions that Lawrence was "always larger-than-life," which fails to acknowledge his military life. Choice C makes a dubious time connection ("While . . . in . . . the Army"), and it also displays redundant phrasing; were it inserted, the sentence would claim that "While being famous . . . Lawrence was also famous." Choice D uses vague phrasing, "Lawrence became well-known for many triumphs," which fails to identify the subject of the first paragraph, namely his military exploits; thus, it does not make an effective transition between these two paragraphs.

45. D. The best statement of the conclusion must include multiple aspects of the discussion, not just a single element. Sentence 14, choice D, best meets this measure, as it touches on many aspects of Lawrence's remarkable life ("lost a great military leader," and "a great writer," "and a great 'man of the people'"). Compared to the ideas in choice D, the ideas in other sentences are all too limited. Sentence 11 (A) only mentions his "meaningless death," and sentence 12 (B) is merely factual ("riding his prized motorcycle"). Choices C and E also fail to provide a summary or conclusion; they merely relate specific factual details of the accident that cost Lawrence his life: "swerving to avoid the boys" (C) and "all of 46 years old" (E). In comparison, sentence 14 (D) presents a far better statement to relate the conclusion of this essay.

Section II: Free-Response Questions

Question 1

Row A: Thesis (0–1 point)	
Scoring Criteria	
0 points for any of the following:	**1 point for**
• Having no defendable thesis. • Only restating the prompt in the thesis. • Only summarizing the issue with no apparent or coherent claim in the thesis. • Presenting a thesis that does not address the prompt.	• Addressing the prompt with a defendable thesis.
Decision Rules and Scoring Notes	
Theses that do not earn this point	**Theses that do earn this point**
• Only restate the prompt. • Are vague or do not take a position. • Equivocate or merely summarize others' arguments. • Simply state obvious facts rather than making a defendable claim.	• Respond to the prompt (rather than restating it) and clearly take a position regarding the influence of the media during disasters instead of simply stating pros and cons.

continued

Additional Notes

- The thesis may be one or more sentences that are in close proximity to each other anywhere in the essay.
- A thesis that meets the criteria can be awarded the point whether or not the rest of the response successfully conveys that line of reasoning.
- For a thesis to be defendable, the sources must have at least minimal evidence that could be used as support.
- A thesis may present a line of reasoning, but it is not required to earn a point.

Row B: Evidence AND Commentary (0–4 points)

Scoring Criteria				
0 points for	**1 point for**	**2 points for**	**3 points for**	**4 points for**
• Simply repeating the thesis (if present). • **OR** restating provided information. • **OR** providing fewer than two references to the provided sources.	• Providing evidence from at least two of the provided sources. • **AND** summarizing the evidence without explaining how the evidence supports the thesis.	• Providing evidence from or references to at least three of the provided sources. • **AND** explaining how some of the evidence relates to the thesis, but the line of reasoning may be nonexistent or faulty.	• Providing specific evidence from or references to at least three of the provided sources to support all claims in the line of reasoning. • **AND** explaining how some of the evidence relates to the thesis and supports the line of reasoning.	• Providing specific evidence from or references to at least three of the provided sources to support all claims in the line of reasoning. • **AND** consistently and explicitly explaining how the evidence relates to the thesis and supports the line of reasoning.
Decision Rules and Scoring Notes				
Typical responses that earn 0 points:	**Typical responses that earn 1 point:**	**Typical responses that earn 2 points:**	**Typical responses that earn 3 points:**	**Typical responses that earn 4 points:**
• Are unclear or fail to address the prompt. • May present mere opinion or repeat ideas from a single source.	• Only summarize or describe sources instead of providing specific details.	• Mix specific details with broad generalities. • May contain simplistic, inaccurate, or repetitive explanations that do not strengthen the argument. Fail to explain the connections between claims and to establish a clear line of reasoning. • May make one point well but fail to adequately support any other claims.	• Consistently offer evidence to support all claims. • Focus on the importance of specific words and details from the sources to build an argument. • Use multiple supporting claims to organize an argument and line of reasoning. • May not integrate some evidence or support a key claim in the commentary.	• Consistently offer evidence to support all claims. • Focus on the importance of specific words and details from the sources to build an argument. • Organize, integrate, and thoroughly explain evidence from sources throughout in order to support the line of reasoning.

Additional Notes

• Writing that suffers from grammatical and/or mechanical errors that interfere with communication cannot earn the fourth point in this row.

Row C: Sophistication (0–1 point)	
Scoring Criteria	
0 points for	**1 point for**
• Not meeting the criteria for 1 point.	• Exhibiting sophistication of thought and/or advancing a complex understanding of the rhetorical situation.
Decision Rules and Scoring Notes	
Responses that do not earn this point:	**Responses that earn this point demonstrate one (or more) of the following:**
• Try to contextualize their argument, but make predominantly sweeping generalizations (*"Throughout all history . . ."* OR *"Everyone believes . . ."*). • Only hint at other possible arguments (*"Some may think . . ."*). • Present complicated or complex sentences or language that is ineffective and detracts from the argument.	• Present a nuanced argument that consistently identifies and examines complexities or tension across the sources. • Illuminate the significance or implications of the argument (either the student's argument or the arguments within the sources) within a broader context. • Make effective rhetorical choices that consistently strengthen the force and impact of the student's argument. • Develop a prose style that is especially vivid, persuasive, resounding, or appropriate to the student's argument.
Additional Notes	
• This point should be awarded only if the demonstration of sophistication or complex understanding is part of the argument, not merely a phrase or brief reference.	

High-Scoring Essay

The media has assumed a reputation of candor, coupled with benevolence, for the media links desperate people in desperate situations to magnanimous audiences, who, theoretically, are only too eager to help. In a media-perpetuated myth, newspapers, radio, internet, and television supposedly serve the distinct purpose of objectively presenting adversity while respecting victims. Thus, the media has tailored for itself an image of an entity that respects victims of disastrous situations, yet simultaneously provides the public with objective reporting. This is not so. The media simply is not able to live up to its self-created reputation. Rather than providing a service to the public and victims following a disaster, the media compromises the integrity of its broadcasts, disregards victims, and alienates audiences, ultimately doing a disservice to the public.

It becomes difficult to regard the traditional media in a favorable light when one considers the information in Patrick Cockburn's article "Catastrophe on camera: Why media coverage of natural disasters is flawed" (Source B). His thesis examines something that we take for granted, namely that "Media coverage of natural disasters . . . is largely accepted as an accurate reflection of what really happened." The author asserts that assumption is clearly misleading, ". . . in my experience, the opposite is true: the reporting of cataclysms or lesser disasters is often wildly misleading." He recounts details of the deceptive reporting of a string of natural disasters, ranging from the floods in Mississippi in the 1990s to the devastation wrought in New Orleans in 2005. In every case, similar patterns emerge: first comes stereotypical reporting, followed by huge exaggeration of the toll, finally ending in a dull, repetitious monotone. Out of this storm of coverage, very little serves to enlighten their viewers or to help to ease the burden for the victims or the responders. Furthermore, Source F details what the media should be doing, namely "provid[ing] a quality service, critiquing claims rather than simply reporting them, and fundamentally, allowing people to make informed decisions." Instead of inadequate and sensationalist coverage such as the Las Vegas mass shooting or the oft-seen photo of the Hindenburg disaster (Source G), the media should be striving for the objective and complete coverage it pretends to present.

In October of 2002, some of America's brightest minds convened for a seminar on effective risk communication (Source C). Effective risk communicators include different aspects of the media; for example, television and radio. The media is an "important channel for risk communication," an asset to authorities, and a source of public information, yet Source C explicitly states that society's "social structure, norms, resources and risk perception" undermine media's post-disaster effectiveness. Meanwhile, Source D focuses on the future, arguing that social media channels are likely to subsume the role of traditional media in disaster relief efforts. Indeed, social media has already played a role in recovery efforts following some recent American disasters. However, as disaster sociologist Jeannette Sutton points out, social media needs to find a way to be more effective and consistent in communicating information about disasters. It is clear that the media has much room for improvement when covering disasters. Thus, in spite of the media's disaster education in Latin America (Source A) and roundtable discussions (Source C), media coverage of disasters does a disservice. Reporting on disasters in an incomplete manner, while intrusively disregarding victims' welfare, and failing to effectively reach the public, the media displays the hallmarks of a public service gone awry.

(576 words)

Analysis of the High-Scoring Essay

This very thorough essay demonstrates just how much argumentation a thoughtful writer can include. Freely synthesizing the sources and contemporary events, this student presents an intelligent discussion of the shortcomings of the media regarding its reporting of disasters. Taking a negative stand, the essay systematically criticizes the media's intrusive nature and poor reporting. The student demonstrates a strong command of diction and syntax, presenting sophisticated phrasing such as "candor coupled with benevolence" and "links desperate people in desperate situations to magnanimous audiences." Additionally, the simple sentence, "This is not so," packs a punch because of its brevity and its being surrounded by longer, more complex sentences. The thesis, which states that, "Rather than providing a service to the public and victims following a disaster, the media compromises the integrity of its broadcasts, disregards victims, and alienates audiences, ultimately doing a disservice to the public," deserves a point for Row A.

The first body paragraph examines a negative aspect of the media's reporting of disasters: Viewers are only shown selected images of devastation, knowing that such coverage sells. This touches on a universal truth: Humanity is compelled to watch images of horror while simultaneously being repelled by them. The student implicitly understands this concept and uses it to further the essay's argument. By citing multiple examples from Source B and from contemporary incidents, the student makes as thorough a case as one can expect in any 40-minute essay. All of the examples are relevant and demonstrate that the student is not merely repeating the information from the sources but instead is digesting the ideas, mulling them over, and then producing an intelligent, albeit one-sided, argument against the media. The inclusion of information from Source F regarding the role that the media should ideally play in a society, plus the brief mention of Source G (the Hindenburg photo) add depth, both by synthesizing multiple sources in the same paragraph and by bringing this particular one to a logical conclusion.

The next paragraph is interesting in its organizational scheme. It chooses to discuss Sources C and D, both of which are more favorable toward the media than other sources. But, keeping in line with the essay's thesis, the student chooses to highlight the negative ideas from each source. The purpose is well-fulfilled. The student points out that the media tries to encourage effective risk communication but follows it up with Source C's criticism that society is not inclined to heed such ideas. This analysis is not terribly strong, as it mainly just reports what Source C has to say. However, it does expand the essay's critique of the media. The inclusion of Source D helps the paragraph's development, but, again, the student could do more critical thinking; it reads a bit too much like mere reporting. The quality of the commentary and evidence are worthy of 3 points in Row B.

The conclusion, too, is brief, basically just a summary that is tacked on to the second body paragraph, but it does bring in another source from the prompt, which highlights the student's overall attention to detail. The essay ends with a poignant phrase: By stating that the media is a "public service gone awry," the student reasserts the essay's thesis with finality and conviction. The quality of the writing is sophisticated and persuasive enough to deserve a point in Row C. Indeed, this essay truly earns its high score; it should receive an overall score of 5.

Medium-Scoring Essay

Media has a powerful influence upon our lives. Not only does it provide us with news; it subtly shapes our opinions. Media, be it television, magazines, or radio, has demonstrated the ability to affect a broad audience. Recent natural disasters and terrorist attacks have been thoroughly reported by the media. When the media portrays a natural disaster it serves one distinct purpose. Over and over, the media has shown that it chooses to consistently display world tragedy in such a way as to convey feelings of closeness and empathy to its audience. Thus, the effects of the media are great, and media attention is beneficial for victims of disasters because it shares their plight with a sympathetic world audience.

The 21st century is an age of technology. Television, radio, and the internet are mediums of media that can convey news quickly and effectively. Source C, an excerpt from a seminar on risk communication, clearly viewed media as an important method to limit the effects of a natural disaster. Media can help limit a disaster's immediate effects, "[media can] track potential disaster agents, alert authorities, and educate and warn the public in a more timely manner" (Source C). Media effectively helps victims of a disaster while helping educate the public in order to limit damage and death in future incidents. The seminar's participants from businesses, industry, and civil services (Source C) exemplified the interest in effectively utilizing media to help in disaster situations.

While Source A acknowledges the importance of media immediately following a disaster, the article emphasizes the importance of educational media that limits the effects of future. The article states, "If people know what to do, they can save their own life." Mr. Briceño, the chairman of the committee that held the forum on disasters, asserted, "The more people are aware of the risks they face, the better chance they have to save their lives when hazards strike" (Source A).

Source F acknowledges that Hurricane Katrina, while a horrible event, at least caused the media to question the administration's ability to help those in need, and in the process of showing the world the devastation from the hurricane, brought tremendous sympathy for those victims of the storm. If we had not seen the images of the people who suffered, we would not have felt for them so much. Therefore, the media helped the victims.

Media has proved itself to be an integral component in disaster relief. Helping people immediately after a disaster and in the ensuing months, media has aided authorities, raised money, and educated potential future victims. Thus, media is a valuable tool in disaster relief.

(439 words)

Analysis of the Medium-Scoring Essay

This essay tries to present a coherent argument about the benefits the media provides after disasters, but it is not terribly convincing because of its simplistic approach. For example, one sentence in the introduction claims that the media serves "one distinct purpose" in reporting disasters: drawing out the audience's sympathy. Surely this naïve thinking exposes an unwarranted assumption; surely the media has many purposes in reporting "world tragedies." A student who displays such one-dimensional thinking early on frequently produces an essay that oversimplifies. Although it is true that media exposure may indeed evoke a sympathetic reaction in the viewers, that alone does not necessarily produce any tangible benefit for the victims. Viewer sympathy alone will not house or feed victims. However, the gist of the thesis, that "media attention is beneficial for victims of disasters," deserves a point in Row A.

The first body paragraph addresses the potential good works that the media can do, such as helping limit the damage from natural disasters by providing warnings to the public and officials of imminent danger. However, the student seems to have forgotten the thesis of the essay; this paragraph includes no evidence for the concept that the media elicits sympathy in a viewing audience. Although this body paragraph does address some good that the media can do, it does not really relate to the introductory paragraph. Unfortunately, this poor organization does not bode well for the essay.

The second body paragraph suffers from similar organizational problems; it does not support the thesis about eliciting sympathy. Just like the previous paragraph, this one focuses on ways in which the media can help circumvent negative effects of disasters with preplanning. Perhaps the student would have been better served had he or she changed the thesis to fit what the body paragraphs actually discuss. Furthermore, the weak development of this paragraph is apparent because it contains only three sentences, two of which are merely quotations from the source. In other words, the student barely hints at any interesting ideas and barely develops them.

The last body paragraph attempts to get back on track and address how the media elicited sympathy for Hurricane Katrina victims. However, the writer uses Source F, which does not really present that idea; this source centers on the concept of how, after the hurricane, the media moved to a more aggressive stance in presenting discrepancies between the Bush administration's statements and actions. Therefore, the student's leap of logic, jumping from an article that criticizes the administration to the idea that photos of hurricane victims elicit sympathy in the viewers, is a flaw no AP Reader can ignore. It appears that the student is grasping at straws, searching for any phrase in the sources that might somehow support the thesis, but he or she falls far short of composing a convincing argument. The quality of the evidence and commentary should earn 2 points in Row B.

The essay concludes too quickly with the concept that "helping people immediately after a disaster and in the ensuing months, media has aided authorities, raised money, and educated potential future victims." Unfortunately, these ideas are simply not proven in this essay.

Overall, the essay demonstrates the logical flaws that occur when a student jumps in and begins writing too quickly, without thinking through his or her positions and how the sources can help establish them. The essay's organization would also benefit from greater sophistication. Instead of using the facile "one-source-per-paragraph" method, the essay could successfully demonstrate more complexity if the writer integrated more sources into each paragraph. It does not deserve a point in Row C. Always keep in mind that this is the synthesis essay. Keep your focus on the concept of synthesis and use it to your advantage as you think deeply about the topic and navigate your way, exploring a variety of ideas. It deserves an overall score of 3.

Question 2

Row A: Thesis (0–1 point)	
Scoring Criteria	
0 points for any of the following: • Having no defendable thesis. • Only restating the prompt in the thesis. • Only summarizing the issue with no apparent or coherent claim in the thesis. • Presenting a thesis that does not address the prompt.	**1 point for** • Addressing the prompt with a defendable thesis that analyzes the writer's rhetorical choices.
Decision Rules and Scoring Notes	
Theses that do not earn this point • Only restate the prompt. • Neglect to address the writer's rhetorical choices. • Simply describe or repeat the passage rather than making a defendable claim.	**Theses that do earn this point** • Respond to the prompt (rather than restating it) <u>and</u> clearly articulate a defendable thesis exploring how Woolf's rhetorical choices reflect her attitude about women in society.
Additional Notes • The thesis may be one or more sentences that are in close proximity to each other anywhere in the essay. • A thesis that meets the criteria can be awarded the point whether or not the rest of the response successfully conveys that line of reasoning. • For a thesis to be defendable, the passage must have at least minimal evidence that could be used as support. • A thesis may present a line of reasoning, but it is not required to earn a point.	

Row B: Evidence AND Commentary (0–4 points)				
Scoring Criteria				
0 points for	**1 point for**	**2 points for**	**3 points for**	**4 points for**
• Simply repeating the thesis (if present). • **OR** restating provided information. • **OR** providing mostly irrelevant and/or incoherent evidence.	• Summarizing the passage without reference or connection to the thesis. • **OR** providing mostly general evidence. • **AND** providing little or no explanation or commentary.	• Providing some specific evidence that is relevant to the thesis. • **AND** explaining how some of the evidence relates to the thesis, but the line of reasoning may be nonexistent or faulty.	• Providing specific evidence to support all claims in the line of reasoning. • **AND** explaining how some of the evidence relates to the thesis and supports the line of reasoning. • **AND** explaining how at least one rhetorical choice in the passage contributes to the writer's thesis.	• Providing specific evidence to support all claims in the line of reasoning. • **AND** providing well-developed commentary that consistently and explicitly explains the relationship between the evidence and the thesis. • **AND** explaining how multiple rhetorical choices in the passage contribute to the writer's thesis.
Decision Rules and Scoring Notes				
Typical responses that earn 0 points:	**Typical responses that earn 1 point:**	**Typical responses that earn 2 points:**	**Typical responses that earn 3 points:**	**Typical responses that earn 4 points:**
• Are unclear or fail to address the prompt. • May present mere opinion with little or no evidence.	• Only summarize or restate ideas from the passage without any analysis. • May mention rhetorical devices with little or no explanation or analysis.	• Mix specific details with broad generalities. • May contain simplistic, inaccurate, or repetitive explanations that do not strengthen the argument. • Fail to explain the connections between claims and establish a clear line of reasoning. • May make one point well but fail to adequately support any other claims.	• Consistently offer evidence to support all claims. • Focus on the importance of specific words and details from the passages to build an argument. • Use multiple supporting claims to organize an argument and line of reasoning. • May not integrate some evidence or support a key claim in the commentary.	• Consistently offer evidence to support all claims. • Focus on the importance of specific words and details from the passages to build an argument. • Use multiple supporting claims with adequate evidence and explanation to organize an argument and line of reasoning. • Explain how the writer's use of rhetorical devices contributes to the student's analysis of the passage.
Additional Notes				
• Writing that suffers from grammatical and/or mechanical errors that interfere with communication cannot earn the fourth point in this row.				

Row C: Sophistication (0–1 point)	
Scoring Criteria	
0 points for • Not meeting the criteria for 1 point.	**1 point for** • Exhibiting sophistication of thought and/or advancing a complex understanding of the rhetorical situation.
Decision Rules and Scoring Notes	
Responses that do not earn this point: • Try to contextualize the text, but make predominantly sweeping generalizations (*"Throughout all history . . ."* OR *"Everyone believes . . ."*). • Only hint at other possible arguments (*"Some may think . . ."*). • Examine individual rhetorical choices but fail to examine the relationship among varying choices throughout the passages. • Oversimplify textual complexities. • Present complicated or complex sentences or language that is ineffective and detracts from the argument.	**Responses that earn this point demonstrate one (or more) of the following:** • Explain the purpose or function of complexities or tension in the passages. • Explain the significance of the writer's rhetorical choices for the given rhetorical situation. • Develop a prose style that is especially vivid, persuasive, resounding, or appropriate to the student's argument.
Additional Notes • This point should be awarded only if the demonstration of sophistication or complex understanding is part of the argument, not merely a phrase or brief reference.	

High-Scoring Essay

The differences between men's and women's colleges were considerable in Virginia Woolf's day. Rather than assert this in a pedestrian, expository way, Woolf uses the respective meals served at each college to illustrate the discrepancies between the schools. The meals are a metaphorical device, akin to a poetic conceit; Woolf makes a far more forceful, profound distinction between the male and female schools through such juxtaposition than if she had merely enumerated their inconsistencies. Woolf details the relative poverty of the women's school, and therefore women's position in society, through varied sentence structure, diction, and imagery between the descriptions of the meals.

Fundamentally different premises underlie each meal. The men's meal is a luxury to be enjoyed, the women's a metabolic necessity to be endured. Woolf, in describing the men's meal, dismisses the notion that ". . . soup and a salmon and ducklings were of no importance whatsoever, as if nobody ever smoked a cigar or drank a glass of wine." She offers a breathless explanation of the sensual joy the meal affords. Diction and sensory detail showcase the piquant pleasure to be taken in foods "spread . . . of the whitest cream," "Sharp and sweet . . . succulent." The men's meal is a catalyst for the "profound, subtle and subterranean glow . . . of rational intercourse." Of course, no similar premium is put on rational intercourse among women, judging by the amenities of the women's meal. They drink not wine "flushed crimson," but rather eat "plain gravy soup . . . transparent liquid." Dry biscuits and water replace partridges, and such victuals provide no stimulus for enlightened conversation; when the eating is done, the women rise and that is all.

Woolf describes the women's meal in plain language, in blunt, staccato, repetitive bursts: "Here was my soup . . . Dinner was ready. Here was the soup. It was a plain gravy soup . . . The plate was plain." All the eloquent wordiness has vanished. The images are those of poverty and ugliness, and the meal is only justified as being superior to that of a coal miner. The prunes are ". . . stringy as a miser's heart and exuding a fluid such as might run in miser's veins . . ." In contrast, the other meal's imagery is that of opulence. The potatoes are "thin as coins," the sprouts "foliated as rosebuds." This is a meal fit for kings, and the diction is suggestive of royalty: "The partridges . . . came with all their retinue . . ." The men are reassured by the meal that they are all going to heaven; the women's meal is a hurried "homely trinity."

As a metaphor for the chasm separating male and female education, and society as a whole, Woolf's piece is mordantly effective. Her point is made with more economy and vivacity through anecdote than it would be through explanation or a propounding of evidence about the inferiority of female schools. By painting the male university as lavish and its female counterpart as lowly, Woolf succeeds in crystallizing her attitude for readers.

(520 words)

Analysis of the High-Scoring Essay

This student addresses the question; he or she also demonstrates a deep understanding of the subtle differences between the two passages. This thesis, "Woolf details the relative poverty of the women's school, and therefore women's position in society, through varied sentence structure, diction, and imagery between the descriptions of the meals," is relevant and on topic and deserves a point in Row A.

The body paragraphs provide ample evidence for ideas, and the quotations are used effectively to prove this student's points. This essay does not merely dwell on the obvious aspects of the passages, but probes more deeply into the ramifications of the two meals. Especially effective is the section in which the student demonstrates how Woolf's diction suggests the meaning of each meal. For example, reread the end of the third paragraph as this student connects the word "retinue" with royalty and goes on to suggest what that royal meal does for the men (it reassures them that they are going to heaven). This type of thinking demonstrates the level of analysis necessary for a high score; the student understands how the language of the essay helps create an effect. Although very well written, this essay could be improved by providing a stronger connection between ideas, evidence, and thesis. Also, a more profound point could be made about the deeper issues involved in the "chasm separating male and female education." In addition, the student could concentrate more on Woolf's attitude as he or she presents the evidence. However, these criticisms are not significant enough to lower the essay's score. The essay earns 3 points in Row B.

The vocabulary and sentence structure are also very sophisticated, as they should be in top-scoring essays. The phrasing is creative and pleasing. Wording such as "akin to a poetic conceit," "a metabolic necessity," "piquant pleasure," and "mordantly effective" are just a few of the phrases that sing to the AP Exam Reader's ear. In addition, this student demonstrates a keen sense of sentence structure and thus adds sufficient variety in both sentence pattern and length. Essays that are this thorough, organized, and well developed in vivid and appropriate prose, indeed, earn a point in Row C. It should earn an overall score of 5.

Low-Scoring Essay

Meals are important, but they are often ignored or not thought of much. People often eat in a hurry, and often they don't pay much attention to the details of what they are actually eating.

Virginia Woolf calls readers' attention to this in the selection about two meals which she had when she was at the university. She had one of these at the men's college and the other at the women's college. They were very different in the food but also in the whole atmosphere of the place where she ate.

Woolf says that though people don't often notice it, the food we eat tells us important things about where we are. She compares the two parts of the university with the different meals. She uses narrative structure, details, and tone to present her attitude about the two meals and inform readers of which one she likes better, and why.

The first meal she describes, which is at the men's college, is the one which Woolf likes better. The reasons become obvious for this, because the food is far more appetizing and the atmosphere is just nicer generally. Woolf uses lots of details and metaphors to describe this meal, and often her descriptions are full of imagery. It is all very fancy, with a uniformed waiter serving roast, and Woolf drinks a lot of wine, which sends a glow down her spine. She comments that all the other eaters were very friendly and everything seemed nice and happy after the meal. "We are all going to heaven" she says after the meal. It is almost a religious experience for them.

The second meal is at the women's college, and Woolf's attitude toward it is not as positive. That is understandable, but the food is not even close to as good. Woolf uses lots of metaphors to make the food seem gross and very repulsive. The beef is like "the rumps of cattle in a muddy market, and sprouts curled and yellowed at the edge" she says. The prunes are stringy and miserly, and instead of the good pudding that she ate at the men's college, she has to eat custard that is not nearly so good. The biscuits are dry and unappetizing, which makes for a meal that is not very appealing. She doesn't talk about friends or smoking at this meal, which makes it far more homely than the men's meal.

Thus, through her metaphors and affective descriptions of the food at the two meals, Woolf compares them and strongly shows her attitude to the readers. She makes one realize that even though we don't often think about meals, they are important. The differences are something to realize, and Woolf's excellent description helps you do just that.

(459 words)

Analysis of the Low-Scoring Essay

This essay earns a low score because it recognizes some of the differences between the two meals. However, it doesn't merit a higher score because it fails to address Woolf's underlying attitude toward women's place in society as displayed through her description of the meals. The introductory remarks go on far too long (for three paragraphs). When the thesis is finally stated, it's bland and obvious, as is the entire essay. This student mentions that Woolf presents her attitudes but never clarifies what he or she thinks these attitudes are. Basically, the thesis merely restates a portion of the prompt and, therefore, does not earn a point in Row A.

This student has chosen to discuss the two meals separately, in two paragraphs, a technique that doesn't allow for strong comparison. This student does accurately present some evidence, but in many cases it is not sufficient. For example, where are the metaphors to which the student refers? Because they aren't included in the essay, the AP Exam Reader is left guessing. The student does see some interesting description in the passages but fails to make an intelligent point about it, and the analysis offered is shallow and obvious. Also, no connection is made between the evidence presented and the major topic of Woolf's attitude.

In addition, this essay demonstrates some stylistic and grammatical problems and is not helped by the use of unsophisticated words and phrases, such as "things," "a lot," and "not . . . as good." Some awkward sentences tend to distract the Reader's attention from this student's ideas. Incorrect word choices, such as "affective" instead of "effective," show that this student doesn't have a strong command of the language. This difficulty is further demonstrated by pronoun problems, such as the improper use of the second-person pronoun "you" in the last sentence and "them" at the end of the fourth paragraph, which also has no antecedent. The essay earns 2 points in Row B.

The positive aspects of this essay are few. It does try to make a point, and it follows many of the conventions of proper writing style. However, its numerous errors and uninteresting, obvious ideas that ignore part of the prompt prevent the essay from earning a point in Row C. It should receive an overall score of 2.

Question 3

Row A: Thesis (0–1 point)	
Scoring Criteria	
0 points for any of the following:	**1 point for**
• Having no defendable thesis. • Only restating the prompt in the thesis. • Only summarizing the issue with no apparent or coherent claim in the thesis. • Presenting a thesis that does not address the prompt.	• Addressing the prompt with a defendable thesis.

Decision Rules and Scoring Notes	
Theses that do not earn this point	**Theses that do earn this point**
• Only restate the prompt. • Are vague or do not take a position. • Simply state obvious facts rather than making a defendable claim.	• Respond to the prompt (rather than restating it) <u>and</u> clearly defend, challenge, or qualify Emerson's ideas about books instead of simply stating pros and cons.
Additional Notes	
• The thesis may be one or more sentences that are in close proximity to each other anywhere in the essay. • A thesis that meets the criteria can be awarded the point whether or not the rest of the response successfully conveys that line of reasoning. • A thesis may present a line of reasoning, but it is not required to earn a point.	

Row B: Evidence AND Commentary (0–4 points)

Scoring Criteria

0 points for	1 point for	2 points for	3 points for	4 points for
• Simply repeating the thesis (if present). • **OR** restating provided information. • **OR** providing mostly irrelevant and/or incoherent examples.	• Summarizing the passage without reference or connection to the thesis. • **OR** providing mostly general evidence. • **AND** providing little or no explanation or commentary.	• Providing some specific evidence that is relevant to the thesis. • **AND** explaining how some of the evidence relates to the thesis, but the line of reasoning may be nonexistent or faulty.	• Providing specific evidence to support all claims in the line of reasoning. • **AND** explaining how some of the evidence relates to the thesis and supports the line of reasoning.	• Providing specific evidence to support all claims in the line of reasoning. • **AND** providing well-developed commentary that consistently and explicitly explains the relationship between the evidence and the thesis.

Decision Rules and Scoring Notes

Typical responses that earn 0 points:	Typical responses that earn 1 point:	Typical responses that earn 2 points:	Typical responses that earn 3 points:	Typical responses that earn 4 points:
• Are unclear or fail to address the prompt. • May present mere opinion with little or no relevant evidence.	• Only summarize or restate ideas from the passage without any analysis.	• Mix specific details with broad generalities. • May contain simplistic, inaccurate, or repetitive explanations that do not strengthen the argument. • Fail to explain the connections between claims and to establish a clear line of reasoning. • May make one point well but fail to adequately support any other claims.	• Consistently offer evidence to support all claims. • Focus on the importance of specific words and details to build an argument. • Use multiple supporting claims to organize an argument and line of reasoning. • May not integrate some evidence or support a key claim in the commentary.	• Engage specific evidence to draw conclusions. • Focus on the importance of specific details to build an argument. • Use multiple supporting claims with adequate evidence and explanation to organize an argument and line of reasoning.

continued

Additional Notes

• Writing that suffers from grammatical and/or mechanical errors that interfere with communication cannot earn the fourth point in this row.

Row C: Sophistication (0–1 point)	
Scoring Criteria	
0 points for	**1 point for**
• Not meeting the criteria for 1 point.	• Exhibiting sophistication of thought and/or advancing a complex understanding of the rhetorical situation.
Decision Rules and Scoring Notes	
Responses that do not earn this point:	Responses that earn this point demonstrate one (or more) of the following:
• Try to contextualize their argument, but make predominantly sweeping generalizations (*"Throughout all history . . ."* OR *"Everyone believes . . ."*). • Only hint at other possible arguments (*"Some may think . . ."*). • Present complicated or complex sentences or language that is ineffective and detracts from the argument.	• Present a nuanced argument that consistently identifies and examines complexities or tension across the sources. • Illuminate the significance or implications of the argument (either the student's argument or the arguments within the sources) within a broader context. • Make effective rhetorical choices that strengthen the force and impact of the student's argument. • Develop a prose style that is especially vivid, persuasive, resounding, or appropriate to the student's argument.

Additional Notes

• This point should be awarded only if the demonstration of sophistication or complex understanding is part of the argument, not merely a phrase or brief reference.

High-Scoring Essay

Ralph Waldo Emerson is perhaps overly strident in his speech, "The American Scholar." But such zeal serves to make a trenchant point about the tendency toward rigid reverence of Great Works, as if each were the Holy Grail itself. He asserts: "Books are the best of things, well used; abused, among the worst." Emerson delivers a stinging indictment of "book-worms." He argues that even the greatest thinkers were once humble students. The danger, Emerson claims, is that of transferring our respect from the venerable acts of creation, of thought, to that endeavor's imperfect product. He believes scholars must not so prostrate themselves before the majesty of profound <u>works</u> that they forget their <u>creators</u>, whom they should emulate in creative thought. They should not idolize the books themselves in a sort of cult of inferiority, Emerson says, but rather write their own books, their own truths, undertake their own sacred acts of creation.

In a strict sense, these points are valid. But Emerson goes beyond these points; he overstates his case. He is treading the ground between the good scholar and the singular genius. Perhaps, given his own stature, it is only fitting that he should hold us to such lofty standards. Nevertheless, his warnings against showing too much respect for books are not altogether true. Such arguments, about the paramount importance of individual thought, can readily be misused to justify a dismissal of the past. Often such self-indulgent, arrogant arguments are used by those less gifted than Emerson as an excuse to disregard the wisdom that has come before them.

A social critic recently said, "It's fine to learn how to think, but what's the point if you have nothing to think about?" The modern education system has sought to shoulder the burden of "teaching students how to think," often elevating such a subjective goal to a status superior to teaching facts and sharing insights about past generations. In short, it focuses more on method and process than what students actually learn.

Some students graduate from American high schools ignorant of when the Civil War occurred or the difference between the Preamble and the Constitution and <u>Das Kapital</u>. Reading and digesting the thoughts of the past is as essential as learning the rules of grammar so as to intelligently violate them. In light of today's high illiteracy rate, society's problems hardly include too many people being "book-worms" or attempting to follow the doctrines of Plato or John Locke or Mahatma Gandhi.

We as Americans share a heritage of ideas. Common assumptions must be examined so that we understand where such "conventional wisdom" came from, for it is only then that we may change the portions of it which may be unjust or clouded by bias. Certainly great books should not be locked away, immune from criticism. Neither, however, should they be lambasted out of visceral ignorance, in the name of "individuality."

Studying and learning from the works of the past, and creating new original writing and thought in the present, are not mutually exclusive propositions. Most scholars lack Emerson's genius, but they will be hard-pressed to find a spark of creativity by meditating in the dark.

Emerson implies that ideas are not great <u>in and of themselves</u>. But ideas <u>can</u> be great. Proof resides in the overwhelming numbers of anonymous poems that fill anthology books. How many aphorisms are repeated daily by speakers who know not whether they generated from the tongue of Winston Churchill or Will Rogers? This is not to suggest that great ideas cannot be proved wrong. That Emerson denies perfection to any ideas is hardly a danger. Since no writer, however brilliant, is perfect, it is perfectly safe to acknowledge certain ideas as great, without granting them perfection and immunity.

When people do not know the past, they face the peril of perpetually re-inventing the wheel—blissfully ignorant of their tendency toward trite alliteration or insipid clichés.

(652 words)

Analysis of the High-Scoring Essay

This thorough, thoughtful, and well-written essay deserves a high score. It begins with the topic and promptly takes a relevant position on the issue of studying from books and ideas of the past, stating that Emerson is "perhaps overly strident," and, later, "he overstates his case." The student then points out a major dilemma inherent in a facile acceptance of Emerson's ideas—that of dismissing the past and the wisdom that have come before. The presence of a defendable thesis earns a point in Row A.

The essay proceeds with a two-paragraph discussion of the state of education today, pointing out the dual needs of teaching both facts and the thinking process. These paragraphs are particularly relevant to the topic, and the examples are presented with insight. The student also acknowledges our American heritage and the necessity of using books to understand that heritage so that the country's great ideas are not hidden away. These paragraphs demonstrate a deep-thinking student, one who is aware of the world and presents complex ideas with clarity and sophistication.

The next paragraph counters Emerson's position with optimism—the student claims that we *can* have it all; we can learn from the past and still become clear, independent thinkers who create new ideas. The essay points out that great new ideas do exist and cites anonymous poems as examples of these new ideas. The student also acknowledges that ideas can be great while being imperfect and that such imperfection is no reason to dismiss them entirely. The quality of the evidence and commentary earns all 4 possible points in Row B.

The essay's brief conclusion reminds the AP Exam Reader that humans may be doomed to repeat their mistakes and to reinvent the wheel unless they learn from the great ideas of the past. Overall, this essay's points are valid. Without dismissing Emerson lightly, the student intelligently discusses his or her concepts, but the presentation is not sophisticated enough to earn a point in Row C. It should earn an overall score of 5.

Medium-Scoring Essay

The process of finding meaningful things in life is not always clear. It is not simple to discover what is true and what is just fancy rhetoric or skirting of the issues. Ralph Waldo Emerson, considered one of our best writers and speakers, gave a speech in Cambridge in 1837, where he talked about books and how they can help us to find the truth which we are seeking in our life.

Emerson said in his speech that books are noble and age-old scholars gave arrangement to the life they saw and organized it. Then they put it into the books that they wrote, and produced a new truth for people to refer to. But he also says that each new generation of Americans has to write their own books. They have to discover their own versions of the truth, and what that truth actually means to them.

He was right. He was also right when he said that we can't just go by what was said then, because the ones who wrote the books that fill our libraries were just young and naïve when they authored those books. How can we be sure they are right, just because they are old? Why are they elevated to the status of classics as if they are perfect?

He says you shouldn't spend all your time in the library, however, I know some people who do just this. The result is that instead of having their own ideas, they just listen to all the old ones, and their creativity is stifled. I agree that it is more important to be a thinking man than one who just accepts everything. You need to have the freedom to have your own ideas, to let them flow without being influenced by principles and underlying ideas already presented in books. These ideas might be right, but if everyone only reads them without thinking for themselves, the country will be full of brainwashed people. They might be well educated, but what will be the price of that education?

He said that books can be best if they are used well, but among the worst of things if they are abused. What this actually encourages is for one to be intelligent about reading and not to believe everything that you read. Also, he says that we should not be bookworms, so caught up in the details of what people said in the past that we don't bother to think our own thoughts about the present or concerning issues of the future that are important to our society. This is the centerpiece of his speech. He means that books have a noble "theory." He also means that in practice we must live up to that theory. We must live up to that theory by not being blind or gullible. Instead, we must be <u>Thinking Men</u> and not <u>thinkers only</u>. He talked about how what we observe has to be filtered in to the truth by our own original ideas. We have to use books wisely, Emerson believed, and I agree wholeheartedly.

(512 words)

Analysis of the Medium-Scoring Essay

This essay begins with a vague introduction that essentially restates a few points from Emerson's speech. The student does not yet state a thesis or take a position.

The second paragraph continues this trend, merely paraphrasing Emerson's speech without thinking critically about those ideas. An essay that only paraphrases the passage will never score in the upper range.

Finally, the third paragraph presents an opinion and takes a position, although it is repetitively worded. The student seems to have finally started thinking, as he or she questions the validity of older books and the pedestal on which the classics have been placed. The idea that "He was right," clarified in the last sentence of the essay, "I agree wholeheartedly," should earn a point in Row A.

The fourth paragraph is probably the best in this essay and saves the score from sinking too low. The student uses personal experience as an example, citing other friends who have become "stifled" in their creativity by spending too much time in the library, consuming old books and old ideas without thinking while they read. The student apparently understands the need for everyone to become an individual thinker, an analyzer of ideas.

However, the next paragraph reverts to simple paraphrasing. It offers no additional commentary and, therefore, falls flat.

The essay reaches an adequate conclusion, explaining the need to read wisely and not be gullible. Ultimately, the student manages to insert enough of his or her own commentary about Emerson's concepts to salvage the score. The evidence and commentary should earn 2 points in Row B.

This essay could be greatly improved by reducing the paraphrasing and including much more analysis and evidence. Remember that this topic specifically directs students to "use appropriate evidence" to develop the essay. This student has barely accomplished that goal and, thus, the score suffers. The essay's sophistication is not sufficient for a point in Row C. It should earn an overall score of 3.

Scoring

Use the following worksheet to arrive at a probable final AP grade on Practice Exam 1. Because being objective enough to estimate your own essay score is sometimes difficult, you might give your essays (along with the sample essays) to a teacher, friend, or relative to score, if you feel confident that the individual has the knowledge necessary to make such a judgment and that he or she will feel comfortable doing so.

Section I: Multiple-Choice Questions

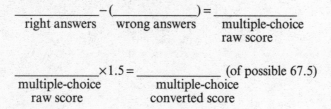

$$\underset{\text{right answers}}{\underline{\hspace{3cm}}} - (\underset{\text{wrong answers}}{\underline{\hspace{3cm}}}) = \underset{\substack{\text{multiple-choice} \\ \text{raw score}}}{\underline{\hspace{3cm}}}$$

$$\underset{\substack{\text{multiple-choice} \\ \text{raw score}}}{\underline{\hspace{3cm}}} \times 1.5 = \underset{\substack{\text{multiple-choice} \\ \text{converted score}}}{\underline{\hspace{3cm}}} \text{ (of possible 67.5)}$$

Section II: Free-Response Questions

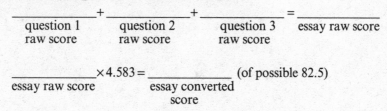

$$\underset{\substack{\text{question 1} \\ \text{raw score}}}{\underline{\hspace{2cm}}} + \underset{\substack{\text{question 2} \\ \text{raw score}}}{\underline{\hspace{2cm}}} + \underset{\substack{\text{question 3} \\ \text{raw score}}}{\underline{\hspace{2cm}}} = \underset{\text{essay raw score}}{\underline{\hspace{2cm}}}$$

$$\underset{\text{essay raw score}}{\underline{\hspace{3cm}}} \times 4.583 = \underset{\substack{\text{essay converted} \\ \text{score}}}{\underline{\hspace{3cm}}} \text{ (of possible 82.5)}$$

Final Score

$$\underset{\substack{\text{multiple-choice} \\ \text{converted score}}}{\underline{\hspace{3cm}}} + \underset{\substack{\text{essay} \\ \text{converted score}}}{\underline{\hspace{3cm}}} = \underset{\substack{\text{final} \\ \text{converted score}}}{\underline{\hspace{3cm}}} \text{ (of possible 150)}$$

Probable Final AP Score

Final Converted Score	Probable AP Score
150–114	5
113–98	4
97–81	3
80–53	2
52–0	1

Chapter 5

Practice Exam 2

Answer Sheet

Section I: Multiple-Choice Questions

1 Ⓐ Ⓑ Ⓒ Ⓓ Ⓔ	21 Ⓐ Ⓑ Ⓒ Ⓓ Ⓔ	41 Ⓐ Ⓑ Ⓒ Ⓓ Ⓔ
2 Ⓐ Ⓑ Ⓒ Ⓓ Ⓔ	22 Ⓐ Ⓑ Ⓒ Ⓓ Ⓔ	42 Ⓐ Ⓑ Ⓒ Ⓓ Ⓔ
3 Ⓐ Ⓑ Ⓒ Ⓓ Ⓔ	23 Ⓐ Ⓑ Ⓒ Ⓓ Ⓔ	43 Ⓐ Ⓑ Ⓒ Ⓓ Ⓔ
4 Ⓐ Ⓑ Ⓒ Ⓓ Ⓔ	24 Ⓐ Ⓑ Ⓒ Ⓓ Ⓔ	44 Ⓐ Ⓑ Ⓒ Ⓓ Ⓔ
5 Ⓐ Ⓑ Ⓒ Ⓓ Ⓔ	25 Ⓐ Ⓑ Ⓒ Ⓓ Ⓔ	45 Ⓐ Ⓑ Ⓒ Ⓓ Ⓔ
6 Ⓐ Ⓑ Ⓒ Ⓓ Ⓔ	26 Ⓐ Ⓑ Ⓒ Ⓓ Ⓔ	
7 Ⓐ Ⓑ Ⓒ Ⓓ Ⓔ	27 Ⓐ Ⓑ Ⓒ Ⓓ Ⓔ	
8 Ⓐ Ⓑ Ⓒ Ⓓ Ⓔ	28 Ⓐ Ⓑ Ⓒ Ⓓ Ⓔ	
9 Ⓐ Ⓑ Ⓒ Ⓓ Ⓔ	29 Ⓐ Ⓑ Ⓒ Ⓓ Ⓔ	
10 Ⓐ Ⓑ Ⓒ Ⓓ Ⓔ	30 Ⓐ Ⓑ Ⓒ Ⓓ Ⓔ	
11 Ⓐ Ⓑ Ⓒ Ⓓ Ⓔ	31 Ⓐ Ⓑ Ⓒ Ⓓ Ⓔ	
12 Ⓐ Ⓑ Ⓒ Ⓓ Ⓔ	32 Ⓐ Ⓑ Ⓒ Ⓓ Ⓔ	
13 Ⓐ Ⓑ Ⓒ Ⓓ Ⓔ	33 Ⓐ Ⓑ Ⓒ Ⓓ Ⓔ	
14 Ⓐ Ⓑ Ⓒ Ⓓ Ⓔ	34 Ⓐ Ⓑ Ⓒ Ⓓ Ⓔ	
15 Ⓐ Ⓑ Ⓒ Ⓓ Ⓔ	35 Ⓐ Ⓑ Ⓒ Ⓓ Ⓔ	
16 Ⓐ Ⓑ Ⓒ Ⓓ Ⓔ	36 Ⓐ Ⓑ Ⓒ Ⓓ Ⓔ	
17 Ⓐ Ⓑ Ⓒ Ⓓ Ⓔ	37 Ⓐ Ⓑ Ⓒ Ⓓ Ⓔ	
18 Ⓐ Ⓑ Ⓒ Ⓓ Ⓔ	38 Ⓐ Ⓑ Ⓒ Ⓓ Ⓔ	
19 Ⓐ Ⓑ Ⓒ Ⓓ Ⓔ	39 Ⓐ Ⓑ Ⓒ Ⓓ Ⓔ	
20 Ⓐ Ⓑ Ⓒ Ⓓ Ⓔ	40 Ⓐ Ⓑ Ⓒ Ⓓ Ⓔ	

CUT HERE

Section II: Free-Response Questions

Question 1

Many NEA Opponents dont think tax payers should fund atragous art. Critics like Patrick Buchanan and Senator Jesse Helms contend that taxpayers unwillingly subsidize obscene and blasphemous art, forced upon them by an out of-touch cultural elite.

The National Endowmen of Arts was created by an act of the U.S Congress in 1965 as an independent agency of the federal government of the U.S goveronment, to support and fund projects displaying artistic excellence. The grant money that the National Endowment of the Arts (NEA) receives comes from American taxpayers, furthermore that money has been used to fund art and more than labled "controversal" (source B). The trump administration made a proposal to eliminate federal funding for the program (Source F). The NEA is a wonderful program that helps bring light to controversial subjects, creates regulations, and free speech. The grants that are given to ej artist helps them create unique pieces of work, creating a light upon conversation subjects being hidden to in the dart. A conversational piece of art helps them has gotten huge amounts of attention is Chris ofili's "Holy Virgin Mary" a representation of the "virgin Mary with elephant dung on her breast". It offended may religious people across the U.S (David).

The goverment is responsibe for regulating trade, waging war, passing laws, and collecting taxes —not

CUT HERE

supporting art, that the job of the people.

Question 2

CUT HERE

CUT HERE

Question 3

Sir tomas More's Utopia discuss fair government and equal social status within our society, and identifies the need for people to give up their Private property is an unesscary. His ideas ~~for written about~~ are valid in light of contemporary standarts.

Initial position that private property is an unnessary evil, within our society at first apparance to be Communistic. His desires to redistribute wealth and property and to makes laws preventing people from earing too much money seem absurd. at first sight. More podicts corruption of the government, something that our nation has been expecting several decades.

Thraught the essay more propossing to the problem of the Private property. He advocates the ideas to our society. He shows the ideas that are relevant to todays society.

CUT HERE

CUT HERE

CUT HERE

Section I: Multiple-Choice Questions

Time: 1 hour

45 questions

Directions: This section consists of selections from prose works with questions about their content, form, and style, plus draft passages with questions about improving their content and clarity. Read each selection carefully. For each question, choose the best answer of the five choices.

Questions 1–14 refer to the following passage from a 20th-century essay.

Here then was I (call me Mary Beton, Mary Seton, or Mary Carmichael or by any name you please—it is not a matter of any importance) sitting on the banks of a river a week or two ago
(5) in fine October weather, lost in thought. That collar I have spoken of, women and fiction, the need of coming to some conclusion on a subject that raises all sorts of prejudices and passions, bowed my head to the ground. To the right and
(10) left bushes of some sort, golden and crimson, glowed with the colour, even it seemed burnt with the heat, of fire. On the further bank the willows wept in perpetual lamentation, their hair about their shoulders. The river reflected
(15) whatever it chose of sky and bridge and burning tree, and when the undergraduate had oared his boat through the reflections they closed again, completely, as if he had never been. There one might have sat the clock round lost in thought.
(20) Thought—to call it by a prouder name than it deserved—had let its line down into the stream. It swayed, minute after minute, hither and thither among the reflections and weeds, letting the water lift it and sink it, until—you know the little
(25) tug—the sudden conglomeration of an idea at the end of one's line: and then the cautious hauling of it in, and the careful laying of it out? Alas, laid on the grass how small, how insignificant this thought of mine looked; the
(30) sort of fish that a good fisherman puts back into the water so that it may grow fatter and be one day worth cooking and eating. I will not trouble you with that thought now, though if you look carefully you may find it for yourselves. . . .
(35) But however small it was, it had, nevertheless, the mysterious property of its kind—put back into the mind, it became at once very exciting and important; and as it darted and sank, and flashed hither and thither, set up such a wash
(40) and tumult of ideas that it was impossible to sit still. It was thus that I found myself walking with extreme rapidity across a grass plot. Instantly a man's figure rose to intercept me. Nor did I at first understand that the gesticulations of a
(45) curious-looking object, in a cut-away coat and evening shirt, were aimed at me. His face expressed horror and indignation. Instinct rather than reason came to my help; he was a Beadle; I was a woman. This was the turf; there was the
(50) path. Only the Fellows and Scholars are allowed here; the gravel is the place for me. Such thoughts were the work of a moment. As I regained the path the arms of the Beadle sank, his face assumed its usual repose, and though turf is
(55) better walking than gravel, no very great harm was done. The only charge I could bring against the Fellows and Scholars of whatever the college might happen to be was that in protection of their turf, which has been rolled for 300 years in
(60) succession, they had sent my little fish into hiding.

What an idea it had been that had sent me so audaciously trespassing I could not now remember. The spirit of peace descended like a
(65) cloud from heaven, for if the spirit of peace dwells anywhere, it is in the courts and quadrangles of Oxbridge on a fine October morning. Strolling through those colleges past those ancient halls the roughness of the present
(70) seemed smoothed away; the body seemed contained in a miraculous glass cabinet through which no sound could penetrate, and the mind, freed from any contact with facts (unless one trespassed on the turf again), was at liberty to
(75) settle down upon whatever meditation was in harmony with the moment. As chance would have it, some stray memory of some old essay about revisiting Oxbridge in the long vacation brought Charles Lamb to mind. . . . Indeed,
(80) among all the dead . . . Lamb is one of the most congenial. . . . For his essays are superior . . . because of that wild flash of imagination that lightning crack of genius in the middle of them which leaves them flawed and imperfect, but
(85) starred with poetry. . . . It then occurred to me that the very manuscript itself which Lamb had

looked at was only a few hundred yards away, so that one could follow Lamb's footsteps across the quadrangle to that famous library where the (90) treasure is kept. Moreover, I recollected, as I put this plan into execution, it is in this famous library that the manuscript of Thackeray's Esmond is also preserved . . . but here I was actually at the door which leads to the library (95) itself. I must have opened it, for instantly there issued, like a guardian angel barring the way with a flutter of black gown instead of white wings, a deprecating, silvery, kindly gentleman, who regretted in a low voice as he waved me back (100) that ladies are only admitted to the library if accompanied by a Fellow of the College or furnished with a letter of introduction.

That a famous library has been cursed by a woman is a matter of complete indifference to a (105) famous library. Venerable and calm, with all its treasures safe locked within its breast, it sleeps forever. Never will I wake those echoes, never will I ask for that hospitality again.

1. According to the passage, the narrator uses several names (lines 1–2) in order to

  A. make a universal statement about all humankind
  B. deemphasize her personal identity
  C. introduce her many pseudonyms as an author
  D. attempt to impress the reader with her literacy
  E. mask her true identity from the reader

2. The dominant literary device used to describe the narrator's contemplation, "Thought—to call it by a prouder name . . . one day worth cooking and eating" (lines 20–32), is

  A. a simile
  B. a metaphor
  C. personification
  D. an apostrophe
  E. hyperbole

3. In the phrase "you know the little tug" (lines 24–25), the narrator refers in the abstract to

  A. a fish's pull on a fishing line
  B. the Beadle's insisting she move off the lawn
  C. the annoying loss of a thought
  D. the sudden awareness of an idea
  E. the pull of her guilty conscience

4. The effect the Beadle has on the narrator is to

  A. encourage her pursuit of knowledge
  B. cause her thoughts to retreat
  C. assure her of correct directions
  D. condemn the women's movement
  E. inquire whether she needs additional assistance

5. It can be inferred that the narrator realizes that she initially cannot remember her thought because

  A. it passes so quickly
  B. the student rowing by interrupts it
  C. it is too undeveloped
  D. it does not compare to a great author's ideas
  E. it is so carefully and slowly thought out

6. The lawn and library serve the purpose of

  A. symbolizing the obstacles that women face
  B. reminding readers of the rigors of university study
  C. contrasting relaxation with research
  D. introducing the existence of equality for women
  E. minimizing the author's point about women's roles

7. The passage contains all of the following rhetorical devices EXCEPT

  A. personification
  B. metaphor
  C. simile
  D. literary allusion
  E. allegory

8. The narrator's purpose in the passage is to

  A. explain her anger at the Beadle
  B. personify nature's splendor
  C. illustrate how men can inhibit women's intellectual pursuits
  D. recall the enticing glory of university study
  E. preach her beliefs about women's roles in society

9. The organization of the passage could be best characterized as

   A. stream of consciousness mixed with narration of specific events
   B. comparison and contrast of two incidents
   C. exposition of the women's movement and the narrator's opinions
   D. description of both the physical setting and the narrator's thoughts
   E. flowing smoothly from general ideas to specific statements

10. The pacing of the sentence, "But however small it was . . . it was impossible to sit still" (lines 35–41)

   A. reflects the acceleration of her thoughts
   B. represents a continuation of the pace of the description of the river
   C. contrasts with the fish metaphor
   D. suggests a sluggishness before the Beadle's interruption
   E. parallels that of the description of the library doorman

11. The narrator's description of the Beadle and the library doorman serves to

   A. confirm the horror of what she has done
   B. frighten women away from universities
   C. encourage women to rebel against men
   D. contrast the men's manners
   E. satirize the petty men who enforce the rules

12. The phrase "for instantly there issued . . . waved me back" (lines 95–99) can best be characterized as containing

   A. obvious confusion from the doorman
   B. metaphorical reference to a jailer
   C. awed wonder at the man's position
   D. humorous yet realistic description
   E. matter-of-fact narration

13. Overall, at the time of the occurrences she describes, the narrator probably felt all of the following EXCEPT

   A. indignation
   B. bewilderment
   C. delight
   D. exasperation
   E. repression

14. The narrator's stylistic technique in the passage can best be described as

   A. alternating depictions of what she sees, what she does, and what she ponders
   B. the presentation of a social problem followed by its resolution
   C. general statements followed by illustrative detail
   D. presentation of a theory followed by exceptions to that theory
   E. comparison and contrast of great authors' ideas

Questions 15–25 refer to the following passage by a 19th-century American author.

The time is coming, I hope, when each new author, each new artist, will be considered, not in his proportion to any other author or artist, but in his relation to the human nature, known to us (5) all, which is his privilege, his high duty, to interpret. "The true standard of the artist is in every man's power" already, as [Edmund] Burke says; Michelangelo's "light of the piazza," the glance of the common eye, is and always was the (10) best light on a statue; . . . but hitherto the mass of common men have been afraid to apply their own simplicity, naturalness, and honesty to the appreciation of the beautiful. They have always cast about for the instruction of some one who (15) professed to know better, and who browbeat wholesome common-sense into the self-distrust that ends in sophistication. . . . They have been taught to compare what they see and what they read, not with the things that they have observed (20) and known, but with the things that some other artist or writer has done. Especially if they have themselves the artistic impulse in any direction they are taught to form themselves, not upon life, but upon the masters who became masters only (25) by forming themselves upon life. The seeds of death are planted in them, and they can only produce the still-born, the academic. They are not told to take their work into the public square and see if it seems true to the chance passer, but (30) to test it by the work of the very men who refused and decried any other test of their own work. The young writer who attempts to report the phrase and carriage of every-day life, who tries to tell just how he has heard men talk and seen (35) them look, is made to feel guilty of something low and unworthy by the stupid people who would like to have him show how Shakespeare's men talked and looked, or Scott's, or Thackeray's,

or Balzac's, or Hawthorne's, or Dickens's; he is
(40) instructed to idealize his personages, that is, to
take the life-likeness out of them, and put the
book-likeness into them. He is approached in the
spirit of the wretched pedantry into which
learning . . . always decays when it withdraws
(45) itself and stands apart from experience in an
attitude of imagined superiority, and which
would say with the same confidence to the
scientist: "I see that you are looking at a
grasshopper there which you have found in the
(50) grass, and I suppose you intend to describe it.
Now don't waste your time and sin against
culture in that way. I've got a grasshopper here,
which has been evolved at considerable pains and
expense out of the grasshopper in general; in
(55) fact, it's a type. It's made up of wire and
cardboard, very prettily painted in a conventional
tint, and it's perfectly indestructible. It isn't very
much like a real grasshopper, but it's a great deal
nicer, and it's served to represent the notion of a
(60) grasshopper ever since man emerged from
barbarianism. You may say that it's artificial.
Well, it is artificial; but then it's ideal too; and
what you want to do is to cultivate the ideal.
You'll find the books full of my kind of
(65) grasshopper, and scarcely a trace of yours in any
of them. The thing that you are proposing to do
is commonplace; but if you say that it isn't
commonplace, for the very reason that it hasn't
been done before, you'll have to admit that it's
(70) photographic."
    I hope the time is coming when not only the
artist, but the common, average man, who always
"has the standard of the arts in his power," will
have also the courage to apply it, and will reject
(75) the ideal grasshopper wherever he finds it, in
science, in literature, in art, because it is not
"simple, natural, and honest," because it is not
like a real grasshopper. But . . . I think the time is
yet far off, and that the people who have been
(80) brought up on the ideal grasshopper, the heroic
grasshopper, the impassioned grasshopper, the
self-devoted, adventureful, good old romantic
cardboard grasshopper, must die out before the
simple, honest, and natural grasshopper can have
(85) a fair field. I am in no haste to compass the end
of these good people, whom I find in the
meantime very amusing. It is delightful to meet
one of them, either in print or out of it—some
sweet elderly lady or excellent gentleman whose
(90) youth was pastured on the literature of thirty or
forty years ago—and to witness the confidence
with which they preach their favorite authors as
all the law and the prophets. They have commonly

read little or nothing since or, if they have, they
(95) have judged it by a standard taken from these
authors, and never dreamed of judging it by
nature; they are destitute of the documents in the
case of the later writers; they suppose that Balzac
was the beginning of realism, and that Zola is its
(100) wicked end; they are quite ignorant, but they are
ready to talk you down, if you differ from them,
with an assumption of knowledge sufficient for
any occasion. The horror, the resentment, with
which they receive any question of their literary
(105) saints is genuine; you descend at once very far in
the moral and social scale, anything short of
offensive personality is too good for you; it is
expressed to you that you are one to be avoided,
and put down even a little lower than you have
(110) naturally fallen.

15. The tone of the passage can best be described as

A. somber
B. ornate
C. didactic
D. critical
E. formal

16. The speaker feels common people make which
of the following mistakes?

A. judging a work of art too quickly
B. letting their own interpretation interfere
   with their reading
C. letting authorities tell them how to
   interpret literature
D. basing their judgments on appearances
   only
E. not modeling their tastes after their
   neighbors

17. The phrase "The seeds of death" (lines 25–26) is
a

A. metaphor for imitative art
B. symbol of the destruction of art
C. metaphor for the art of an older age
D. reference to Michelangelo's art
E. symbol of artistic immaturity

18. The author's criticism of those who read only older literature is tempered by the fact that he

    A. is certain their ideas will die out quickly
    B. finds them entertaining and delightful
    C. dismisses them as unimportant
    D. alleges they do little harm to the average reader
    E. acknowledges that they have great knowledge

19. The idealized grasshopper is a symbol for

    A. the quest to merge art and science
    B. the human search for perfection
    C. art that lasts through the ages
    D. artificial rather than realistic art
    E. the scientist's folly in trying to describe nature

20. According to the author, the irony of the idealized grasshopper is that

    A. it ceases to be realistic
    B. scientists will find it useful
    C. it blends science and art into one
    D. it cannot be distinguished from a real grasshopper
    E. it has not been created

21. Which of the following types of grasshopper does the author feel will be the slowest to become integrated into mainstream literature?

    A. the heroic grasshopper
    B. the ideal grasshopper
    C. the simple, honest, and natural grasshopper
    D. the impassioned grasshopper
    E. the good old romantic cardboard grasshopper

22. The story of the grasshopper contains

    A. hidden hyperbole
    B. satiric humor
    C. overstated oxymoron
    D. ruthless criticism
    E. remarkable realism

23. In context, which of the following best represents the author's main idea about art appreciation?

    A. "simplicity, naturalness, and honesty" (line 12)
    B. "people who would like to have him show how Shakespeare's men talked" (lines 36–38)
    C. "an attitude of imagined superiority" (lines 45–46)
    D. "it is artificial; but then it's ideal too" (line 62)
    E. "witness the confidence with which they preach their favorite authors" (lines 91–92)

24. What similarity is suggested between the scientist and artist who discuss the grasshopper?

    A. The models of their studies will both be artificial.
    B. They both love to observe nature.
    C. They both look to old masters for inspiration.
    D. Both of their methods will become obsolete.
    E. They both spend too much time on research.

25. Which of the following devices is NOT used in the passage?

    A. irony
    B. metaphor
    C. caricature
    D. allusion
    E. analogy

Questions 26–33 refer to the following draft.

(1) A famous literary disagreement between Richard Wright and Zora Neale Hurston epitomized some of the philosophical differences within the African-American community of the 1930s. (2) Wright, with barely any formal education, believed that literature was a political tool that should be used to fight against racism, not used to debase blacks. (3) He objected to Hurston's fictional portrayal of blacks during the time period. (4) He felt it degraded their race. (5) Some critics find irony in the fact that the man who had so little education became one of the most eloquent spokesmen against racism, while Hurston, educated at Howard University and Barnard College, chose to use common colloquialisms as the vehicle for her characters. (6) Indeed, the power of

language to provide inspiration or to produce anger can never be denied.

(7) Wright felt that Hurston's most famous work "carries no theme, no message, no thought" because he felt that she wrote not for the black audience, but for the white audience. (8) He derided Hurston for continuing the tradition of presenting the Negro in the guise of a minstrel, designed to make whites laugh at the black experience. (9) Ultimately, Wright felt Hurston appeared to support the status quo of blacks instead of helping to further any social cause. (10) Her supporters claim she used natural language with the finesse of Mark Twain. (11) Esteemed critic Harold Bloom even claimed Hurston represented a continuum from the Wife of Bath to Falstaff and to Whitman.

(12) In turn, Hurston accused Wright of writing too much about hatred, without displaying any understanding or sympathy. (13) She also claimed that any attempt he made at natural black vernacular came across as tone deaf.

(14) Ultimately, it can be said that the two authors' approaches to the literature were immensely different, but their final goal was the same. (15) They both wanted to promote the literature of black people. (16) While they shared this goal, Hurston tried to bridge the cultural gap between blacks and whites, while Wright moved beyond this to promote equality between the races. (17) Perhaps it is telling that Wright died in Paris, far away from his original home, while Hurston died in poverty in the South, where she was born.

26. To add interest for readers who may be unfamiliar with Wright and Hurston, the writer wants to provide a brief introduction to these authors. Where in the first paragraph (sentences 1–6) would such information be best placed?

    A.   before sentence 1
    B.   after sentence 1
    C.   after sentence 2
    D.   after sentence 5
    E.   after sentence 6

27. The writer is considering adding a transition to the opening of sentence 3 (reprinted below), adjusting the capitalization as needed, to better shift to the information in the sentence.

He objected to Hurston's fictional portrayal of blacks during the time period.

Which of the following transitions best accomplishes that goal?

    A.   However,
    B.   In other words,
    C.   In general,
    D.   Similarly,
    E.   On the other hand,

28. In sentence 3 (reprinted below), the writer is considering replacing the underlined section, adjusting punctuation as necessary, with a convincing explanation of why Wright objected to Hurston's depiction of blacks in her literature, one that is consistent with the argument of the passage as a whole.

He objected to Hurston's fictional portrayal of blacks <u>during the time period</u>.

Which of the following versions of the underlined text best serves that purpose?

    A.   (as it is now)
    B.   although she later understood and agreed with Wright and admitted she would have liked to change the manner in which she portrayed blacks in her literature
    C.   because it incited negative passions among fellow black writers
    D.   since she portrayed blacks as ambitious but thwarted in their quest for racial equality during a time of intense racial tension
    E.   as ignorant commoners who worked the fields, but his strongest criticism was directed at her use of black vernacular as the language of the people

29. The writer wants to add a sentence before sentence 7 to introduce the ideas of the second paragraph. Which of the following options best accomplishes this goal?

  A. Wright focused his criticism specifically on Hurston's 1937 novel, *Their Eyes Were Watching God.*

  B. Hurston was strong and stood up to male authors who criticized her writing.

  C. Wright and Hurston would continue their literary feud for most of their respective careers.

  D. Wright was a budding author when he attacked Hurston in his angry essay.

  E. The two authors never saw the world with the same eyes; it is understandable that they disagreed on how to portray the black experience.

30. The writer wants to add a phrase at the beginning of sentence 10 (reprinted below), adjusting the capitalization as needed, to introduce the critics who disagreed with Wright.

Her supporters claim she used natural language with the finesse of Mark Twain.

Which of the following choices best accomplishes that purpose?

  A. Consequently,
  B. In fact,
  C. In contrast,
  D. Accordingly,
  E. Indeed,

31. The writer is considering deleting sentence 11 (reprinted below).

Esteemed critic Harold Bloom even claimed Hurston represented a continuum from the Wife of Bath to Falstaff and to Whitman.

Should the writer make this deletion?

  A. Yes, because it distracts from the information in the paragraph.

  B. Yes, because an esteemed critic does not necessarily add credence to the writer's point.

  C. Yes, because the older literature mentioned in the sentence is irrelevant to Hurston's 20th-century fiction.

  D. No, because Harold Bloom adds an authoritative outside voice and pertinent examples that support the writer's claims.

  E. No, because Harold Bloom is such an important critic in 20th-century literary criticism.

32. The writer wants to further develop the third paragraph (sentences 12–13) by adding relevant information. All of the following pieces of accurate information help achieve this purpose EXCEPT that Hurston

  A. was able to stand up to her critics and give as good as she got

  B. centered her criticism of Wright in a review of his four novellas, titled *Uncle Tom's Children*

  C. condescendingly commented that she wondered where Wright got the ability to write in black vernacular

  D. felt that it was Wright who pandered to the white readers, not herself

  E. brought new life to characters with her use of black vernacular

33. The writer is considering deleting sentence 17 (reproduced below).

Perhaps it is telling that Wright died in Paris, far away from his original home, while Hurston died in poverty in the South, where she was born.

Should the writer make this deletion?

A. No, because it adds interesting information.

B. No, because it serves as an appropriate conclusion to the passage.

C. No, because it is consistent with the flow of the passage.

D. Yes, because it is irrelevant to the content of the passage.

E. Yes, because readers will find it unremarkable.

Questions 34–40 refer to the following draft.

(1) Dawson City, Canada, which became famous during the Yukon Klondike Gold Rush of 1897, received quite a surprise in the summer of 1978. (2) While bulldozing an old sports hall, workers discovered a most unusual treasure-trove in the bottom of the facility's swimming pool: more than 500 reels of ancient nitrate films, including feature films and newsreels dating from the 1910s and '20s that had survived in the frozen conditions.

(3) Film-maker Bill Morrison has pieced together some of this footage into a mesmerizing documentary. (4) *Dawson City: Frozen Time* traces the growth of Dawson City during its most colorful years. (5) Morrison's film also incorporates another lost-and-found tale: a collection of astoundingly evocative still photographs taken in the Dawson City vicinity during the late 19th century by Eric Hegg, who later used 200 of these glass-plate negatives, then deemed valueless, as insulation in the walls of his Dawson City photography studio. (6) They were only rediscovered in the 1950s.

(7) Morrison's project also focuses on the growth of the fledgling motion picture industry in Dawson City, identifying fascinating connections between the "stampeders" who went looking for gold in the Yukon and the hustlers and showmen who conquered Hollywood. (8) For example, in the late 1890s, when thousands descended on Dawson City, both Sid Grauman (who would later build LA's famous Grauman's Chinese Theater) and vaudeville tycoon Alexander Pantages lived and worked there.

(9) Although motion pictures became the primary entertainment for the remote Dawson City miners, motion picture studios soon realized that there was no money in having their film reels shipped back to them. (10) Dawson City was so geographically isolated that it was the last stop on the film distribution line. (11) As the unreturned reels stacked up, many were burned in bonfires or chucked into the river. (12) Only a tiny fraction of the nitrate silent films were wheelbarrowed into the bottom of that fateful filled-in swimming pool.

(13) The damage to the ancient footage is distinctive, and Morrison's documentary deploys these damaged fragments to haunting effect, laying bare the fragility and impermanence of a young art form. (14) In many ways, the negligence of the film industry mirrored the damage done to the Yukon by the gold rush miners: Both were stories of opportunity and innovation colored by tragic carelessness.

34. Which of the following sentences, if placed before sentence 1, would help capture the audience's interest and also introduce an important element of the Dawson City enigma?

A. Gold miners in the Great White North needed entertainment and eagerly sought out any possible distractions to endure the long winter nights.

B. Small towns sometime get big surprises in forms no one could have possibly anticipated.

C. Sub-zero temperatures are usually destructive, but they can also serve to preserve some items in unexpected ways.

D. The Klondike Gold Rush left quite a lasting legacy, both on the land and the people who tried to find their fortune quickly.

E. You never know what you'll find in a new construction project in an old town; amazing things are often found in the least-likely places.

35. The writer is considering deleting the underlined portion of sentence 2 (reprinted below).

While bulldozing an old sports hall, workers discovered a most unusual treasure-trove in the bottom of the facility's swimming pool: more than 500 reels of ancient nitrate films, <u>including feature films and newsreels dating from the 1910s and '20s</u> that had survived in the frozen conditions.

Should the writer delete the underlined portion?

A. Yes, because the information is too vague to add anything of importance.

B. Yes, because it provides unnecessary information about the buried material.

C. Yes, because it distracts from the paragraph's main point.

D. No, because it provides important context for the recovered films.

E. No, because people can relate to feature films from any time period.

36. In the context of the overall structure of the passage, which of the following choices best describes the purpose of the second paragraph (sentences 3–6)?

A. It provides an explanation to resolve a paradox in the first paragraph.

B. It further develops the ideas about Dawson City that were introduced in the first paragraph.

C. It provides a metaphor about filmmaking to help balance the remainder of the passage.

D. It provides a convincing argument for why the ancient films were preserved.

E. It provides details of the new documentary as well as the film industry of old Dawson City.

37. In paragraph three (sentences 7–8), the writer wants to add commentary to bolster the paragraph's point. All of the following would make an appropriate addition EXCEPT

A. The sports hall that contained the old swimming pool in which the ancient films were later found was actually quite a status symbol in old Dawson City.

B. The documentary illustrates how this location in the far north went from unsettled native land, to a small, remote frontier settlement, then to a boomtown, and later an entertainment hub, and then finally back to a tiny remote town.

C. The story of miners near Dawson City is frequently a story of loss, and that is reflected in the later loss of photographic quality in the preserved films.

D. In the heady days of the Yukon Gold Rush, Dawson City was the destination of more than 100,000 would-be gold miners.

E. The films that were discarded included work by major stars like Lionel Barrymore, Lon Chaney, and Douglas Fairbanks, and long-forgotten features with evocative titles like *A Sagebrush Hamlet* and *The Bludgeon*.

38. The writer wants to add the following sentence to the fourth paragraph (sentences 9–12) to provide additional information.

Thus, it is estimated that 99% of all the movies that were sent to Dawson City during the 1910s and '20s were simply destroyed when they were no longer needed.

Where is the best location to place this new sentence?

A. before sentence 9
B. after sentence 9
C. after sentence 10
D. after sentence 11
E. after sentence 12

39. The writer is considering adding information to further develop the ideas of the fifth paragraph (sentences 13–14). Which of the following would be the most appropriate addition?

    A. which films were most popular with Dawson City residents

    B. an explanation of the common exploitation of the mining industry and the film industry

    C. discussion of how Morrison's film exposes the fragility of the old film

    D. examples of other industries that took advantage of vulnerable people in the time period

    E. clarification of the economic impact Dawson City had on the region during its heyday

40. The writer is considering moving the fifth paragraph (sentences 13–14) and placing it between paragraphs two and three. Should the writer make this change?

    A. Yes, because the information relates to the second paragraph.

    B. Yes, because sentence 13 relates to the end of the second paragraph so well.

    C. Yes, because it enhances the organization of the passage.

    D. No, because it best serves as an appropriate conclusion in its current location.

    E. No, because the change would confuse readers about the damage done to the films.

Questions 41–45 refer to the following draft.

(1) Vietnam's intricate system of caves has long been a mystery, a largely unexplored enigma. (2) During decades of war, it was well-known that Vietnamese fighters hid in caves that were all but invisible to the untrained eye. (3) But the recent discovery of one of the longest river caves in the world, the amazing 12-mile-long Hang Khe Ry, has helped foster the creation of Phong Nha-ke Bang National Park, which attracts hundreds of thousands of visitors a year. (4) In the same vicinity, cave explorers were helped by a local villager who remembered hiding in caves when he was a child during the war, and they found Hang Son Doong, a colossal limestone passage over 5.6 miles long and estimated to be 600–800 feet high. (5) The immensity of this cave is mind-boggling.

(6) Inside this capacious space you could not just park a 747 jetliner; you could also fit an entire block of 40-story modern skyscrapers. (7) Midway through the passage, two sinkholes let in shafts of daylight and 100-foot-tall trees sprout from the cave floor. (8) The scale of everything in the cave appears unearthly; one of the sinkholes is an amazing 300 feet across, a stalagmite calcite column towers more than 300 feet above the floor of the cave, and clouds form near the ceiling.

(9) While explorers have discovered longer caves—the Mammoth Cave system in Kentucky—and discovered deeper caves—Veryovkina in Abkhazia, Georgia—it appears that the explorers of Hang Son Doong have found the largest cave in the world.

41. The writer wants to add a new opening sentence before sentence 1 to help attract the reader's attention. Which of the following best accomplishes that goal?

    A. There are many unexplained mysteries in the natural world, and here is one of them.

    B. The small country of Vietnam has many natural attractions; many are well known, such as the islands of Ha Long Bay and the French Colonial architecture of Hanoi.

    C. Most large cave systems on Earth, such as the Mammoth Cave system in Kentucky, have been extensively explored, but a few large caves have not.

    D. People were initially drawn to caves for shelter, but today they are also driven by a sense of curiosity about what may lie in the unexplored deeper recesses.

    E. One of the world's last unexplored mysteries lies in southeastern Asia.

42. In context, which of the following best describes the primary purpose of the second paragraph (sentences 6–8)?

    A. comparing the cave's interior to more recognizable objects

    B. detailing the immensity of Hang Son Doong

    C. suggesting the cave has more secrets that have not yet been revealed

    D. exploring the cave's sites from one opening to the other

    E. specifying the difficulty of exploring Hang Son Doong

43. The writer is considering adding the following sentence to contribute another fact about Hang Son Doong's incredible size.

Hang Son Doong also houses some of the world's tallest stalagmites, which are up to 300 feet tall.

Should this new sentence be added, and, if so, where would it best be placed?

A. after sentence 5
B. after sentence 6
C. after sentence 7
D. after sentence 8
E. The sentence should not be added.

44. The writer wants to add supplemental information that is relevant to the discovery of Hang Son Doong. Which of the following would make the most appropriate addition?

A. Vietnam resident Ho Khanh initially discovered the cave in 1991.
B. Ho Khanh did not find the entrance again until 2009.
C. The British Cave Research Association funded the initial exploration of the cave.
D. A trio of British divers who helped rescue the trapped Thailand soccer team in 2018 explored the cave's waterways in 2019.
E. British divers think the cave's waters reach a depth of 120 meters.

45. The writer wants to add a brief sentence before sentence 9 to better introduce and develop the final paragraph. Which of the following best meets that purpose?

A. Visitors report that exploring the cave is a once-in-a-lifetime adventure.
B. Explorers have already discovered longer caves, so Hang Son Doong is not the longest in the world.
C. One of the original British explorers claims that any other cave in the world will be able to fit comfortably inside Hang Son Doong.
D. Explorers have already discovered deeper caves, so Hang Son Doong is not the deepest.
E. The tremendous importance of this discovery will be a boon to the Vietnamese economy and to scientific exploration.

IF YOU FINISH BEFORE TIME IS CALLED, CHECK YOUR WORK ON THIS SECTION ONLY. DO NOT WORK ON ANY OTHER SECTION IN THE TEST.

Section II: Free-Response Questions

Time: 2 hours, 15 minutes
3 questions

Question 1

(Suggested writing time—40 minutes. This question counts for one-third of the total free-response section score.)

The National Endowment for the Arts (NEA) is an independent federal agency that has been awarding grants to contemporary visual and performing artists since 1965. This grant money comes from American taxpayers. Much of the visual art that is funded by federal grants has been labeled controversial. Should such controversy continue being funded by unsure taxpayers? How does society today look at art as a contribution to culture, and how does it affect the public's view of the spending habits of the government?

Considering the pros and cons of NEA funding, read the following seven sources (including any introductory information) carefully. Then, write an essay that synthesizes material from at least three of the sources and develops your position on the claim that a government should award grants to artists.

> Source A (Brooks)
> Source B (Cole)
> Source C (Walters)
> Source D (Horwitz)
> Source E (NEA chart)
> Source F (Knochel)
> Source G (graphic)

In your response, you should do the following:

- Respond to the prompt with a thesis that presents a defensible position.
- Select and use evidence from at least three of the provided sources to support your line of reasoning. Indicate clearly the sources used through direct quotation, paraphrase, or summary. Sources may be cited as Source A, Source B, etc., or by using the description in parentheses.
- Explain how the evidence supports your line of reasoning.
- Use appropriate grammar and punctuation in communicating your argument.

Source A

Brooks, Arthur C. "Do Public Subsidies Leverage Private Philanthropy for the Arts?" Nonprofit and Voluntary Sector Quarterly. Mar. 1999: 28: 32–45. Print.

The following passage is excerpted from an article about the relationship between government funding and private donations to the arts.

The idea that private philanthropy depends positively on public subsidies has commonly been heard of late in the debate over the need for government participation in the provision of the arts in the United States. According to the American Arts Alliance (1995), "Last year [1994], $123 million in [National Endowment for the Arts (NEA)] grants leveraged more than $1.3 billion." This statement imputes causality to the NEA grants: They were in some way responsible for the generation of more than 10 times as much in non-NEA donations.

This argument relies principally on the assumption that donors respond to the added incentives that matching funds from government grants provide: Because NEA dollars require at least equal matching from other sources, these dollars must have elicited at least that amount in donations from the private sector. Other explanations are also commonly heard as to why there should be a positive relationship between public funding and private philanthropy. For example, it has been argued that grants from the government to an organization can bring that organization to the attention of private donors as the object of support. Similarly, being a recipient of government funding requires a certain level of financial accountability and responsibility, which private donors find attractive.

Is it reasonable to claim that government funding to the arts will have this leveraging effect? Some might say not and make the argument that just the opposite effect should obtain: Public funds should tend to "crowd out" private donations, so private donations are likely made in spite of the NEA subsidies rather than because of them. There are three general reasons why this crowding out might occur.

First, the sense of responsibility and public enthusiasm to support a social cause might be diminished if the government takes responsibility for its funding.

Second, subsidies to arts firms may indeed be a signal of quality but not good quality: They might appear to be a bailout of arts firms in dire straits. Although this may attract some donors, others may be driven away by the prospect of a failed project.

Finally, to the extent that higher government subsidies are paid for with higher taxes, individuals have less disposable income and hence do not donate as much as they otherwise might. This is probably insignificant in the United States, where tax revenues (at all levels of government) allocated to the arts in 1987 amounted to just $3.30 per person.

Source B

Cole, David. "The Culture War; When the Government Is a Critic." *Los Angeles Times.* 3 Oct. 1999, home ed.: pg. 1. Print.

The following article discusses the government's role in funding controversial art.

New York City Mayor Rudolph W. Giuliani, who threatened in true New York fashion to bring the Brooklyn Museum to its knees if it went ahead with an art exhibition that he finds "sick," is only the latest in a none-too-distinguished line of government officials who decide to become art critics. The mayor's most prominent precursor is Sen. Jesse Helms (R-N.C.), who, in 1989, objected vociferously to federal funding of a Robert Mapplethorpe exhibition on the ground that it was homoerotic, thereby launching a decade-long cultural battle over the National Endowment for the Arts. Five years earlier, Rep. Mario Biaggi of New York objected to NEA funding of a Metropolitan Opera production of Verdi's "Rigoletto," which he considered denigrating to Italians. Long before that, there was the Inquisition, which tried the painter Paolo Veronese in 1573 for his allegedly sacrilegious depiction of the Last Supper.

This cast of characters should be enough to illustrate why we need to limit government officials' ability to mandate "politically correct" art. Giuliani's heavy-handed tactics underscore the point. His objection apparently focuses on a single painting in a Brooklyn Museum exhibit that opened yesterday, Chris Ofili's "Holy Virgin Mary," a representation of the Virgin Mary with elephant dung on her breast. The mayor objects that the painting is anti-Catholic, which it may or may not be. (Ofili is himself a Catholic who attends church.) When ordinary people decide they don't like such a painting, they generally stay away or turn away. But that's not enough for the mayor. He dislikes this painting so much he doesn't want anyone else to see it.

In light of the prevalence of government subsidies, if the state were free to deny funds to those whose speech it finds disagreeable, freedom of expression would be rendered meaningless. The postmaster could deny subsidies to newspapers that criticized the president. Broadcast stations could be put off the air, nonprofit groups denied their tax exemptions and university faculty fired for expressing controversial views.

This is not a hypothetical concern. Such arguments were widely advanced in the 1950s and 1960s to justify legislative efforts to exclude suspected communists from public universities. The Supreme Court, however, ruled that such claims could not be squared with the principle of academic freedom protected by the 1st Amendment. As a result, even though no professor has a right to be on the government payroll, the court struck down as unconstitutional efforts to deny jobs to those who declined to take an oath against communism.

Two years ago, the Supreme Court had an opportunity to make clear that the same principle applied to public funding of the arts, in National Endowment for the Arts vs. Finley, which challenged a law that required the NEA to "take into consideration general standards of decency" in allocating arts grants. The lower courts held the law unconstitutional. But the Supreme Court ducked the issue, interpreting the statute not to bar funding of indecent or offensive art to be merely advisory. In doing so, however, the majority rejected the view, adopted by Justices Antonin Scalia and Clarence Thomas, that the government has a free hand when subsidizing speech.

Source C

Walters, Scott E. "Some observations on NEA grants." Theatreideas.blogspot.com. Theatre Ideas. 19 May 2011. Web. 3 June 2011.

The following excerpt, written by a professor who teaches drama and theater history at UNC Asheville and serves as the director of the Center for Rural Arts Development and Leadership Education, discusses inequalities in NEA funding.

Last night and this morning, I posted some number crunching of the latest theatre grants given by the NEA. I'd like to do more, and maybe I will, but the next step—examining the populations of the places where grants were given—requires a great deal more time, and I'm not certain it is worth the effort. A quick glance through the list ought to make it pretty clear that most of the grants went to metropolitan areas. But if I get the urge, maybe I'll pull that information together.

Nevertheless, the listing of the grants in a geographic list does make a pretty clear point: five states pulled down over 50% of the theatre grant money. Again. The average grant size is substantially larger for those places, to the tune of about 25%.

As is usually the case when confronted with actual data that confirms an inequality, there is a quick rush to, well, demand more data. How many applications came from each state? We don't know. The NEA says in its press release "Through the Access to Artistic Excellence category, 789 grants out of 1,415 eligible applications are recommended for funding for a total of $24.9 million." That doesn't break it down according to discipline, nor does it indicate where the other eligible applications were from. But given the 55.7% funding rate, let's assume that the proportion of submitted applications was probably pretty similar to those funded. "Aha!" the theatrical birthers pounce, "So that's not really geographical bias, but just the reality of who submitted grants!" Perhaps so. But that's not the point. I'm not claiming, say, bias on the part of the peer review panels—although I suspect that bias is there. What I am claiming is much simpler.

The point is that the theatre has become increasingly centralized (the top five states that received money are also the top five states that have the highest number of TCG-member theatres, for instance), and the NEA is simply reinforcing that centralization through its funding patterns. The question is not whether "that's the way things are," but rather whether "that's the way things ought to be." And if you answer, as I do, that it is not the way things ought to be, if you believe that the arts ought to reflect the diversity of the nation, a diversity which includes not only race but also things like class and geography, then the next question is what the NEA ought to be doing to change the map.

The "N" in NEA stands for "national," but to have more than one-third of the states in the nation receiving no theatre funding at all undermines that claim. Perhaps those states are cleaning up in the other categories, but I doubt it. Regardless, a centralized theatre scene diminishes the theatre's scope, influence, and overall health. It is something we, as theatre people, ought to be concerned about. It reinforces the disconnect between the populace and the arts, and gives credence to those who would claim that the arts are an urban elitist pastime serving a small portion of the nation and therefore unworthy of government funding.

Source D

Horwitz, Andy. "Who Should Pay for the Arts in America?" *The Atlantic.* 31 Jan. 2016. Web. 19 Sept. 2017.

The following excerpt examines the need for diversity in NEA-funded art projects.

One morning last August I visited Williams College in Massachusetts to teach a workshop on "building a life in the arts" with a group of racially, geographically, and economically diverse young people working at the Williamstown Theatre Festival. Later that night I attended a show at the theater, where I saw these idealistic apprentices taking tickets from, ushering, and selling merchandise to an overwhelmingly white audience—mostly over 60 and, judging by appearances, quite well-off. The social and cultural distance between the aspiring artists at Williamstown and their theater-going audience couldn't have been more pronounced. This gulf is quite familiar to most producers and practitioners of the performing arts in America; it plays out nightly at regional theaters, ballets, symphonies, and operas across the country.

The current state of the arts in this country is a microcosm of the state of the nation. Large, mainstream arts institutions, founded to serve the public good and assigned non-profit status to do so, have come to resemble exclusive country clubs. Meanwhile, outside their walls, a dynamic new generation of artists, and the diverse communities where they live and work, are being systematically denied access to resources and cultural legitimation.

Fifty years ago, the National Endowment for the Arts was created to address just such inequity. On September 29, 1965, President Lyndon B. Johnson signed the National Endowment for the Arts into existence, along with a suite of other ambitious social programs, all under the rubric of the Great Society. Johnson imagined these programs as ways to serve "not only the needs of the body and the demands of commerce but the desire for beauty and the hunger for community."

Half a century later, the ethos upon which the NEA was founded—inclusion and community—has been eroded by consistent political attack. As the NEA's budget has been slashed, private donors and foundations have jumped in to fill the gap, but the institutions they support, and that receive the bulk of arts funding in this country, aren't reaching the people the NEA was founded to help serve. The arts aren't dead, but the system by which they are funded is increasingly becoming as unequal as America itself.

* * *

The NEA was founded to "nurture American creativity, to elevate the nation's culture, and to sustain and preserve the country's many artistic traditions." In an inclusive, pluralistic society, arts funding should reflect our increasingly diverse communities. Deliberately excluding art made by and for underrepresented communities goes against the spirit on which the NEA was founded.

If you look at the more than 1,000 projects set to receive NEA funding this year, you can see the historical (and present) richness of American culture that all but demands to be preserved and supported. A small literary press in Hawaii that mostly publishes works by Asian American and native Hawaiian authors. A Chicago children's theater that puts on performances that can be enjoyed by visually impaired audiences or those on the autism spectrum. Songwriting workshops to teach Tlingit children in Hoonah, Alaska, about their culture. A New Orleans film festival for Louisiana filmmakers. Art reflects the values, aspirations, and questions of a culture; it's a mechanism for a society to articulate how it imagines itself. The projects funded by the NEA reflect the growing diversity—and beautiful complexity—of America itself.

Source E

"How the United States Funds the Arts." *National Endowment for the Arts*. Nov. 2012. Web. 13 Sept. 2017.

The following chart explores the amount per capita spent on the arts by agencies in different countries.

Comparison of Funding by Selected Arts Councils and Agencies

	Budget per Capita (U.S. Dollars)	Data Year
Arts Council of Wales	$17.80	2012/2013
Arts Council (Ireland)	$16.96	2012
Scottish Arts Council	$14.52	2009/2010
Arts Council of England	$13.54	2010
Arts Council of Northern Ireland	$12.36	2011/2012
Australian Council	$8.16	2010/2011
Canada Council for the Arts	$5.19	2011
Creative New Zealand	$2.98	2009/2010
National Endowment for the Arts	$0.47	2012

Source F

Knochel, Aaron. "Why Do Conservatives Want the Government to Defund the Arts?" *The Conversation.* 5 Feb. 2017. Web. 1 Oct. 2017.

The following excerpt briefly presents the history of the NEA and explores the current controversy over continued funding for the arts.

Recent reports indicate that Trump administration officials have circulated plans to defund the National Endowment for the Arts (NEA), putting this agency on the chopping block—again.

Historically, the relationship between the state and culture is as fundamental as the idea of the state itself. Prior to the formation of the NEA in 1965, the federal government strategically funded cultural projects of national interest. For example, the Commerce Department subsidized the film industry in the 1920s and helped Walt Disney skirt bankruptcy during World War II. The same could be said for the broad range of New Deal economic relief programs, like the Public Works of Art Project and the Works Progress Administration, which employed artists and cultural workers. The CIA even joined in, funding Abstract Expressionist artists as a cultural counterweight to Soviet Realism during the Cold War.

The NEA came about during the Cold War. In 1963, President John F. Kennedy asserted the political and ideological importance of artists as critical thinkers, provocateurs and powerful contributors to the strength of a democratic society. His attitude was part of a broader bipartisan movement to form a national entity to promote American arts and culture at home and abroad. By 1965, President Johnson took up Kennedy's legacy, signing the National Arts and Cultural Development Act of 1964—which established the National Council on the Arts—and the National Foundation on the Arts and Humanities Act of 1965, which established the NEA.

Since its inception, the NEA has weathered criticism from the left and right. The right generally argues state funding for culture shouldn't be the government's business, while some on the left have expressed concern about how the funding might come with constraints on creative freedoms.

But today, it's not about the art itself. It's about limiting the scope and size of the federal government. And that ideological push presents real threats to our economy and our communities.

Organizations like the Heritage Foundation fail to take into account that eliminating the NEA actually causes the collapse of a vast network of regionally controlled, state-level arts agencies and local councils. In other words, they won't simply be defunding a centralized bureaucracy that dictates elite culture from the sequestered halls of Washington, D.C. The NEA is required by law to distribute 40 percent of its budget to arts agencies in all 50 states and six U.S. jurisdictions.

Therein lies the misguided logic of the argument for defunding: It targets the NEA but in effect threatens funding for programs like the Creede Repertory Theatre—which serves rural and underserved communities in states like Colorado, New Mexico, Utah, Oklahoma and Arizona—and Appalshop, a community radio station and media center that creates public art installations and multimedia tours in Jenkins, Kentucky, to celebrate Appalachian cultural identity.

While the present administration and the conservative movement claim they're simply trying to save taxpayer dollars, they also ignore the significant economic impacts of the arts. The Bureau of Economic Analysis reported that the arts and culture industry generated $704.8 billion of economic activity in 2013 and employed nearly five million people. For every dollar of NEA funding, there are seven dollars of funding from other private and public funds. Elimination of the agency endangers this economic vitality.

Ultimately, the Trump administration needs to decide whether artistic and cultural work is important to a thriving economy and democracy.

Source G
Pixy. N.D. Web. 2 Nov. 2019.

The following graphic depicts the debate regarding the NEA.

Soapstone passage 1
S- MFK fisher
O- on the french port of Marseille
A- people living in Marseille, people targeted
P - to show reality, how the other side lives
S- Stereotypes
tone- frank, sarcastic

Soapstone passage 2
S- Maya Angelou
O- small town of Stamp, Arkansas.
A - people reading this passage
P- to show reality
S- sterio types, reality.
Tone-

Question 2

(Suggested writing time—40 minutes. This question counts for one-third of the total free-response section score.)

The following passages contain comments on two places: M. F. K. Fisher on the French port of Marseille and Maya Angelou on the small town of Stamps, Arkansas.

Read both carefully and write an essay that analyzes the rhetorical choices the authors make to create both similar and different effects in the two passages.

In your response, you should do the following:

- Respond to the prompt with a thesis that analyzes the writer's rhetorical choices.
- Select and use evidence to support your line of reasoning.
- Explain how the evidence supports your line of reasoning.
- Demonstrate an understanding of the rhetorical situation.
- Use appropriate grammar and punctuation in communicating your argument.

Passage 1

One of the many tantalizing things about Marseille is that most people who describe it, whether or not they know much about either the place or the languages they are supposedly using, write the same things. For centuries this has been so, and a typically modern opinion could have been given in 1550 as well as 1977.

(5) Not long ago I read one, mercifully unsigned, in a San Francisco paper. It was full of logistical errors, faulty syntax, misspelled French words, but it hewed true to the familiar line that Marseille is doing its best to live up to a legendary reputation as world capital for "dope, whores, and street violence." It then went on to discuss, often erroneously, the essential ingredients of a true bouillabaisse! The familiar pitch had been made, and idle readers dreaming of a great seaport dedicated to heroin, prostitution, and rioting could easily skip the clumsy details of marketing for fresh fish. . . .

(10) "Feature articles" like this one make it seem probable that many big newspapers, especially in English-reading countries, keep a few such mild shockers on hand in a back drawer, in case a few columns need filling on a rainy Sunday. Apparently people like to glance one more time at the same old words: evil, filthy, dangerous.

Sometimes such journalese is almost worth reading for its precociously obsolete views of a society too easy to forget. In 1929, for instance, shortly before the Wall Street Crash, a popular travel writer named Basil

(15) Woon published *A Guide to the Gay World of France: From Deauville to Monte Carlo* (Horace Liveright, New York). (By now even his use of the word "gay" is quaintly naïve enough for a small chuckle. . . .)

Of course Mr. Woon was most interested in the Côte d'Azur, in those far days teeming and staggering with rich English and even richer Americans, but while he could not actively recommend staying in Marseille, he did remain true to his journalistic background with an expectedly titillating mention of it:

(20) If you are interested in how the other side of the world lives, a trip through old Marseilles—by daylight—cannot fail to thrill, but it is not wise to venture into this district at night unless dressed like a stevedore and well armed. Thieves, cutthroats, and other undesirables throng the narrow alleys, and sisters of scarlet sit in the doorways of their places of business, catching you by the sleeve as you pass by. The dregs of the world are here, unsifted. It is Port Said, Shanghai, Barcelona, and Sydney combined.

(25) Now that San Francisco has reformed, Marseilles is the world's wickedest port.

Passage 2

There is a much-loved region in the American fantasy where pale white women float eternally under black magnolia trees, and white men with soft hands brush wisps of wisteria from the creamy shoulders of their lady loves. Harmonious black music drifts like perfume through this precious air, and nothing of a threatening nature intrudes.

(30) The South I returned to, however, was flesh-real and swollen-belly poor. Stamps, Arkansas, a small hamlet, had subsisted for hundreds of years on the returns from cotton plantations, and until World War I, a creaking

[handwritten margin notes: "speaks of reality" "then shots it down"]

lumbermill. The town was halved by railroad tracks, the swift Red River and racial prejudice. Whites lived on the town's small rise (it couldn't be called a hill), while blacks lived in what had been known since slavery as "the Quarters."

(35)   In my memory, Stamps is a place of light, shadow, sounds and entrancing odors. The earth smell was pungent, spiced with the odor of cattle manure, the yellowish acid of ponds and rivers, the deep pots of greens and beans cooking for hours with smoked or cured pork. Flowers added their heavy aroma. And above all, the atmosphere was pressed down with the smell of old fears, and hates, and guilt.

    On this hot and moist landscape, passions clanged with the ferocity of armored knights colliding. Until I

(40)   moved to California at thirteen I had known the town, and there had been no need to examine it. I took its being for granted and now, five years later, I was returning, expecting to find the shield of anonymity I had known as a child.

Question 3

(Suggested writing time—40 minutes. This question counts for one-third of the total free-response section score.)

The following essay comes from Sir Thomas More's *Utopia* (1516). Read the passage carefully and then write an essay that argues your position on the validity of More's ideas in light of contemporary standards.

In your response, you should do the following:

- Respond to the prompt with a thesis that presents a defensible position.
- Provide evidence to support your line of reasoning.
- Explain how the evidence supports your line of reasoning.
- Use appropriate grammar and punctuation in communicating your argument.

On Communal Property

By this I am persuaded that unless private property is entirely done away with, there can be no fair distribution of goods, nor can the world be happily governed. As long as private property remains, by far the largest and the best part of mankind will be oppressed with an inescapable load of cares and anxieties. This load, I admit, may be lightened somewhat, but cannot be entirely removed. Laws might be made that no one should own more than a certain amount of land nor possess more than a certain sum of money. Or laws might be passed to prevent the prince from growing too powerful and the populace from becoming too strong. It might be made unlawful for public offices to be solicited, or sold, or made burdensome for the officeholder by great expense. Otherwise officeholders are tempted to reimburse themselves by dishonesty and force, and it becomes necessary to find rich men for those offices which ought rather be held by wise men. Such laws, I say, may have as much effect as good nursing has on men who are dangerously sick. Social evils may be allayed and mitigated, but so long as private property remains, there is no hope at all that they may be healed and society restored to good health. While you try to cure one part, you aggravate the disease in other parts. In redressing one evil another is committed, since you cannot give something to one man without taking the same thing from another.

IF YOU FINISH BEFORE TIME IS CALLED, CHECK YOUR WORK ON THIS SECTION ONLY. DO NOT WORK ON ANY OTHER SECTION IN THE TEST.

Answer Key

Section I: Multiple-Choice Questions

1. B	**10.** A	**19.** D	**28.** E	**37.** A
2. B	**11.** E	**20.** A	**29.** A	**38.** E
3. D	**12.** D	**21.** C	**30.** C	**39.** B
4. B	**13.** C	**22.** B	**31.** D	**40.** D
5. C	**14.** A	**23.** A	**32.** E	**41.** D
6. A	**15.** D	**24.** A	**33.** D	**42.** B
7. E	**16.** C	**25.** C	**34.** C	**43.** E
8. C	**17.** A	**26.** B	**35.** D	**44.** A
9. D	**18.** B	**27.** C	**36.** E	**45.** C

Section II: Free-Response Questions

Essay scoring rubrics, student essays, and analysis appear beginning on page 192.

Answer Explanations

Section I: Multiple-Choice Questions

The passage referred to in questions 1–14 is from Virginia Woolf's A Room of One's Own *(1929).*

1. **B.** The narrator uses several names in order to deemphasize her personal identity, choice B. The phrase that follows the list of names explains this answer: "call me . . . by any name you please—it is not a matter of any importance." The narrator is not trying to make any statement about all humankind (A), introduce any pseudonyms (C), attempt to impress (D), or mask her identity (E).

2. **B.** The narrator primarily uses a metaphor, choice B, as she describes her thought, imagining it to be on a fishing line that "swayed . . . among the reflections." The thought morphs into a metaphorical fish that she hauls to shore on that line. The device is not personification (C) because in this case an abstract idea is given animal characteristics rather than human (her thought is compared to a fish caught on a line). While one may consider her thought to be personified, it is surely not the dominant literary device Woolf uses. The remaining choices are not used in this part of the passage.

3. **D.** The narrator is referring in the abstract to the sudden awareness of an idea, choice D. The phrase that follows the quotation clearly identifies the answer: "the sudden conglomeration of an idea at the end of one's line." Choice A names not the abstract meaning but the literal meaning on which the metaphor is based. Choices B, the Beadle's interruption, and C, the annoying loss of her thought, mention later occurrences unrelated to this "tug." There is no suggestion that the narrator has a guilty conscience (E).

4. **B.** The Beadle causes the narrator's thoughts to retreat, choice B. Being made aware that she is in an area in which only "Fellows and Scholars" are allowed to walk sends her metaphorical "fish into hiding." The Beadle doesn't encourage (A), direct (C), or ask her questions (E). The women's movement (D) is not addressed in the passage.

5. **C.** In the fish metaphor, the narrator points out "how small, how insignificant" her thought is when examined; at this point, her thought is undeveloped, choice C. Later she realizes that the thought "became at once very exciting and important," and she mulls it over as she walks across the lawn. However, the Beadle's refusing to let her walk on the lawn again sent her "little fish into hiding." There is no evidence that the thought passes very quickly (A), or is carefully thought out (E), or that either has to do with her forgetting. Notice of the rower (B) occurs before mention of the thought and does not cause her to forget. Finally, the passage does not hint that her thought does not compare to a great author's ideas (D).

6. **A.** The lawn, on which the narrator is forbidden to walk, and the library, where she is forbidden to enter, are symbols of the obstructions all women face, choice A. Neither choice B nor choice C accurately identifies the intended symbolism. Choice D contradicts the purpose of the passage—to point out inequality. Choice E is incorrect because these two symbols reinforce, and do not distract from, the narrator's point.

7. **E.** There is no allegory (the use of characters to symbolize truths about humanity), choice E, in this passage. The passage does use personification ("willows wept in perpetual lamentation," choice A), metaphor (the "fish" sequence, choice B), simile ("like a guardian angel," choice C), and literary allusion (to Thackery's *Esmond*, choice D).

8. **C.** The vignettes demonstrate how men have told women where they may and may not go. On a deeper level, they suggest that men's attitudes inhibit women in their intellectual pursuits, choice C. The narrator is angry (A) and touches on nature (B), but neither fact states the purpose of the passage. Choice D contradicts the passage; women have been kept away from university study. Choice E overstates; the narrator neither preaches nor discusses society and women's roles in general.

9. **D.** The passage presents external reality, such as the descriptions of the environs of the university and the actions of the Beadle and the doorman, while interspersing the narrator's thoughts about the events, choice D. The passage is too logical and grammatical to be classified as a stream of consciousness (A), which is a narrative technique, not a structural element. The passage doesn't compare or contrast two incidents (B) or address the women's movement (C). Although choice E might be a method of organization, it is not used in this passage.

10. **A.** The sentence accelerates, as do her thoughts, choice A—"it became at once very exciting and important; . . . it darted and sank . . . flashed hither and thither . . . tumult of ideas . . . impossible to sit still." Choice B is incorrect because the sentence describes her thought, not the river. Choice C is incorrect because the sentence is her fish metaphor, not a contrast to it. The speed of the sentence is the opposite of being sluggish (D). Nothing suggests that the pace of this sentence parallels the library doorman (E).

11. **E.** The description of the men, of their pompous behavior and dress, satirically emphasizes how trifling are the narrator's supposed crimes—walking on the grass and attempting to enter the library—and how foolish is the men's self-important enforcement of discriminatory rules, choice E. Choices A and B contradict the passage. The narrator doesn't consider what she's done a "horror," nor would she intend to frighten women away from universities. Choice C is not addressed. Choice D is incorrect because the men's manners are similar, not contrasting.

12. **D.** The description of the gentleman is realistic but also takes a humorous turn in describing a simple doorman as "like a guardian angel barring the way with a flutter of black gown instead of white wings . . . deprecating" as he bars the narrator from entering the library, choice D. The doorman is not confused (A), and the reference is not to a jailer (B) but to a guardian angel. Both choices C and E are unreasonable.

13. **C.** It is highly unlikely that the events described produced an overall feeling of delight, choice C. The events ultimately are described with a negative tone, even though some of the details are definitely pleasing. Notice that all answer choices except choice C are negative.

14. **A.** The narrator blends a presentation of what she sees, what actions she takes, and her thoughts as she walks, choice A. For example, she sees the river, the trees, the Beadle, and the library doorman; she walks across the forbidden lawn and to the library; she ponders about such things as the indignity of being shooed off the lawn and refused entrance to the library. Choice B is incorrect because there is no resolution to her problem. The narrator's stylistic technique does not include making a generality and following it with detail (C), presenting a theory and any exceptions to it (D), or comparing and contrasting great authors' ideas (E).

The passage referred to in questions 15–25 is from "Criticism and Fiction" (1891) by William Dean Howells.

15. D. The best term to describe the tone of this passage is "critical," choice D. The author's purpose is to criticize those who do not think for themselves, imitating older works in pursuit of art. Some examples of this critical tone include "men have been afraid to apply their own simplicity," "seeds of death are planted," "spirit of the wretched pedantry," "decays when it withdraws itself," "they are destitute of the documents," "they are quite ignorant," "you descend . . . in the moral and social scale," and "you are one to be avoided." "Somber" (A) is too strong, as evidenced by the playful grasshopper analogy and the fun the author pokes at old readers. The sentences are not complex enough nor the diction flamboyant enough to be called "ornate" (B). The author's purpose is not "didactic" (C); that is, he does not mean to teach, and his diction is not pedantic. Choice E, "formal," like "ornate," is too strong. The tone is more conversational than formal.

16. C. Howells feels that the common people don't place enough trust in their own abilities to interpret literature but rather rely on "some one who professed to know better and who browbeat wholesome common-sense" into them (lines 14–16), choice C. Choices A and D are not mentioned. Choices B and E contradict the passage. Howells feels that common people should attempt to make their own judgments rather than copy anyone else's taste.

17. A. "The seeds of death" is a metaphor for imitative art, choice A—art formed from studying older masters who themselves imitated the life of their time. According to Howells, this practice produces dead art, imitative art. The author doesn't deal with the destruction of art (B) but rather with the imitation of art. "The seeds of death" does not refer to the art of an older age (C), to Michelangelo's art (D), or to artistic immaturity (E).

18. B. While Howells feels that readers who restrict their reading to older literature are narrow-minded, he also finds them "very amusing . . . delightful," choice B. The author claims that these old ideas will die out slowly, not quickly (A), that "the time is yet far off." He doesn't dismiss these readers as unimportant (C), suggesting only that they are far too limited in their approach. Howells does attribute harm to them (D) in their narrow approach and characterizes their knowledge as assumed rather than great (E).

19. D. The idealized grasshopper, made of cardboard and wire, is symbolic of the artificial, choice D. No quest to merge art and science is mentioned (A); the passage presents only an artist talking to a scientist, and no reference is made to the search for perfection—the cardboard grasshopper is far from perfection (B). Although this cardboard grasshopper is said by the artist to be indestructible, it will not last through the ages of art (C) because it is divorced from reality (although the artist seems to think that it will). Choice E is incorrect because the scientist doesn't produce the idealized grasshopper, the artist does.

20. A. In the quest for the ideal, the grasshopper is created out of wire, cardboard, and paint, ironically becoming in the process a lesser thing because it does not resemble reality, choice A. Even if true (and there is no evidence that they are), choices B and C are not ironic. Common sense tells us that everyone can tell a cardboard grasshopper from a real one (D), and the passage suggests that the cardboard grasshopper has, indeed, been created (E).

21. C. In lines 71–85, Howells claims that the natural, simple grasshopper, choice C, will eventually be recognized. The remaining choices are types of grasshoppers that he hopes will disappear as the natural one emerges.

22. B. Howells' satire, choice B, makes fun of those who believe that they can create an idealized copy of nature when, obviously, nature's product is alive, real, and superior. It is also humorous to think of this silly cardboard grasshopper as a realistic imitation of life. The other answer choices are either stated too strongly (C and D) or are not evident in the passage (A and E).

23. A. The author believes that one should use simplicity, naturalness, and honesty in art and in its appreciation, choice A. The remaining answer choices involve attitudes that Howells criticizes.

24. A. Although the artist creates an idealized version of the grasshopper and the scientist's description (version) of the grasshopper will be based on reality, both of their creations remain artificial, choice A, both representations rather than reality. It is true that Howells presents the scientist's creation as preferable because it approaches reality more closely, but the fact remains that neither creation is itself reality. He suggests that "what [the scientist] want[s] to do is cultivate the ideal," which is also artificial. Both the artist and the scientist are victims of the "wretched pedantry into which learning . . . always decays when it withdraws itself and stands apart from experience in an attitude of imagined superiority." There is no evidence in the passage for the remaining answer choices.

25. **C.** A caricature, choice C, is an exaggerated depiction of a character's features and, by extension, the character's personality—a device not found in the passage. The remaining devices are present. Some examples include irony (A)—the grasshopper analogy (while the artist professes that the cardboard grasshopper is to be preferred to the real one, Howells would have the reader understand that the opposite is true); metaphor (B)—"The seeds of death" (lines 25–26); allusion (D)—to Shakespeare, Thackeray, Hawthorne, and others; and analogy (E)—extended analogy in the grasshopper segment.

The draft referred to in questions 26–33 discusses a literary squabble between Richard Wright and Zora Neale Hurston.

26. **B.** The writer wants to pique the interest of readers who may be unfamiliar with these authors by providing a brief introduction, so the new material would be best placed after sentence 1, choice B. Read the whole paragraph carefully to determine its organization and, therefore, the best placement for an addition. Sentence 1 sets the stage for the passage, announcing the "famous literary disagreement" between Wright and Hurston that "epitomized some of the philosophical differences within the African-American community of the 1930s," and thus it would make no sense to introduce the two authors before this general opening sentence; this eliminates choice A. It also would make no sense to place new introductory information about the two novelists after sentence 2 (C) because sentence 2 begins to explain Wright's objections to Hurston's style, and that commentary is continued in sentences 3 and 4. Adding new background information in between these three sentences would be distracting. Adding introductory information about the novelists after sentence 5 (D) would also be disruptive, and it would appear too late in the paragraph. Sentence 6 provides a conclusion to the entire first paragraph, so it would not be appropriate to place new information after it (E).

27. **C.** Sentence 2 establishes Richard Wright's opinion about literature, that it should be used as a political tool to fight racism. Then sentence 3 begins to delineate Wright's overall objection to Hurston's fictional depictions of blacks; the transition "in general," choice C, would set it up appropriately. This transition would help explain why the information in sentence 3 is located in the overall introductory paragraph instead of paragraph two, in which the writer delineates Wright's particular complaints about a specific Hurston novel. The transition "however," (A), which is used to set up contrast, makes no sense because sentence 3 does not present an idea that opposes sentence 2. The phrase "in other words" (B) is the equivalent of writing "simply put," or "this means," or "put differently," which are ideas that do not logically transition to the idea in sentence 3. "Similarly," (D) also does not make sense because sentence 3 has no information that is similar to what is stated before it. "On the other hand," (E) is a transition that shows contrast, which is improper for sentence 3. Transitions always need to be logical and fit the context of surrounding sentences.

28. **E.** As it is written, sentence 3 is quite vague, and it seems to not fit in with the other sentences in the paragraph; however, choice E adds substantial information about Wright's specific objections to Hurston's characters, particularly her use of black vernacular as their language. Choice A, leaving the sentence as it is, does not address the question, which asks for a convincing *explanation* of Wright's criticism; as originally written, sentence 3 provides no explanation at all. Choice B has no support in the passage as a whole; rather, by claiming Hurston later agreed with Wright, it contradicts everything in the passage, specifically that the two authors disagreed vehemently. Choice C has no evidence in the passage, which offers no hint that other black writers felt negative passions about Hurston's characters; thus, it would not make an appropriate addition. Choice D is incorrect for a similar reason; the passage as a whole does not support the idea that Hurston's characters were "ambitious but thwarted in their quest for racial equality," so it too is not a proper addition.

29. **A.** The second paragraph explores Wright's criticism of "Hurston's most famous work," and choice A both identifies the novel and specifies its publication date. This information is most appropriately placed before

introducing Wright's objections. All of the other answer choices are irrelevant to the second paragraph; none would make an appropriate opening. Choice B states that Hurston's strong personality could stand up to male critics, but it does not address the specific novel that Wright criticized, nor does it logically introduce sentence 7. Choice C explains that the two authors continued their feud for most of their careers, but that information is not related to this paragraph. Equally off topic is the idea in choice D, that Wright was a budding author when he attacked Hurston; the fact that he was indeed a fairly new author does not help introduce this paragraph's ideas. Choice E, explaining that the two authors disagreed on how to portray the black experience, also does not specifically relate to this paragraph.

30. **C.** Sentence 10 would be improved if the writer were to add the transitional phrase "In contrast," choice C, because this sentence changes direction from the preceding sentences. The paragraph presents Wright's criticisms in sentences 7–9, but then sentence 10 switches abruptly to a rebuttal from Hurston's supporters; without any transition, it takes the reader by surprise. "Consequently," as in choice A, makes no sense; it is equivalent to claiming "therefore," or "subsequently," and it does not fit the context of sentence 10. The phrase "in fact" (B) should properly be used as a clarifying phrase that helps prove an idea, not to signal a shift in thinking. "Accordingly" (D) is a transition that is used to summarize or show how something is the logical result of the preceding ideas; it makes little sense within the context of sentence 10. "Indeed" (E) should always be used to add emphasis, but sentence 10 instead needs a signal of contrast.

31. **D.** Sentence 11, with its erudite proclamations from "*Esteemed* critic Harold Bloom," adds an authoritative and respected viewpoint from a professional, while also bringing in pertinent examples for the writer's claims, namely that Hurston's supporters have the backing of someone as influential as Harold Bloom. It should not be deleted, for doing so would weaken the one sentence about Hurston's supporters, choice D. Choices A, B, and C all erroneously claim the sentence should be deleted, so they can be quickly eliminated. Choice A states the sentence distracts from the information in the paragraph, but rather it adds support at the end of the paragraph. Choice B erroneously states that an esteemed critic does not necessarily add credence to the writer's point; obviously, an esteemed professional's claim *can* help as long as it is relevant, as is Bloom's contribution. Choice C makes the silly claim that Bloom's examples of older literature are not relevant to Hurston's 20th-century fiction; in fact, Bloom's point is that Hurston has presented characters that *do* relate and continue the traditions of previous literature. Choice E accurately votes for keeping sentence 11, but for the wrong reason; Harold Bloom is an important critic, but this is not the most significant reason that sentence 11 fits in appropriately with the paragraph's progression.

32. **E.** The third paragraph deals with Hurston's rebuttal to Wright's criticism, and choice E is the only answer choice that does *not* address that subject; instead, it relates how she brought new life to characters with her use of black vernacular. While this is considered to be true, it is irrelevant to the particular paragraph in question. All of the remaining answer choices *do* add relevant information to further develop the paragraph. Choice A directly states how Hurston "was able to stand up to her critics and give as good as she got," which implies how she stood up for herself, defended her literary choices, and, in turn, criticized Wright's work. Choice B names the specific Wright work she criticized, which adds context for her rebuttal and provides further development. Choice C would also aid the development of the paragraph and help pinpoint Hurston's criticism of Wright, by way of her condescending comment wondering where he got the ability to write black vernacular. Choice D also adds interest by detailing Hurston's counterargument that it was Wright, not she, who pandered to white readers, and it addresses a point made previously in the passage.

33. **D.** The question simply asks whether the last sentence should be deleted. Yes, it should, because it has no major bearing or relevance on the passage as a whole, choice D. Although it is true that Wright died in Paris, far away from his Mississippi birthplace, while Hurston died in poverty in Florida, these details are irrelevant as a concluding sentence; the passage deals with the two authors' opposing viewpoints about character, not their respective biographies. Choices A, B, and C all claim that the sentence should not be deleted, which is not accurate; it should be cut. Choice A erroneously claims that sentence 17 adds interesting information; while some may find sentence 17 interesting, it is still irrelevant to the passage. Choice B wrongly claims it serves as an appropriate conclusion; a proper conclusion should wrap up the information and summarize the passage, not bring up unrelated information. Choice C inaccurately states sentence 17 is consistent with the flow of the passage, when instead it interrupts the flow of ideas. Choice E also votes to delete sentence 17, but it does so for the wrong reason; whether or not readers find it "unremarkable" is irrelevant to the question.

The draft referred to in questions 34–40 discusses the surprising discovery of damaged but viewable films that were frozen in a swimming pool in the Yukon at Dawson City.

34. C. The question asks for an opening sentence that would help capture the audience's attention and also introduce an important element of the Dawson City enigma. Choice C fulfills both requirements; audiences will be intrigued to find out how sub-zero temperatures can both destroy and preserve, an enigma that the passage explores. Additionally, it introduces the "surprise" that is mentioned in the first sentence. Choice A barely fits the topic of the passage; while it is undoubtedly true that gold miners, like all people, need entertainment, it is hardly an intriguing idea to entice readers, and it does not relate to the enigma of the age-old films that were preserved in the Dawson City swimming pool for decades. Choice B may sound nice at first; indeed, small towns do get big surprises at times in unanticipated ways, but this idea is too simplistic and general to fit the point of the passage, and it does not relate to the enigma of the frozen films that were found. Choice D is likely true in reality; surely the Klondike Gold Rush had a lasting legacy on the land and the people who lived in the region, but this idea does not relate to the passage specifically enough to be a correct answer, and it does not address the enigma that the question asks about. Choice E is weak, beginning with the clichéd phrase "you never know what . . . ," the inappropriate and informal use of the second-person pronoun, and its failure to address what the question requires, namely the enigma encompassed in the Dawson City cache of films.

35. D. The underlined portion of sentence 2 provides important context for the passage and, therefore, should not be deleted. Without knowing that the found films were actually feature films and newsreels from the 1910s and '20s, the discovery of the frozen cache would not have such significance; they might have been early nitrate films of any subject, any quality, or any decade. This information gives the sentence much more context to appreciate the discovery of the films, choice D. Choice A incorrectly wants to discard the underlined portion of the sentence, and it erroneously claims the information is too vague to add importance. Instead, the underlined portion identifies the time period and genre of the films. Choice B also negates the underlined portion, claiming it offers unnecessary information; instead, it provides significant knowledge about the films, including their dates and subjects. Choice C is simply wrong because the underlined portion does not distract from the paragraph's main point; it enhances it. Without the knowledge of the films' dates and content, the readers would not understand the importance of the discovery. Choice E agrees that the underlined portion should be included, but for a weak reason. While it is perhaps true that people can relate to feature films, that idea alone is not a convincing reason for its inclusion; choice D offers a much more compelling reason.

36. E. The second paragraph provides information about two aspects of the films found in Dawson City: It identifies Bill Morrison's documentary about the films' discovery and their historical importance to Dawson City, and it reveals the additional discovery of the glass-plate negatives of Eric Hegg. Choice E pinpoints these two ideas. Choice A makes no sense; the first paragraph does not present a paradox, so the second paragraph cannot resolve it. Choice B is too vague, simplistic, and generic to be the correct response; it fails to identify what ideas of the first paragraph are further developed. Choice C makes two incorrect claims: that the second paragraph contains a metaphor and that it helps balance the remainder of the passage. Instead, the second paragraph introduces Morrison's documentary that is further explored in the remaining paragraphs. Choice D cannot be the correct response because neither the second paragraph nor the entire passage offers any convincing argument about the films' preservation.

37. A. The question asks you to find which information does *not* provide appropriate commentary to bolster the third paragraph. Choice A may be somewhat interesting, but it is not relevant to the subject of the third paragraph; this information about the status of the sports hall that housed the Dawson City swimming pool might be appropriate for the first paragraph in a longer piece, but it does not fit the third paragraph. Choice B fits the paragraph's content and would add interesting information about the rise and fall of Dawson City's significance in the late 19th century. Choice C nicely draws a parallel between the losses that miners in Dawson City faced with the loss in the quality of the films that had been buried for decades in the swimming pool. It would make an interesting addition to the paragraph. Choice D would bolster the paragraph's point by explaining how many potential miners flooded the city; the addition of 100,000 people helps explain why film studios would send motion pictures to the area theaters. Choice E adds emphasis by naming specific, well-known movie stars who were featured in the discarded films, which reinforces how important film stars were involved in the films discovered in Dawson City.

38. E. The suggested additional sentence would be best placed at the end of the fourth paragraph, after sentence 12. The exclamation that an estimated 99% of films were destroyed when no longer needed reinforces the information in sentence 12 that "only a tiny fraction of the nitrate silent films were wheelbarrowed into the bottom of that fateful filled-in swimming pool." It provides an appropriate conclusion to the paragraph. The addition would make no sense if placed before sentence 9 (A) because the reader does not yet know that any films were destroyed, let alone why. Choice B also would make no sense; the additional information should not follow sentence 9 because it would completely disrupt the continuity of information in sentences 9 and 10. Sentence 9 explains that movie studios realized the futility of having films shipped back, and sentence 10 explains the reason: that Dawson City was the very remote last destination of distribution. Choice C, which suggests placing the new information after sentence 10, also disrupts the continuity of the paragraph. Sentence 11 logically follows sentence 10 by stating how the films, now at the end of the distribution line, stacked up and were burned or chucked in the river for disposal. Placing the additional information after sentence 11 (D) would not be the best placement for the additional information either because the new sentence serves as a conclusion to both sentences 11 and 12. It cannot be placed before sentence 12.

39. B. The fifth paragraph concludes with the idea that the neglectful film industry mirrors the damage done to the Yukon by gold miners, and choice B suggests adding explanation of this exploitation by different industries. Such an addition would certainly further develop the paragraph by connecting the two sentences. Choice A, suggesting which films were popular with Dawson City residents, might be well-placed in the third paragraph (at best), but it does not relate to the last paragraph. Choice C does not add anything germane to the last paragraph because it fails to connect the distinct damage of the films to the damage done to the area by miners; therefore, the way in which Morrison shows the fragility of old film is irrelevant at this point in the passage. Choice D would be irrelevant at the end of the passage; one cannot justify bringing up new examples of other industries that took advantage of vulnerable people. In addition, the passage deals with the damage done to the environment, not to people. Choice E is basically immaterial; understanding the economic impact of Dawson City in its prime does not relate to the passage.

40. D. It would be an unwise choice to relocate the current concluding paragraph between paragraphs two and three. As it is written, sentences 13–14 provide an appropriate conclusion to the passage by suggesting a greater context, such as claiming the damaged films "[lay] bare the fragility and impermanence of a young art form," and connecting the "negligence of the film industry" to "the damage done to the Yukon by the gold rush miners." Choices A, B, and C all incorrectly suggest the paragraph should be moved. Choice A's reasoning is flawed; the information in the last paragraph does not relate to the second paragraph, which finishes with mention of a photography studio owned by a Dawson City resident, not the damaged film found in the swimming pool. Choice B is wrong for a similar reason; sentence 13 does not relate to the information at the end of the second paragraph. Choice C erroneously claims that moving the paragraph would enhance the organization of the passage; it would instead disrupt it. Choice E correctly votes for leaving the paragraph where it is, but for the wrong reason; moving it would not necessarily confuse readers about the damage done to the films, but it would cause them to wonder about the placement of the information because it does not relate to the second paragraph.

The draft referred to in questions 41–45 discusses the recent discovery in Vietnam of the world's largest cave system.

41. D. This question asks for a new opening line, one that is specifically designed to attract the reader's attention; it calls for a sentence that makes the reader *want* to continue reading. Choice D is the best choice because it alludes to a universal truth: People have a tendency to be curious about things unknown and unseen, like deep caves. All of the other answer choices take too narrow of a viewpoint, and they don't hook the reader's attention quite as well. Choice A is far too vague with its phrase "unexplained mysteries," which is neither true nor attention-getting, and the bland phrase "here is one of them" does not entice a reader to continue. Choice B veers off topic; the essay discusses the caves of Vietnam, not every tourist attraction in the country. Choice C perhaps brings up an interesting point by claiming that a few large caves have not been explored, but it does not apply to the Hang Son Doong cave, which *has* been explored; therefore, it is not an appropriate opening sentence. Choice E is questionable with its vague phrase "One of the world's last unexplored mysteries" because the cave has been discovered and explored, and the passage has no reference to the number of unexplored mysteries the world may hold.

42. B. The second paragraph details the immensity of Hang Son Doong in several ways, choice B. It compares its size to well-known visual objects, such as a 747 jetliner and a block of modern skyscrapers; it describes sinkholes so large that 100-foot-tall trees grow inside them; it chronicles the width of one sinkhole, the height of a calcite column, and the fact that clouds form inside the cave. These cumulative details help the audience picture the incredible interior size of the cave. Choice A is just too limited to address the primary purpose of the paragraph. Sentence 6 indeed compares the cave's interior to recognizable objects, namely a 747 jetliner and a block of 40-story-tall skyscrapers, but these comparisons are only a small part of the paragraph; this thread is not sufficiently global to clarify its overall purpose. Choice C does not describe the paragraph's purpose; while it is undoubtedly true that the cave still has unrevealed secrets, this paragraph does not hint at such secrets. It describes what has already been discovered there, not what is still unknown. Choice D is unreasonable; the paragraph does not mention exploring the cave from one end to another, so this idea cannot be the paragraph's purpose. Choice E is also not contained in the paragraph, so it cannot articulate its purpose; surely the cave is difficult to explore, but the second paragraph does not mention that fact.

43. E. The information in the suggested new sentence is a redundant addition because its information about the height of the stalagmites is already contained in sentence 8, which states, ". . . a stalagmite calcite column towers more than 300 feet above the floor of the cave. . . ." Therefore, no need exists for stating that the cave's "stalagmites . . . are up to 300 feet tall." Because the information is already contained in the passage, it would not be wise to add it; thus, all other answer choices are incorrect. It should not be placed after sentence 5 (A), or sentence 6 (B), or sentence 7 (C), or sentence 8 (D). It does not improve the passage, so it should not be added at all.

44. A. The information in each of the answer choices is interesting, but the supplemental information that is most relevant to the *discovery* of the cave is choice A, which reveals both the name of the cave discoverer (Vietnam resident Ho Khanh) and the date of the discovery (1991). Regarding this initial discovery, the passage does not need to explain how long it took for Ho Khanh to find its entrance again (B). And, while it is true that the British Cave Research Association funded and initially helped explore the cave (C), this information is not necessary to the passage. Some may find it intriguing that members of the diving team who rescued the Thailand soccer team in 2018 explored the cave in 2019 (D), but this is not vitally relevant to the content of the passage. Choice E is also interesting, but not really necessary, especially because the British divers apparently only "think" they know the depth of the waters; they have not yet accurately measured it.

45. C. Sentence 9 discusses how other caves are longer and deeper (Mammoth Cave and Veryovkina, respectively) but labels Hang Son Doong as the largest cave. Choice C would make the best introduction to the third paragraph because it introduces the idea of Hang Son Doong being the largest, stating that any other cave in the world could fit comfortably inside it. It leads into sentence 9 very well. Choice A, that visitors report exploring the cave is a once-in-a-lifetime adventure, is very likely true, but it does not relate to the content of sentence 9. Choice B merely repeats some of the information in sentence 9 by stating that other caves are longer and, therefore, is certainly not necessary. Choice D suffers from the same fault; it too only states something that is already in sentence 9, that other caves are deeper. Choice E may also be true; surely the discovery of the cave will aid Vietnam's economy and scientific exploration, but that, too, is not relevant to the content of sentence 9.

Section II: Free-Response Questions

Question 1

Row A: Thesis (0–1 point)	
Scoring Criteria	
0 points for any of the following: • Having no defendable thesis. • Only restating the prompt in the thesis. • Only summarizing the issue with no apparent or coherent claim in the thesis. • Presenting a thesis that does not address the prompt.	**1 point for** • Addressing the prompt with a defendable thesis.
Decision Rules and Scoring Notes	
Theses that do not earn this point • Only restate the prompt. • Are vague or do not take a position. • Equivocate or merely summarize others' arguments. • Simply state obvious facts rather than making a defendable claim.	**Theses that do earn this point** • Respond to the prompt (rather than restating it) <u>and</u> clearly take a position on the issue of governments funding grants to artists, instead of simply stating pros and cons.
Additional Notes • The thesis may be one or more sentences that are in close proximity to each other anywhere in the essay. • A thesis that meets the criteria can be awarded the point whether or not the rest of the response successfully conveys that line of reasoning. • For a thesis to be defendable, the sources must have at least minimal evidence that could be used as support. • A thesis may present a line of reasoning, but it is not required to earn a point.	

Row B: Evidence AND Commentary (0–4 points)				
Scoring Criteria				
0 points for	**1 point for**	**2 points for**	**3 points for**	**4 points for**
• Simply repeating the thesis (if present). • **OR** restating provided information. • **OR** providing fewer than two references to the provided sources.	• Providing evidence from at least two of the provided sources. • **AND** summarizing the evidence without explaining how the evidence supports the thesis.	• Providing evidence from or references to at least three of the provided sources. • **AND** explaining how some of the evidence relates to the thesis, but the line of reasoning may be nonexistent or faulty.	• Providing specific evidence from or references to at least three of the provided sources to support all claims in the line of reasoning. • **AND** explaining how some of the evidence relates to the thesis and supports the line of reasoning.	• Providing specific evidence from or references to at least three of the provided sources to support all claims in the line of reasoning. • **AND** consistently and explicitly explaining how the evidence relates to the thesis and supports the line of reasoning.

Decision Rules and Scoring Notes				
Typical responses that earn 0 points:	**Typical responses that earn 1 point:**	**Typical responses that earn 2 points:**	**Typical responses that earn 3 points:**	**Typical responses that earn 4 points:**
• Are unclear or fail to address the prompt. • May present mere opinion or repeat ideas from a single source.	• Only summarize or describe sources instead of providing specific details.	• Mix specific details with broad generalities. • May contain simplistic, inaccurate, or repetitive explanations that do not strengthen the argument. • Fail to explain the connections between claims and to establish a clear line of reasoning. • May make one point well but fail to adequately support any other claims.	• Consistently offer evidence to support all claims. • Focus on the importance of specific words and details from the sources to build an argument. • Use multiple supporting claims to organize an argument and line of reasoning. • May not integrate some evidence or support a key claim in the commentary.	• Consistently offer evidence to support all claims. • Focus on the importance of specific words and details from the sources to build an argument. • Organize, integrate, and thoroughly explain evidence from sources throughout in order to support the line of reasoning.

Additional Notes

• Writing that suffers from grammatical and/or mechanical errors that interfere with communication cannot earn the fourth point in this row.

Row C: Sophistication (0–1 point)

Scoring Criteria	
0 points for	**1 point for**
• Not meeting the criteria for 1 point.	• Exhibiting sophistication of thought and/or advancing a complex understanding of the rhetorical situation.

Decision Rules and Scoring Notes	
Responses that do not earn this point:	**Responses that earn this point demonstrate one (or more) of the following:**
• Try to contextualize their argument, but make predominantly sweeping generalizations (*"Throughout all history . . ."* OR *"Everyone believes . . ."*). • Only hint at other possible arguments (*"Some may think . . ."*). • Present complicated or complex sentences or language that is ineffective and detracts from the argument.	• Present a nuanced argument that consistently identifies and examines complexities or tension across the sources. • Illuminate the significance or implications of the argument (either the student's argument or the arguments within the sources) within a broader context. • Make effective rhetorical choices that consistently strengthen the force and impact of the student's argument. • Develop a prose style that is especially vivid, persuasive, resounding, or appropriate to the student's argument.

continued

Additional Notes

• This point should be awarded only if the demonstration of sophistication or complex understanding is part of the argument, not merely a phrase or brief reference.

High-Scoring Essay

Our world is far from that of Renaissance Florence where all was abuzz with the revival of humanitarian philosophy and a rapidly changing society. This was a time of radical development in art, coupled with major shifts in social values and views. However, much has changed in the five hundred years since this rebirth. The twenty-first century is driven by technological advancement and rational thinking more than any time before; these priorities have the result, whether intended or not, of placing funding for the arts in jeopardy. However, at the heart of mankind lies an appreciation for the arts and all they do to improve our world. Thus, it is necessary for government spending, through the National Endowment for the Arts (NEA), to step in and help provide the arts to a society that has forgotten the importance of art in fostering self-discovery and the progression of mankind.

It is only natural for art to be controversial. Art is often an expression of internal strife, a stinging criticism of society, a challenge to what is accepted, or a dare to humanity to look at our everyday world with a new perspective. Indeed, art is at the very cusp of social change. When Praxiteles sculpted the first female nude sculpture in Ancient Greece it produced as much uproar as Chris Ofili's "Holy Virgin Mary" that Giuliani objected to (Source B). Yet today we look back at the countless nude figures in art as beautiful, not scornful. Art is a necessity that is very rarely accepted without conflict. So it remains today. But, if artists have been under attack for hundreds of years and have continued to persist, why must they still require the support of our government?

The answer is a complex one. Art and government have always been intertwined. Before cameras, television, or the internet, art was a main form of propaganda used by the government and even the church. From the Great Pyramids to the frescos in the Sistine Chapel, from the Nazi recruiting posters to the murals of Diego Rivera, leaders of all times and regions have employed art for political and social purposes. As Aaron Knochel notes, even the CIA funded "Abstract Expressionist artists as a cultural counterweight to Soviet Realism during the Cold War" (Source F). However, government-sponsored propaganda-art was often more subdued, and thus more ethically acceptable, than was non-governmental propaganda-art of the time. No government needed to worry about issuing formal guidelines to control obscenity for the art it sponsored. However, what the NEA seeks to achieve is quite different than any previous government institution and it is this that concerns people. Instead of supporting art that benefits the government they are supporting art that supposedly benefits the people. The NEA claims to be protecting "freedom of expression" (Source B), and generating a "positive relationship between public funding and private philanthropy" (Source A).

What necessitates this fusion of art and government is the changing ethos of the American people. Nowadays, there is very little emphasis placed on the humanities, personal expression, or creativity. Our world is changing rapidly, and many feel there is simply no time for these frivolous pursuits. Math, science, and reason are emphasized as the pathways to success, fortune, fame, and the advancement of humanity. However, while humans are making huge strides with their minds, they are leaving their hearts and emotions underdeveloped. Many seem as if they are mentally stuck in the Age of Enlightenment, a time when reason was emphasized as the solution to all problems over all other human capabilities. Today people are much more willing to invest their money in economic ventures than in the more intangible experiments of artists. The government has perceived this change and, fortunately, has deemed the arts important enough to be saved, albeit at meager levels. Unfortunately, in the United States, arts funding lags far, far behind other developed countries. If the U.S. were to quadruple arts funding, we'd still fall short of New Zealand's budget, and if we were to multiply it tenfold, we'd still not even reach the funding of Northern Ireland (Source E). Scott E. Walters decries the inequity in funding throughout all the states; clearly the NEA grants help fulfill this need (Source C). Andy Horwitz adds to Walters' worry, noting that "the institutions they support, and that receive the bulk of arts funding in this country, aren't reaching the people the NEA was founded to help serve." However, the fact that the NEA was created to fulfill the "desire of beauty and the hunger for community" (Source D) reminds us that the NEA must adhere to its founding principles.

The NEA must continue to award grants to artists to support the social change we value so much. Perhaps some art works will be better received than others, and perhaps some works will make people "sick" (Source

B), while others will delight them. But, no matter what, the work of artists will keep our society awake and changing. It is for this reason that the NEA must strive to "reflect our increasingly diverse communities" so that we can continue to see "the historical (and present) richness of American culture that all but demands to be preserved and supported" (Source D). If we lose our art, we will lose our ability to express ourselves and expand our minds, and we will lose the essence of our humanity. In our bustling modern world, the art supported by the NEA is an essential connection back to our internal experience.

(918 words)

Analysis of the High-Scoring Essay

This thoughtful and insightful essay clearly addresses the prompt and thoroughly develops the idea that the NEA should continue to fund grants for public art. It is far more developed than most essays, but an AP Reader will quickly sense that the student is well-versed in the topic. The student's knowledge of the history of art gives him or her a chance to shine. By using most available sources, the student efficiently integrates both implicit and explicit evidence to bolster his or her position. The introduction blends a historical perspective, noting the Florentine Renaissance, with an examination of 21st-century priorities. The student logically demonstrates that current funding for the arts has become a lower priority than funding for technology. The precept that humanity has a fundamental need for the arts in order to make societal progress sets up the thesis that the NEA should, indeed, continue to fund grants in the arts. This thesis deserves a point in Row A.

The second paragraph explores the idea that art has always had a component of controversy, and it effectively uses an example from ancient Greek art, comparing the public reception for Praxiteles' sculpture to the objection posed in modern times by Mayor Giuliani to an art exhibit. The student accepts that art will always entail controversy but acknowledges that art is necessary to bring social advancement. Leaving the Reader with a thought-provoking question, the student wonders why artists need government support, given that their work will be "under attack." This paragraph encourages the Reader to pause and contemplate the answer. By demonstrating both the ability to engage the Reader's intellect and to pose thought-provoking questions, the student is already earning a high score.

The third paragraph readily acknowledges that "the answer is a complex one" and proceeds to demonstrate how intricate the issue really is. The effective use of examples from throughout art history, all of which involve some degree of controversy, demonstrates the student's overall awareness of the world and of how its political history affects the art world; this skill will impress any AP Reader. Although the student acknowledges the role governments have played in funding the arts, he or she also acknowledges that the arts have sometimes been misused by governments as official tools of propaganda. The student then rightfully differentiates NEA funding from previous government-sponsored art by specifying that NEA-funded projects are designed to "benefit the people," not to promulgate government propaganda. This paragraph, although a bit rough in its construction, presents sound ideas while differentiating the purpose of NEA grants from previous government-sponsored art. Given that this essay was written under a time limit, it is easy to overlook minor wording issues that would likely be clarified in a more polished draft. The fact that the student integrates three sources into this paragraph is also an effective demonstration of his or her writing skill.

The next paragraph advances the progress of the argument by exploring contemporary needs for arts funding. The comparison of our current society to the Age of Enlightenment demonstrates this student's grasp of humanity's intellectual development and the similarities between today and an era hundreds of years ago. The idea that humanity is too ensconced in becoming successful at the expense of the arts is an interesting thought; it causes the Reader to ponder this philosophical issue. The essay uses ample evidence from the sources to back up its assertion of the lack of adequate funding for the arts in the U.S. and the inequities of funding distribution. The student's choice to end the paragraph by emphasizing the positive role the NEA should play is also effective. The thorough development of evidence and commentary deserve 4 points in Row B.

The student concludes by lobbying on behalf of all humanity, by acknowledging that "we value" the social change that the arts represent. This application works well because it uses the classical rhetorical appeal of ethos, an appeal that makes the Reader appreciate the shared aims of humanity. Overall, this essay truly earns its high score because it is specifically on topic, it demonstrates superior organizational skills, and it has splendid development. The student's command of language is also outstanding; the syntax is varied, and the diction is accurate and concise. These traits earn a point in Row C. It would be hard for any Reader to ask for more success in a timed essay than is displayed here, and it deserves its overall score of 6.

Medium-Scoring Essay

The National Endowment for the Arts (NEA) must stop awarding grants to artists because it takes society out of the picture, allows the public no say in what is produced, and crowds out public investment.

For as long as art has existed so has the strenuous relationship between art and society. It is a natural part of the production of art—that artists must struggle and search out support in society. The NEA takes the place of society and ruins this relationship: "the sense of responsibility and public enthusiasm to support a social cause might be diminished if the government takes responsibility for its funding" (Source A). Government interference is only hurting the production of art by hindering the centuries-old method of artistic production.

It is dangerous to let a bureaucracy control something as creative as art. This is clear with Mayor Rudolph Giuliani who relied on "a none-too-distinguished line of government officials who decide to become art critics" (Source B) for advice. Our country was founded on the ideas of freedom of expression and no taxation without representation. It is not right that people's money is being used for projects they do not support. Source F is accurate when it argues "state funding for culture shouldn't be the government's business." Politicians are representative of society and its interests. The NEA is headed down a slippery-slope toward too much government control.

Finally, the NEA discourages people to donate to the arts because they think it has already been taken care of by the government. Many might have thought that this was enough. It is not unreasonable to think that "public funds tend to 'crowd out' private donations" (Source A). People no longer feel the moral obligation to support the arts. This separates people from the art of our society, therefore decreasing its power, meaning, and effectiveness.

The National Endowment for the Arts hinders the public's involvement in the development and production of art. Furthermore, it is systematizing a creative progress and allocating funds in an irresponsible manner. The government is responsible for regulating trade, waging war, passing laws, and collecting taxes—not supporting art. That is the job of the people.

(361 words)

Analysis of the Medium-Scoring Essay

This essay makes a few good points, but it is impaired by brevity and logical flaws. Simply put, it does not exhibit the development and clarity of thought that are required to earn a high score. The introductory paragraph takes a clear stand, albeit simplistic, stating that the NEA should simply stop funding all grants, and for that it earns a point in Row A. Several of the assumptions underlying this one-sentence paragraph are questionable at best. One example is the assumption that the "public [has] no say" in NEA decisions; no evidence is presented to substantiate this claim. Another questionable assumption is that NEA funding will indeed "crowd out public investment," despite any actual evidence of this. These unsubstantiated assertions indicate that this student is not as aware of the world as one would hope, and they lead the AP Exam Reader to fear that the essay will merely present an oversimplified view of a very complex issue. Alas, that fear is realized.

The second paragraph simplistically states that artists must struggle, another questionable assertion that is heavily laden with the student's preconceived notions about artists. Next, it claims that NEA funding somehow "ruins" this struggle. Presumably, this student believes that, since the NEA helps an artist to some degree with some form of funding, the artist is free to create art without any other pressures. The student's conclusion is questionable because the logic is full of holes. He or she offers neither concrete examples nor logical explanation; therefore, the paragraph fails to convince the Reader.

The next paragraph is riddled with unfortunate logical errors that distract the Reader's attention from the points the student is trying to make. For example, the student leaps from the idea that bureaucratic control is dangerous to the unrelated idea of "no taxation without representation." This jarring jump in logic leaves the Reader's head spinning, wondering how the student is trying to connect these two ideas. It comes across as if the student suddenly remembered the "no taxation without representation" phrase from a history class and tried to work it into the essay, regardless of its relevance. Although it might be possible to construct a convincing argument for this student's ideas, this oversimplified presentation does not work in the student's favor. The student seems to be composing without considering what he or she had previously stated. For example, in this paragraph, the student claims that "politicians are representative of society." If this were true, then it directly contradicts the student's statements in the first paragraph, which claim that the NEA takes "society out of the picture." If politicians are representative of society, then society is indeed "in the picture." The student's word choices would benefit from clarification and consistency.

The fourth paragraph contains more examples of awkward wording, such as the phrase "discourages people to donate." Perhaps with more time the student might have improved this diction. In addition, the muddled thinking and leaps of logic that the student demonstrated previously crop up again in this paragraph. For example, the student equates "moral obligation" with financial funding, which is not necessarily the same; a moral obligation to the arts does not necessarily include a financial obligation. Additionally, the student never addresses the important questions of how a lack of funding will "separate people from the art of our society" or why a decrease in arts funding would bring a decrease in art's "power, meaning, and effectiveness." The student does not seem to have thought through these positions well enough to understand their logical ramifications. The evidence and commentary in the essay only earn 2 points in Row B.

The concluding paragraph does present a very interesting opinion, that NEA funding of the arts may be "systematizing a creative progress." If the student developed this idea in more detail and explored its implications, the essay might have come out stronger. However, as the essay is presented, it appears that the student thought of this new idea just as time was running out. Overall, this essay demonstrates how a student can begin with potentially good ideas and arguments, but unless they are thought through to their logical conclusions and supported with relevant evidence from the sources, they can fall far short of producing a convincing argument. Finally, the student's repeated problems with diction and poor development definitely hold this essay back from a higher score. It does not earn a point in Row C, and its overall score should be 3.

Question 2

Row A: Thesis (0–1 point)	
Scoring Criteria	
0 points for any of the following: • Having no defendable thesis. • Only restating the prompt in the thesis. • Only summarizing the issue with no apparent or coherent claim in the thesis. • Presenting a thesis that does not address the prompt.	**1 point for** • Addressing the prompt with a defendable thesis that analyzes the writer's rhetorical choices.
Decision Rules and Scoring Notes	
Theses that do not earn this point • Only restate the prompt. • Neglect to address the writer's rhetorical choices. • Simply describe or repeat the passage rather than making a defendable claim.	**Theses that do earn this point** • Respond to the prompt (rather than restating it) <u>and</u> clearly articulate a defendable thesis exploring how the two authors' rhetorical strategies create both similar and different effects in the two passages.
Additional Notes • The thesis may be one or more sentences that are in close proximity to each other anywhere in the essay. • A thesis that meets the criteria can be awarded the point whether or not the rest of the response successfully conveys that line of reasoning. • For a thesis to be defendable, the passage must have at least minimal evidence that could be used as support. • A thesis may present a line of reasoning, but it is not required to earn a point.	

Row B: Evidence AND Commentary (0–4 points)

Scoring Criteria				
0 points for	**1 point for**	**2 points for**	**3 points for**	**4 points for**
• Simply repeating the thesis (if present). • **OR** restating provided information. • **OR** providing mostly irrelevant and/or incoherent evidence.	• Summarizing the passages without reference or connection to the thesis. • **OR** providing mostly general evidence. • **AND** providing little or no explanation or commentary.	• Providing some specific evidence that is relevant to the thesis. • **AND** explaining how some of the evidence relates to the thesis, but the line of reasoning may be nonexistent or faulty.	• Providing specific evidence to support all claims in the line of reasoning. • **AND** explaining how some of the evidence relates to the thesis and supports the line of reasoning. • **AND** explaining how at least one rhetorical choice in the passages contributes to the writer's thesis.	• Providing specific evidence to support all claims in the line of reasoning. • **AND** providing well-developed commentary that consistently and explicitly explains the relationship between the evidence and the thesis. • **AND** explaining how multiple rhetorical choices in the passages contribute to the writer's thesis.
Decision Rules and Scoring Notes				
Typical responses that earn 0 points:	**Typical responses that earn 1 point:**	**Typical responses that earn 2 points:**	**Typical responses that earn 3 points:**	**Typical responses that earn 4 points:**
• Are unclear or fail to address the prompt. • May present mere opinion with little or no evidence.	• Only summarize or restate ideas from the passages without any analysis. • May mention rhetorical devices with little or no explanation or analysis.	• Mix specific details with broad generalities. • May contain simplistic, inaccurate, or repetitive explanations that do not strengthen the argument. • Fail to explain the connections between claims and establish a clear line of reasoning. • May make one point well but fail to adequately support any other claims.	• Consistently offer evidence to support all claims. • Focus on the importance of specific words and details from the passages to build an argument. • Use multiple supporting claims to organize an argument and line of reasoning. • May not integrate some evidence or support a key claim in the commentary.	• Consistently offer evidence to support all claims. • Focus on the importance of specific words and details from the passages to build an argument. • Use multiple supporting claims with adequate evidence and explanation to organize an argument and line of reasoning. • Explain how the writer's use of rhetorical devices contributes to the student's analysis of the passages.

Additional Notes

• Writing that suffers from grammatical and/or mechanical errors that interfere with communication cannot earn the fourth point in this row.

Row C: Sophistication (0–1 point)	
Scoring Criteria	
0 points for	**1 point for**
• Not meeting the criteria for 1 point.	• Exhibiting sophistication of thought and/or advancing a complex understanding of the rhetorical situation.
Decision Rules and Scoring Notes	
Responses that do not earn this point:	**Responses that earn this point demonstrate one (or more) of the following:**
• Try to contextualize the text, but make predominantly sweeping generalizations (*"Throughout all history . . ."* OR *"Everyone believes . . ."*). • Only hint at other possible arguments (*"Some may think . . ."*). • Examine individual rhetorical choices but fail to examine the relationship among varying choices throughout the passages. • Oversimplify textual complexities. • Present complicated or complex sentences or language that is ineffective and detracts from the argument.	• Explain the purpose or function of complexities or tension in the passage. • Explain the significance of the writer's rhetorical choices for the given rhetorical situation. • Develop a prose style that is especially vivid, persuasive, resounding, or appropriate to the student's argument.
Additional Notes	
• This point should be awarded only if the demonstration of sophistication or complex understanding is part of the argument, not merely a phrase or brief reference.	

Medium-Scoring Essay

Although M. F. K. Fisher's description of Marseille and Maya Angelou's description of Stamps both seek to dispel illusions of their places, they differ in the use of technique, tone, and diction. In the first passage, Fisher uses a satiric style to poke fun at Marseille's misconceived reputation as "the world's wickedest port." In the other passage, Maya Angelou uses fantastic imagery to also reveal a faulty reputation, this time, of the South. Both authors are attempting to reform mistaken opinions of their places, but they both use extremely different techniques.

In her passage, M. F. K. Fisher seeks only to quell Marseille's misrepresentation. By wryly examining articles describing Marseille, Fisher never directly gives her impression of this French port, but instead she reveals the spurious nature of these descriptions. Throughout the passage, a satiric tone is employed. Before introducing Basil Woon's piece on Marseille, Fisher writes "Sometimes such journalese is almost worth reading for its precociously obsolete views." This statement ridicules Woon's work even before it is introduced. Contributing to the tone of the piece, Fisher not only derides the descriptions of Marseille, but also the backgrounds of their writers. Although Woon did not recommend visiting Marseille, "he did remain true to his journalistic background with an expectedly titillating mention of it." Fisher masks an otherwise intense diatribe with the light-hearted, humorous use of satire.

The use of precise and informal diction also contributes to the effects of the first passage. In describing newspaper descriptions of Marseille, the words "mild shockers" are used. The concise image formed by these words contributes to the informal mood of the passage. Also, instead of employing the more conservative and respected word "journalism," Fisher chose to use the word "journalese." This simple substitution embodies the essence of the passage. Like the word journalese, the passage continually ridicules writers' misrepresentations of Marseille.

Using an opposite style of attack, Maya Angelou does not mock the faulty representation of the South. Instead she contrasts both a description of the "American fantasy" of the South with her own vivid impressions. The dream-like tone of the first paragraph is aided by the rich choice of diction. "Women float eternally" among "wisps of wisteria." Like paradise, the word "eternally" allows this scene of gentle alliteration to last forever.

This fantasy is contrasted in the remaining paragraphs with an intense, passionate tone of life. The descriptions, like smells "spiced with the odor of cattle manure, the yellowish acid of the ponds and rivers, the deep pots of greens and beans," are all concrete. These concrete images sharply contrast the ethereal images of women floating eternally. The misrepresentation of the South is easily dispelled by the reality of Maya Angelou's observations. Furthermore, the choice of diction is superb. Angelou's South was "flesh-real and swollen-belly poor." These words easily bring to mind the harshness of black life in the South. Toward the end of the passage, a metaphor is used to change the direction of the passage from concreteness into memories ". . . passions clanged with the ferocity of armored knights colliding." After erasing the erroneous images of the South, the passage prepares to tell Angelou's story.

Though these passages are similar in their goals, their distinct uses of diction and tone drastically differ in their methods of dispelling illusions.

(550 words)

Analysis of the Medium-Scoring Essay

The essay begins by directly addressing the topic with a relevant comparison of the passages, pointing out that each "seek[s] to dispel illusions" of the perception of a location. This student recognizes that, although the passages have the same purpose, their differences lie in their stylistic choices. Such interesting ideas as these engage the AP Exam Reader, and the thesis deserves a point in Row A.

The next two paragraphs analyze the Fisher passage on Marseille and, together, demonstrate a clear understanding of Fisher's use of humor and satire to ridicule those who have painted Marseille as "the world's wickedest port." The student supports the point with appropriate quotations from the passage. The second paragraph specifically analyzes and gives evidence for Fisher's purpose—to dispel the myths about Marseille— while the third paragraph explores how the language of the passage contributes to the effect. The student here uses effective organization and sophisticated diction, making this a strong section.

The fourth and fifth paragraphs deal with the Angelou passage, again analyzing the author's effect and the language used to create it. The analysis begins with Angelou's first paragraph, noting its differences from the Fisher passage—specifically, that she "does not mock the faulty representation" as Fisher does and noting that Angelou creates a "dream-like tone" contrasting with her own impressions. The analysis continues with a discussion of diction, noting how effectively Angelou dispels the misrepresentation of the South with her use of concrete images, an exploration of Angelou's use of metaphor, and an explanation of the metaphor's effect in introducing the realistic treatment that follows in the work. A Reader might perhaps wish that the student would explore the effect of racial comments in Angelou's description, but, because it is not mentioned in the prompt, a Reader cannot fault the student for not mentioning it. The body paragraph development is sufficient to earn 3 points in Row B.

The essay concludes with a brief summary of its main point—that the authors have similar goals but different techniques. Although the statement is not itself thought-provoking, it is an adequate end to the essay. Overall, this student makes points clearly while demonstrating a competent command of language. The essay prompt asks specifically for analysis of the rhetorical choices that create effects in the two pieces, and this essay can be faulted because, to some degree, it confuses effect with purpose. The essay also misreads the tone of the Fisher passage as an "intense diatribe" and could benefit from additional evidence from the passages. On the whole, however, the essay is intelligent, articulate, and substantiated with enough evidence to score in the upper-half range. However, its sophistication is not mature enough to warrant a point in Row C. It earns an overall score of 4.

Low-Scoring Essay

Although both passages describe places, their styles are very different. The first passage illustrates how most descriptions of Marseille treat this city unfairly. This is accomplished through the author's humiliation of these articles. The second passage shows how most people's description of the South is wrong. But rather than through satire, this is accomplished through the use of imagery. Thus, both pieces are similar in their effect, but are different in their author's handling of the resources of language.

The first piece by M. F. K. Fisher about the French port of Marseille succeeds in showing that writers about this place only tell the wrong side of the story. Although Marseille like all cities has its attractions and its good points, these writers unfairly give it "a legendary reputation as a world capital for 'dope, whores, and street violence.'" Thus this piece humiliates and satirizes those writers. The tone of this piece is very light and humorous, but it hides the meaning of the author's words. For instance, "The familiar pitch had been made, and idle readers dreaming of a great seaport dedicated to heroin, prostitution, and rioting could easily skip the clumsy detail of marketing for fresh fish." By including the talk of fresh fish in the sentence, this passage is making a parody of the article where dope, whores, and street violence are combined with how to make a true bouillabaisse. The other article that this passage also talks about says "Marseilles is the world's wickedest port." The passage ridicules this piece with the satiric sentence "Sometimes such journalese is almost worth reading for its preciously obsolete views of a society too easy to forget." This piece is sarcastically saying that readers should read this article because it is a great example of something bad. Therefore, this passage is able to use sarcasm, satire, and humiliation to show how Marseille is improperly represented by writers.

The second piece by Maya Angelou about the small town of Stamps, Arkansas, tries to show how this place is also improperly represented. This is done by using imagery. First, that passage describes the South as "a much-loved region in the American fantasy where pale white women float eternally under black magnolia trees." These images show that the American fantasy is a peaceful, relaxed South where white people linger around. In fact, this image is wrong. In the next part of the passage, the South is shown in the harsh light of reality. "The South I returned to, however, was flesh-real and swollen-belly poor." These images succeed in showing the harshness of life the African Americans led in the South. This sentence also shows this point. "And above all, the atmosphere was pressed down with the smell of old fears, and hates, and guilt." The use of atmosphere adds to the depressingly real tone created by these images. Also a metaphor is used "passions clanged with the ferocity of armored knights colliding." This adds to the electrical atmosphere of the passage. By using such strong images to create the electrical atmosphere of the passage, the illusion of the first paragraph is shown for what it truly is. Therefore, this passage is able to use images, words, and atmosphere to show how Stamps, Arkansas, is improperly represented by the American fantasy of the South. The style of this passage is different from the other, which humiliates the improper representation. Therefore, both passages use their authors' handling of the resources of language in a different way to talk about the same effect.

(588 words)

Analysis of the Low-Scoring Essay

The essay's introduction accurately addresses the topic. However, the student's writing style and depth of thought do not demonstrate the sophistication needed for a high-scoring essay. To claim merely that the two passages are "similar in effect, but . . . different" in their use of language barely touches on the topic and does not present a defendable thesis. It will not earn a point in Row A.

The second paragraph concentrates on Fisher's article and points out that Fisher humiliates (an inaccurate word in this context) and satirizes the authors who have presented Marseille as the "wickedest port." The student seems to recognize Fisher's effect but doesn't extend the observation, merely stating that Fisher is "making a parody" through use of sarcasm. Some examples from the passage are included, but they are treated perfunctorily and obviously, without depth or strong analysis.

The last paragraph also is accurate in its discussion, but the presentation is simplistic and uninteresting. For example, "This sentence also shows this point" fails to connect the two examples effectively, and the claim that the use of metaphor creates an "electrical atmosphere" doesn't explain in what way "armored knights colliding" does so. The phrase "which humiliates the improper representation" is simply baffling. This paragraph, as those preceding it, makes valid points but doesn't explore them in enough depth to engage or convince the AP Exam Reader. The evidence and commentary only earn 2 points in Row B. This essay could be greatly improved with the use of deeper analysis and more sophisticated presentation. It does not deserve a point in Row C, and its overall score is a 2.

Question 3

Row A: Thesis (0–1 point)	
Scoring Criteria	
0 points for any of the following: • Having no defendable thesis. • Only restating the prompt in the thesis. • Only summarizing the issue with no apparent or coherent claim in the thesis. • Presenting a thesis that does not address the prompt.	**1 point for** • Addressing the prompt with a defendable thesis.
Decision Rules and Scoring Notes	
Theses that do not earn this point • Only restate the prompt. • Are vague or do not take a position. • Simply state an obvious fact rather than making a defendable claim.	**Theses that do earn this point** • Respond to the prompt (rather than restating it) <u>and</u> clearly evaluate the validity of More's ideas about communal property instead of simply stating pros and cons.
Additional Notes • The thesis may be one or more sentences that are in close proximity to each other anywhere in the essay. • A thesis that meets the criteria can be awarded the point whether or not the rest of the response successfully conveys that line of reasoning. • A thesis may present a line of reasoning, but it is not required to earn a point.	

Row B: Evidence AND Commentary (0–4 points)				
Scoring Criteria				
0 points for	**1 point for**	**2 points for**	**3 points for**	**4 points for**
• Simply repeating the thesis (if present). • **OR** restating information. • **OR** providing mostly irrelevant and/or incoherent examples.	• Summarizing the passage without reference or connection to the thesis. • **OR** providing mostly general evidence. • **AND** providing little or no explanation or commentary.	• Providing some specific evidence that is relevant to the thesis. • **AND** explaining how some of the evidence relates to the thesis, but the line of reasoning may be nonexistent or faulty.	• Providing specific evidence to support all claims in the line of reasoning. • **AND** explaining how some of the evidence relates to the thesis and supports the line of reasoning.	• Providing specific evidence to support all claims in the line of reasoning. • **AND** providing well-developed commentary that consistently and explicitly explains the relationship between the evidence and the thesis.

Decision Rules and Scoring Notes				
Typical responses that earn 0 points:	**Typical responses that earn 1 point:**	**Typical responses that earn 2 points:**	**Typical responses that earn 3 points:**	**Typical responses that earn 4 points:**
• Are unclear or fail to address the prompt. • May present mere opinion with little or no relevant evidence.	• Only summarize or restate ideas from the passage without any analysis.	• Mix specific details with broad generalities. • May contain simplistic, inaccurate, or repetitive explanations that do not strengthen the argument. • Fail to explain the connections between claims and establish a clear line of reasoning. • May make one point well but fail to adequately support any other claims.	• Consistently offer evidence to support all claims. • Focus on the importance of specific words and details to build an argument. • Use multiple supporting claims to organize an argument and line of reasoning. • May not integrate some evidence or support a key claim in the commentary.	• Engage specific evidence to draw conclusions. • Focus on the importance of specific details to build an argument. • Use multiple supporting claims with adequate evidence and explanation to organize an argument and line of reasoning.

Additional Notes

• Writing that suffers from grammatical and/or mechanical errors that interfere with communication cannot earn the fourth point in this row.

Row C: Sophistication (0–1 point)	
Scoring Criteria	
0 points for	**1 point for**
• Not meeting the criteria for 1 point.	• Exhibiting sophistication of thought and/or advancing a complex understanding of the rhetorical situation.
Decision Rules and Scoring Notes	
Responses that do not earn this point:	**Responses that earn this point demonstrate one (or more) of the following:**
• Try to contextualize their argument, but make predominantly sweeping generalizations (*"Throughout all history . . ."* OR *"Everyone believes . . ."*). • Only hint at other possible arguments (*"Some may think . . ."*). • Present complicated or complex sentences or language that is ineffective and detracts from the argument.	• Present a nuanced argument that consistently identifies and examines complexities or tensions. • Illuminate the significance or implications of the argument (either the student's argument or an argument related to the prompt) within a broader context. • Make effective rhetorical choices that consistently strengthen the force and impact of the student's argument. • Develop a prose style that is especially vivid, persuasive, resounding, or appropriate to the student's argument.

continued

Additional Notes

• This point should be awarded only if the demonstration of sophistication or complex understanding is part of the argument, not merely a phrase or brief reference.

High-Scoring Essay

Sir Thomas More's <u>Utopia</u> discusses ideas and conflicts still relevant to society today. He manages to perceptively express the nature of wealth and material goods; and although written over 400 years ago, his essay still reveals essential truths about the attitudes in our contemporary society.

More primarily addresses the issue of ownership of private property and its hindrance upon the fair distribution of wealth. More points out that ownership of private wealth hurts those who have little or none themselves, which makes up the majority of the population. More perceives that "As long as private property remains, by far the largest and the best part of mankind will be oppressed with an inescapable load of cares and anxieties." In today's society, More's idea still holds true. The majority of the population does control less than their fair amount of wealth and goods. This is evident not just in America, but also among competing nations of the world. Each day, in countries like Mexico, the poor struggle to keep from getting poorer, while the wealth of many of the rich grows more opulent. Because of this unfair distribution of wealth, the poor have little opportunity to change their worsening situations.

More's concerns also go beyond the poor and encompass another major realm of controversy: politics. More correctly predicts the nature of politics that exists in a society where not everyone is of the same economic class. He suggests that "It might be made unlawful for public offices to be solicited, or sold, or made burdensome for the officeholder by great expense. Otherwise officeholders are tempted to reimburse themselves by dishonesty and force, and it becomes necessary to find rich men for those offices which ought rather be held by wise men." This prediction has certainly come true in contemporary America, where the vast number of politicians tends to come from the upper echelons of society; conversely, one would be hard-pressed to name a top office-holder who rose from the ranks of the poor under-class. In addition, just as Plato saw the needs for wise, rational men to fill the position of philosopher-king, More also realizes the danger of public offices held by rich men rather than wise men, an event fostered by a society in which unequal distribution of goods exists. Both Plato and More have made a valid point here, and the voting public should be constantly cautioned to question a potential leader's wisdom and rational thinking before they vote.

While More's essays define the evils that burden a private property-owning society, More fails to see some of the problems that would follow with completely eradicating the system. More suggests several legal reforms to stop and prevent the amassing of goods by citizens. When this is stopped, however, all incentive to work is taken away. People rarely have the time, the energy, or the interest to work solely for the merit of working. In contemporary society, human nature drives people to work to earn something tangible—be it wealth, or goods, or love. More's reforms are also unfair. While at first glance they may sound fair and equal, in reality they are not. This system would be unfair to hard workers who do deserve a reward, and unfair to lazy workers who don't earn what they receive. Instead of promoting equality, this system would promote laziness and remove the incentive to work. In theory, this would be a good system. But, in reality, Sir Thomas More's Utopia does not work. The breakdown of the Soviet Union alone disproves More's system.

More's essay perceptively observes some of the major injustices and corruptions within a private property-owning society. While these are valid, pertinent issues, More overlooks some of the inherent pitfalls within the system of a society that bans the ownership of private property.

(632 words)

Analysis of the High-Scoring Essay

This thoughtful essay immediately addresses the topic in its first sentence and takes a defendable stand in the second sentence. It deserves a point in Row A. The student uses contemporary examples to buttress points and also insightfully comments that More addresses more concepts than money and land distribution.

The student's inclusion of Plato in the third paragraph relevantly extends this idea. In the fourth paragraph, the student acknowledges that More fails to accurately predict all the consequences of his proposals—the problem that the need for reward is inherent in human nature. Showing both advantages and disadvantages of More's proposal demonstrates the skill of close reading and a high degree of maturity in this student. The development of evidence and commentary are worthy of 4 points in Row B.

To improve this essay, the student could have worked on a stronger thesis that more accurately addresses his or her points; notice that the thesis does not allude to any criticism of More's ideas. Some of the vague wording could be made more specific, such as the statements, "More's reforms are also unfair. While at first glance they may sound fair and equal, in reality they are not." In general, the essay's ideas are more sophisticated than their presentation.

This essay is well organized, and the ideas are supported by examples from contemporary society, but it is not sophisticated enough to earn a point in Row C. Overall, this essay deserves a score of 5.

Medium-Scoring Essay

Sir Thomas More's <u>Utopia</u> discusses fair government and equal social status within our society, and identifies the need for people to give up their private property. His ideas (as written about in the essay) are valid in light of contemporary standards.

More's initial position that private property is an unnecessary evil within our society at first appears to be blatantly Communistic. His desires to redistribute wealth and property and to make laws preventing people from earning too much money seem absurd at first glance. However, on further inspection, the reader realizes that some of More's views are valid and relevant to society. More predicts corruption of the government, something that our nation has been experiencing for several decades. This corruption is a result of politicians feeling obligated to remunerate themselves for the great expense they go through as a part of their job. More sums this up very nicely and accurately as he points out that rich men (instead of wise men) take over the offices of government.

Not only do we see the validity of More's views in our current day and age, but personally speaking, I agree with More's beliefs. The greed and self-interest associated with Capitalism are two symptoms of the sickness that comes with private property. It is wrong for a country's government to allow some people to starve on the streets while others are living like kings. More sympathizes with the great majority of people who do not have much private property.

Throughout his essay More proposes solutions to the problem of private property. He advocates altruism and his ideas are shown to be relevant to our society. His essay is very valid in light of today's social standards.

(284 words)

Analysis of the Medium-Scoring Essay

This medium-scoring essay attempts to address the topic. The first paragraph produces a thesis that claims that More's ideas are valid for contemporary society, but little else is presented here. The thesis is not highly thought-provoking, and it contains some redundancy ("as written about in the essay"), but it is sufficiently defendable to warrant a point in Row A.

The student devotes almost half of the second paragraph to explaining his or her first impression of More, only to reverse it after a deeper analysis. This student should be commended for looking below the surface, but no evidence is offered to support the student's opinions. This paragraph would be stronger if the student were to include some specific examples of government corruption, rather than merely alluding to them.

The third paragraph becomes a forum for the student's personal beliefs. Once again, the student presents relevant ideas but little evidence for them. The only example included, the idea that the government allows poor people to starve while others live like kings, may indeed be true, but it is not specific. Stronger development of both ideas and examples would improve this paragraph. The body paragraphs earn 2 points in Row B.

The concluding paragraph merely summarizes the essay's only point, that the student finds More's ideas valid. There's not much of substance here, and the conclusion doesn't help to convince the AP Exam Reader of the validity of the student's opinions.

Although this essay does take a stand, it offers only weak support and sometimes simplistic and redundant wording. It does not deserve a point in Row C. This essay would be stronger if the student were to include more of More's ideas and test their validity by today's standards. Overall, this essay is adequate, but it is not persuasive enough to merit a higher score. It should receive an overall score of 3.

Scoring

Use the following worksheet to arrive at a probable final AP grade on Practice Exam 2. Because being objective enough to estimate your own essay score is sometimes difficult, you might give your essays (along with the sample essays) to a teacher, friend, or relative to score, if you feel confident that the individual has the knowledge necessary to make such a judgment and that he or she will feel comfortable doing so.

Section I: Multiple-Choice Questions

$$\underline{\hspace{3cm}} - (\underline{\hspace{3cm}}) = \underline{\hspace{3cm}}$$
right answers   wrong answers   multiple-choice raw score

$$\underline{\hspace{3cm}} \times 1.5 = \underline{\hspace{3cm}} \text{ (of possible 67.5)}$$
multiple-choice raw score   multiple-choice converted score

Section II: Free-Response Questions

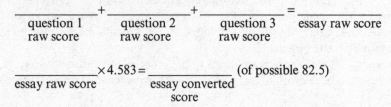

$$\underline{\hspace{2cm}} + \underline{\hspace{2cm}} + \underline{\hspace{2cm}} = \underline{\hspace{2cm}}$$
question 1 raw score   question 2 raw score   question 3 raw score   essay raw score

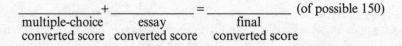

$$\underline{\hspace{2cm}} \times 4.583 = \underline{\hspace{2cm}} \text{ (of possible 82.5)}$$
essay raw score   essay converted score

Final Score

$$\underline{\hspace{2cm}} + \underline{\hspace{2cm}} = \underline{\hspace{2cm}} \text{ (of possible 150)}$$
multiple-choice converted score   essay converted score   final converted score

Probable Final AP Score

Final Converted Score	Probable AP Score
150–114	5
113–98	4
97–81	3
80–53	2
52–0	1

Chapter 6

Practice Exam 3

Answer Sheet

Section I: Multiple-Choice Questions

1	Ⓐ Ⓑ Ⓒ Ⓓ Ⓔ	21	Ⓐ Ⓑ Ⓒ Ⓓ Ⓔ	41	Ⓐ Ⓑ Ⓒ Ⓓ Ⓔ
2	Ⓐ Ⓑ Ⓒ Ⓓ Ⓔ	22	Ⓐ Ⓑ Ⓒ Ⓓ Ⓔ	42	Ⓐ Ⓑ Ⓒ Ⓓ Ⓔ
3	Ⓐ Ⓑ Ⓒ Ⓓ Ⓔ	23	Ⓐ Ⓑ Ⓒ Ⓓ Ⓔ	43	Ⓐ Ⓑ Ⓒ Ⓓ Ⓔ
4	Ⓐ Ⓑ Ⓒ Ⓓ Ⓔ	24	Ⓐ Ⓑ Ⓒ Ⓓ Ⓔ	44	Ⓐ Ⓑ Ⓒ Ⓓ Ⓔ
5	Ⓐ Ⓑ Ⓒ Ⓓ Ⓔ	25	Ⓐ Ⓑ Ⓒ Ⓓ Ⓔ	45	Ⓐ Ⓑ Ⓒ Ⓓ Ⓔ
6	Ⓐ Ⓑ Ⓒ Ⓓ Ⓔ	26	Ⓐ Ⓑ Ⓒ Ⓓ Ⓔ		
7	Ⓐ Ⓑ Ⓒ Ⓓ Ⓔ	27	Ⓐ Ⓑ Ⓒ Ⓓ Ⓔ		
8	Ⓐ Ⓑ Ⓒ Ⓓ Ⓔ	28	Ⓐ Ⓑ Ⓒ Ⓓ Ⓔ		
9	Ⓐ Ⓑ Ⓒ Ⓓ Ⓔ	29	Ⓐ Ⓑ Ⓒ Ⓓ Ⓔ		
10	Ⓐ Ⓑ Ⓒ Ⓓ Ⓔ	30	Ⓐ Ⓑ Ⓒ Ⓓ Ⓔ		
11	Ⓐ Ⓑ Ⓒ Ⓓ Ⓔ	31	Ⓐ Ⓑ Ⓒ Ⓓ Ⓔ		
12	Ⓐ Ⓑ Ⓒ Ⓓ Ⓔ	32	Ⓐ Ⓑ Ⓒ Ⓓ Ⓔ		
13	Ⓐ Ⓑ Ⓒ Ⓓ Ⓔ	33	Ⓐ Ⓑ Ⓒ Ⓓ Ⓔ		
14	Ⓐ Ⓑ Ⓒ Ⓓ Ⓔ	34	Ⓐ Ⓑ Ⓒ Ⓓ Ⓔ		
15	Ⓐ Ⓑ Ⓒ Ⓓ Ⓔ	35	Ⓐ Ⓑ Ⓒ Ⓓ Ⓔ		
16	Ⓐ Ⓑ Ⓒ Ⓓ Ⓔ	36	Ⓐ Ⓑ Ⓒ Ⓓ Ⓔ		
17	Ⓐ Ⓑ Ⓒ Ⓓ Ⓔ	37	Ⓐ Ⓑ Ⓒ Ⓓ Ⓔ		
18	Ⓐ Ⓑ Ⓒ Ⓓ Ⓔ	38	Ⓐ Ⓑ Ⓒ Ⓓ Ⓔ		
19	Ⓐ Ⓑ Ⓒ Ⓓ Ⓔ	39	Ⓐ Ⓑ Ⓒ Ⓓ Ⓔ		
20	Ⓐ Ⓑ Ⓒ Ⓓ Ⓔ	40	Ⓐ Ⓑ Ⓒ Ⓓ Ⓔ		

Section II: Free-Response Questions

Question 1

In one's democratic society, voting is the most major form of communication in telling how they feel about particular issues and view points. Because of a ballot's potential power to change the course of public policy, it is important to make informed choices.

Political opinion poll is usually a flawed process. "polls are used to gather information" (Source D) A push poll is an interactive marketing technique, most commonly employed during political campaigning, in which an individual or organization attemps to influence prospective voters' views under the appearence of conducting an optional polls. "Are polls accurate" (source E), limited respondent questions, lack of information, difficulty measuring intensity, and lack of intrest in political issues. People socialization is the process through which indivisual learn their political beliefs. Indivisual may impact government policy by joining public Intrest groups.

Public Opinion is a vital part of the political process. It identifies issues for resolution, brings views into political debate, helps choose the political candidate and gives policymakers some ideas of what the voters want. "selection Bias" (source D) is introdused by the selection of individuals, groups, or data for analysis, selecting your sample or your data wrong.

Opinion polls are usually designed to represent the opinions of a population by conducting a series of questions and then generals in ratio or within intervals. A person who conducts polls is referred to as a pollster.

CUT HERE

Question 2

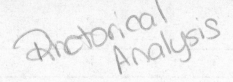
Rhetorical Analysis

In the essay "The first Kiss", John Updike shows the game baseball as a love-hate Relationship. John shows the relationship of baseball by appealing to pathos using metaphors and personification.

John Updike opens with a metaphor saying "The many headed monster called the fenway faithful yesterday resumed its romance with 25 youngish men in red socks who last year broke its monsterous big heart". His describes baseball fans, as aggressive from the passion that they feel for that spot. He expresses how the love turns to hate by saying "braced for the first Kiss of another prolonged enlanged" he then a the rhetorical question, who can forget the ups and downs of last year's flings?" he makes a reference to the first hit as the first Kiss. He then uses personification saying that baseball did the "crulest tease", he referse to their win streak against their number one enemy.

Thus by using metaphors and personifications about the love and hate in the relationship he sends a message that there is a balanced love hate relations between baseball and its fans.

CUT HERE

CUT HERE

Question 3

Argument

Men usually go fishing all of their lives without knowing that it not fish they are after. fishing takes time and patience, with that theres time to think meditate and focus. Fishing is a form of release, escape, time to sit an find the root of our problems, but for the commercial fisherman it's a living he is after there after the money.

Men fish for the pleasure of being outdoors, the joys of being with friends or family, and for the callange of the sport. The Humans greatest desire is to experience something good. People are going out fishing to learn patience andsee the beauty of water where the fish are some want to feel success and others go for quiet reflection.

In conclution men usually go fishing all their lives without knowing that it not fish they are after. They are mostly after the feelings and rebese it comes with.

A

CUT HERE

Section I: Multiple-Choice Questions

Time: 1 hour

45 questions

Directions: This section consists of selections from prose works with questions about their content, form, and style, plus draft passages with questions about improving their content and clarity. Read each selection carefully. For each question, choose the best answer of the five choices.

Questions 1–11 refer to the following passage written by an 18th-century British author.

This single stick, which you now behold ingloriously lying in that neglected corner, I once knew in a flourishing state in a forest; it was full of sap, full of leaves, and full of boughs; but
(5) now, in vain, does the busy art of man pretend to vie with nature, by tying that withered bundle of twigs to its sapless trunk; 'tis now, at best, but the reverse of what it was, a tree turned upside down, the branches on the earth, and the root in the air;
(10) 'tis now handled by every dirty wench, condemned to do her drudgery, and, by a capricious kind of fate, destined to make other things clean, and be nasty itself; at length, worn to the stumps in the service of the maids, either
(15) thrown out of doors, or condemned to the last use, of kindling a fire. When I beheld this, I sighed, and said within myself: *Surely Man is a Broomstick!* Nature sent him into the world strong and lusty, in a thriving condition, wearing
(20) his own hair on his head, the proper branches of this reasoning vegetable, until the axe of intemperance has lopped off his green boughs, and left him a withered trunk; he then flies to art, and puts on a periwig, valuing himself upon an
(25) unnatural bundle of hairs (all covered with powder) that never grew on his head; but now should this our broomstick pretend to enter the scene, proud of all those birchen spoils it never bore, and all covered with dust, though the
(30) sweepings of the finest lady's chamber, we should be apt to ridicule and despise its vanity. Partial judges that we are of our own excellences, and other men's defaults!

But a broomstick, perhaps you will say, is an
(35) emblem of a tree standing on its head; and pray, what is a man but a topsy-turvy creature, his animal faculties perpetually mounted on his rational, his head where his heels should be, groveling on the earth! And yet, with all his
(40) faults, he sets up to be a universal reformer and corrector of abuses, a remover of grievances, rakes into every slut's corner of nature, bringing hidden corruption to the light, and raises a mighty dust where there was none before; sharing
(45) deeply all the while in the very same pollutions he pretends to sweep away; his last days are spent in slavery to women, and generally the least deserving; till, worn out to the stumps, like his brother broom, he is either kicked out of doors,
(50) or made use of to kindle flames for others to warm themselves by.

1. All of the following are present in the opening sentence of the passage EXCEPT

   A. syntactically complex structure
   B. parallel construction
   C. a pedantic tone
   D. the narrative of a broomstick's life
   E. subordinate clauses

2. According to the author, both a broomstick and a man

   A. cleanse the world
   B. become corrupted by the evil in society
   C. can be proud of their humble accomplishments
   D. symbolize integrity in the world
   E. were untainted in their natural state

3. According to the passage, the broomstick symbolizes

   A. society's corruption of the youth
   B. the goodness in nature that man uses and discards
   C. the triumph of nature over man's evil tendencies
   D. the evil inherent in man's soul
   E. the tremendous power of nature that man fears

4. The "axe of intemperance" (lines 21–22) can be interpreted as

    A.   an understatement of man's dominance over nature

    B.   a metaphor for nature's nourishing elements

    C.   a simile comparing man and tree

    D.   a hyperbole describing man's destruction

    E.   a metaphor for man's excesses

5. The author's attitude toward mankind can best be described as

    A.   disillusionment at man's deeds

    B.   perplexed concern for man's future

    C.   guarded optimism for man's soul

    D.   anger at the society man has created

    E.   sincere praise for man's use of nature

6. Which of the following does NOT demonstrate a negative attitude by this author?

    A.   "a flourishing state in a forest" (line 3)

    B.   "the axe of intemperance" (lines 21–22)

    C.   "an unnatural bundle of hairs" (lines 24–25)

    D.   "sweepings of the finest lady's chamber" (line 30)

    E.   "sharing . . . the very same pollutions he pretends to sweep away" (lines 44–46)

7. The word referred to by the phrase "this reasoning vegetable" (line 21) is

    A.   "*Man*" (line 17)

    B.   "hair" (line 20)

    C.   "head" (line 20)

    D.   "branches" (line 20)

    E.   "green boughs" (line 22)

8. In context, "this our broomstick" (line 27) is a

    A.   symbol for the thriving forest

    B.   metaphor for man's pretentious character

    C.   link between nature and society

    D.   demonstration of nature's control

    E.   representation of man's intelligence

9. What does the author imply about man's ability to be a "corrector of abuses" (line 41)?

    A.   Man easily solves his own problems.

    B.   Man effectively improves society.

    C.   Man can act as a fair arbitrator in disputes.

    D.   Man readily accepts his role as a social reformer.

    E.   Man causes problems where none previously existed.

10. The tone of the passage can best be described as

    A.   neutral toward society

    B.   condescending toward nature

    C.   cynical toward mankind

    D.   bellicose toward mankind

    E.   dogmatic toward society

11. Which of the following represents the strongest statement of the author's theme?

    A.   "condemned to do her drudgery" (line 11)

    B.   "destined to make other things clean" (lines 12–13)

    C.   "the axe of intemperance has lopped off his green boughs" (lines 21–22)

    D.   "Partial judges that we are of our own excellences" (lines 31–32)

    E.   "his last days are spent in slavery" (lines 46–47)

Questions 12–25 refer to the following passage by a 19th-century American author.

It is remarkable that there is little or nothing to be remembered written on the subject of getting a living; how to make getting a living not merely honest and honorable, but altogether
(5) inviting and glorious; for if *getting* a living is not so, then living is not. One would think, from looking at literature, that this question had never disturbed a solitary individual's musings. Is it that men are too much disgusted with their
(10) experience to speak of it? The lesson of value which money teaches, which the Author of the Universe has taken so much pains to teach us, we are inclined to skip altogether. As for the means of living, it is wonderful how indifferent men of
(15) all classes are about it, even reformers, so called,—whether they inherit, or earn, or steal it. I think that Society has done nothing for us in this respect, or at least has undone what she has done. Cold and hunger seem more friendly to my

(20) nature than those methods which men have adopted and advise to ward them off.

The title *wise* is, for the most part, falsely applied. How can one be a wise man, if he does not know any better how to live than other (25) men?—if he is only more cunning and intellectually subtle? Does Wisdom work in a tread-mill? or does she teach how to succeed *by her example*? Is there any such thing as wisdom not applied to life? Is she merely the miller who (30) grinds the finest logic? Is it pertinent to ask if Plato got his living in a better way or more successfully than his contemporaries,—or did he succumb to the difficulties of life like other men? Did he seem to prevail over some of them merely (35) by indifference, or by assuming grand airs? Or find it easier to live, because his aunt remembers him in her will? The ways in which most men get their living, that is, live, are mere makeshifts, and a shirking of the real business of life,—chiefly (40) because they do not know, but partly because they do not mean, any better.

The rush to California, for instance, and the attitude, not merely of merchants, but of philosophers and prophets, so called, in relation (45) to it, reflect the greatest disgrace on mankind. That so many are ready to live by luck, and so get the means of commanding the labor of others less lucky, without contributing any value to society! And that is called enterprise! I know of (50) no more startling development of the immorality of trade, and all the common modes of getting a living. The philosophy and poetry and religion of such a mankind are not worth the dust of a puffball. The hog that gets his living by rooting, (55) stirring up the soil so, would be ashamed of such company. If I could command the wealth of all the world by lifting my finger, I would not pay *such* a price for it. Even Mahomet knew that God did not make this world in jest. It makes (60) God to be a moneyed gentleman who scatters a handful of pennies in order to see mankind scramble for them. The world's raffle! A subsistence in the domains of Nature a thing to be raffled for! What a comment, what a satire, on (65) our institutions! The conclusion will be, that mankind will hang itself upon a tree. And have all the precepts in all the Bibles taught men only this? And is the last and most admirable invention of the human race only an improved muck-rake? (70) Is this the ground on which Orientals and Occidentals meet? Did God direct us so to get our living, digging where we never planted,—and He would, perchance, reward us with lumps of gold?

(75) God gave the righteous man a certificate entitling him to food and raiment, but the unrighteous man found a *facsimile* of the same in God's coffers, and appropriated it, and obtained food and raiment like the former. It is (80) one of the most extensive systems of counterfeiting that the world has ever seen. I did not know that mankind was suffering for want of gold. I have seen a little of it. I know that it is very malleable, but not so malleable as wit. A (85) grain of gold will gild a great surface, but not so much as a grain of wisdom.

The gold-digger in the ravines of the mountains is as much a gambler as his fellow in the saloons of San Francisco. What difference (90) does it make whether you shake dirt or shake dice? If you win, society is the loser. The gold-digger is the enemy of the honest laborer, whatever checks and compensations there may be. It is not enough to tell me that you worked (95) hard to get your gold. So does the Devil work hard. The way of transgressors may be hard in many respects. The humblest observer who goes to the mines sees and says that gold-digging is of the character of a lottery; the gold thus obtained (100) is not the same thing with the wages of honest toil. But, practically, he forgets what he has seen, for he sees only the fact, not the principle, and goes into trade there, that is, buys a ticket in what commonly proves another lottery, where the fact (105) is not so obvious.

12. In his opening sentence, the author asserts that "getting a living" should be both

A. moral and pious
B. ethical and admirable
C. accessible and sensible
D. desirable and attainable
E. humble and profitable

13. According to the author, although man must earn money, he is indifferent to

A. religion
B. society
C. cold and hunger
D. lessons of value
E. laborers

14. The author asserts that

    A. we have forgotten the proper value of money

    B. good, hard work will save mankind

    C. the world operates solely on luck

    D. religion fails to address the merit of labor

    E. gold-digging is acceptable under certain conditions

15. The "Author of the Universe" (lines 11–12) can be interpreted as a

    A. symbol for cosmic consciousness

    B. metaphor for a contemporary writer

    C. symbol for judgment

    D. metaphor for all artists

    E. metaphor for God

16. The author's rhetorical purpose in referring to Plato is to

    A. make the point about gold-digging more universal and timeless

    B. qualify the assertions about gold-diggers and their luck

    C. question whether ancient philosophers faced the same dilemmas that others do

    D. consider the ancient philosopher's premises about morality in society

    E. create an authoritative tone to lend credence to the argument

17. What is the antecedent for "it" (line 58)?

    A. "immorality" (line 50)

    B. "philosophy" (line 52)

    C. "hog" (line 54)

    D. "wealth" (line 56)

    E. "world" (line 57)

18. Which of the following is the best example of aphorism?

    A. "The ways in which most men . . . any better." (lines 37–41)

    B. "Nature a thing to be raffled for!" (lines 63–64)

    C. "A grain of gold . . . a grain of wisdom." (lines 84–86)

    D. "What difference does it make . . . shake dice?" (lines 89–91)

    E. "So does the Devil work hard." (lines 95–96)

19. An unstated assumption of the author is that

    A. philosophers should work harder to apply their teachings

    B. a pig would be mortified by some men

    C. society is gradually improving

    D. true wisdom comes only through hard work

    E. what appears honest to one can be harmful to society

20. The author's comments about the California gold rush serve the purpose of

    A. comparing gold-diggers to the ancient Greeks

    B. illustrating how immorally men are earning a living

    C. explaining the relationship of Orientals to Occidentals

    D. sensationalizing a topical and popular occupation

    E. criticizing those who think gold-digging is romantic

21. Which of the following negative phrases is, in context, a qualified negative?

    A. "men are . . . disgusted with their experience" (lines 9–10)

    B. "Cold and hunger" (line 19)

    C. "the greatest disgrace on mankind" (line 45)

    D. "the unrighteous man" (lines 76–77)

    E. "society is the loser" (line 91)

22. The sentence "A grain of gold . . . a grain of wisdom" (lines 84–86) can best be restated as

    A. knowledge is more valuable than gold

    B. gold-diggers must work harder than philosophers

    C. gold will last longer than knowledge

    D. erudition takes longer to achieve than money

    E. money has no practical purpose

23. The tone of the passage can best be described as

    A. condescending

    B. skeptical

    C. worried

    D. indignant

    E. pedestrian

24. Which of the following is NOT part of the author's argument against gold-digging?

    A. "The hog . . . would be ashamed of such company." (lines 54–56)

    B. "digging where we never planted" (line 72)

    C. "I know that it is very malleable" (lines 83–84)

    D. "the enemy of the honest laborer" (line 92)

    E. "of the character of a lottery" (lines 98–99)

25. Which of the following is NOT discussed in the passage?

    A. Man can learn to improve his lot in life.

    B. Authors have not addressed "getting a living."

    C. Gamblers have damaged society.

    D. The title "wise" may be misapplied.

    E. Men are too easily lured by monetary rewards.

Questions 26–33 refer to the following draft.

(1) In the long and enduring history of the British peoples, there are times when the fate of the entire Empire seems to depend on a single individual, someone who is called upon unexpectedly, yet who absolutely *must* be successful in rising to the occasion. (2) The improbable life-story of Albert, Prince of Wales, who ascended the British throne as King George VI in 1936, is just such a story. (3) He was born into royalty in 1895, a son of then-reigning King George V, but since he was the King's second son, neither he nor anyone else expected him to ascend the throne. (4) Prince Albert, frail and shy, instead grew up in the large shadow cast by his older brother, the King's first-born son, Edward.

(5) Albert's life as a young adult was further complicated by a speech impediment, his verbal stuttering; he had a seemingly-incurable stammer that impaired his public speaking, his only official duty. (6) Prince Albert tried all the traditional cures, but he found no relief until he received a series of highly unusual treatments, sometimes called "the talking-cure," administered by an unlicensed Australian, Lionel Logue. (7) This unorthodox approach worked, and, after that, Albert finally mastered his problem and gained confidence in his public-speaking performances. (8) Then, in 1936, Albert's older brother, now the reigning King Edward VIII, abdicated impetuously and, although it was never Albert's ambition, he suddenly ascended the Throne of England as King George VI and faced more public speaking. (9) In 1939, the United Kingdom declared war on Germany,

and the King, with Logue's guidance and assurance, took to the radio airwaves, making a successful series of courageous wartime radio speeches, urging Britons everywhere to be steadfast, strong and united.

(10) Thus, in the end, Britain was saved by a most improbable hero, one who started as an under-nourished and under-appreciated little brother, said to have an "incurable" stutter, but who nobly rose to the occasion and became the courageous, successful leader that the nation needed during the dark days of World War II and its aftermath.

26. The writer wants to ensure that the first sentence provides the most effective introduction. Which of the following best meets that aim?

    A. (as it is now)

    B. In the British Empire, someone always has to rise to the occasion and save the people from some unexpected threat to the monarchy.

    C. At times in the enduring history of the British Isles, the fate of the empire seems to depend on a single individual who is called to duty unexpectedly, and who absolutely *must* successfully rise to the occasion.

    D. All countries face strife, and in Britain, the empire has confronted such difficulty, needing one single individual to rise to the occasion and successfully save the empire.

    E. In the British kingdom, difficult times have required that a single individual rise up and save the fate of the entire empire; when this unexpected conflict arises, one person must be successful.

27. The writer wants to add a transition at the beginning of sentence 4 (reprinted below) that emphasizes how Prince Albert was treated as "second-best" in the family.

Prince Albert, frail and shy, instead grew up in the large shadow cast by his older brother, the King's first-born son, Edward.

Which of the flowing choices best accomplishes this goal?

    A. Additionally,

    B. Furthermore,

    C. Subsequently,

    D. Indeed,

    E. Similarly,

28. The writer is considering adding the following sentence after sentence 4.

Prince Edward shone over Albert in most areas, like sports.

Should the writer make this addition?

A. Yes, because sports fans will relate to the information.

B. Yes, because it adds necessary information about the brothers' relationship.

C. Yes, because it brings Prince Edward to life.

D. No, because it does not clarify any information about Albert's sporting activities.

E. No, because it is redundant information.

29. The writer is considering revising sentence 6 (reprinted below) for precision and clarity.

Prince Albert tried all the traditional cures, but he found no relief until he received a series of highly unusual treatments, sometimes called "the talking-cure," administered by an unlicensed Australian, Lionel Logue.

Which of the following versions best achieves this purpose?

A. (as it is now)

B. After having no success with traditional treatments, Prince Albert found relief via an unlicensed Australian, Lionel Logue, who administered a series of treatments sometimes called "the talking-cure."

C. Prince Albert found no help, until he discovered an Australian who, although untrained, administered a series of treatments called "the talking-cure" that worked for Albert and gave him relief.

D. Surprisingly, an untrained Australian came to Prince Albert's attention, and after receiving his "talking-cure" treatments, Albert found relief from his embarrassing stutter.

E. Surely Prince Albert was frustrated when he tried all traditional cures for stuttering and found none of them helped; then he discovered an untrained Australian who introduced the prince to a series of unusual treatments called "the talking-cure" that actually helped.

30. The writer wants to revise sentence 8 (reprinted below) to provide a historical explanation for King Edward VIII's abdication.

Then, in 1936, Albert's older brother, now the reigning King Edward VIII, abdicated impetuously and, although it was never Albert's ambition, he suddenly ascended the Throne of England.

Which version of the underlined text best achieves this purpose?

A. abdicated impetuously so that he could marry his mistress, Wallis Simpson, an American divorcee; subsequently, although it was never Albert's ambition, he suddenly ascended the Throne of England.

B. resigned so that he could marry the love of his life, and, although it was never Albert's ambition, he suddenly ascended the Throne of England.

C. quit suddenly because of private issues, and, although it was never Albert's ambition, he suddenly ascended the Throne of England.

D. left his post and, consequentially, Albert (who was called Bertie informally by his family) ascended the Throne of England.

E. resigned because he disliked the role he had to play, paving the way for Albert to become king.

31. The writer wants to add relevant information about Lionel Logue to the second paragraph (sentences 5–9). Which of the following ideas would best fit this goal?

A. Logue settled in London, teaching elocution to rich and poor alike.

B. Logue and his wife had traveled the world studying speech patterns.

C. Logue and King George VI remained friends throughout their lives.

D. Logue had studied elocution, speech therapy, and public speaking for years.

E. Logue believed humor and patience helped stutterers.

32. The writer wants to add the following sentence to the second paragraph (sentences 5–9) to provide additional relevant information.

Unfortunately, he notably stumbled through his closing speech at the British Empire Exhibition at Wembley on 31 October 1925, an embarrassing ordeal for the speaker and listeners alike.

Where would this sentence be best placed?

    A. before sentence 5
    B. before sentence 6
    C. before sentence 7
    D. before sentence 8
    E. before sentence 9

33. The writer is considering adding the following sentence after sentence 10 to add another interesting piece of historical information that relates to King George VI being "a most improbable hero."

Another improbable outcome of King George VI's ascension to the throne is that his daughter became first-in-line to the throne; and that daughter is now Queen Elizabeth II, the longest-serving monarch in British history.

Should the writer make this addition?

    A. Yes, because Queen Elizabeth is more famous than her father was.
    B. Yes, because everyone knows how popular Queen Elizabeth II is with her subjects.
    C. Yes, because many are unaware that Queen Elizabeth II is King George VI's daughter.
    D. No, because the information does not relate to King George VI's stuttering.
    E. No, because it does not matter who Queen Elizabeth's father was.

Questions 34–40 refer to the following draft.

(1) In the earliest development of the U.S. space shuttle, a fierce debate raged over the optimal design which would balance capability vs. the costs of development and operations. (2) Initially, a fully reusable design was preferred: a manned orbiter and a large manned booster. (3) However, studies showed that the size required for a manned booster would be absolutely enormous and have an equally enormous cost. (4) Eventually, the idea was abandoned due to several factors: high price, technical complexity, and development risk.

(5) Another debate was over the nature of the 1st-stage booster's huge rocket engines, which needed to lift the entire rocket and its payload from the ground and then accelerate to several thousand miles per hour. (6) NASA examined multiple solutions to this challenge: redevelopment of the existing Saturn rocket, but with simplified liquid-fuel engines; or one large single solid rocket; or multiple smaller ones. (7) The final design incorporated two very large solid-fuel booster rockets, which were reusable.

(8) Another major change to the initial plans rejected the idea of the orbiter carrying its liquid fuel on board. (9) Instead, using an external disposable fuel tank that would feed liquid fuel to the shuttle's built-in main engine allowed for a larger payload bay in a relatively smaller craft. (10) Plus, the solid-fuel booster rockets could be strapped onto the external liquid-fuel tank, which would be discarded after each launch, while the booster rockets would be refurbished for reuse, and the orbiter would fly again and again.

(11) But the most significant change to the early designs questioned the need for the winged orbiter to have additional jet engines to maneuver the craft after reentry. (12) NASA ultimately axed the jet engines, based partially on experience from previous rocket-then-glider vehicles such as the X-15, and they decided on a purely gliding orbiter. (13) However, this design meant astronauts would have to control the orbiter's re-entry without any engine power for maneuvering, flying it in a high-speed glide from orbit to landing, every single flight.

(14) Finally, the initial design was complete: A relatively small gliding shuttle, attached to an external disposable fuel tank, mated with two huge reusable solid-fuel boosters, became the basis for what eventually was the successful fleet of U.S. space shuttles.

34. The writer is considering further development of the first paragraph (sentences 1–4). Which of the following ideas would NOT be relevant for the writer to include?

    A. an explanation of the difference between a manned booster and a manned orbiter
    B. clarification of the task performed by the booster and the orbiter
    C. a cost analysis of the manned booster
    D. an explanation of the technical complexity of the booster
    E. an overview of the development risk

35. The writer is considering adding the following sentence to the first paragraph (sentences 1–4).

This plan for full reusability would provide lower operating costs.

If the writer adds the sentence, where would it be best placed?

A. after sentence 1
B. after sentence 2
C. after sentence 3
D. after sentence 4
E. The sentence should not be added.

36. In sentence 6 (reprinted below), the writer wants to further clarify the proposed solutions.

NASA examined multiple solutions to this challenge: <u>redevelopment of the existing Saturn rocket, but with simplified liquid-fuel engines; or one large single solid rocket; or multiple smaller ones</u>.

Which of the following revisions best revises the underlined portion?

A. redeveloping the existing Saturn rocket by simplifying its engines, or using one large single solid rocket, or using multiple smaller rockets
B. redeveloping the current Saturn lower stage booster, redeveloping the Saturn liquid-fuel engines, using one big solid rocket, and/or using multiple smaller rockets
C. redesigning Saturn rockets, simplifying Saturn rockets, engaging one large solid rocket, or using multiple smaller rockets
D. redeveloping current Saturn rockets, streamlining Saturn engines, producing one large rocket, or producing multiple smaller ones
E. renovating the existing Saturn rocket design, simplifying the current Saturn liquid-fuel engine, adding one large solid rocket, or substituting multiple smaller rockets

37. In the third paragraph (sentences 8–10), the writer wants to provide additional explanatory information about the fuel tanks. Which of the following ideas, if added, would best resolve unanswered questions?

A. why the external liquid fuel tanks were not reused
B. how the external tank provided structural support for the space shuttle's solid rocket boosters and orbiter
C. how the booster rockets were reused, even though they were strapped to the external liquid fuel tank that was destroyed upon re-entry
D. how much the increased shuttle payload allowed parts to be delivered to the International Space Station
E. what arguments supported carrying liquid fuel on board

38. Which of the following best clarifies the writer's rationale for the gliding shuttle?

A. sentence 3
B. sentence 7
C. sentence 9
D. sentence 12
E. sentence 13

39. The writer wants to revise sentence 12 (reprinted below), adjusting the punctuation as needed, to further explain the relevance of the X-15 to the space shuttle.

NASA ultimately axed the jet engines, based partially on experience from previous rocket-then-glider vehicles <u>such as the X-15</u>, and they decided on a purely gliding orbiter.

Which of the following versions of the underlined portion best meets the writer's goal?

A. such as the X-15, which was a hypersonic rocket-powered experimental aircraft
B. such as the X-15, the vehicle that set speed and altitude records in the 1960s
C. such as the X-15, which captured essential data used in aircraft and spacecraft design, including the space shuttle
D. such as the X-15, the first flight test program to make extensive use of simulators to work out aviation-related problems and train pilots
E. such as the X-15, which proved that a vehicle could re-enter the atmosphere and glide down to a precision landing

40. The writer wants to embellish the final paragraph (sentence 14) with additional information. Which of the following additions would be most relevant to the passage as a whole?

    A. In the following decades, the shuttles ultimately launched satellites, interplanetary probes, and the Hubble Space Telescope.

    B. NASA had reviewed 29 potential designs before choosing the initial design.

    C. The *Challenger* disaster of 1986 set the program back considerably.

    D. The vertical launch resembled a conventional rocket.

    E. The shuttle was designed after NASA and the Air Force determined the need for a reusable, heavy-lift spacecraft.

Questions 41–45 refer to the following draft.

(1) One of our most deeply-held cultural beliefs is the notion that when a public speaker such as a politician breaks into tears, it is a sign of sincerity, a display of authentic feeling. (2) Our intellect may remind us that some people have the ability to cry "crocodile tears" on demand, but our emotions still lead us to believe that we are seeing a window into the speaker's true, pure emotional center.

(3) When we observe this phenomenon, we tend to think the speaker is "losing emotional control"; otherwise, he or she would never "break down into tears." (4) Thus, we interpret this uncharacteristic display as an indication of the depth, truth, and purity of the emotion felt by the speaker for his subject.

(5) However, scientific research into this phenomenon suggests an entirely different conclusion: Crying is most often the result of excruciatingly mixed emotions. (6) Many people weep when overwhelmed by contradictions, when they cannot reconcile the conflicting pull of incompatible ideas. (7) A loving mother may be bewildered at her own weeping at her daughter's wedding, as she cannot reconcile her genuine joy for her daughter's happiness with her equally-genuine feelings of loss. (8) A mourner crying uncontrollably at a funeral is seen as expressing his genuine feelings of grief and loss, but at the same time, he may also be anguished by perceived guilt or pending loneliness, or he may possibly cry in secret relief that the loved one's suffering has ended.

(9) Overall, many studies confirm that such "uncontrollable" crying in public is usually not correlated with the speaker's believing what he is saying; rather, it shows that he is suffering from dissonance, from the conflict between equally compelling, deeply felt emotions.

41. The writer is considering adding a new opening question to the beginning of the first paragraph (sentences 1–2) to build suspense and pique the reader's curiosity. Which of the following would best achieve that purpose?

    A. Why are our instincts often wrong?

    B. How should we react when a public speaker breaks into tears?

    C. Why should we place our trust in any public speaker who cannot control emotions?

    D. What is it about crying that makes people so believable?

    E. How can we tell if we are witnessing true emotions?

42. The writer wants to add a transitional sentence that bridges the idea in sentence 3 and the conclusion reached in sentence 4 (both reprinted below).

(3) When we observe this phenomenon, we tend to think the speaker is "losing control"; otherwise, he or she would never "break down into tears." (4) Thus, we interpret this uncharacteristic display as an indication of the depth, truth, and purity of the emotion felt by the speaker.

Which of the following sentences best serves the writer's goal?

    A. When a speaker is losing control, it is an indication that the person is telling the truth.

    B. Breaking down into tears is an indication that the speaker has something shameful to hide.

    C. However, we mistake a speaker's tears as revelatory of truth, rather than other strong emotions.

    D. A person who is crying obviously cannot hold back the truth.

    E. We tend to believe breaking down into tears is something that a speaker cannot control.

43. The writer is considering revising the underlined portion of sentence 5 (reprinted below) to make its point more effectively.

However, scientific research into this phenomenon suggests an entirely different conclusion: Crying is most often the result of excruciatingly mixed emotions.

Which of the following revisions to the underlined portion best achieves the writer's goal?

A. (as it is now)

B. However, scientific research into this phenomenon suggests a somewhat different conclusion

C. However, quite to the contrary, scientific research into this phenomenon suggests an unexpected and entirely different conclusion

D. On the other hand, some scientific research into this phenomenon could suggest a different conclusion

E. However, a review of the scientific research into this phenomenon might advocate a different conclusion

44. Which of the following provides the strongest criticism of the third paragraph's development (sentences 5–8)?

A. The paragraph as a whole contradicts the previous paragraphs.

B. No proof of the scientific research is provided; therefore, it cannot be believed.

C. The instances described are common occurrences that cause people to cry.

D. The examples provided do not appropriately illustrate the overall subject of the passage.

E. The paragraph is hard to follow because it provides too little explanatory logic.

45. To provide a stronger conclusion, the writer wants to add a closing sentence. Which of the following would best meet the writer's goal?

A. In conclusion, although most people believe that crying public speakers are telling the truth, it is more likely that they are actually hiding something.

B. It appears that we should distrust our natural inclinations when we see public speakers cry, and instead use our intellect to try to understand the strong pull of conflicting emotions.

C. In conclusion, many of our deeply held cultural beliefs may be wrong; believing the statements of public speakers just because they cry is a good example.

D. Thus, we always need to reassess our deeply held cultural beliefs, lest they lead us astray of reality as demonstrated by scientific research.

E. At the end of the day, it is always better to reserve judgment whenever you listen to a public speaker and to not let your emotions control you.

IF YOU FINISH BEFORE TIME IS CALLED, CHECK YOUR WORK ON THIS SECTION ONLY. DO NOT WORK ON ANY OTHER SECTION IN THE TEST.

Section II: Free-Response Questions

Time: 2 hours, 15 minutes

3 questions

Question 1

(Suggested writing time—40 minutes. This question counts for one-third of the total free-response section score.)

Polling has become an integral part of election processes. The media, as well as the voting population, take into great consideration the results of various political polls. But are these polls truly accurate? Have voters been relying too heavily on the often inaccurate data of political polling?

Considering the role that political polls play in elections, read the following six sources (including any introductory information) carefully. Then, write an essay that synthesizes material from at least three of the sources and develops your position on the claim that political polls do not accurately represent the views of a population.

> Source A (photo)
> Source B (Triola)
> Source C (Fund)
> Source D (Morgan)
> Source E (Patterson)
> Source F (Ponnuru)

In your response, you should do the following:

- Respond to the prompt with a thesis that presents a defensible position.
- Select and use evidence from at least three of the provided sources to support your line of reasoning. Indicate clearly the sources used through direct quotation, paraphrase, or summary. Sources may be cited as Source A, Source B, etc., or by using the description in parentheses.
- Explain how the evidence supports your line of reasoning.
- Use appropriate grammar and punctuation in communicating your argument.

Source A

Dewey Defeats Truman. 5 Nov. 1948. Photograph. Library of Congress, New York World-Telegram and Sun Newspaper Photograph collection. loc.gov. Web. 5 Oct. 2017.

The following photograph, published on November 3, 1948, shows President Truman, jubilant after winning the 1948 election, holding up a copy of the Chicago Daily Tribune *newspaper with the erroneous headline stating that Truman's opponent, New York Governor Thomas Dewey, had won the election. The newspaper relied on political polls to predict the "winner," but in this case the polls were clearly wrong.*

The pridiction and election of the "winner".

Source B

Triola, Mario F. *Elementary Statistics,* 7th ed. Reading: Addison Wesley Longman, Inc., 1998. Print.

The following passage is taken from a statistics textbook that examines the uses and abuses of statistics.

    Abuses of statistics have occurred for some time. For example, about a century ago, statesman Benjamin Disraeli famously said, "there are three kinds of lies: lies, damned lies, and statistics." It has also been said that "figures don't lie; liars figure," and that "if you torture the data long enough, they'll admit to anything." Historian Andrew Lang said that some people use statistics "as a drunken man uses lampposts—for support rather than illumination." These statements refer to abuses of statistics in which data are presented in ways that may be misleading. Some abusers of statistics are simply ignorant or careless, whereas others have personal objectives and are willing to suppress unfavorable data while emphasizing supportive data. We will now present a few examples of the many ways in which data can be distorted.

    Loaded Questions: Survey questions can be worded to elicit a desired response. A famous case involves presidential candidate Ross Perot, who asked this question in a mail survey: "Should the president have the line item veto to eliminate waste?" The results included 97% "yes" responses. However, 57% said "yes" when subjects were randomly selected and asked this question: "Should the president have the line item veto, or not?" Sometimes questions are unintentionally loaded by such factors as the order of the items being considered. For example, one German poll asked these two questions:

- Would you say that traffic contributes more or less to air pollution than industry?
- Would you say that industry contributes more or less to air pollution than traffic?

When traffic was presented first, 45% blamed traffic and 32% blamed industry; when industry was presented first, those percentages changed dramatically to 24% and 57%, respectively.

[handwritten note: Abuses of statistics are used for lies damned lies and statistics.]

Source C

Fund, John. "Polling Isn't Perfect." *The Wall Street Journal.* 14 Nov. 2002: n. pag. Print.

The following passage is excerpted from an article in a national newspaper about problems facing pollsters.   +

America has too many political polls, and Americans pay too much attention to them. Many people have believed that for a long time. What's different now is that some pollsters are starting to agree.

"We have falsely raised expectations about polling," says John Zogby, who is famous for having called Bill Clinton's margin in the 1996 presidential race almost exactly and having been virtually the only pollster to give Al Gore a slight popular-vote edge on election eve in 2000. But this year Mr. Zogby saw three of his final 11 statewide polls indicate the wrong winner. He says it would be helpful if people discovered the limitations of polling. In a speech and interview in Washington yesterday he described some of the problems his profession faces:

- The nightly tracking polls that both candidates and reporters fixate on are less reliable than larger polls +
  taken over a longer period of time. "I probably should have used larger samples," admits Mr. Zogby, who
  thought that Democrat Jeanne Shaheen would win an open New Hampshire Senate seat and that
  Republican Jim Ryan was tied for the governor's race in Illinois. (She lost by four points and he by seven.)

Dave Winston, a Republican pollster, says one problem with nightly tracking polls is that a pollster doing them doesn't have the time to make innumerable repeat calls to people who won't pick up the phone. Mr. Zogby says that he now has to make an average of seven calls to get just one person willing to spend the 20 minutes or so it takes to answer his polling questions.

- *Pollsters can't poll on Election Day.* Surveys this year found that between 4% and 12% of voters in key states made up their mind who to vote for on Election Day. Although challengers tend to pick up most of the undecided vote, it doesn't always work out that way—making last-minute votes impossible to predict.

- *Answering machines, caller ID and other screening devices make pollsters easier to avoid.* Some phones won't even ring unless they recognize the number of the caller. Scott Adler, University of Colorado political scientist, says pollsters are now concerned that the people who do finally agree to answer a pollster's questions are no longer representative of the voters as a whole.

Whit Ayres, a GOP pollster, told the *Atlanta Journal-Constitution* that "I can't fathom 20 years from now the telephone remaining the primary means of data collection. This industry is in a transition from telephone data collection to Internet data collection." In the meantime, look for polls to be more variable and less reliable than ever. Perhaps it's time that we spend more time listening to the candidates and having people make up their own mind who's doing well.

America has too
many polls

Source D

Morgan, Lee. "The Disadvantages of Public Polling." *Classroom.* N.D. Web. 17 Sept. 2017.

The following article explores reasons for polls being inaccurate.

Public opinion polls are used to gather information about the attitudes of a population regarding politics and other social issues. While they often prove to be useful in determining outcomes of elections or persuading politicians or business owners to take a particular action on an issue, the public opinion poll is a flawed process that has its own unique set of disadvantages.

The Leading Option

According to Surveys.com.au, one major disadvantage of public opinion polling is the tendency of the person taking the survey to go with "the leading option." The leading option is the answer to a polling question that the researcher suggests is the popular answer while asking someone else. For example, a pollster may tell a person that research has shown that Candidate A is the most common answer when people are asked who they think will win the election between Candidates A, B, and C. When the poll question is actually asked, it is phrased, "Among Candidates A, B, and C, who do you believe will win the election?" Having already heard what the supposed most popular answer is, those who do not have a strong opinion about the matter are likely to go with Candidate A because most other people have apparently done the same. This leads to inaccurate public opinion and is a way that pollsters with an agenda can help get the results they want.

Sampling Errors

If you've seen poll results on the news, there is usually a disclaimer that lets the viewer know that there is a plus or minus 3 percent margin of error. This may occasionally be the case, but there is no solid way to tell just how big the error margin is, according to PollingReport.com. Sampling errors take place in a number of different ways. If a pollster is conducting a sidewalk survey, there is a strong possibility several people will refuse to take part in it. If the poll was about attitudes toward public opinion polls, for example, a very significant portion of the population may not be represented. And, of course, there is outright dishonesty by pollsters. If the poll is driven by an agenda, little stops them from doctoring the results to fit that agenda or wording questions in a way that is likely to provoke a certain response.

Selection Bias

Selection bias happens when the people intentionally selected to take part in a poll may not be representative of the entire population. If a conservative talk radio station is conducting a call-in opinion poll from its listeners concerning their opinion on a liberal political candidate, the results are fairly predictable. The liberal politician is likely to be viewed as unfavorable to the station's conservative listeners. In addition, in the above example, the people who feel strongly about a subject are likely to call in multiple times to vote. According to the Skeptic's Dictionary website, a poll conducted by Alfred Kinsey about homosexuality showed that 10 percent of the American population is gay. Later studies suggested the number is more like 2 percent. Kinsey's numbers were subject to selection bias because he conducted the survey with people in prisons and those who attended his lectures. Neither was representative of the entire population.

Public opinion Pobl is a flawed Process

Source E

Patterson, Dan. "Numbers lie all the time: How political polls work." *TechRepublic.* 23 Aug. 2016. Web. 17 Sept. 2017.

The following excerpt is from an article about how political polls are conducted.

Numbers lie all the time. Yet the business of numbers is big business. Big data helps companies make better decisions by extracting key insights from piles of information. Polling does the same for politics.

And like big data for business, though results can be ambiguous and notoriously hard to interpret, polls are essential tools for political campaigns. When pundits and politicos talk about "the polls," they're referring to a bevy of companies and universities that perform specialized research.

Modern political polls are generally conducted through telephone surveys that target population samples based on demographic and psychographic criteria. Poll recipients are run through a barrage of carefully worded questions about personalities, messaging, and policy.

Quality polls use random sampling to determine who is called. Random digit dialing, a widely used tactic, is based on manual selection of the area code and phone number prefix, then picks the last four digits of a phone number at random. This tactic is great at getting usable local responses to questions, but bad because it doesn't exclude business, Skype, and other non-human numbers.

Registration-based sampling, another common polling method, is based on available data, usually voter registration lists and other data provided by the party. These polls can be less expensive, because voter data is already captured.

Tracking, policy, benchmark, and opinion polls are often commissioned by campaigns digging for information about voter segments. The final product, presented to the campaign or client, is typically a document that breaks down recipient responses by age, gender, location, income, and political association.

Big data played a major role in informing the Ted Cruz campaign who to microtarget and poll during the primaries. Computers are prohibited from calling cell phones, but humans can manually dial numbers from spreadsheets generated by computers.

Are polls accurate? Poll results can seem inconsistent because the business of polling is diverse. Gallup, a respected data firm that provides deep analytics to large organizations, routinely publishes a survey on its election polling accuracy.

Data site FiveThirtyEight tracks the accuracy of dozens of polling agencies, ranging from local regional specialists to national firms and large research universities. While accuracy depends on the type of poll and the agency conducting poll research, political polls have been fairly accurate.

A Bloomberg survey seems to confirm that, during the 2016 political cycle campaign, polls have been reliable. Bloomberg used RealClearPolitics aggregate polling data in a month-long survey during the primaries, which showed that 86 percent of polls accurately forecast election winners.

Though polls have been accurate this cycle, the industry appears to be in a period of transition. Mobile devices have had a significant impact on poll response rates. Because many polls are conducted over the phone, consumers are more able to block or dismiss unknown calls. A Vanderbilt survey found that response rates to robocalls are abysmal.

Big data companies are hungry for political dollars and attempting to augment or supplant polling data with web and mobile user data. During the recent Republican National Convention, several polling experts indicated that the polling and big data industries could someday merge. A number of private data companies . . . already provide campaigns with mission critical data. Several political data companies see politics as a stepping-stone to other industries.

"Numbers lie"

Source F

Ponnuru, Ramesh. "Margin of Error." Review of Mobocracy: How the Media's Obsession with Polling Twists the News, Alters Elections, and Undermines Democracy, by Matthew Robinson. *National Review.* 6 May 2002: 49. Print.

The following passage is excerpted from a book review of Mobocracy: How the Media's Obsession with Polling Twists the News, Alters Elections, and Undermines Democracy, *by Matthew Robinson.*

Reporters lean on polls because they provide the illusion of numerical certainty amid all the spin. In political campaigns, reporters are torn between the conflicting desires to stay with the herd and to write a new story: Changes in the poll numbers provide the pivot point that lets everyone know when to make the switch together. Now the candidate whose campaign was brilliant last week is revealed as a sad-sack loser. His initiative on health care has bombed. How do we know that? Because he's down in the polls. Why is he down in the polls? Because his health-care initiative has bombed.

The over reliance on polls has the effect of overestimating public support for small policies that seem innocuous to voters. But it kills big ideas in the crib. Voters' initial reaction to any sweeping change is likely to be negative, so the first polls on it will show that it is unpopular. From then on, the idea can be dismissed as such. Polls can interfere with the formation of public opinion.

They can also create the illusion that public opinion exists when it does not. Reports that discuss what the public thinks about stem-cell research, or the Middle East peace process, are pointless because the public has no coherent, consolidated view on these matters, at least at the level of specificity needed to guide action. Polls, and media summaries of them, routinely gloss over the vast public ignorance and apathy that makes them so fluid.

Reporters use polls for thore own benefts.

Question 2

(**Suggested writing time—40 minutes. This question counts for one-third of the total free-response section score.**)

In the following excerpt, John Updike, in his essay "The First Kiss," describes the opening of a new baseball season, including reflecting on the past season and the attitude of the fans as the new season begins.

Read the following narrative carefully. Then, write an essay that analyzes the rhetorical choices Updike makes to convey an audience's attitude toward a sporting event.

In your response you should do the following:

- Respond to the prompt with a thesis that analyzes the writer's rhetorical choices.
- Select and use evidence to support your line of reasoning.
- Explain how the evidence supports your line of reasoning.
- Demonstrate an understanding of the rhetorical situation.
- Use appropriate grammar and punctuation in communicating your argument.

The many-headed monster called the Fenway Faithful yesterday resumed its romance with twenty-five youngish men in red socks who last year broke its monstrous big heart. Just showing up on so dank an Opening Day was an act of faith. But the wet sky dried to a mottled pewter, the tarpaulin was rolled off the infield and stuffed into a mailing tube, and we Faithful braced for the first kiss of another prolonged entanglement.

(5)   Who can forget the ups and downs of last year's fling? First, the Supersox; then, the unraveling. Our eyeballs grew calluses, watching Boomer swing from the heels and Hobson throw to the stars. Dismal nights watching the Royals play pinball with our heroes on that plastic prairie in Kansas City. Dreadful days losing count of Yankee singles in the four-game massacre. Fisk standing ever more erect and stoic at the plate, looking more and more like a Civil War memorial financed with Confederate dollars. The Noble Lost Cause.

(10)   In September, the mini-resurrection, Zimmer's last stand, the miraculous last week of no losses, waiting for the Yankees to drop one. Which they did. And then, the cruelest tease, the playoff game surrendered to a shoestring catch and a shortstop's cheap home run. Enough. You'll never get us to care again, Red Sox.

But monsters have short memories, elastic hearts, and very foolable faculties, as many an epic attests. From natty-looking to nasty-looking, the fans turned out. "We Miss Louis and Bill," one large cardboard
(15)   complained. "Windsor Locks Loves the Sox!" a bedsheet benignly rhymed. Some fellow behind us exhaled a sweetish smell, but the dragon's breath was primarily flavored with malt.

Governor King was booed royally. Power may or may not corrupt, but it does not win friends. A lady from Dedham not only sang all the high notes in "The Star-Spangled Banner" but put in an extra one of her own, taking "free" up and out of the ballpark. We loved it. Monsters love high notes and hoards of gold.

(20)   The two teams squared off against each other in a state of statistical virginity. Every man in both lineups was batting .000. On the other hand, both pitchers had earned-run averages of 0.00. And every fielder there had thus far played errorless ball.

Eckersley looked quick. A moment of sun made some of the windows of the Prudential Center sparkle. The new Red Sox uniforms appeared tight as outfits for trapeze artists but otherwise struck the proper conservative
(25)   note, for a team of millionaires: buttons on the shirt and a single red pinstripe. Eckersley yielded a double and then struck out two. The first nicks in statistical virginity had been taken. The season had begun. . . .

We witnessed a little by-play at the beginning that may tell it all. After the Cleveland lineup had been called out, the Red Sox roll began with Zimmer. Out he trotted, last year's anti-hero, the manager who watched ninety-nine victories be not quite enough, with his lopsided cheeks and squint, like a Popeye who
(30)   has let the spinach settle to his middle. The many-headed monster booed furiously, and Zimmer laughed, shaking hands with his opposite manager, Torborg.

That laugh said a strange thing. It said, *This is fun.* Baseball is meant to be fun, and not all the solemn money men in fur-collared greatcoats, not all the scruffy media cameramen and sour-faced reporters that crowd around the dugouts can quite smother the exhilarating spaciousness and grace of this impudently
(35)   relaxed sport, a game of innumerable potential redemptions and curious disappointments. This is fun.

A hard lesson for a hungry monster to master, but he has six months to work on it. So let's play ball.

Question 3

(Suggested writing time—40 minutes. This question counts for one-third of the total free-response section score.)

> Henry David Thoreau wrote, "Many men go fishing all of their lives without knowing that it is not fish they are after."

Write an essay that argues your opinion about the accuracy of Thoreau's aphorism in modern society.

In your response, you should do the following:

- Respond to the prompt with a thesis that presents a defensible position.
- Provide evidence to support your line of reasoning.
- Explain how the evidence supports your line of reasoning.
- Use appropriate grammar and punctuation in communicating your argument.

IF YOU FINISH BEFORE TIME IS CALLED, CHECK YOUR WORK ON THIS
SECTION ONLY. DO NOT WORK ON ANY OTHER SECTION IN THE TEST.

Answer Key

Section I: Multiple-Choice Questions

1. C	**10.** C	**19.** E	**28.** E	**37.** C
2. E	**11.** D	**20.** B	**29.** B	**38.** D
3. B	**12.** B	**21.** B	**30.** A	**39.** E
4. E	**13.** D	**22.** A	**31.** D	**40.** B
5. A	**14.** A	**23.** D	**32.** B	**41.** D
6. A	**15.** E	**24.** C	**33.** C	**42.** C
7. A	**16.** C	**25.** A	**34.** C	**43.** C
8. B	**17.** D	**26.** C	**35.** B	**44.** D
9. E	**18.** C	**27.** D	**36.** A	**45.** B

Section II: Free-Response Questions

Essay scoring rubrics, student essays, and analysis appear beginning on page 247.

Answer Explanations

Section I: Multiple-Choice Questions

The passage referred to in questions 1–11 is from "Meditations upon a Broomstick" by Jonathan Swift (1701).

1. **C.** The sentence is not pedantic (overly scholarly), choice C. The sentence is syntactically complex (A), and it has parallel construction (B), ". . . full of sap, full of leaves, and full of boughs. . . ." It contains a narrative of the broomstick's life (D), from tree sapling to death in a fireplace. Finally, the sentence has subordinate clauses (E), such as ". . . which you now behold ingloriously lying in that neglected corner. . . ."

2. **E.** According to the author, both a broomstick and a man were untainted in their natural state, choice E. The broomstick began life in nature in a "flourishing state . . . full of sap, full of leaves, and full of boughs." Man began life in youth "strong and lusty, in a thriving condition." Choices A, C, and D contradict the passage. Choice B is not addressed.

3. **B.** The broomstick symbolizes the goodness in nature that man uses and discards, choice B. It starts life as a flourishing tree, but after man uses it up, he throws it away or burns it. Choice A has no support in the passage. Choices C and E contradict the passage. Nature does not triumph over man's evil tendencies, and man does not fear nature but rather destroys it. The evil inherent in man's soul (D) is not addressed.

4. **E.** Intemperance is a lack of moderation in behavior, and the "axe of intemperance" is a metaphor for those excesses, choice E. It is the "axe" that chops man down like a tree. Before that, man had "green boughs"; after, he has but a "withered trunk." The phrase does not refer to "man's dominance over nature" (A). Nature is not shown as providing much nourishment (B); rather, it is destroyed. "Axe of intemperance" is neither a simile (C) nor hyperbole (D).

5. A. The author is saddened and disillusioned by man's behavior, choice A. Choice B is incorrect because man's future is not addressed. Choices C and E contradict the tone of the passage—there is no optimism or praise here. This author is angry with man and his nature, not the society man has created (D).

6. A. The phrase "a flourishing state in a forest" refers to pure, untouched nature (before man chops down trees) and has positive connotations, choice A. All other answer choices are negative within the passage's context.

7. A. The phrase "this reasoning vegetable" refers to "Man," choice A. Notice how the author claims that "Nature sent him [man] into the world . . . this reasoning vegetable." Do not be confused when the author adds that man was sent into the world "wearing his own hair on his head," because the hair (B) refers to "the proper branches of this reasoning vegetable," and that "reasoning vegetable," which happens to have hair on his head, is man. The head itself (C) is not the reasoning vegetable; man is. The remaining answer choices do not refer to the "reasoning vegetable."

8. B. In context, "this our broomstick" (line 27) is a metaphor for man's pretentious character, choice B. Man pretends to solve the problems of the world but only makes them worse. Choice A is inaccurate—the broomstick represents decline, not thriving. Choice C is also inaccurate; the broomstick is a metaphor for man, not society. There is no evidence for choice D; nature doesn't exert control in this author's world, man does. Choice E is obviously incorrect; the broomstick is an analogy for man's physical state, not his intellectual state.

9. E. The author implies that man causes problems where none previously existed, choice E. It is only man's presentation that allows him to believe that he can correct abuses. In fact, he "raises a mighty dust where there was none before." All incorrect answer choices are positive ideas; the correct response needs a negative one.

10. C. Swift is cynical toward mankind, choice C, and all of man's works, believing that mankind is motivated wholly by self-interest and therefore not to be trusted. This author takes a strong position, not a neutral one (A), and while he may be condescending, the condescension is directed toward man, not nature (B). "Bellicose" (D) means quarrelsome and warlike and is too strong a term to accurately describe the tone here. Finally, "dogmatic" (E) fails to adequately convey the negative, cynical tone of the passage.

11. D. "Partial judges that we are of our own excellences" (lines 31–32), choice D, represents the strongest statement of the author's theme. Swift appears to concentrate on how inappropriate it is for man to try to reform nature while thinking of himself in such grand terms while, in reality, being the corrupter of nature. Choices A and E are too narrow in their scope. Choices B and C do not articulate the author's overall theme.

The passage referred to in questions 12–25 is from Henry David Thoreau's "Life Without Principle" (1863).

12. B. Thoreau insists that "getting a living" should be ethical ("honest and honorable," line 4) and admirable ("altogether inviting and glorious," lines 4–5), choice B. All of the other choices contain at least one disqualifying word; Thoreau does not stress aspects such as "pious" (A), nor "accessible" (C), nor "attainable" (D), nor "profitable" (E).

13. D. Thoreau explains that "the lesson of value which money teaches . . . we are inclined to skip altogether" (lines 10–13), choice D. Although all of the other answer choices are mentioned in the passage, man is not indifferent to these ideas; therefore, they do not answer the question.

14. A. A major assertion of the passage is that people no longer understand the proper value of money, choice A. The author claims that people get money in the wrong way and use it based on the wrong principles. Thoreau never addresses what will "save mankind" (B). And while he acknowledges that gold-digging may be "hard work," "gold thus obtained is not the same thing with the wages of honest toil" and "society is the loser." Although Thoreau believes that gold-diggers rely on luck to find gold, he doesn't believe that the entire world operates this way (C). Neither choice D nor E is suggested in the passage.

15. E. To Thoreau, the "Author of the Universe" is God, choice E. None of the other choices is a reasonable answer.

16. **C.** The author wonders whether Plato had to face the same dilemmas that others do, choice C, if Plato lived his life more admirably than did his contemporaries. The author's points about gold-digging—choices A and B—are not addressed in the discussion of Plato. Thoreau doesn't mention Plato's premises about morality (D). Mentioning Plato does nothing to change the tone of the passage (E), and it is highly unlikely that the author uses Plato merely to impress his readers.

17. **D.** Thoreau claims that he would not raise a finger for "all the wealth of the world." The pronoun "it" refers to this wealth, choice D.

18. **C.** An aphorism, a brief, pointed statement of fundamental truth, is similar to a proverb. Choice C fits this definition, as it addresses how gold can cover a great surface but cannot cover one grain of wisdom. Choice A essentially claims that most men get their living through improvised means; it is an opinion, not a statement of truth. Choice B is also not an aphorism; in fact, Thoreau states that answer B's quotation is a "comment . . . a satire." Choice D follows Thoreau's opinion that gamblers and gold-diggers are alike; again, it is an opinion, not an aphorism. Finally, answer E, that claims the Devil works hard, clarifies Thoreau's analogy between gold-diggers and gamblers, but it is not an aphorism.

19. **E.** An unstated assumption of the author is that what appears honest to one can be harmful to society, choice E. Thoreau suggests that, although gold-digging may appear to be an honest way to earn "food and raiment" to some, it harms society in the same way that gambling does; it "is not the same thing with the wages of honest toil." The author never implies that philosophers should work harder (A), that society is improving (C), or that hard work produces wisdom (D). In fact, he suggests the opposite: Hard work can be the "enemy." Choice B is not an unstated assumption but a paraphrase of an explicit statement.

20. **B.** The California gold rush, which some saw as an example of hard-working men diligently trying to get ahead, is used by this author as an example of immorality, of gambling in life, choice B. Thoreau doesn't compare gold-diggers to Greeks (A), explore relations of Orientals and Occidentals (C) (that relationship is only touched on), sensationalize (D), or criticize those who saw the gold rush as romantic (E) (he directly criticizes those who participate in the gold-digging).

21. **B.** Thoreau states that "cold and hunger seem more friendly to my nature." Cold and hunger, choice B, generally undesirable states, are here seen as better than man's methods of warding them off. The other answer choices are not *qualified* negative ideas; they are truly negative.

22. **A.** Knowledge is more valuable than gold, choice A; wisdom will metaphorically gild more surface than gold. The remaining answer choices are unreasonable because they do not offer accurate interpretations of the sentence.

23. **D.** The author is angry, indignant at humanity's unseemly pursuit of money, choice D. The tone is not condescending (A), which means haughty and arrogant. Skeptical (B) is too weak a word for the author's tone, as is worried (C). Choice E, pedestrian, which means humdrum and unimaginative, does not apply to the tone.

24. **C.** The quotation in choice C is not part of the argument against gold-digging. It simply states a fact about gold. All of the other answer choices do indeed help further the author's argument.

25. **A.** Thoreau doesn't directly address man's improving his lot in life, choice A, although one can infer that he probably believes man should do so. All of the other answer choices are addressed in the passage.

The draft referred to in questions 26–33 discusses Prince Albert's difficulties with stuttering.

26. **C.** When asked for the most effective answer, look for the choice that is most accurate to the passage as well as direct and succinct. Choice C supplies the most effective introduction because it presents all of the necessary information in the most concise manner. It is superior to choice A, which calls for the original sentence. Let's compare the two: Choice A begins with a series of long and redundant phrases ("In the long and enduring history of the British peoples, there are times . . .") all of which choice C condenses to the essential and more accurate information ("At times in the enduring history of the British Isles . . ."). Choice A continues with the wordy phrase, ". . . times when the fate of the entire Empire seems to depend on a single individual, someone who. . . ." Choice C improves upon this with its succinct "the fate of the empire seems to depend on a single individual who. . . ." Choice A also presents long-winded phrasing, ". . . who absolutely *must* be successful in rising to the occasion." Choice C is again more concise with direct phrasing, "who absolutely *must* successfully rise to the occasion." Meanwhile, choice B is inaccurate because of both the absolute word "always" and the erroneous phrase "save the people from some unexpected threat to the monarchy." Choice D goes astray by bringing in "all countries," which is not the subject of the passage. Choice E is redundant with its phrase "a single individual . . . one person." Choice E also misuses a key word; it is not that *the conflict* arises unexpectedly; rather, it is *the individual* who is unexpectedly called upon to lead the nation.

27. **D.** The transition "indeed" adds intensity, emphasis, and a tone of assurance; it is the equivalent of writing "certainly," or "as a matter of fact," and it fits the context of the passage between sentences 3 and 4. No other choices add this type of emphasis. Choice A, "additionally," is a transition that signals new information, but it does not necessarily add emphasis. Choice B, "furthermore," rather indicates a continuance of ideas; it may perhaps add some small degree of emphasis, but it does not fit well in the context of sentence 4. Choice C, "subsequently," deals with something that occurs at a different time, like the word "later," or "afterward," and it too does not fit in the context of sentence 4. Choice E, "similarly," is used for things that are similar or equal. It is the equivalent of writing "in the same way" or "likewise"; it does not add emphasis, nor does it fit the context of the passage.

28. **E.** The writer would be better served by not adding this new sentence about Prince Edward. Sentence 4 already states that Prince Albert "grew up in the large shadow cast by his older brother," so it is redundant to add a sentence that also claims how the older prince "shone over Albert in most areas"; plus, mentioning that Edward excelled in sports is not really relevant to the passage as a whole. For all these reasons, choice E is correct. Choice A votes for adding the new sentence and claims sports fans will relate to the information about Edward; this is hardly a reason for adding the sentence, and it is certainly not compelling, because sports is not germane to the passage as a whole. Choice B also votes for adding the sentence, claiming that its information is necessary. This idea is simply untrue; the reader already knows Edward cast a large shadow over his younger brother, and the addition of sports is a new, but certainly not a necessary, bit of information. Choice C is incorrect because mentioning that Edward bested Albert in sports does not necessarily bring him to life; it merely states one of the areas in which Edward was better than Albert. Choice D accurately votes against adding the sentence, but for the wrong reason: The new sentence cannot "*clarify* . . . Albert's sporting activities," because sports are never mentioned in the passage.

29. **B.** Choice B is superior to the original sentence (A) because it is more concise, and it gets right to the point while still including all of the essential information. It cuts down the wordiness contained in the original sentence in phrasing such as "Prince Albert tried all the traditional cures, but he found no relief . . ." and replaces it with the more streamlined phrase, "After having no success with traditional treatments, Prince Albert found relief. . . ." Remember that the question asks for a clear and precise sentence; choice B provides just that. On the other hand, choice C is no more precise or clear than the original; in fact, it fails to mention that Albert tried all of the traditional cures. In addition, choice C inaccurately claims that Lionel Logue was "untrained," which is certainly not the same as "unlicensed." Choice D likewise does not mention traditional cures and erroneously adds that it was surprising that Albert found help with the "untrained" (not *unlicensed*) Australian. Plus, the passage offers no proof that eventually finding relief should be surprising, whether or not Logue was licensed. Choice E is far too wordy, adding nine words onto the original and fourteen more than choice B, and it too mistakenly identifies Logue as "untrained."

30. **A.** Choice A precisely addresses the question by adding historical information that better explains King Edward's decision to abdicate, namely his desire to marry his mistress, the American divorcee Wallis Simpson. Choice A also effectively turns the second half of the original sentence into a dependent clause followed by an independent clause, beginning with the appropriate transition, "subsequently," and this spotlights the idea of Albert being suddenly thrust onto the Throne of England. Choice B mentions King Edward's desire to "marry the love of his life," but that is not as factually accurate as choice A, which not only names Wallis Simpson but also identifies her as his mistress *and* an American *and* a divorcee. Choice C adds no substantial historical explanation, instead merely claiming he "quit suddenly because of private issues." Also, King Edward did not simply "quit" his job; he abdicated the throne, he renounced his titles, and he relinquished his position of ultimate power. Likewise, choice D suffers from the same fault, simply stating that King Edward "left his post." Additionally, choice D mentions that Albert was called Bertie

informally, which is historically true, but it does not add any explanation for King Edward's abdication. Choice E completely misses the mark; it provides no historical explanation, and instead it simplistically states that King Edward "disliked the role he had to play." Plus, the last phrase, stating that Edward's abdication "[paved] the way for Albert to become king," completely loses the impact of the original wording that acknowledges Albert did indeed ascend to the throne, regardless of his never hoping to do so.

31. D. The question asks which piece of information about Lionel Logue is most relevant to add to the second paragraph, and choice D best fits that goal. It addresses the fact that Logue had studied elocution, speech therapy, and public speaking for years, information that indeed helps explain why the "unlicensed" Australian was successful in ameliorating Prince Albert's symptoms. Choice A may indeed be true; Logue did treat rich and poor alike in London, but this fact is not particularly relevant to his work with Prince Albert. Choice B is even more off topic, informing us that Logue and his wife traveled the world studying speech patterns; this may be interesting, but it does not specifically relate to his work with Prince Albert. Choice C presents another interesting tidbit, but knowing that Logue and King George VI remained lifelong friends is simply a nice side note; it is not the most relevant information about Logue. Choice E is another interesting tidbit of information, that Logue believed in humor and patience to help stutterers, but it is not useful or particularly relevant to the second paragraph overall.

32. B. The new sentence adds a particularly trenchant historical example of Prince Albert stuttering in a major public speech, and choice B correctly identifies that it would best be placed between sentences 5 and 6. Sentence 5 introduces the idea that stuttering impaired Albert's public speaking, and the new sentence gives a poignant example of that impairment. Sentence 6 continues this thought by recounting the various cures that Albert tried. Choice A incorrectly suggests placing the new information before sentence 5, but this would make no sense; it would place the example before the introductory information. Choice C suggests placing the information before sentence 7, but doing so would break up the logical flow of sentences 6 and 7 that ties together the unusual treatments (sentence 6) and how well they worked (sentence 7). Choice D suggests placing the information before sentence 8, which also makes no sense; sentence 8 explains how Albert came to the throne, and inserting this embarrassing Wembley speech from 11 years earlier would be quite misplaced in this location. Choice E, placing the new addition at the end of the paragraph, makes even less sense because sentence 9 gives information about the United Kingdom's entry into WWII and King George's successful speeches to the country. It would be very distracting to place a 1925 event after an event that occurred 14 years later.

33. C. The addition of a new sentence explaining that Queen Elizabeth is actually King George VI's daughter will add interest and a historical footnote to her father becoming such "a most improbable hero." If Albert had not become King George VI, his daughter would have never become Queen Elizabeth II, the longest-serving monarch in British history. The sentence should be added to elucidate this point to the many readers who are unaware that her ascension to the throne began with her father's sudden and improbable rise to become king, choice C. Choice A rightfully adds the sentence, but merely stating that Queen Elizabeth is more famous now than her father does not relate to his being such an improbable hero and, therefore, to her also being an even more improbable ruler. Ruling the British Empire was not her destiny until her uncle unexpectedly abdicated the throne. Choice B also votes for including the sentence, but the reasons it cites are irrelevant; yes, Queen Elizabeth is indeed extremely popular with her subjects, but that does not relate to her father's improbable rise to power. Additionally, choice B includes an incorrect absolute word, indicating that "everyone" knows this fact. Choice D wrongly votes against adding the sentence. It may be true that mentioning Queen Elizabeth is not relevant to her father's stuttering, but the question asks what would be an "interesting piece of historical information" that ties in to King George being an "improbable hero." It is precisely that improbable rise to power that makes the long rule of his daughter relevant. Choice E is simply wrong; it *does* matter who Queen Elizabeth's father was, and adding the new sentence fulfills the writer's desire to include "interesting . . . historical information."

The draft referred to in questions 34–40 discusses some controversies in the initial design of the U.S. space shuttle.

34. C. This question asks you to find the one answer choice that is *not relevant* to be included in the first paragraph; therefore, on the contrary, all of the incorrect choices *would* make a relevant addition to the paragraph. A cost analysis of the manned booster, choice C, would be inappropriate to include because the manned booster idea was eventually scrapped; therefore, an additional *analysis* of its costs is a moot point.

We only need to know the bottom line, that it was too expensive, not the details of the analysis used to reach that conclusion. On the other hand, it would be appropriate to include an explanation of the difference between a manned booster and a manned orbiter (A) because those with little or no knowledge of the space shuttle or spacecraft may not understand these terms in the first place. Choice B, which suggests adding clarification of the tasks performed by the booster and orbiter, is also appropriate for the same reason as choice A; some readers may not otherwise understand the terminology. Choice D, explaining the technical difficulty of developing a manned booster, would be an applicable addition to the paragraph to help explain why it was too challenging for the program. Choice E, an overview of the development risk, like choice D, would be beneficial because it could help justify abandoning the idea of a manned booster.

35. **B.** When asked where to place a new sentence, examine the paragraph's overall organization, looking for an existing logical gap that the new sentence could fill. In this question, the new sentence that claims a fully reusable shuttle design would lower costs would best fit after sentence 2, choice B. The first sentence introduces that a debate existed regarding the design of the space shuttle, and bringing up lower cost at this point makes no sense, which makes choice A incorrect. Choice C, inserting the new sentence after sentence 3, also makes no sense because the third sentence transitions to the fact that one component of the fully reusable shuttle, the manned booster, would be physically too large and too expensive. It would be contradictory and disruptive to insert the new sentence here. Choice D, adding the new sentence at the end of the paragraph, would be equally illogical because sentence 4 explains the manned booster was abandoned; lower operating costs are irrelevant to an abandoned idea. Choice E suggests not adding the sentence at all; however, it is relevant to know why the fully reusable design was attractive in the first place, so the new sentence should be included in the paragraph, and the best location is after sentence 2.

36. **A.** As it is written, the underlined portion of sentence 6 is confusing; it is unclear how many solutions NASA considered to overcome the difficulty of lifting and accelerating the space shuttle. Choice A clears up this dilemma by presenting three succinct solutions: (1) redeveloping the existing Saturn rocket by simplifying its engines, OR (2) using one large single solid rocket, OR (3) using multiple smaller rockets. Choice B confuses the information about the Saturn rocket boosters by stating that redeveloping the current rocket is separate from redeveloping the Saturn's liquid-fuel engines; instead, simplifying the engines fulfills the redevelopment of the rocket itself. Choice C is wrong for two reasons: Like choice B, it confuses the information about the Saturn rocket's redevelopment; plus, it incorrectly uses the term "engaging" when it mentions one large solid rocket. Choice D likewise confuses the information about the Saturn rockets, separating redeveloping them from streamlining their engines, when the act of streamlining the engines completes the redevelopment. Choice E also makes the error of misrepresenting the redevelopment of the Saturn rocket into two tasks, and it adds more confusion by claiming one solution was "adding one large solid rocket," making it unclear whether or not that would be *in addition* to a preexisting rocket.

37. **C.** As the third paragraph is currently written, sentence 10 is unclear; it claims the solid-fuel booster rockets could be strapped to the external liquid fuel tank, which would be discarded after each launch, but then the sentence also claims the solid-fuel boosters would be reused. The reader can't help but wonder how that occurs. If how the booster rockets were reused, even though they were strapped to the external liquid fuel tank that was destroyed upon re-entry, choice C, were addressed properly, it would clear up the confusion. (Incidentally, the booster rockets separated from the external tank within minutes of liftoff and parachuted into the ocean for recovery, while the external tank was jettisoned later, after the shuttle had reached orbital altitude, and the tank then disintegrated upon re-entry.) Choice A is not a reasonable question to ask; reading between the lines allows one to realize that the external disposable tank had to stay attached to the shuttle until the shuttle was high enough to no longer need the fuel, and discarding it at such a great height would inevitably lead to the destruction of the external tank upon re-entry. Choice B brings up an accurate fact; the external tank did provide structural support for the shuttle and its booster rockets, but how it did so is not particularly relevant to the purpose of the third paragraph. Choice D is irrelevant to the paragraph; while it is interesting that the space shuttle was instrumental in delivering parts to the International Space Station, it is inconsequential to know how much its payload was increased due to the development of the external fuel tank. Choice E, what arguments supported carrying liquid fuel onboard, is entirely irrelevant because that idea was scrapped in early development.

38. **D.** Sentence 12, choice D, explicitly clarifies the writer's rationale for the decision to create a gliding shuttle. It claims "NASA ultimately axed the jet engines . . . and they decided on a purely gliding orbiter." Sentence 3 (A) is irrelevant to the decision to create a glider because it deals with the manned booster and the realization that it would be too large and expensive. It does not relate to the shuttle itself but rather to a method of getting it to its orbital altitude. Sentence 7 (B) relates to the decision to use two reusable solid-fuel booster rockets, which is irrelevant to the decision to make the shuttle a glider. Sentence 9 (C) relates to the advantage of using the external disposable tank that allowed for a larger payload, but it does not relate to the decision for a gliding shuttle. Sentence 13 (E) is the second-best option, but it only deals with the result of the decision to make the shuttle a glider, that astronauts would have to control the orbiter's re-entry, but it does not answer the question about clarifying the rationale for making that decision.

39. **E.** Sentence 12 would better explain the relevance of mentioning the X-15 if it were to connect it to the final shuttle design, and choice E does that by specifically explaining that the X-15 provided proof that a vehicle could re-enter the atmosphere and glide to a precision landing, which is exactly what the shuttle was designed to do. All of the other answer choices bring up true facts about the X-15, but they are not relevant to this specific question. Choice A merely identifies the X-15 as a hypersonic rocket-powered aircraft, but that does not explain its relevance. Choice B tells us that the X-15 set speed and altitude records, but that does not connect it to the space shuttle. Choice C provides the interesting notion that the X-15's data were used in other aircraft and spacecraft designs, including the shuttle, but that alone does not make it particularly relevant. Choice D is the least relevant of the answer choices, simply letting us know that the X-15 was the first flight test program to use flight simulators. Remember that the question asks which of the answer choices most clearly relates the X-15 to the space shuttle, and choice E provides the best connection.

40. **B.** To answer this question, remember the focus of the passage as a whole, which briefly summarizes some of the debates over the initial design of the space shuttle, ending with NASA's final decisions to use an external fuel tank and two solid-rocket boosters and make the shuttle an unpowered glider for re-entry. Knowing that NASA had actually reviewed 29 potential designs, choice B, would be relevant to this discussion because it would give greater importance to the wide-ranging process of designing the shuttle. The alternate answer choices are not nearly as relevant. Choice A is interesting because it informs of some of the space shuttle's future accomplishments, but those feats take place after the initial design was chosen and do not relate to the passage as a whole, which instead discusses the shuttle's initial design. Choice C, which brings up the disastrous end of the *Challenger* shuttle, is completely off topic; this catastrophe surely affected future designs of the shuttle, but not its original design. Choice D is equally off topic; the vertical launch indeed resembles a conventional rocket, but that has nothing to do with the subject of this passage. Choice E is barely relevant; while it is true that if NASA and the Air Force did not determine the need for the shuttle in the first place, it would not have been built, why would the passage need that information? It does not add anything of substance.

The draft referred to in questions 41–45 discusses people's perceptions about public speakers who cry.

41. **D.** The writer wants to include a new opening line, a question that helps build suspense and pique the reader's curiosity, so the correct answer must have more than a dry recitation of the facts. Choice D is the best choice because it does entice one to read on and understand more about why crying people seem so believable. The passage immediately addresses that we feel public speakers' crying "is a sign of sincerity, a display of authentic feeling." While all of the other choices are correctly formed as questions, most simply restate an aspect that is mentioned in the argument; none goes beyond to build suspense and pique curiosity. Choice A, that wonders why our instincts are often wrong, might seem attractive at first. Indeed, the passage explains why our instinct when seeing public speakers cry can be inaccurate, but this answer choice incorrectly pluralizes the word "instincts" and, therefore, suggests that it applies to other situations in which our instincts may indeed be reliable. Choice B merely wonders how we should react when faced with a crying public speaker, an idea that does not pinpoint the main idea of the passage. Instead of dealing with our reaction, the passage deals with opening our mind to the possibility that conflicting emotions are likely being felt by the speaker. Choice C goes off track by questioning why we should trust *any* public speaker, not just someone who cries; this passage is not about whether or not we can trust any speaker. Choice E is overly broad; the argument is about realizing that public speakers who cry have conflicted emotions, not whether or not we can judge true emotions.

42. **C.** This question calls for a transition between the idea in sentence 3, about someone losing control or breaking down into tears, and the false conclusion in sentence 4, that it must be an indication of truly felt, deep emotions. Choice C provides the best transition, by pointing out that this is a misinterpretation and also by postulating an alternative explanation, namely that "other strong emotions" may have triggered the crying. Choice A is incorrect because it merely restates the false conclusion of sentence 4, that "the person is telling the truth." Choice B does not provide a transition; rather, by reversing the stated conclusion and exaggerating it (the speaker has something shameful to hide), it contradicts sentence 4. Choice D is yet another restatement of the false conclusion in sentence 4; it does not provide a transition between the two sentences. Choice E, in stating that "breaking down into tears is something that a speaker cannot control," simply rephrases sentence 3, which claims, "we tend to think the speaker is 'losing control.'" This statement also does not provide a transition to sentence 4.

43. **C.** Choice C makes the point most effectively because it emphasizes the meaning of "however" by adding "quite to the contrary" and adding that the result of the scientific research is "unexpected." Choice A, which leaves the underlined portion as originally written, is not bad, but it does not address the writer's potential desire to make the point *more* effective. The idea in choice B, "suggests a *somewhat* different conclusion," is actually weaker than the original, which states *entirely* different." Choices D and E also present weaker statements because they both delete the word "entirely." Additionally, choice D uses the weak phrase "could suggest," while choice E merely states "might advocate."

44. **D.** The question requires that you understand the overall topic of the passage before choosing the strongest criticism of the third paragraph's development. Because the passage discusses our reaction to public speakers who cry, choice D presents the strongest criticism of the third paragraph because it directly attacks how the examples that are provided do not apply. The passage is about public speakers' crying, but the examples in this paragraph are not about public speakers; instead, they present a mother crying at her daughter's wedding and a mourner crying at a funeral. Choice A incorrectly claims the third paragraph contradicts the previous paragraphs, but it does not. Its first sentence does suggest a different conclusion about crying, but that cannot, by itself, represent the whole paragraph. Choice B is unreasonable; the proof provided by scientific research does not have to be presented in order for it to be believable. If the scientific research is reasonable enough to follow, it does not require detailed proof in the passage. Choice C is irrelevant; it is true that the instances of the mother and mourner are common enough, but that does not represent a criticism of the paragraph as it relates to the passage overall. Choice E is unreasonable; the paragraph is not hard to follow, although its examples are not applicable to the passage, and it does provide ample explanatory logic, especially in sentences 5 and 6.

45. **B.** This essay already includes a conclusion, albeit a brief one, and this question asks you to make it stronger. Choice B meets this task well; it includes several ideas from the passage, specifying that we should distrust our natural inclinations when we observe crying public speakers and concluding with a strong statement that we should "use our intellect to try to understand . . . conflicting emotions." Choice A contradicts the intent of the passage by stating that "most people believe that crying public speakers are telling the truth." Choice C does include the concept of questioning cultural beliefs, but that alone does not make for a strong conclusion, and its final phrase is particularly weak. Choice D is too simple, merely asserting that we must reassess our cultural beliefs to avoid being led astray from scientific research, and it incorrectly includes the absolute word "always." Likewise, choice E uses the same incorrect absolute word "always" and feebly asserts that we must "reserve judgment" when listening to a public speaker, but it ignores too many of the ideas in the passage; it fails to mention our incorrect assumptions about people crying, or the scientific evidence, or the idea of mixed, conflicting emotions.

Section II: Free-Response Questions

Question 1

Row A: Thesis (0–1 point)	
Scoring Criteria	
0 points for any of the following: • Having no defendable thesis. • Only restating the prompt in the thesis. • Only summarizing the issue with no apparent or coherent claim in the thesis. • Presenting a thesis that does not address the prompt.	**1 point for** • Addressing the prompt with a defendable thesis.
Decision Rules and Scoring Notes	
Theses that do not earn this point • Only restate the prompt. • Are vague or do not take a position. • Equivocate or merely summarize others' arguments. • Simply state obvious facts rather than making a defendable claim.	**Theses that do earn this point** • Respond to the prompt (rather than restating it) <u>and</u> clearly take a position about how accurately political polls reflect the views of a population instead of simply stating pros and cons.
Additional Notes • The thesis may be one or more sentences that are in close proximity to each other anywhere in the essay. • A thesis that meets the criteria can be awarded the point whether or not the rest of the response successfully conveys that line of reasoning. • For a thesis to be defendable, the sources must have at least minimal evidence that could be used as support. • A thesis may present a line of reasoning, but it is not required to earn a point.	

Row B: Evidence AND Commentary (0–4 points)				
Scoring Criteria				
0 points for	**1 point for**	**2 points for**	**3 points for**	**4 points for**
• Simply repeating the thesis (if present). • **OR** restating provided information. • **OR** providing fewer than two references to the provided sources.	• Providing evidence from at least two of the provided sources. • **AND** summarizing the evidence without explaining how the evidence supports the thesis.	• Providing evidence from or references to at least three of the provided sources. • **AND** explaining how some of the evidence relates to the thesis, but the line of reasoning may be nonexistent or faulty.	• Providing specific evidence from or references to at least three of the provided sources to support all claims in the line of reasoning. • **AND** explaining how some of the evidence relates to the thesis and supports the line of reasoning.	• Providing specific evidence from or references to at least three of the provided sources to support all claims in the line of reasoning. • **AND** consistently and explicitly explaining how the evidence relates to the thesis and supports the line of reasoning.

continued

Decision Rules and Scoring Notes				
Typical responses that earn 0 points:	**Typical responses that earn 1 point:**	**Typical responses that earn 2 points:**	**Typical responses that earn 3 points:**	**Typical responses that earn 4 points:**
• Are unclear or fail to address the prompt. • May present mere opinion or repeat ideas from a single source.	• Only summarize or describe sources instead of providing specific details.	• Mix specific details with broad generalities. • May contain simplistic, inaccurate, or repetitive explanations that do not strengthen the argument. • Fail to explain the connections between claims and to establish a clear line of reasoning. • May make one point well but fail to adequately support any other claims.	• Consistently offer evidence to support all claims. • Focus on the importance of specific words and details from the sources to build an argument. • Use multiple supporting claims to organize an argument and line of reasoning. • May not integrate some evidence or support a key claim in the commentary.	• Consistently offer evidence to support all claims. • Focus on the importance of specific words and details from the sources to build an argument. • Organize, integrate, and thoroughly explain evidence from sources throughout in order to support the line of reasoning.

Additional Notes

• Writing that suffers from grammatical and/or mechanical errors that interfere with communication cannot earn the fourth point in this row.

Row C: Sophistication (0–1 point)	
Scoring Criteria	
0 points for	**1 point for**
• Not meeting the criteria for 1 point.	• Exhibiting sophistication of thought and/or advancing a complex understanding of the rhetorical situation.
Decision Rules and Scoring Notes	
Responses that do not earn this point:	**Responses that earn this point demonstrate one (or more) of the following:**
• Try to contextualize their argument, but make predominantly sweeping generalizations (*"Throughout all history . . ."* OR *"Everyone believes . . ."*). • Only hint at other possible arguments (*"Some may think . . ."*). • Present complicated or complex sentences or language that is ineffective and detracts from the argument.	• Present a nuanced argument that consistently identifies and examines complexities or tension across the sources. • Illuminate the significance or implications of the argument (either the student's argument or the arguments within the sources) within a broader context. • Make effective rhetorical choices that consistently strengthen the force and impact of the student's argument. • Develop a prose style that is especially vivid, persuasive, resounding, or appropriate to the student's argument.

Additional Notes

• This point should be awarded only if the demonstration of sophistication or complex understanding is part of the argument, not merely a phrase or brief reference.

High-Scoring Essay

In modern elections, candidates are under constant pressure to stay in the public eye. Long gone are the days when candidates would traverse the country by train, for instance, visiting city after city on a pre-set itinerary. To be competitive today, candidates for national office must crisscross the country many times; their image must be seen and heard relentlessly. One factor that helps modern candidates and their managers decide what route to travel and which issues to highlight is the modern political poll. Recall the 2016 presidential election in the final weeks and days before the voting. Hillary Clinton and Donald Trump traversed the country, showing up at carefully planned rallies to muster more support. Both the locations and attendees were carefully chosen, based on the most up-to-date poll information about likely voters and their ballot choices. Attaining success in any close political contest is difficult; candidates must utilize many voting tactics, and no tactic is more prevalent, albeit less precise, than political polls. These polls theoretically provide candidates with an accurate assessment of public opinion. Unfortunately, political polls tend to be unreliable; their results are sometimes intentionally skewed; they yield inaccurate information and provide a poor indicator of public opinion.

Designed to ascertain general public opinion by querying a small number of individuals, then multiplying the individual's answers to project a population's opinion, polls inherently rely upon statistics. However, Benjamin Disraeli, the famous British Prime Minister, succinctly stated, "'there are three kinds of lies: lies, damned lies, and statistics'" (Source B). Common sense indicates that polls should be taken with the proverbial grain of salt; polls often display a specific margin of error, an explicit admission of fallibility. Unfortunately, far too many rely on the results of polls while ignoring their potential inaccuracies. Perhaps this stems from mankind's tendency to "trust numbers" as if they are facts that are actually true. Ramesh Ponnuru, in a book review, commented that "reporters lean on polls because they provide the illusion of numerical certainty" (Source F). Indeed, this "illusion" also persuades the public to rely on and trust in polls, simply because they appear to be so accurate. But when the logic behind any political poll is faulty, the integrity of the poll's results is compromised.

Often a poll's accuracy is compromised by its authors. The intentional skewing of questions and audiences is a significant factor that adversely affects a poll's results. For example, identical questions pertaining to Ross Perot's platform resulted in a 40 percent variance between answers when the questions were subtly reworded (Source B). Unfortunately, polls suffer from a "unique set of disadvantages" (Source D). According to Source D, polls' accuracy falls prey to "The Leading Option," plus sampling errors and selection bias. Naturally, those who conduct and write polls are extremely aware of these ways to skew the results and use these techniques to their advantage. Polls exhibiting the aforementioned faults provide inaccurate information for a variety of reasons, only one of which is antagonizing the respondent. "Because many polls are conducted over the phone, consumers are more able to block or dismiss unknown calls. A Vanderbilt survey found that "response rates to robocalls are abysmal" (Source E).

While the published poll results attempt to appear "fair and balanced," for instance, by revealing the number of people polled and what part of the country they live in, the public rarely thinks about the important questions one needs to know about any given poll before judging its accuracy. The public needs to question who wrote the poll, who administered it and under what conditions, how many people were sampled at what time of day, how many questions the poll had, what order they were given in, etc. Regrettably, we do not take the time to even think of these questions, let alone search out the answers; we just accept the numbers.

The advent of modern technology has increasingly enabled target audiences to elude pollsters. Caller ID and answering machines enable people to circumvent time-consuming political polls (Source C), therefore reducing the potential variety of opinions from those who do respond. Additionally, pollsters find that it takes seven calls to find one participant who is "willing to spend the 20 minutes or so it takes to answer his polling questions" (Source C), thus further compromising a poll's accuracy. Similar to the number of people who have opinions about governmental matters but do not take the time to write letters to the editor of their local newspaper, those who do not answer the phone when approached by a pollster can add to the inaccuracy of a poll merely by keeping their opinions to themselves.

Polls are ubiquitous in national publications; however, their value is debatable. Source E asks "Are polls accurate? Poll results can seem inconsistent because the business of polling is diverse." However, "A Bloomberg survey seems to confirm that, during the 2016 political cycle campaign, polls have been reliable" (Source E).

Perhaps the promise and pitfalls of polling are most aptly summarized by Lee Morgan: "While they often prove to be useful in determining outcomes of elections or persuading politicians or business owners to take a particular action on an issue, the public opinion poll is a flawed process that has its own unique set of disadvantages" (Source D). A long track record of unreliability, perpetuated by inherent flaws in the creation and administration of polls, has consistently yielded inaccurate data, thus making polls a poor representation of a population's opinion.

(917 words)

Analysis of the High-Scoring Essay

This essay is praiseworthy for its development and its thoughtful discussion of the role that political polls play in American elections. The introductory paragraph successfully juxtaposes the campaigns of "long gone" elections with the tactics of contemporary politicians. Although this comparison is apt, the presentation could be a bit stronger in drawing connections; as it is, the AP Exam Reader must implicitly understand the student's point. The thesis follows: "Although candidates in modern elections must rely heavily on political polls, these polls do not provide an accurate assessment of the populace's opinions." Because the essay includes a defendable thesis, it earns a point in Row A.

Next, in discussing the reliability of polls, the essay skillfully includes both the humorous quotation from Disraeli and the interesting notion that numbers seem so trustworthy to humanity. This idea is a fascinating one that helps capture the Reader's attention. This idea points out one of the underlying reasons why polls are trusted by politicians and the public alike, which demonstrates that this student is incorporating more than just the information in the sources. This paragraph synthesizes the sources well, presenting more than one reference in the same paragraph to advance the student's points.

The third paragraph discusses the ways in which polls can elicit inaccurate information, based on examples from the sources. Clearly this student understands the problematic nature of polls and data gathering. The student also presents information appropriately and uses logical reasoning to demonstrate a good grasp of human psychology.

Next, the essay explores an additional factor that contributes to inaccurate poll results. This fourth paragraph focuses on the fact that many people simply avoid responding to polls; this factor alone indicates that polls cannot represent all people's opinions. In the sixth paragraph, with the example of those who never write letters to the editor, the student makes an appropriate analogy to those who have opinions but never share them. Then the student extends this logic to show that the accuracy of polls is diminished with fewer respondents. The thinking is sound and the presentation valid.

By the seventh paragraph, this essay seems to lose some of the energy and forcefulness of the beginning paragraphs, almost as if the student is both running out of steam and running out of time to develop ideas thoroughly. This paragraph has only four sentences, and it's hard to understand how they connect. The Reader wonders where the student got the idea about polls being "ubiquitous" in national publications and what connection that has to the inaccurate poll predictions in the recent elections. If the student were to have expanded this paragraph and explored the controversies of the elections in more depth, this paragraph would have more to offer. As written, it falls flat. Overall, however, the evidence and commentary are strong enough to earn 4 points in Row B.

The concluding paragraph neatly summarizes the essay. Adding the quotation from Source D works well, as it precisely fits the student's thesis. The Reader may wish the essay's conclusion would have had more to offer than a recapitulation of the essay's main ideas, but again, this issue is most likely due to the limited time, not the student's inability to think. However, overall, the essay is consistently on topic, decently organized, well developed, and appropriate in its use of language. The writing is not strong enough throughout the essay to earn a point in Row C, although the essay as a whole does deserve a high score of 5.

Medium-Low-Scoring Essay

In the United States, where politics is heavily bank-rolled, political races are tight, and (in the presidential election) the victor becomes the world's most powerful man, candidates seek every advantage. Polls are regarded as a source of information regarding potential voters. After subscribing to a political poll, parties will attempt to tailor their campaigns to reach voters who indicated they were disaffected on the poll. Thus, political campaigns consider polls to be valuable assets that indicate a population's opinion. Unfortunately for the political parties, polls have proved to be unreliable indicators of opinion; effectively rendering them useless.

One major fault of the polls is that they are misleading. According to Source B, a statistics textbook, "survey questions can be worded to elicit . . . desired response[s]." Important factors such as diction and the order of the statements in the question can heavily affect the response. For example, Ross Perot asked, "'should the president have the line item veto to eliminate waste?'" 97 percent of respondents said "yes" (Source B). Conversely when the same question was rephrased to "'should the president have a line item veto, or not?'" only 57 percent of respondents indicated "yes" (Source B). The big difference between the first poll's results and the second's (which asked essentially the same question) indicate that polls are unreliable because of their intentional loaded questions.

Polls are designed by experts in order to establish accurate information. According to Source D, "the public opinion poll is a flawed process that has its own unique set of disadvantages." Also, "one major disadvantage of public opinion polling is the tendency of the person taking the survey to go with "the leading option" (Source D). In addition, "there is usually a disclaimer that lets the viewer know that there is a plus or minus 3 percent margin of error . . . but there is no solid way to tell just how big the error margin is" (Source D). Another problem happens when "Selection bias happens when the people intentionally selected to take part in a poll may not be representative of the entire population" (Source D).

Rather than providing a public service, polls actually limit the infusion of new ideas into society. Source F states that because initial reactions to reform are almost always negative, early polls will present reform as "unpopular" and ultimately "interfere with the formation of public opinion."

Polls do not accurately reflect a population's views for a variety of reasons. First, polls are filled with loaded questions designed to trick the participant and elicit a wrong answer. Secondly, polls suffer from a variety of handicaps such as sampling bias, interview bias, and wording bias. Finally, polls are often used improperly, clouding the true intentions of the poll's subject. Thus, it is fair to conclude that polls do not provide an accurate representation of the population's opinions.

(477 words)

Analysis of the Medium-Low-Scoring Essay

This essay attempts to present an adequate response to the prompt but suffers from simplistic thinking and presentation. In the first paragraph, the student establishes a thesis, that political polls are "useless" and "unreliable indicators of public opinion," which is sufficient to earn a point in Row A. However, the writing demonstrates numerous errors that begin to distract the AP Exam Reader. The first sentence contains a subject-verb error: "politics is bank-rolled." The second sentence includes odd and repetitive diction that essentially says nothing, such as, "Polls are regarded as a source of information regarding potential voters." The third sentence displays additional problems with diction: First, political parties do not "subscribe" to polls; second, the phrase "disaffected on the poll" is simply inaccurate and inexact language. The fourth sentence has no grammatical or diction errors, but the final sentence uses the semicolon inappropriately. The Reader is left with a fairly disappointing introduction, so the first impression of this essay is not a strong one. The student takes a stand, claiming that political polls are "useless," but failed to provide any details to back it up.

The second paragraph is adequate, but only in restating the facts in Source B. Basically, this paragraph paraphrases Source B but offers no strong ideas that help prove the student's thesis. It does make the point that diction and the order of questions can affect responses to polls, but that information is already in the source. The paragraph would be stronger if the student were to integrate more sources and develop more analytical ideas. Unfortunately, as it reads now, the paragraph is undeveloped and overly simplistic.

The third paragraph gets off to a bad start with an unsubstantiated assumption that the goal of polls is, in fact, to design ones that elicit "accurate information." However, this idea contradicts this essay's overall point, that polls are "useless." The student seems to ignore the first sentence in this paragraph and continues to paraphrase Source D, pointing out the many ways in which polls can be misleading. This paragraph, just like the previous one, would be much stronger were it to contain additional ideas, incorporated from more sources, and more insightful analysis from the student.

The fourth paragraph, containing only two sentences, presents an underdeveloped idea: Polls tend to limit the spread of new ideas in a society. The student basically copies the information in Source F, and the paragraph ends clumsily. The Reader cannot avoid the impression that the student felt compelled to produce five paragraphs, focusing a body paragraph on one of the sources, but by now was running out of time. The evidence and commentary is adequate enough to warrant 2 points in Row B.

The essay finishes with a simplistic summary of the three body paragraphs; it displays no new insights. Overall, the entire essay is held back from a higher score by the continual lack of analytical depth. The essay would be more impressive if the student were to actually synthesize the information in the sources and then present a more engaging argument.

This essay clearly demonstrates the oversimplification that is typical of medium- to low-scoring essays, and it does not earn a point in Row C. Remember, the synthesis essay offers students an open opportunity to truly demonstrate how they think and how well they interact with the world. Every student should try to seize this opportunity and present well-developed ideas in a sophisticated manner. The extra effort will be rewarded with a higher score than this sample essay earns, which currently stands at an overall score of 3.

Question 2

Row A: Thesis (0–1 point)	
Scoring Criteria	
0 points for any of the following: • Having no defendable thesis. • Only restating the prompt in the thesis. • Only summarizing the issue with no apparent or coherent claim in the thesis. • Presenting a thesis that does not address the prompt.	**1 point for** • Addressing the prompt with a defendable thesis that analyzes the writer's rhetorical choices.
Decision Rules and Scoring Notes	
Theses that do not earn this point • Only restate the prompt. • Neglect to address the writer's rhetorical choices. • Simply describe or repeat the passage rather than making a defendable claim.	**Theses that do earn this point** • Respond to the prompt (rather than restating it) and clearly articulate a defendable thesis exploring how Updike's rhetorical strategies convey an audience's attitude toward sporting events.
Additional Notes • The thesis may be one or more sentences that are in close proximity to each other anywhere in the essay. • A thesis that meets the criteria can be awarded the point whether or not the rest of the response successfully conveys that line of reasoning. • For a thesis to be defendable, the passage must have at least minimal evidence that could be used as support. • A thesis may present a line of reasoning, but it is not required to earn a point.	

Row B: Evidence AND Commentary (0–4 points)

Scoring Criteria

0 points for	1 point for	2 points for	3 points for	4 points for
• Simply repeating the thesis (if present). • **OR** restating provided information. • **OR** providing mostly irrelevant and/or incoherent evidence.	• Summarizing the passage without reference or connection to the thesis. • **OR** providing mostly general evidence. • **AND** providing little or no explanation or commentary.	• Providing some specific evidence that is relevant to the thesis. • **AND** explaining how some of the evidence relates to the thesis, but the line of reasoning may be nonexistent or faulty.	• Providing specific evidence to support all claims in the line of reasoning. • **AND** explaining how some of the evidence relates to the thesis and supports the line of reasoning. • **AND** explaining how at least one rhetorical choice in the passage contributes to the writer's thesis.	• Providing specific evidence to support all claims in the line of reasoning. • **AND** providing well-developed commentary that consistently and explicitly explains the relationship between the evidence and the thesis. • **AND** explaining how multiple rhetorical choices in the passage contribute to the writer's thesis.

Decision Rules and Scoring Notes

Typical responses that earn 0 points:	**Typical responses that earn 1 point:**	**Typical responses that earn 2 points:**	**Typical responses that earn 3 points:**	**Typical responses that earn 4 points:**
• Are unclear or fail to address the prompt. • May present mere opinion with little or no evidence.	• Only summarize or restate ideas from the passage without any analysis. • May mention rhetorical devices with little or no explanation or analysis.	• Mix specific details with broad generalities. • May contain simplistic, inaccurate, or repetitive explanations that do not strengthen the argument. • Fail to explain the connections between claims and to establish a clear line of reasoning. • May make one point well but fail to adequately support any other claims.	• Consistently offer evidence to support all claims. • Focus on the importance of specific words and details from the passage to build an argument. • Use multiple supporting claims to organize an argument and line of reasoning. • May not integrate some evidence or support a key claim in the commentary.	• Consistently offer evidence to support all claims. • Focus on the importance of specific words and details from the passage to build an argument. • Use multiple supporting claims with adequate evidence and explanation to organize an argument and line of reasoning. • Explain how the writer's use of rhetorical devices contributes to the student's analysis of the passage.

continued

Additional Notes

• Writing that suffers from grammatical and/or mechanical errors that interfere with communication cannot earn the fourth point in this row.

Row C: Sophistication (0–1 point)

Scoring Criteria	
0 points for	**1 point for**
• Not meeting the criteria for 1 point.	• Exhibiting sophistication of thought and/or advancing a complex understanding of the rhetorical situation.

Decision Rules and Scoring Notes	
Responses that do not earn this point:	**Responses that earn this point demonstrate one (or more) of the following:**
• Try to contextualize the text, but make predominantly sweeping generalizations (*"Throughout all history . . ."* OR *"Everyone believes . . ."*). • Only hint at other possible arguments (*"Some may think . . ."*). • Examine individual rhetorical choices but fail to examine the relationships among varying choices throughout the passage. • Oversimplify textual complexities. • Present complicated or complex sentences or language that is ineffective and detracts from the argument.	• Explain the purpose or function of complexities or tension in the passage. • Explain the significance of the writer's rhetorical choices for the given rhetorical situation. • Develop a prose style that is especially vivid, persuasive, resounding, or appropriate to the student's argument.

Additional Notes

• This point should be awarded only if the demonstration of sophistication or complex understanding is part of the argument, not merely a phrase or brief reference.

High-Scoring Essay

In this passage, John Updike's juxtaposition of two central metaphors, combined with his occasional bellicose diction, allows him to emphasize the vicissitudes and the simple grandeur of baseball and the game's ability to reveal our humanity. Symbolic of our life and love, baseball offers prospective liberation along with possible disillusionment.

Both the monster and romance metaphors are used throughout the passage, creating a sense of continuity and allowing the author to thematically connect all the elements—from opening day to the action of the field to the real significance of the passage. Phrases like "its monstrous big heart," "act of faith," and "the first kiss of another prolonged entanglement" sustain imagery that the monster is altogether human and thus forgiving and loving. The contrast of the typical monster and the one portrayed as the "Fenway Faithful" not only adds interest to the piece, but also mirrors the roller coaster ride experienced by the fans. From "Supersox" to "dreadful days," the metaphors' inherent contrasts allow Updike to emphasize the same in the hearts of the fans. The author relies on us to draw upon our own life experiences, as we know romance, too, is full of disagreements and perfect moments, of triumphs and disappointments, truly a "hard lesson for a hungry monster to master." And yet, by the end of the passage, the author recognizes the simple beauty of baseball. Updike implies the innocent joy and magnificence in the way these "twenty-five youngish men" manipulate the hearts of fans. Indeed, it is so much like a romance, with its simplicity and complexity, perfectly summed up in the words, "You'll never get us to care again." However, Updike's voice clearly implies the opposite, that this game of love and hate will continue.

Indeed, the author seems to use the game of baseball as a microcosm of the outside world. His use of warlike diction elevates the game to a near life-or-death struggle. A four-game sweep by the Yankees becomes a "massacre"; a winning streak becomes a "mini-resurrection"; and players seem to be "Civil War memorial[s]" who are fighting for a "Noble Lost Cause" in "Zimmer's last stand." Interestingly enough, this supposed struggle between life and death that is fought out on the baseball diamond ultimately turns into Updike's commentary on life itself. For, in reality, it is not war, but instead, to quote the manager Zimmer, "This is fun." Ultimately, his metaphors using the monster and romance only seek to simplify the relationship between the game and the fans. Like baseball, life, the author implies, should be fun at its core element, stripped of "solemn money men . . . scruffy media cameramen and sour-faced reporters." It is, in the end, a game of "innumerable potential redemptions and curious disappointments." In our attempts to understand, influence, and record these vicissitudes, perhaps Updike's intention is to leave us with some sense of the here and now. Perhaps it's best that we just jeer, holler, boo, and cheer as we enjoy ourselves in the sun. Perhaps that special moment is a little of what that "many-headed monster" feels that makes it come back again and again.

(523 words)

Analysis of the High-Scoring Essay

This essay does an excellent job of addressing the topic. It thoroughly explores metaphors and the connotation of Updike's "warlike diction," showing in the process how these elements create not only Updike's attitude toward baseball, but toward life itself. The introduction clearly tells the AP Exam Reader what to expect and ends with a graceful statement of how baseball symbolizes life. Updike would agree that this student truly comprehends his point, and its defendable thesis earns a point in Row A.

The first body paragraph examines the monster and romance metaphors, showing how the two are intricately connected. The student offers ample examples of each and then ties them together with appropriate logic and interesting ideas. The student makes noteworthy points about how Updike relies on his audience to connect his ideas about baseball to their own life experiences, which we will find to be "full of disagreements and perfect moments, of triumphs and disappointments. . . ." The student's poise in using parallelism in this sentence also demonstrates his or her polish as a writer, which a Reader will certainly notice and appreciate. The student's final idea in this paragraph, that baseball is a "game of love and hate" that "will continue," serves effectively not only as a clinching sentence to this paragraph but also as a transition to the next paragraph, which explores the author's diction.

The second body paragraph scrutinizes how Updike's diction, especially the references to war, emphasizes the "life-or-death struggle" of the game. The student presents virtually every example of "warlike diction" that the excerpt offers but does not stop at merely listing them. He or she makes a larger point about how this diction helps establish Updike's attitude: that although it may seem like war on the baseball diamond, it is really just a game played for fun. The student has a good perspective on language analysis and on life itself. The quality of the evidence and commentary are sufficient to earn 3 points in Row B.

Overall, this essay covers the topic very well; it is organized logically and develops ideas substantially. The student also demonstrates a very nice flair for language, as witnessed in the use of parallelism (notice it not only in the first body paragraph, as previously noted, but also in the closing two sentences with the repetition of the word "Perhaps . . ."). The student's sentence structure is varied, vocabulary is sophisticated, and a sense of rhythm is present. These strengths throughout the essay warrant a point in Row C. This essay indeed deserves a high score of 5.

Medium-Scoring Essay

The author's use of the monster metaphor allows him to paint the fans as having similar hopes and reactions to the Boston Red Sox's at times rocky season.

By incorporating the monster metaphor throughout the passage, the author calls the fans both hopeful and disappointed. He writes that last years team had broken its "monstrous big heart," and that showing up was "an act of faith." Clearly, the fans cannot help but come back and watch the Boston Red Sox, despite the multitude of horrifying disappointments, often at the hands of the Yankees. "Monsters," the author writes, "have short memories, elastic hearts, and very foolable faculties." The fans, interestingly, in all their differences, have a singular attitude and wish that unites them. It is this wish for the Boston Red Sox to win that enables the author to group these people into an entity, what he calls the "many-headed monster." What is the focus of much of the passage, however, is a description of the fundamental essence of the game of baseball.

It is decidedly from a baseball fans point of view. It is focused on the fun of baseball, how little things within the game bring so much enjoyment and pleasure. It is, to this author, more than just a game of baseball, but rather a celebration of life and an atmosphere. As the author writes, "Monsters love high notes and hoards of gold," referring to "The Star-Spangled Banner" performance and the governor's appearance. The fans, represented as a whole by the monster, love everything about the atmosphere of baseball. From the pure essence of "statistical virginity" to the manager, "last year's anti-hero," the fans love the effect it has on their lives. They keep coming back, it makes no difference because of the elevation of baseball to a more important level—a staple of their lives. The author may be saying to us that the wonderfulness of baseball is, in itself, good enough.

(325 words)

Analysis of the Medium-Scoring Essay

This essay essentially attempts to tackle the topic but does not accomplish much more than paraphrasing the original passage. The student recognizes that Updike uses a metaphor, but there is little else in this essay that is praiseworthy. The introduction/thesis is somewhat vague. For example, when the student writes that the fans have "similar hopes and reactions," the AP Exam Reader wonders exactly what they are similar to; are they similar to the "rocky season"? A clearer thesis statement would certainly help this essay.

The first body paragraph identifies the monster metaphor and correctly identifies that it represents the baseball audience, but the student offers no strong analysis of that metaphor. Instead, the student paraphrases Updike: Yes, the fans are "both hopeful and disappointed"; yes, the fans come back to watch over and over; yes, the fans have a "singular . . . wish that unites them," but the student merely lists these ideas and never analyzes how Updike's metaphor establishes his attitude. It is not convincing to merely state the attitude and drop in a quotation or two from the author. However, in this paragraph, the writer does produce a defendable thesis and earns a point in Row A.

The second body paragraph, too, is basically accurate in its paraphrasing of Updike; indeed, to Updike the game is a "celebration of life." However, once again, the student offers little more than a string of quotations and examples of the behavior and attitude of fans from the passage. For a stronger essay, the student needs to have a reason for presenting all of this information, an analytical point about how these examples work in this excerpt. The weak quality of the writer's commentary earns 2 points in Row B.

Also compounding the student's weak analytical skills is his or her weak command of written English. Apostrophe errors abound ("last years team had broken . . ." and "a baseball fans point of view," to name two), plus run-on sentences ("They keep coming back, it makes no difference . . .") and weak wording ("things," "the author writes," and so on) do not help demonstrate sophistication in the writing. Top-scoring essays address the topic, have clear organization, develop ideas thoroughly, and demonstrate strong control over written English. This essay simply does not show those traits, and it does not earn a point in Row C. It deserves an overall score of 3.

Question 3

Row A: Thesis (0–1 point)	
Scoring Criteria	
0 points for any of the following:	**1 point for**
• Having no defendable thesis. • Only restating the prompt in the thesis. • Only summarizing the issue with no apparent or coherent claim in the thesis. • Presenting a thesis that does not address the prompt.	• Addressing the prompt with a defendable thesis.

Decision Rules and Scoring Notes	
Theses that do not earn this point	**Theses that do earn this point**
• Only restate the prompt. • Are vague or do not take a position. • Simply state obvious facts rather than making a defendable claim.	• Respond to the prompt (rather than restating it) <u>and</u> clearly evaluate the accuracy of Thoreau's aphorism in modern society instead of simply stating pros and cons.
Additional Notes	
• The thesis may be one or more sentences that are in close proximity to each other anywhere in the essay. • A thesis that meets the criteria can be awarded the point whether or not the rest of the response successfully conveys that line of reasoning. • A thesis may present a line of reasoning, but it is not required to earn a point.	

Row B: Evidence AND Commentary (0–4 points)

Scoring Criteria				
0 points for	**1 point for**	**2 points for**	**3 points for**	**4 points for**
• Simply repeating the thesis (if present). • **OR** restating information. • **OR** providing mostly irrelevant and/or incoherent examples.	• Summarizing the passage without reference or connection to the thesis. • **OR** providing mostly general evidence. • **AND** providing little or no explanation or commentary.	• Providing some specific evidence that is relevant to the thesis. • **AND** explaining how some of the evidence relates to the thesis, but the line of reasoning may be nonexistent or faulty.	• Providing specific evidence to support all claims in the line of reasoning. • **AND** explaining how some of the evidence relates to the thesis and supports the line of reasoning.	• Providing specific evidence to support all claims in the line of reasoning. • **AND** providing well-developed commentary that consistently and explicitly explains the relationship between the evidence and the thesis.
Decision Rules and Scoring Notes				
Typical responses that earn 0 points:	**Typical responses that earn 1 point:**	**Typical responses that earn 2 points:**	**Typical responses that earn 3 points:**	**Typical responses that earn 4 points:**
• Are unclear or fail to address the prompt. • May present mere opinion with little or no relevant evidence.	• Only summarize or restate ideas from the passage without any analysis.	• Mix specific details with broad generalities. • May contain simplistic, inaccurate, or repetitive explanations that do not strengthen the argument. • Fail to explain the connections between claims and to establish a clear line of reasoning. • May make one point well but fail to adequately support any other claims.	• Consistently offer evidence to support all claims. • Focus on the importance of specific words and details to build an argument. • Use multiple supporting claims to organize an argument and line of reasoning. • May not integrate some evidence or support a key claim in the commentary.	• Engage specific evidence to draw conclusions. • Focus on the importance of specific details to build an argument. • Use multiple supporting claims with adequate evidence and explanation to organize an argument and line of reasoning.

continued

Additional Notes

• Writing that suffers from grammatical and/or mechanical errors that interfere with communication cannot earn the fourth point in this row.

Row C: Sophistication (0–1 point)	
Scoring Criteria	
0 points for	**1 point for**
• Not meeting the criteria for 1 point.	• Exhibiting sophistication of thought and/or advancing a complex understanding of the rhetorical situation.
Decision Rules and Scoring Notes	
Responses that do not earn this point:	Responses that earn this point demonstrate one (or more) of the following:
• Try to contextualize their argument, but make predominantly sweeping generalizations (*"Throughout all history . . ."* OR *"Everyone believes . . ."*). • Only hint at other possible arguments (*"Some may think . . ."*). • Present complicated or complex sentences or language that is ineffective and detracts from the argument.	• Present a nuanced argument that consistently identifies and examines complexities or tensions. • Illuminate the significance or implications of the argument (either the student's argument or an argument related to the prompt) within a broader context. • Make effective rhetorical choices that strengthen the force and impact of the student's argument. • Develop a prose style that is especially vivid, persuasive, resounding, or appropriate to the student's argument.

Additional Notes

• This point should be awarded only if the demonstration of sophistication or complex understanding is part of the argument, not merely a phrase or brief reference.

Medium-Scoring Essay

Henry David Thoreau aptly described the nature of mankind by expressing man's tendency to become lost in unimportant pursuits in today's society. Using fish as a symbol for what people believe they are searching for, Thoreau describes a problem of human nature which is seen in all of society: the problem of continually searching while not recognizing what one truly desires in life.

This problem is clouded by the confusing mist of appearances. This shroud hangs over what society has taught one to see as success: money, fancy cars, large houses, to name a few. In the pursuit of what society deems symbolic of success, one is trapped in the conflict of appearance versus reality. All too often someone craves a material object, only to find it boring shortly after it was acquired. This, of course, causes the person to want more possessions, always with the same result. This endless cycle continues, the result being dissatisfaction; as Thoreau might note, this person looks for still more fish, not knowing that fish will not satisfy.

This conflict leads only to the greater problem of getting lost in the race for success and losing sight of life's full meaning. In a society such as America, it is easy to forget that inner happiness cannot to be bought with material goods. With so many opportunities for one to flaunt wealth, it is not difficult to understand how people get caught up in trivial pursuits which do not satisfy their actual desire for success. The necessity to discern between needs and wants then becomes apparent within society. Today this confusion of true desire and false success is seen as the divorce rate increases, as drug abuse rises, as people continue to look for permanent happiness and inner success in temporary feelings and actions. Thoreau was accurate as he used this aphorism to describe human tendencies. Sad yet true, Thoreau's comment is still truthful in regard to the earnest search for false success.

(328 words)

Analysis of the Medium-Scoring Essay

This essay is concisely articulate in its exploration of Thoreau's aphorism in relation to modern society. It clearly takes a stand and buttresses it with discussion and examples, which earns a point in Row A. The student is not sidetracked into irrelevance and keeps the commentary specific.

The second paragraph presents its insights with a nice flair. Phrases such as "clouded by the confusing mist of appearances" and the "shroud [that] hangs over" are negative images appropriate to the student's assertions and reinforce the theme of the deceit of "success" as our society defines it. By returning to Thoreau's symbol of fish, the student completes the paragraph logically and effectively links it to the topic.

The third paragraph continues the philosophical discussion, adding additional relevant, contemporary examples and expanding the notion that people are never satisfied with what they have. Divorce and drugs are especially apt illustrations. The essay would be stronger if it included more such examples, but those used are convincing. As it is, the evidence and commentary are strong enough to earn 3 points in Row B.

Overall, the essay deserves a fairly high score because it is clearly on topic, is well organized, shows sufficient paragraph development, and demonstrates maturity in style, even if only sporadically. It would earn a higher score if it offered stronger evidence and development and used more precise language. The repetition of ideas is a problem, but one that is sometimes seen when writing on philosophical topics under time pressure. It does not earn a point in Row C. Overall, it should score a total of 4 points.

Low-Scoring Essay

Thoreau's quote relating to man's futile search for fish is applicable to modern society today. I think this quote especially relates to materialism, which is rampant within our greedy, American, self-centered society. Many values today revolve around selfishness and instant gratification, and the big picture of life isn't really seen. This drive for ownership and power and wealth often materializes itself in the mad rush to buy things. Credit cards only encourage this behavior, and the trip for the fish is not what they need. Materialism is a perfect example of this behavior, since many people feel the need to fill their lives with <u>something</u>, whether it's love or money or things. Thoreau sums up this observation about human nature so well, and this statement related not only to Thoreau's society, but to our society in modern America as well. The difference between needs and wants are easily confused, and those who are consumed by materialism cannot see the forest for the trees. I think Thoreau was reminding people not to forget what the important things in life are, and to express the importance of searching for what really matters in life, not settling for temporary things like material goods.

(200 words)

Analysis of the Low-Scoring Essay

This essay has some merit: It attempts to discuss the topic, and its semblance of a defendable thesis earns a point in Row A. The paragraph is acceptable and some of the points are relevant, but the essay falls short of thoroughly convincing the AP Exam Reader. The student's one-paragraph format leads to a rambling, unfocused result. It isn't necessarily the essay's ideas alone that lower the score but the presentation. The student uses pertinent examples from contemporary life, such as the use of credit cards and "materialism," but lapses into vague terms like "things."

The student should be commended for trying to connect the essay to Thoreau's "fish" aphorism, but that important connection should be incorporated more smoothly. For example, the sudden jump from "credit cards" to "fish" in the fifth sentence needs a transitional phrase so that the Reader can follow the student's argument. The quality of the commentary earns 2 points in Row B. In addition, demonstrating more sophisticated skills in the fundamentals of the essay form and more effective diction would significantly improve this essay. As written, it does not warrant a point in Row C, and it should earn an overall score of 3 points.

Scoring

Use the following worksheet to arrive at a probable final AP grade on Practice Exam 3. Because being objective enough to estimate your own essay score is sometimes difficult, you might give your essays (along with the sample essays) to a teacher, friend, or relative to score, if you feel confident that the individual has the knowledge necessary to make such a judgment and that he or she will feel comfortable doing so.

Section I: Multiple-Choice Questions

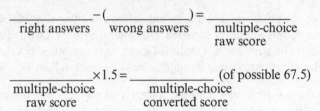

$$\underline{\hspace{3cm}} - (\underline{\hspace{3cm}}) = \underline{\hspace{3cm}}$$
right answers   wrong answers   multiple-choice
raw score

$$\underline{\hspace{3cm}} \times 1.5 = \underline{\hspace{3cm}} \text{ (of possible 67.5)}$$
multiple-choice   multiple-choice
raw score   converted score

Section II: Free-Response Questions

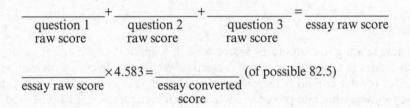

$$\underline{\hspace{2cm}} + \underline{\hspace{2cm}} + \underline{\hspace{2cm}} = \underline{\hspace{2cm}}$$
question 1   question 2   question 3   essay raw score
raw score   raw score   raw score

$$\underline{\hspace{3cm}} \times 4.583 = \underline{\hspace{3cm}} \text{ (of possible 82.5)}$$
essay raw score   essay converted
score

Final Score

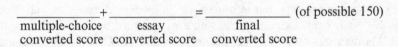

$$\underline{\hspace{3cm}} + \underline{\hspace{3cm}} = \underline{\hspace{3cm}} \text{ (of possible 150)}$$
multiple-choice   essay   final
converted score   converted score   converted score

Probable Final AP Score

Final Converted Score	Probable AP Score
150–114	5
113–98	4
97–81	3
80–53	2
52–0	1

Chapter 7

Practice Exam 4

Answer Sheet

Section I: Multiple-Choice Questions

1	Ⓐ Ⓑ Ⓒ Ⓓ Ⓔ	21	Ⓐ Ⓑ Ⓒ Ⓓ Ⓔ	41 Ⓐ Ⓑ Ⓒ Ⓓ Ⓔ
2	Ⓐ Ⓑ Ⓒ Ⓓ Ⓔ	22	Ⓐ Ⓑ Ⓒ Ⓓ Ⓔ	42 Ⓐ Ⓑ Ⓒ Ⓓ Ⓔ
3	Ⓐ Ⓑ Ⓒ Ⓓ Ⓔ	23	Ⓐ Ⓑ Ⓒ Ⓓ Ⓔ	43 Ⓐ Ⓑ Ⓒ Ⓓ Ⓔ
4	Ⓐ Ⓑ Ⓒ Ⓓ Ⓔ	24	Ⓐ Ⓑ Ⓒ Ⓓ Ⓔ	44 Ⓐ Ⓑ Ⓒ Ⓓ Ⓔ
5	Ⓐ Ⓑ Ⓒ Ⓓ Ⓔ	25	Ⓐ Ⓑ Ⓒ Ⓓ Ⓔ	45 Ⓐ Ⓑ Ⓒ Ⓓ Ⓔ
6	Ⓐ Ⓑ Ⓒ Ⓓ Ⓔ	26	Ⓐ Ⓑ Ⓒ Ⓓ Ⓔ	
7	Ⓐ Ⓑ Ⓒ Ⓓ Ⓔ	27	Ⓐ Ⓑ Ⓒ Ⓓ Ⓔ	
8	Ⓐ Ⓑ Ⓒ Ⓓ Ⓔ	28	Ⓐ Ⓑ Ⓒ Ⓓ Ⓔ	
9	Ⓐ Ⓑ Ⓒ Ⓓ Ⓔ	29	Ⓐ Ⓑ Ⓒ Ⓓ Ⓔ	
10	Ⓐ Ⓑ Ⓒ Ⓓ Ⓔ	30	Ⓐ Ⓑ Ⓒ Ⓓ Ⓔ	
11	Ⓐ Ⓑ Ⓒ Ⓓ Ⓔ	31	Ⓐ Ⓑ Ⓒ Ⓓ Ⓔ	
12	Ⓐ Ⓑ Ⓒ Ⓓ Ⓔ	32	Ⓐ Ⓑ Ⓒ Ⓓ Ⓔ	
13	Ⓐ Ⓑ Ⓒ Ⓓ Ⓔ	33	Ⓐ Ⓑ Ⓒ Ⓓ Ⓔ	
14	Ⓐ Ⓑ Ⓒ Ⓓ Ⓔ	34	Ⓐ Ⓑ Ⓒ Ⓓ Ⓔ	
15	Ⓐ Ⓑ Ⓒ Ⓓ Ⓔ	35	Ⓐ Ⓑ Ⓒ Ⓓ Ⓔ	
16	Ⓐ Ⓑ Ⓒ Ⓓ Ⓔ	36	Ⓐ Ⓑ Ⓒ Ⓓ Ⓔ	
17	Ⓐ Ⓑ Ⓒ Ⓓ Ⓔ	37	Ⓐ Ⓑ Ⓒ Ⓓ Ⓔ	
18	Ⓐ Ⓑ Ⓒ Ⓓ Ⓔ	38	Ⓐ Ⓑ Ⓒ Ⓓ Ⓔ	
19	Ⓐ Ⓑ Ⓒ Ⓓ Ⓔ	39	Ⓐ Ⓑ Ⓒ Ⓓ Ⓔ	
20	Ⓐ Ⓑ Ⓒ Ⓓ Ⓔ	40	Ⓐ Ⓑ Ⓒ Ⓓ Ⓔ	

CUT HERE

Section II: Free-Response Questions

Question 1

Some of the ~~obvious~~ ~~benefits~~ lowest paid workers, including employees of retail giant walwart and fast food workers. Some of the obvious beneficiaries such as CEO's of major corporations, draw compensation that work the gap wages, but other high-paid indivisuals, including Hollywoool stars, athletes Ceos make so much money you can only dream of.

Hollywood stars draw amazing salaries, although ponder this : male stars greatly out-earn their female counterparts. Nonetheless, even while they earn far less than male stars, female A- listeners are still doing pretty well. "This is true whether their annual earnings or per-fitm salaries are measured", according to the hollywood reporter (Source A).

Superstar athletes draw huge salaries ranging well into seven and even eight figures. But those figures tell only part of the story. Even "when those astronomical salaries are broken down into pre-game figures as Business Insider did in 2013." (source A) the totals exceed what many average workers make in a year.

The average salary for cheif Executive Officers ranges comfortably into six figures, with many CEO's earning millions in bonuses and share holdings, and while the compresation of big names such as "larry Ellison" of Oracle and Marissa Mayer of Yahoo "[almost 25 million in 2013]" is stunning (sorce A), the highest compensation packages are reserved for executives whoes names are virtually unknown.

CUT HERE

CUT HERE

Question 2

Barack Obama's win for President in 2009 was a historical moment for the United States. His inaugral speech was special because it set the tone for his presidency. His speech was said to tell Americans people that improving the economy is one of his priorities, improving health care and education system also was at the top of the list.

In the beginning of the speech President obama said "My fellow citizens". This was an emotional turn in the citizens eyes the president has goals and aims in common. Goals and aims that helping to solve the current problems that most of the citizens had. The president connected himself to the public through his speech, he stands as Citizens like them. President obama proved how American citizens able to change he provided an provided example "why a man whose father less than 60 years agoo". The president used pathos and ethos to strenghts and raise confidence. He stated "we build, we will rebuild, we will recover". President obama promised that "as soon as I took office, I asked this Congress to send me a recovery plan by Presidents day that would put people back to work and put money in their pockets". Here he used ethos was used to show qualifications of the President and what he capable of, while it touched emotionally the public using his common connection.

President Obama connected and moved his audience and promised a better life and because of this he had many rely and hope in him.

CUT HERE

CUT HERE

CUT HERE

Question 3

CUT HERE

CUT HERE

Section I: Multiple-Choice Questions

Time: 1 hour

45 questions

Directions: This section consists of selections from prose works with questions about their content, style, and form, plus draft passages with questions about improving their content and clarity. Read each selection carefully. For each question, choose the best answer of the five choices.

Questions 1–12 refer to the following passage by a a 20th-century American author.

When I was first aware that I had been laid low by the disease, I felt a need, among other things, to register a strong protest against the word "depression." Depression, most people (5) know, used to be termed "melancholia," a word which appears in English as early as the year 1303 and crops up more than once in Chaucer, who in his usage seemed to be aware of its pathological nuances. "Melancholia" would still (10) appear to be a far more apt and evocative word for the blacker forms of the disorder, but it was usurped by a noun with a bland tonality and lacking any magisterial presence, used indifferently to describe an economic decline or a (15) rut in the ground, a true wimp of a word for such a major illness. It may be that the scientist generally held responsible for its currency in modern times, a Johns Hopkins Medical School faculty member justly venerated—the Swiss- (20) born psychiatrist Adolf Meyer—had a tin ear for the finer rhythms of English and therefore was unaware of the semantic damage he had inflicted by offering "depression" as a descriptive noun for such a dreadful and raging disease. (25) Nonetheless, for over seventy-five years the word has slithered innocuously through the language like a slug, leaving little trace of its intrinsic malevolence and preventing, by its very insipidity, a general awareness of the horrible intensity of (30) the disease when out of control.

As one who has suffered from the malady in extremis yet returned to tell the tale, I would lobby for a truly arresting designation. "Brainstorm," for instance, has unfortunately (35) been preempted to describe, somewhat jocularly, intellectual inspiration. But something along these lines is needed. Told that someone's mood disorder has evolved into a storm—a veritable howling tempest in the brain, which is indeed (40) what a clinical depression resembles like nothing else—even the uninformed layman might display sympathy rather than the standard reaction that "depression" evokes, something akin to "So what?" or "You'll pull out of it" or "We all have (45) bad days." The phrase "nervous breakdown" seems to be on its way out, certainly deservedly so, owing to its insinuation of a vague spinelessness, but we still seem destined to be saddled with "depression" until a better, sturdier (50) name is created.

1. Which of the following clarifies one reason why the author would prefer to use the word "melancholia" instead of the word "depression"?

  A. It suggests a more acceptable condition.
  B. It seems a gentler word.
  C. It would bring a contemporary lightness to the condition.
  D. It would make the condition more well known.
  E. Its meaning is limited to its reference to a mental condition.

2. In line 14, the word "indifferently" can be best defined as

  A. apathetically
  B. neither particularly well nor badly
  C. indiscriminately
  D. ardently
  E. with no understanding

3. The author objects to the word "depression" to describe the disease because

  A. it has been used for only about 75 years
  B. its other meanings are nondescript and too euphemistic
  C. it evokes an irrational fear in those who hear it
  D. it is applied too strictly to a specific malady
  E. the psychiatrist who coined the term had a tin ear

4. The phrases "wimp of a word" (line 15) and "tin ear" (line 20) are two different examples of

    A. paradox
    B. colloquialism
    C. euphemism
    D. mixed metaphor
    E. parody

5. All of the following words or phrases contribute to creating the same meaning and effect EXCEPT

    A. "semantic damage" (line 22)
    B. "dreadful and raging disease" (line 24)
    C. "intrinsic malevolence" (lines 27–28)
    D. "horrible intensity" (line 29)
    E. "howling tempest in the brain" (line 39)

6. The word "brainstorm" (line 34) can probably not be used to replace the word "depression" because

    A. it does not adequately suggest what depression is like
    B. it is more misleading than the term "depression"
    C. the public is slow to adapt to new terminology
    D. it already has another very different meaning
    E. psychiatrists do not support any such change

7. In the sentence in lines 37–45 ("Told that someone's . . . have bad days"), the author

    A. suggests a possible way of changing the conventional response to a victim of depression
    B. exaggerates the unsympathetic response in order to increase sympathy for the mentally ill
    C. exaggerates the suffering of the victim of depression in order to increase the sympathetic response
    D. suggests possible responses people can use for those who suffer from depression
    E. questions his own idea of a more accurate term

8. In line 45, the speaker refers to the phrase "nervous breakdown" in order to

    A. suggest that the phrase is more evocative that the word "depression"
    B. give an example of an inadequate phrase that is losing its currency
    C. offer a second example of a bland and unevocative phrase
    D. contrast a well-chosen name for mental illness with the ill-chosen word "depression"
    E. show that the uninformed layman is unsympathetic to mental illness

9. Of the following, which would the author probably prefer to use to describe a person suffering from acute depression?

    A. dispirited
    B. down-at-the-mouth
    C. utterly desolated
    D. gloomy
    E. low

10. Of the following, which best describes the author's overall attitude toward the use of the word "depression"?

    A. resigned approval
    B. amused disapproval
    C. casual disinterestedness
    D. cool dislike
    E. strong resentment

11. Which of the following best describes the rhetorical purpose of the passage?

    A. to record the history of the word "depression"
    B. to criticize the inadequacy of the word "depression"
    C. to explain the multiple meanings of the word "depression"
    D. to demonstrate the shortcomings of medical language
    E. to argue for the use of the word "melancholia" in place of the word "depression"

12. Which of the following is a central idea of this passage?

    A. The denotation of a word may not adequately represent what it really means.

    B. The healthy do not properly sympathize with victims of mental illness.

    C. The changes in meanings of words over time are unpredictable.

    D. The scientific understanding of depression is incomplete.

    E. Words are an inadequate means of describing reality.

Questions 13–24 refer to the following passage from a 17th-century British essay.

First, he that hath words of any language, without distinct ideas in his mind to which he applies them, does, so far as he uses them in discourse, only make a noise without any sense
(5) or signification; and how learned soever he may seem by the use of hard words, or learned terms, is not much more advanced thereby in knowledge than he would be in learning, who had nothing in his study but the bare titles of books, without
(10) possessing the contents of them. For all such words, however put into discourse, according to the right construction of grammatical rules, or the harmony of well turned periods, do yet amount to nothing but bare sounds, and
(15) nothing else.

Secondly, he that has complex ideas, without particular names for them, would be in no better case than a bookseller, who had in his warehouse volumes that lay there unbound, and without
(20) titles; which he could therefore make known to others only by showing the loose sheets, and communicating them only by tale. This man is hindered in his discourse for want of words to communicate his complex ideas, which he is
(25) therefore forced to make known by an enumeration of the simple ones that compose them; and so is fain often to use twenty words to express what another man signifies in one.

Thirdly, he that puts not constantly the same
(30) sign for the same idea, but uses the same words sometimes in one, and sometimes in another signification, ought to pass in the schools and conversation for as fair a man as he does in the market and exchange, who sells several things
(35) under the same name.

Fourthly, he that applies the words of any language to ideas different from those to which the common use of that country applies them,

however his own understanding may be filled
(40) with truth and light, will not by such words be able to convey much of it to others, without defining his terms. For however the sounds are such as are familiarly known, and easily enter the ears of those who are accustomed to them; yet
(45) standing for other ideas than those they usually are annexed to, and are wont to excite in the mind of the hearers, they cannot make known the thoughts of him who thus uses them.

Fifthly, he that imagined to himself substances
(50) such as never have been, and filled his head with ideas which have not any correspondence with the real nature of things, to which yet he gives settled and defined names, may fill his discourse, and perhaps another man's head, with the
(55) fantastical imaginations of his own brain, but will be very far from advancing thereby one jot in real and true knowledge.

He that hath names without ideas, wants meaning in his words, and speaks only empty
(60) sounds. He that hath complex ideas without names for them, wants liberty and dispatch in his expressions, and is necessitated to use periphrases. He that uses his words loosely and unsteadily, will either be not minded, or not understood. He
(65) that applies his names to ideas different from their common use, wants propriety in his language, and speaks gibberish. And he that hath the ideas of substances disagreeing with the real existence of things, so far wants the materials of
(70) true knowledge in his understanding, and hath instead thereof chimeras.

13. As it is used in line 13, the word "periods" may be best defined as

    A. sound conclusions

    B. complete sentences

    C. musical measures

    D. marks of punctuation

    E. times

14. In line 26, the word "ones" refers to

    A. words

    B. books

    C. ideas

    D. discourse

    E. names

15. In the second paragraph, the shift from the first sentence (lines 16–22) to the second sentence (lines 22–28) can be best described as one from

A. objective to subjective
B. indicative to interrogative
C. analytical to discursive
D. figurative to literal
E. speculative to assertive

16. The comparison in lines 16–22 ("Secondly . . . only by tale") likens words to

A. the pages of a book
B. the contents of a warehouse
C. complex ideas
D. booksellers
E. the bindings of books

17. In the first and second paragraphs, the author supports his arguments by the use of

A. analogies
B. personifications
C. understatements
D. rhetorical questions
E. hyperbole

18. In line 33, the word "fair" is best understood to mean

A. equitable
B. attractive
C. clement
D. unblemished
E. average

19. In line 49, "substances" are contrasted with

A. shadows
B. ideas
C. imaginings
D. realities
E. names

20. Based on the content of the first five paragraphs, which of the following best clarifies how their ideas are united?

A. paragraph one; paragraphs two and three; paragraphs four and five
B. paragraph one; paragraphs two, three, and four; paragraph five
C. paragraphs one, two, and three; paragraphs four and five
D. paragraphs one and two; paragraph three; paragraphs four and five
E. paragraphs one and two; paragraphs three and four; paragraph five

21. Which of the following best describes the relation of the last paragraph to the rest of the passage?

A. It comments on and develops the arguments of the first five paragraphs.
B. It calls into question the arguments of the preceding paragraphs.
C. It raises new issues about language that the preceding paragraphs have not addressed.
D. It sums up the contents of the first five paragraphs.
E. It develops the ideas raised in the fourth and fifth paragraphs.

22. Which of the following is the meaning of the word "chimeras" that can be inferred from its use in the last sentence of the passage (line 71)?

A. fanciful illusions
B. confused conundrums
C. religious revelations
D. logical conclusions
E. philosophical distinctions

23. Which paragraph describes a person who misunderstands the meaning of the word "refuse" and instead uses it to mean agree?

A. first paragraph (lines 1–15)
B. second paragraph (lines 16–28)
C. third paragraph (lines 29–35)
D. fourth paragraph (lines 36–48)
E. fifth paragraph (lines 49–57)

24. In which paragraph does the passage deal with a speaker or writer who would use the word "apple" to denote a fruit, an animal, and an article of footwear?

    A. first paragraph (lines 1–15)
    B. second paragraph (lines 16–28)
    C. third paragraph (lines 29–35)
    D. fourth paragraph (lines 36–48)
    E. fifth paragraph (lines 49–57)

Questions 25–33 refer to the following draft.

(1) Karl Marx famously predicted that the rise of automation would result in mass unemployment; however, that was ultimately not the case. (2) Marx failed to anticipate that the new technology would also bring increased demand for workers. (3) It is interesting to note that by the end of the 19th century, more than four times the number of factory weavers had jobs than in 1830. (4) Additionally, with improved technology, weavers had greater output and the cost of cloth was reduced. (5) Consumers, in turn, bought more cloth. (6) This increased demand for cloth equaled increased jobs for weavers regardless of automation. (7) In 1803, the United Kingdom had 2,400 looms in operation, but by 1857, that number had risen to 250,000. (8) In the long term, by making cloth more affordable, the power loom increased demand and stimulated exports, causing a growth in industrial employment, albeit low-paid. (9) The power loom also opened up opportunities for female mill workers.

(10) This pattern can be seen in many more modern examples. (11) Since the 1970s, some note in alarm that bank tellers have given way to Automatic Teller Machines (ATMs) and in-store sales clerks have been sacrificed to e-commerce, while switchboard operators and secretaries have been lost to voice recognition technology. (12) All of these examples suggest that newer, automated technologies are leading to persistent unemployment. (13) But, in fact, the world saw more bank tellers, sales clerks, receptionists, and secretaries in 2009 than in 1999. (14) Demand explains this. (15) There is no doubt that it takes fewer bank tellers to operate a bank branch, thanks to the ATMs. (16) In turn, this makes it less costly to operate a bank branch, and banks opened more of them. (17) With more branches, banks expanded their markets. (18) Obviously, more branches increased demand for tellers, offsetting the loss in the number of tellers per branch. (19) Clearly ATMs have not eliminated teller jobs.

25. Which of the following sentences, if placed before sentence 1, would both arouse interest and provide an effective introduction to the passage?

    A. Even though some may think so, the world of commerce is not in dire straits.
    B. Automation will always pose a threat to workers.
    C. History proves that automation can be seen from more than one viewpoint in the business environment.
    D. Contrary to popular belief, automation does not necessarily eliminate jobs.
    E. Workers rightfully feared losing employment when mechanization began.

26. In order to make the first paragraph flow better, the writer is considering deleting sentence 5 (reprinted below).

Consumers, in turn, bought more cloth.

Should the writer make this deletion?

    A. Yes, because it adds unimportant information to the paragraph.
    B. Yes, because it distracts from the writer's argument.
    C. No, because it is a logical connection between sentence 4 and sentence 6.
    D. No, because the audience will be interested in the consumers' actions.
    E. No, because the paragraph would make no sense without the information about the cost of cloth.

27. The writer is considering revising the underlined portion of sentence 6 (reprinted below) for greater accuracy and clarity.

This increased demand for cloth equaled increased jobs for weavers <u>regardless of automation</u>.

Which of the following best meets the writer's goal?

    A. because of automation
    B. in spite of automation
    C. no matter that automation had increased
    D. although automation continued to grow
    E. despite the fact that automation was going to stay

28. The writer wants to add an appropriate phrase to introduce sentence 7 (reprinted below), adjusting capitalization as necessary.

In 1803, the United Kingdom had 2,400 looms in operation, but by 1857, that number had risen to 250,000.

Which of the following phrases best introduces sentence 7?

A. In fact,
B. Regardless,
C. It is interesting to know that
D. Historians are quick to note that
E. Notwithstanding,

29. The writer is considering moving sentence 7 (reprinted below) to improve the organization of the first paragraph's ideas.

In 1803, the United Kingdom had 2,400 looms in operation, but by 1857, that number had risen to 250,000.

Where would be the best placement of sentence 7, considering the first paragraph as a whole?

A. after sentence 2
B. after sentence 3
C. after sentence 4
D. after sentence 5
E. Leave it where it is.

30. Which of the following ideas would NOT moderate the optimism of the first paragraph?

A. Female workers were forced to work for less money than males.
B. Automation also brought the rise of child labor in factories.
C. Workers essentially became indebted to the factory owner.
D. Factory workers faced longer work hours under exhausting conditions.
E. Artisans could see the result of their labor.

31. The writer is considering adding the following sentence after sentence 11.

As of 2015, close to 3.5 million ATMs were in use worldwide.

Should the writer add this sentence?

A. Yes, because it adds interesting data to support the writer's argument.
B. Yes, because the paragraph fails to provide adequate supporting statistics.
C. No, because the information diverts attention from the flow of the sentences.
D. No, because the new sentence is redundant.
E. No, because the addition is unconcerned with the writer's argument.

32. The writer is considering revising sentence 14 (reprinted below) to better support the overall argument contained in both paragraphs in the passage.

Demand explains this.

Which of the following is the best revision to achieve this goal?

A. (as it is now)
B. The increased demand that accounted for more 19th-century weavers is analogous to the increased demand that accounted for more 20th-century bank tellers.
C. The increased number of bank tellers and other workers is because of increased demand.
D. Demand will always dictate the number of jobs available.
E. The public fails to understand how higher demand affects the employment market.

33. The writer is considering adding a concluding sentence at the end of the second paragraph that summarizes the overall argument. Which of the following provides the best conclusion for the passage as a whole?

A. Industry in general will always face increased automation, and management has to predict the consequent changes to the workforce.

B. Obviously, one cannot predict whether or not future industries will benefit from increased automation.

C. Economists should be aware of the effect that automation has had on the salaries and working hours of employees.

D. The experience in the textile and banking industries demonstrates that technology and automation sometimes interact with society in surprising ways.

E. People need to remember that their first impressions of the effects of automation may not necessarily be accurate.

Questions 34–40 refer to the following draft.

(1) There is an ongoing debate about the merits of handwriting vs. typing on a keyboard or other electronic devices.

(2) Producing words via handwriting is very different than typing on a keyboard. (3) Handwriting requires various skills, such as feeling the pen and paper, moving the pen and directing that movement with thought to create each different letter. (4) This precise motor exercise takes children years to master. (5) Operating a keyboard, however, is not the same; all one has to do in typing is touch the correct key, and the hand movement is the same for every letter. (6) Children can learn typing more easily because the movement does not vary from letter to letter as in handwriting.

(7) Studies show that cursive handwriting increases brain synapses and synchronicity between the brain's hemispheres, which does not happen when typing or printing. (8) On a related note, a study, published in *Psychological Science,* focused on university students' in-class note-taking across the country. (9) The results consistently showed that those who took handwritten class notes were better able to answer questions about a lecture than those who used a laptop. (10) Why? (11) Although handwriting is slower for most, those who handwrite notes while in class have to think while they write, think about what is important and how to best articulate it. (12) They have to slow down enough to comprehend and summarize. (13) Those who take laptop notes too often try to copy the professor's words verbatim, or at least literally, with less cognitive connection. (14) What happens is a lack of meaningful understanding and application of information. (15) While typing may be faster and more convenient, handwriting has unique advantages.

(16) Handwritten notes aid short- and long-term memory by activating parts of your brain involved in thinking and working memory, and allow you to store and manage information.

(17) However, typing via a keyboard has advantages, especially in producing a finished product. (18) Typed words look professional, margins are uniform, and one hardly need worry about spelling and grammar. (19) Editing is also much easier on a computer, since you can copy and paste, as well as track your changes. (20) And, if one is a good typist, typing saves paper and time.

(21) You are exposed to more critical thinking when you handwrite than when you type; handwriting requires you to think more while writing and allows you to expand on your ideas and form connections between them.

34. The writer wants to revise sentence 1 (reprinted below) for greater precision.

There is an ongoing debate about the merits of handwriting vs. typing on a keyboard or other electronic devices.

Which of the following sentences best meets the writer's goal?

A. Some people prefer to handwrite, while others prefer to type.

B. There is an ongoing debate over whether to handwrite or type.

C. A controversy over whether to handwrite or type is constantly brewing.

D. People debate about handwriting vs. typing on a keyboard or other electronic devices all the time.

E. An ongoing debate exists regarding the merits of handwriting vs. typing.

35. The writer wants to further develop the first paragraph. Which of the following would be the LEAST important addition to meet this goal?

A. a mention of note-taking in an academic setting

B. an explanation of the difference between using a keyboard and laptop

C. the inclusion of a thesis that clarifies the scope of the passage

D. a brief reference to the tools and media used in writing through history

E. some remarks about the various kinds of writing that will be discussed in the passage

36. The writer is considering deleting sentence 4 (reprinted below) to improve the flow of the second paragraph.

This precise motor exercise takes children years to master.

Should the writer delete this sentence?

A. Yes, because it distracts from the paragraph's content.

B. Yes, because the paragraph does not present information about learning typing skills.

C. Yes, because the passage is not about children's learning.

D. No, because it is balanced with information about children's learning curve in typing.

E. No, because the information reminds the reader of the difficulties children have when learning to handwrite.

37. The writer is considering revising the underlined portion of sentence 11 (reprinted below) to make it more precise.

Although handwriting is slower for most, those who handwrite notes while in class have to think while they write, think about what is important and how to best articulate it.

Which of the following revisions to the underlined portion best accomplishes this goal?

A. students who handwrite class notes have to think about what is important and how to best articulate it while writing

B. those who prefer handwriting their notes have to think about the important content while writing

C. the people who handwrite notes have to think much more while taking them than those who type

D. when students are in class and taking notes in handwriting, they have to think about what is being said before they can think about what to write down

E. the people who handwrite class notes have a harder task because they have to think before they can write anything

38. The writer wants to revise the underlined portion of sentence 14 (reprinted below) for stronger impact.

What happens is a lack of meaningful understanding and application of information.

To meet this goal, which of the following is the best version of the underlined portion?

A. (as it is now)

B. A lack of meaningful understanding results

C. Consequentially, the student has less meaningful understanding

D. Therefore, there is a lack of meaningful understanding

E. The final result is a lack of meaningful understanding

39. The writer is considering moving sentence 15 (reprinted below) to another location to improve the flow of ideas in the third paragraph.

While typing may be faster and more convenient, handwriting has unique advantages.

Where would be the best placement for sentence 15?

A. after sentence 7
B. after sentence 8
C. after sentence 10
D. after sentence 11
E. Leave it where it is.

40. The writer is concerned about the overall balance of ideas in the passage. Which of the following, if implemented, would best address that concern?

A. Complement the information with interviews with those who favor typing class notes.
B. Add more information about the specific benefits of typing over handwriting.
C. Present testimony from those who favor typing over handwriting.
D. Delete sentence 16 entirely.
E. Revise the last paragraph to present the other side of the issue.

Questions 41–45 refer to the following draft.

(1) Cartoonist Charles M. Schulz popularized the term "security blanket" through his character Linus, the best friend of Charlie Brown and the younger brother of Lucy van Pelt in the comic strip *Peanuts*; Linus was rarely seen without his. (2) We can all relate to the child who needs something to hold onto.

(3) Donald Woods Winnicott, a British pediatrician and psychoanalyst, studied childhood development and introduced the concept of a "transitional object" that serves as a very important bridge between infancy and childhood. (4) Infants see themselves and their mothers as a whole. (5) The mother brings the baby what he or she wants and, in doing so, satisfies the baby's needs, giving the baby a sense of, as Winnicott calls it, subjective omnipotence.

(6) Objective reality soon interferes as the baby comes to realize that the mother is a separate entity, which tells the child he or she has lost something and is dependent on others. (7) This causes frustration and anxiety, which is the perfect opportunity for the transitional object to enter the child's life.

(8) The transitional object is often the first "not me" possession of the child, and it often takes a physical shape, such as a teddy bear, a doll, or a security blanket like Linus'. (9) It can also take the form of a melody or single word. (10) In any case, the object represents all the components of "mothering" and allows the child to create what he or she needs as well. (11) Symbolically, the child can still have a bond with the mother when she gradually separates herself for longer periods of time. (12) The transitional object is especially important at the time of going to sleep and acts as a defense against anxiety.

(13) Charles Schultz was appropriate in naming Linus' constant companion a "security blanket." (14) Children do indeed get comfort from their chosen object, and the object helps them to adapt to new situations and to cope with not being the center of their universe.

41. The writer wants to add a thesis statement after sentence 2. Which of the following best clarifies the writer's main point?

A. The importance of having an object that brings comfort cannot be denied.
B. A security blanket plays an important role in helping infants grow.
C. The strong bond between infants and their mothers creates difficulties when it is broken.
D. All children have the need for security, and the objects they use to achieve it are psychologically understandable.
E. Children constantly need assurance that they are safe, and a security blanket provides that assurance.

42. In order to better develop the argument, it would be most effective if the writer would include all of the following in the second paragraph EXCEPT

A. definition of the term "transitional object"
B. explanation of how the transitional object serves as a bridge between infancy and childhood
C. biographic information about Winnicott
D. clarification of subjective omnipotence
E. description of how the transitional object takes the place of the mother-child relationship

43. The writer is considering revising the underlined portion of sentence 10 (reprinted below) to present its ideas more logically.

In any case, the object represents all the components of "mothering" <u>*and allows the child to create what he or she needs as well.*</u>

Which of the following revisions best meets the writer's goal?

- **A.** (as it is now)
- **B.** which allows the child to substitute the object for the mother, thereby creating security and safety
- **C.** and teaches the child to understand how the object can take the place of mommy and supply all she usually does
- **D.** and ultimately permits children to gain independence faster
- **E.** and psychologically encourages the child to learn that mother will not always be available

44. The writer is considering deleting sentence 13 (reprinted below) that opens the last paragraph.

Charles Schultz was appropriate in naming Linus' constant companion a "security blanket."

Should the writer make this deletion?

- **A.** No, because readers will relate to the famous comic strip character.
- **B.** No, because it appropriately ties in with the introduction.
- **C.** Yes, because the information has already been established in the passage.
- **D.** Yes, because it fails to move the passage's ideas forward.
- **E.** Yes, because it offers no pertinent information.

45. Which of the following presents the strongest refutation of the passage as a whole?

- **A.** Fathers can be the primary source of comfort for a child, making the need for a transitional object obsolete.
- **B.** Some children normally fall asleep without the need of a teddy bear or security blanket.
- **C.** A transitional object can also be a cause of great stress for the growing child when it is lost or left behind.
- **D.** Mothers who are aware of this phenomenon are better able to cope when their children cry at night.
- **E.** Studies show that children rarely use transitional objects in cultures in which the mother is always present.

IF YOU FINISH BEFORE TIME IS CALLED, CHECK YOUR WORK ON THIS SECTION ONLY. DO NOT WORK ON ANY OTHER SECTION IN THE TEST.

Section II: Free-Response Questions

Time: 2 hours, 15 minutes

3 questions

Question 1

(Suggested writing time—40 minutes. This question counts for one-third of the total free-response section score.)

Throughout recent years, professional athletes' salaries have skyrocketed. Do you find that today's athletes are overpaid? Or are professional athletes paid an appropriate amount for their physical talents?

Considering the salaries that are paid to professional athletes, read the following six sources (including any introductory information) carefully. Then, write an essay that synthesizes material from at least three of the sources and develops your position on the claim that professional athletes are overpaid.

> Source A (Henderson)
>
> Source B (Callahan)
>
> Source C (Morss)
>
> Source D (PK)
>
> Source E (Hollway)
>
> Source F (graphic)

In your response, you should do the following:

- Respond to the prompt with a thesis that presents a defensible position.
- Select and use evidence from at least three of the provided sources to support your line of reasoning. Indicate clearly the sources used through direct quotation, paraphrase, or summary. Sources may be cited as Source A, Source B, etc., or by using the description in parentheses.
- Explain how the evidence supports your line of reasoning.
- Use appropriate grammar and punctuation in communicating your argument.

Source A

Henderson, Audrey. "Who Makes More Money: Athletes, Actors, National Leaders, or CEOs?" *Supermoney*. 26 Aug. 2017. Web. 18 Sept. 2017.

This excerpt from a financial website compares salaries from professions that are perceived as high-paying ones.

The income inequality gap is huge—and growing. Some of the obvious beneficiaries, such as CEOs of major corporations, draw compensation that drives much of the wage gap. But other high-paid individuals, including Hollywood stars and athletes, also make more than any American can dream of. On the other hand, many national government leaders draw surprisingly modest salaries.

Hollywood stars draw amazing salaries, although ponder this: male stars greatly out-earn their female counterparts. Nonetheless, even while they earn far less than male stars, female A-listers are still doing pretty well. This is true whether their annual earnings or per-film salaries are measured, according to the *Hollywood Reporter*. For instance, Dwayne Johnson, perhaps better known as wrestling superstar The Rock, has built a solid action film career, earning an estimated 52 million dollars between June 2013 and June 2014, commanding an average 15 million per picture. Leading man Leonardo DiCaprio earned 45 million dollars between June 2013 and June 2014, but routinely averages 20 million dollars per film, according to the *Hollywood Reporter*.

By contrast, Jennifer Lawrence, the highest-paid female actress mentioned by the *Hollywood Reporter*, earned a not-bad 35 million dollars between June 2013 and June 2014. But the Oscar-winning actress also got a big raise for her most recent films. Lawrence's paycheck jumped from 500,000 dollars to a cool 10 million dollars between the filming of the first two installments of the blockbuster *Hunger Games* franchise.

Superstar athletes draw huge salaries ranging well into seven and even eight figures. But those figures tell only part of the story. Even when those astronomical salaries are broken down into per-game figures as *Business Insider* did in 2013, the totals far exceed what many average workers make in an entire year.

For instance, quarterback Peyton Manning earns a reported 15 million dollars from the Denver Broncos. Manning took a 4 million dollar pay cut for his team in 2015, meaning he made 19 million in 2014. But since football players only play once every week, his weekly salary translates to an eye-popping 937,500 dollars.

By contrast, basketball superstar Kobe Bryant earns 25 million dollars from the Los Angeles Lakers, a pay cut from his 30.4 million in 2014. But since basketball players play many more games each season than football players, Kobe Bryant averages "only" 304,000 dollars per game, according to *Business Insider*.

Baseball star Alex Rodriguez is paid right there with Bryant: 25 million dollars. But baseball players play even more games each season than basketball players—which translates to a per-game average paycheck of only 154,000 dollars for Alex Rodriguez.

The average salary for Chief Executive Officers ranges comfortably into six figures, with many CEOs earning millions in bonuses and shareholdings. And while the compensation of big names such as Larry Ellison of Oracle (more than 78 million in 2013) and Marissa Mayer of Yahoo! (almost 25 million in 2013) is stunning, the highest compensation packages are reserved for executives whose names are virtually unknown. For instance, the very top earning CEO in 2013 was someone named Charif Souki of Cheniere Energy, whose compensation totaled an amazing 141,949,280 dollars.

And while many CEOs log more working hours than the standard 40-hour work week, they are well compensated for their time and efforts. The average CEO earned more than 331 times the salary of everyday workers in 2013. Compare that figure with salaries for rank-and-file employees, which averaged just $16.94 per hour in 2013, or $35,239 annually, according to figures compiled by the AFL-CIO.

With his country sinking into recession in response to intense pressure from international sanctions, Russian Federation president Vladimir Putin cut his own salary by 10 percent, according to CNN Money. His remaining salary is 8.2 million rubles annually, which translates to about 136,000 US dollars. French President François Hollande gave himself a 30 percent salary haircut when he took office in 2012, reducing his annual earnings from 255,600 Euros (274,522 US dollars) to 194,251 dollars.

By contrast, CNN Money reports that German Chancellor Angela Merkel and her cabinet received a 2.2 percent pay rise in March 2015. The raise increased her annual salary to 213,000 Euros, or the equivalent of 234,383 US dollars. China's President Xi Jingping also obtained a raise at the beginning of 2015. But even after a 60 percent boost, his annual salary is still shockingly low—the equivalent of only 22,000 US dollars annually, according to CNN Money.

For the record, United States President Barack Obama is the highest-paid world leader. He earns 400,000 dollars annually, and also has a tax-free 50,000 dollar expense account. Not too shabby.

Source B

Callahan, Gene. "Athletes' Salaries Too High? Sports Fans, Blame Yourselves." *The Foundation for Economic Education.* Fee. 1 July 2007. Web. 29 Sept. 2017.

This excerpt from a financial website presents the idea that high salaries in professional sports are directly caused by sports fans.

It is the very fans who often grumble about the "ridiculous" wages paid to top athletes who in effect set their salaries. That's because in a market economy the price paid for any factor of production (including labor services) arises from the choices consumers make about the items they wish to buy and how much they are willing to pay. Producers face costs in providing a good, and if they estimate that buyers will not pay at least enough for their output to cover their costs plus some profit, the good will not be produced. Those estimates can turn out to be over-optimistic: producers are often mistaken in gauging consumer demand, and many a business has gone under because it spent more to manufacture its offerings than consumers were willing to pay. But competition among entrepreneurs for buyers' dollars rewards those entrepreneurs whose forecasts are generally most accurate with profits that allow them to remain in business and invest even more in the future.

Consumers must bid enough to prompt producers into action, and the price of every good—industrial products as well as consumption items—can be traced to consumer choice. Producers of items needed for the production of consumer goods will find it rewarding to produce those items only if consumers value the final goods enough to pay for the resources and work necessary to create them.

What's more, the costs producers face in their operations are not determined by nonhuman factors such as energy expenditures, chemical transformations, or the abundance or scarcity of various raw materials; rather they are the consequence of the producers' evaluation of alternative ways in which they might earn their livings by meeting consumer demand. Of course, producers must not ignore physical reality in their business decisions: it will clearly require far more time and energy to manufacture skillets from iron mined on Mars than from the same metal mined on earth. However, unless consumers value "Martian skillets" more than the terrestrial variety, expending all that effort to procure otherworldly metal will not result in a higher price being paid for it. It is the preferences of consumers that drive the formation of prices all the way backwards along the production chain. If some resource could be used in the creation of a consumer good, but producers judge that their efforts to acquire it will not add enough to the value of the final product to be worth their while, they simply will choose not to employ it; they have no power to drive up the price of the end product by picking an extravagant way of manufacturing it.

This aspect of the market economy, which has been termed "consumer sovereignty," is entirely independent of how concerned a proprietor is about the welfare of his customers. One entrepreneur may start a firm because of a sincere conviction that the product or service he plans to provide will bring immense benefits to his clientele. Another may be motivated solely by his desire to become fabulously wealthy. But to succeed, both will be equally bound to judge accurately as to how much consumers will value his offerings. Certainly, an unscrupulous businessman may try to deceive consumers about the true nature of what he is selling, but that is more accurately classified as theft rather than commerce and properly is subject to legal sanctions.

Nevertheless, the enormous salaries earned by sports stars are chiefly the result of the willingness of their fans to pay to see them play. If my neighbors in the sports bar are seriously distressed that star athletes make so much more than educators, the power to alter that situation lies with them. They can stop paying so much for ESPN and tickets to ballgames and instead spend the money they save on their children's schooling. I certainly would not complain about such a shift in people's priorities. But it is the only way a free people can address the situation.

Source C

Morss, Elliot. "The Global Economics of Professional Sports." *Global Finance*. 9 May 2012. Web. 17 Sept. 2017.

This chart compares average salaries in different sports around the world.

This table presents data on average salaries by sport and country. US basketball (NBA) tops the list, with Indian Cricket in second place. The National Football League is in a very strong position relative to its players. Not only is the average salary relatively low, but salaries are not guaranteed. That means if you can't play because of an injury, the team does not have to pay you.

Sport/League	Average Salary
Basketball - NBA	**4,375,735**
Cricket - India	**3,612,726**
Baseball - Total	**3,218,840**
Baseball - MLB	3,415,772
Baseball - Japan	841,208
Soccer - Total	**2,338,081**
Soccer - Britain	3,184,110
Soccer - Germany	2,380,330
Soccer - Spain	1,970,263
Soccer - Italy	1,960,080
Soccer - Scotland	446,571
Soccer - Australia	202,291
Soccer - US	192,689
Hockey - NHL	**2,311,733**
Football - Total	**2,188,374**
Football - NFL	2,208,364
Football - Canada	102,812

Source D

PK. "Athletes Are Underpaid: The Economics of Player Salaries." *Don't Quit Your Day Job . . .* DQYDJ. 26
Sept. 2017. Web. 1 Oct. 2017.

This excerpt examines ways in which athletes' salaries are not as high as many think.

The problem with painting every sports contract with the "overpaid" brush is there is an army of athletes who
will never touch the salaries that make us do a double take—we contend that, as a whole, **athletes are underpaid.**

Starting with Pee Wee sports, there is a pretty well-defined route to professional leagues. Kids start from as
young as 4 or 5 to learn the fundamentals of the game, and play for the sports teams of their schools or pickup
games in their neighborhoods. As athletes progress in age, there are sports camps, AAU teams, college camps, and
other competitive travel teams that can get young athletes onto scouting radars. Next up is usually (with the notable
exception of baseball, which has two paths to the pros) recruitment to an NCAA school. Finally, a few of those
athletes will go on to be drafted by teams—and fewer still will get the huge contracts that we so often dismiss as
absurd and obscene.

What am I saying here? The first reason that "athletes" are underpaid is because the odds are so stacked against
"athlete" as a career it is reasonable to think that those who make it should draw a large salary. What we are
missing out on are the millions of children who grew up dreaming they'd be the next Michael Jordan, Emmitt
Smith, or Babe Ruth (or Wayne Gretzky. Or . . . Pelé). It's a bias against the unseen—there has to be a reasonable
reward at the end of the road for the number of athletes who actually make it out of the various stages of the game.
There are cuts at every stage—it's a pyramid.

How large is the pool that the draft ends up drawing from? In 2006, this CNN article pegged youth participation
at 41 million. Athletes (not just the four major sports) in the NCAA number 400,000. As for the pros? Let's look at
the four major sports:

Football (NFL): 32 players a round, 7 rounds means 224 players a year from the draft, plus a smattering of
free agents—generally place kickers, punters, and the occasional retiree.

Basketball (NBA): 30 players a round, 2 rounds means 60 players a year are drafted.

Baseball (MLB): Baseball is the exception to our draft rule, due to its nicely varied league levels and
development teams (Low-A, High-A, AA, AAA, Majors). It's tough to pin down a hard number for draft
size, but in 2006, 1,503 players were selected. Most of them will never make a major league roster.

Hockey (NHL): 30 players a round, 7 rounds means 210 players are drafted.

Of the four majors, the NHL comes in with the highest minimum salary at $525,000. Basketball players pull in
$490,180 annually. Baseball players pull in a minimum of $414,000. Football players will make at least $375,000
annually. Those numbers are huge—the 2010 median household income in the United States was $49,445. However,
when talking about career longevity we tend to cherry pick the most durable players we can think of—Robert
Parish (21 seasons in NBA), Brett Favre (20 seasons in NFL), Wayne Gretzky (16 seasons, NHL), or Tim Wakefield
(17 seasons and still active, MLB). The truth is most players will see nowhere near the sorts of contracts we see
from the Peyton Mannings and the Alex Rodriguezes of the sports world—most will be closer to the minimum,
and play out much shorter careers.

From what I can find, NHL players average 5.66 seasons, NFL players 6.86, NBA players 4.81, and MLB
players (again, skewed by the minor league system) 5.6. All else being equal, the NBA would pay the highest
minimum salary and the NFL the least.

Remember that a college athlete drafted at 21 and out of the league 5 years later is still 26 years old. Even with
5 years of large salaries, his future is not guaranteed. It's one of the reasons so many former players are broke, even
some of the ones with salaries near the top of the ranges.

There is no doubt in my mind that some of the contracts in the sports world grate on the nerves of my fellow
members of the 9–5 crowd. When we hear of guys making millions a dollar a year on police blotters, it's normal to
be a bit disgusted. However, salaries are high but rational—in aggregate, we still argue athletes are underpaid.

The extreme difficulty of developing the skills necessary to be a professional, *staying injury-free* until you can
demonstrate those skills at the pro level, then maintaining the skills for a reasonable number of years is so extreme
that the salaries we see make a little more sense.

Source E

Hollway, Cameron. "Bargain or Bust?" *St. Louis Post-Dispatch.* 3 Aug. 2005: D2. Print.

This newspaper article questions the validity of professional sports salaries.

Since Bobby Hull became the first reported million-dollar man in 1972, salaries in professional sports have escalated to out-of-control proportions. Tuesday, Shaquille O'Neal's restructured contract worth $100 million over five years was barely a blip on the radar screen in the NBA, where $100 million deals are common. Bryant Reeves makes $7.8 million a year and LeBron James pockets $90 million for wearing Nike skids.

Athlete contracts have become more about "respect" and one-upping a rival player than about the money—seriously, besides Mike Tyson, who can really spend $100 million? Tiger Woods might actually be worth his reported $1-billion-plus bank account, but are any of the other milestone millionaires deserving of their loot?

From Hull to O'Neal, we take a look at a few big-money payouts and whether they were worth the risk.

Alex Rodriguez (baseball)

The money: A-Rod's 10-year, $252-million contract delivered by Texas in December 2000 is the richest in professional sports history. In January, Carlos Beltran became the 10th big-league player to sign a $100 million contract.

Bust: Babe Ruth's $50,000 contract in 1922 was a record that took 25 years to double (Hank Greenberg, $100K, 1947). After Mike Piazza signed for $13 million annually in 1998, it took only two years for A-Rod to pull in more than double at $27 million.

Shaquille O'Neal (NBA)

The money: The game's most dominant big man opted out of his one-year contract for $30.6 million, saying through his agent that he preferred the "stability" of a long-term deal. Five years, $100 million buys a stable of stability.

Bust: Remember when Magic Johnson signed a 25-year deal for $25 million in 1984? Shaq Daddy is too fat, too injury-prone and too dramatic to draw $20 million per, even if he is the most physically dominant player in NBA history.

The following image represents some of the sports that are affected by player salaries.

Question 2

(Suggested writing time—40 minutes. This question counts for one-third of the total free-response score.)

The following passage is excerpted from President Barack Obama's first inaugural address on January 21, 2009. In it, he calls for a new era of responsibility. Read the passage carefully and write an essay in which you analyze how the rhetorical choices that President Obama uses develop his message.

In your response, you should do the following:

- Respond to the prompt with a thesis that analyzes the writer's rhetorical choices.
- Select and use evidence to support your line of reasoning.
- Explain how the evidence supports your line of reasoning.
- Demonstrate an understanding of the rhetorical situation.
- Use appropriate grammar and punctuation in communicating your argument.

Forty-four Americans have now taken the presidential oath. The words have been spoken during rising tides of prosperity and the still waters of peace. Yet, every so often, the oath is taken amidst gathering clouds and raging storms. At these moments, America has carried on not simply because of the skill or vision of those in high office, but because we, the people, have remained faithful to the ideals of our forebears and true
(5) to our founding documents.

So it has been; so it must be with this generation of Americans.

. . .

Today I say to you that the challenges we face are real. They are serious and they are many. They will not be met easily or in a short span of time. But know this America: They will be met.
(10) . . .

In reaffirming the greatness of our nation we understand that greatness is never a given. It must be earned. Our journey has never been one of short-cuts or settling for less. It has not been the path for the faint-hearted, for those that prefer leisure over work, or seek only the pleasures of riches and fame. Rather, it has been the risk-takers, the doers, the makers of things—some celebrated, but more often men and women
(15) obscure in their labor—who have carried us up the long rugged path towards prosperity and freedom.

For us, they packed up their few worldly possessions and traveled across oceans in search of a new life. For us, they toiled in sweatshops, and settled the West, endured the lash of the whip, and plowed the hard earth. For us, they fought and died in places like Concord and Gettysburg, Normandy and Khe Sahn.

Time and again these men and women struggled and sacrificed and worked till their hands were raw so
(20) that we might live a better life. They saw America as bigger than the sum of our individual ambitions, greater than all the differences of birth or wealth or faction.

. . .

The question we ask today is not whether our government is too big or too small, but whether it works—whether it helps families find jobs at a decent wage, care they can afford, a retirement that is dignified. Where
(25) the answer is yes, we intend to move forward. Where the answer is no, programs will end. And those of us who manage the public's dollars will be held to account, to spend wisely, reform bad habits, and do our business in the light of day, because only then can we restore the vital trust between a people and their government.

. . .

(30) Our challenges may be new. The instruments with which we meet them may be new. But those values upon which our success depends—honesty and hard work, courage and fair play, tolerance and curiosity, loyalty and patriotism—these things are old. These things are true. They have been the quiet force of progress throughout our history.

What is demanded, then, is a return to these truths. What is required of us now is a new era of
(35) responsibility—a recognition on the part of every American that we have duties to ourselves, our nation and the world; duties that we do not grudgingly accept, but rather seize gladly, firm in the knowledge that there is nothing so satisfying to the spirit, so defining of our character than giving our all to a difficult task.

. . .

(40) So let us mark this day with remembrance of who we are and how far we have traveled. In the year of America's birth, in the coldest of months, a small band of patriots huddled by dying campfires on the shores of an icy river. The capital was abandoned. The enemy was advancing. The snow was stained with blood. At the moment when the outcome of our revolution was most in doubt, the father of our nation ordered these words to be read to the people:

(45) "Let it be told to the future world . . . that in the depth of winter, when nothing but hope and virtue could survive . . . that the city and the country, alarmed at one common danger, came forth to meet [it]."

America: In the face of our common dangers, in this winter of our hardship, let us remember these timeless words. With hope and virtue, let us brave once more the icy currents, and endure what storms may come. Let it be said by our children's children that when we were tested we refused to let this journey end, that we did not turn back nor did we falter; and with eyes fixed on the horizon and God's grace upon us, we carried forth (50) that great gift of freedom and delivered it safely to future generations.

Question 3

(Suggested writing time—40 minutes. This question counts for one-third of the total free-response score.)

The following excerpt is taken from *The Autobiography of Benjamin Franklin* (1791). Read the passage carefully and write an essay that argues your position on Franklin's assertions about the ability to justify one's actions through reasoning.

In your response, you should do the following:

- Respond to the prompt with a thesis that presents a defensible position.
- Provide evidence to support your line of reasoning.
- Explain how the evidence supports your line of reasoning.
- Use appropriate grammar and punctuation in communicating your argument.

I believe I have omitted mentioning that in my first voyage from Boston, being becalmed off Block Island, our people set about catching cod and hauled up a great many. Hitherto I had stuck to my resolution of not eating animal food; and on this occasion I considered with my Master Tryon, the taking of every fish as a kind of unprovoked murder, since none of them had or ever could do us any injury that might justify the slaughter. All this seemed very reasonable. But I had formerly been a great lover of fish, and when this came hot out of the frying pan, it smelled admirably well. I balanced some time between principle and inclination: till I recollected, that when fish were opened, I saw smaller fish taken out of their stomachs: Then, thought I, if you eat one another, I don't see why we mayn't eat you. So I dined upon cod very heartily and continued to eat with other people, returning only now and then occasionally to a vegetable diet. So convenient a thing it is to be a *reasonable creature,* since it enables one to find or make a reason for everything one has a mind to do.

IF YOU FINISH BEFORE TIME IS CALLED, CHECK YOUR WORK ON THIS SECTION ONLY. DO NOT WORK ON ANY OTHER SECTION IN THE TEST.

Answer Key

Section I: Multiple-Choice Questions

1. E	10. E	19. D	28. A	37. A
2. C	11. B	20. E	29. B	38. C
3. B	12. A	21. D	30. E	39. C
4. B	13. B	22. A	31. C	40. B
5. A	14. A	23. D	32. B	41. D
6. D	15. D	24. C	33. D	42. C
7. A	16. E	25. D	34. E	43. B
8. B	17. A	26. C	35. B	44. B
9. C	18. A	27. A	36. D	45. E

Section II: Free-Response Questions

Essay scoring rubrics, student essays, and analysis appear beginning on page 302.

Answer Explanations

Section I: Multiple-Choice Questions

The passage referred to in questions 1–12 is from the American novelist William Styron's Darkness Visible *(1990), an autobiographical account of his suffering from clinical depression.*

1. **E.** The first paragraph of the passage explains that the word "depression" has far too many varied definitions and uses; "melancholy" is more specifically appropriate to the mental condition, choice E. Choice A contradicts the author's intent; he feels that melancholia is "a far more apt and evocative word for the blacker forms of the disorder" than is depression, but he does not claim that calling the condition melancholia would give it wider acceptance. The author does not want a gentler word (B); he wants a more accurate one. The phrase "contemporary lightness" makes choice C incorrect; the term "melancholy" was used since the 1300s, so it is not "contemporary," and the disease is anything but "light." The passage offers no evidence that the author thinks changing the term would make it better known (D).

2. **C.** Though "indifferent" can mean "apathetic" (A) or "average" (B), in this context the word has another of its several meanings: "showing no preference or bias, indiscriminate," choice C. The author's point is that a word that can be equally well used to denote a rut or financial hard times should not be used to describe a disease as terrible as depression. Choice D, ardently, means to do something passionately, enthusiastically, which does not fit the context of the passage. Choice E is too much of a stretch; the author's point that the word "depression" is applied to so many different situations does not mean that the word is used without any understanding.

3. **B.** The author objects to using a word with two other commonplace meanings, a "bland tonality," and a euphemistic effect, choice B. The author believes the word "depression" is less expressive, less shocking than is necessary to denote the condition accurately. Because the passage suggests replacing "depression" with

another word, the length of time the word has been in use cannot be held against it. The 75 years mentioned in choice A are too long rather than too short a time. The author states nothing about people feeling fear when they hear the word "depression" (C). The author does not imply that the term is applied too strictly (D). Finally, the author indeed makes fun of the Swiss-born psychiatrist who coined the term for having a tin ear (E), but that is hardly the reason why he objects to the term.

4. **B.** Both "wimp" and "tin ear" are colloquialisms—that is, words, phrases, or idioms used in conversation or informal writing, choice B. Choice A, paradox, is simply not accurate; this term refers to two seemingly contradictory statements that actually do have some truth, and the phrases in this question are not contradictory. Choice C is incorrect because the phrases are not euphemisms, kind phrases for harsh realities. The phrase "wimp of a word" is metaphorical—the word is compared to a type of person—but it is not a mixed metaphor (D), which might compare a word to a person and to a tree at the same time, for example. Finally, choice E is blatantly inaccurate; the phrases are not a parody, nor is the passage as a whole a parody.

5. **A.** The phrase "semantic damage," choice A, refers to harm done by the use of the word "depression," but not to the effect of the illness. The phrases in the rest of the answer choices all refer to the fierce power of depression, the disease itself.

6. **D.** The passage says that "brainstorm" describes the disease well, but that it cannot be used because it already has a different established meaning, one of "intellectual inspiration," choice D. Choices A and B are both contradictions; the author feels "brainstorm" is a more accurate term for the disease. Choices C and E have no evidence in the passage; it never alludes to how quickly the public may or may not adopt a new term or to psychiatrists' reticence to change terms.

7. **A.** The sentence argues that a better word than "depression" might change the conventional response to the illness, choice A. The author insists that he is not exaggerating ("veritable," "indeed," "like nothing else") what the victim suffers (C), and we have no reason to assume his examples of the "standard reaction" are inaccurate (B). Choices D and E are completely off base, misreading the passage. The author decries the "standard responses" (D), and he never questions his own idea of a better term (E).

8. **B.** The author alludes to "nervous breakdown" as a phrase that, like "depression," is ill-chosen, but, unlike it, is passing out of use, choice B. His objection to "nervous breakdown" is not because it is "bland" but because it appears to blame the victims for their illness. He never suggests the term is more evocative (A). Choice C is incorrect because the author's purpose in bringing up the term "nervous breakdown" is not merely to add another example of a poor phrase. He does not contrast the two terms (D), and he does not connect "nervous breakdown" to what the uninformed layman feels (E).

9. **C.** Because the author presents depression as "dreadful and raging," as horrible and malevolent, we can assume he would choose the most powerful adjective of the five, "utterly desolated," choice C, and reject the four other choices as too weak to describe its "horrible intensity."

10. **E.** The passage uses the phrase "strong protest" in its first sentence, and this position does not change, choice E. Choice A is incorrect because the author does not approve of the term "depression," although he is unhappily resigned to its use. Both words are inaccurate in choice C. While choices B and D do have one negative word, "disapproval" and "dislike," they are not strong enough for the author's overall attitude, and each is preceded by an inaccurate word, "amused" and "cool."

11. **B.** Though the passage does incidentally give the history of the word (A) and some of its meanings (C), its central idea is to protest the "bland tonality" of the term "depression," choice B. The author reveals his dislike of the phrase "nervous breakdown," and he does mention the archaic word "melancholia" (E), but the passage is focused on the word "depression," not on the shortcomings of medical language (D) in general.

12. **A.** Though the author would probably agree with choices B, C, and D, the central issue of the passage is the misleading meaning of the word "depression" when it refers to the illness, choice A. Choice E is inaccurate because the passage complains about the one word, not about all words.

The passage referred to in questions 13–24 is from John Locke's "An Essay Concerning Human Understanding" (1690).

13. **B.** Any of these five choices can technically define the word "periods," but in this context, the best choice is "complete sentences," choice B. In most multiple-choice exams, a question calling for the definition of a word will ask about a word with several legitimate meanings, and you must look carefully at the context in the passage to determine your answer and, in particular, the specific sentence in which the word appears. Notice how the entire paragraph supports that words put together with "the right construction of grammatical rules" would become sentences. Choice A may deceive some, but the author's point in the first paragraph eliminates it. Because the paragraph's idea is that one who uses words without having ideas behind them "only make[s] a noise without any sense or signification" and simply produces "bare sounds and nothing else," the phrase "sound conclusions" (A) can be considered a contradiction to the passage's context. Choices C, D, and E do not fit the context of the passage.

14. **A.** The antecedent of "ones" is "words" in line 23, choice A. The "them" that follows ("that compose them") refers to "ideas" (C).

15. **D.** In the second paragraph, the shift can best be described as one from figurative to literal, choice D. The first sentence uses a figure of speech, a simile, which pictures an imagined bookseller who has a warehouse of unbound volumes without titles. The second sentence is literal, describing a man who has complex ideas but cannot find the words to express them. The other answer choices do not accurately describe the shift between the two sentences. If you need a definition for any of the terms listed in the answer choices, look in Appendix A.

16. **E.** The simile compares the man who lacks the words to express his complex ideas to the bookseller whose books are only loose sheets of paper, with no means of binding them together, choice E. The other answer choices are images within the sentence, but they do not accurately answer the question.

17. **A.** The author uses analogies (comparisons) to support his arguments, choice A. In the first paragraph, he compares a man who has words but no thoughts to books with titles and no words inside. In the second paragraph, he compares a man who has complex ideas but no words to express them to a bookseller who has volumes of pages that are not bound into any books. The remaining answer choices are not in both paragraphs.

18. **A.** In this context, the word "fair" means equitable or honest, choice A. The other answer choices do not fit the context of the paragraph.

19. **D.** The "substances" are imagined thoughts that "never have been" and do not have "any correspondence with the real nature of things" and are therefore contrasted with realities, choice D, the things that represent "real and true knowledge." Shadows (A), if anything, compares to the use of "substances" because shadows have little substance. Ideas (B) and the author's use of "substances" are similar; he claims substances are imagined ideas. That reasoning also makes choice C inaccurate, as imaginings, in context, are the substances that don't reflect the real truth. In context, names (E) also refers to the imagined substances.

20. **E.** The grouping in choice E best clarifies how the ideas of the first five paragraphs are united: paragraphs one and two; paragraphs three and four; paragraph five. Paragraphs one and two are related; the first presents someone who has words but no ideas, and the second, someone who has ideas but no words. Paragraphs three and four describe two related misuses of words: using one word to mean many things and using words with meanings different from those that are commonly accepted. The fifth paragraph discusses imaginary notions.

21. **D.** The last paragraph recapitulates the contents of the first five, choice D. It does not develop the arguments (A) or question the validity of the arguments (B). No new issues are raised in the last paragraph (C). Choice E is incorrect for two reasons: The last paragraph does not develop ideas, it summarizes them, and the last paragraph summarizes all previous paragraphs, not just the fourth and fifth.

22. **A.** In classical myth, a chimera was a monster with the head of a lion, the body of a goat, and the tail of a serpent. The word has come to mean an impossible fantasy, and the adjective "chimerical" means imaginary, unreal, or absurd, choice A. Even if you are not familiar with the word, notice how the other

answer choices simply do not fit the context accurately, if at all. In choice B, conundrum means an intricate and complicated problem to be solved, which does not relate to the passage's content. The passage does not discuss religious revelations (C) or philosophical distinctions (E). Logical conclusions (D) contradicts the passage, which discusses illogical use of language.

23. **D.** The fourth paragraph, choice D, describes the man who uses familiar words to mean something different from what everyone else understands them to mean.

24. **C.** The third paragraph, choice C, describes the man who uses a word "sometimes in one, sometimes in another signification."

The draft referred to in questions 25–33 discusses the degree to which automation has replaced workers.

25. **D.** The passage explores how some people inaccurately lament that increased automation unavoidably results in workers losing their jobs; instead, it offers examples to argue that increased automation can actually increase jobs. Choice D arouses interest by questioning those who think that increased automation decreases the number of jobs, and it provides an effective lead-in to the Karl Marx example that begins the passage. Additionally, Choice A begins with a plausible idea, positing that "some" people believe an idea that is mistaken, but it then veers wildly off topic by incorrectly addressing "the world of commerce," which is certainly not the subject of the passage. Choice B completely contradicts the passage by claiming that "automation will always pose a threat to workers." Also, notice its problematic use of the absolute word "always." Remember to check the use of absolute and qualifying words for their accuracy. Choice C is only partially accurate for this passage; while it is true that "automation can be seen from more than one viewpoint," the passage is not about seeing the business environment from multiple viewpoints; rather, it is about automation creating new jobs. Choice E may be historically accurate; indeed, workers did fear "losing employment when mechanization began," but this passage deals with the opposite idea—the way that mechanization can actually create more jobs. Thus, choice E too is not an accurate or effective introduction to the passage.

26. **C.** Sentence 5 makes a required point, that consumers bought more cloth *because* of its reduced cost, and thus this sentence is necessary to the passage. It provides a logical connection between the idea in sentence 4, which brings up *how* the cost of cloth was reduced with more factory workers increasing the output, and sentence 6, which asserts that the *increased demand* for cloth equaled more jobs, choice C. Without the link in sentence 5, the ideas in sentences 4 and 6 do not logically follow one another. Choice A incorrectly elects to delete sentence 5, claiming that it adds unimportant information; but in fact, the information *is* necessary. Choice B also votes inaccurately for deleting the sentence, claiming that it distracts from the writer's argument, when, instead, it is a necessary part of the argument. Choice D accurately votes for keeping the sentence, but for the wrong reason; the decision to keep the sentence in question should not be based on whether or not the reading audience might be interested in consumers' actions. Choice E also correctly votes for keeping the sentence and seems to have accurate reasoning at first; it is true that "the paragraph would make no sense without the information," but then it adds incorrect information, "the cost of cloth." That idea was actually expressed in sentence 4, and what sentence 5 provides is the logical next step, the effect: When the cost of cloth went down, consumer buying went up.

27. **A.** Choice A accurately changes the original sentence to show cause and effect; it is precisely *because of automation* that the number of weaving jobs increased. The original phrasing, "regardless of automation," could be read as contradicting the writer's overall point about increased automation. Choice B, "in spite of automation," is synonymous with the original, and it also seems to contradict the overall point. Choice C is awkward, creating a cumbersome and unidiomatic sentence. Notice how unwieldy it is to read ". . . increased jobs for weavers no matter that automation had increased." Choice D may sound potentially good, but it fails to establish the idea of cause and effect that the sentence needs. It is precisely *because of automation* that weavers had more jobs; the word "although" in choice D simply means that the growth was parallel, for jobs increased while automation was increasing. In choice E, the term "despite" is synonymous with the original phrase "regardless of" and incorrectly ignores the causal relationship between increased automation leading to increased jobs.

28. **A.** Sentence 7 would be improved with the addition of the transitional phrase "in fact," choice A, which acts as an intensifier to help verify the accuracy and increase the power of the facts in the sentence. Choice B,

"regardless," is completely contrary to the ideas contained in this sentence. Choice C blandly states that the following information may be "interesting to know," which does nothing to appropriately introduce the sentence; this vacuous wording says nothing significant. Choice D may sound good at first because it gains strength from the supposed credibility of historians, but simply stating that historians note something does not really provide an on-topic and appropriate introductory phrase. Choice E, "notwithstanding," is synonymous to "nevertheless" or "although," and thus it is not a sensible transition to the facts in sentence 7.

29. B. The best placement for sentence 7 would be after sentence 3, choice B. Notice that sentence 3 brings up how, at the end of the 19th century, the number of factory weavers had quadrupled since 1830. If sentence 7 is moved to follow sentence 3, it will add another relevant fact of the increased number of looms for those weavers to work on. Choice A, following sentence 2, is not appropriate; sentence 2 introduces the idea of increased demand for workers, which leads into the example presented in sentence 3 perfectly. Placing sentence 7 in this location would disturb the logical flow of ideas. Choice C suggests placing sentence 7 after sentence 4, but this too would not be appropriate because sentences 4–6 initiate the ideas that need to follow each other: greater output = lower cost of cloth = consumers buying more cloth = increased jobs for workers because of increased demand. Thus, sentence 7 would make a cumbersome insertion after sentence 4. Choice D is wrong for the same reason; sentence 7 cannot follow sentence 5 because it would interrupt the flow of ideas in sentences 4–6. Choice E suggests leaving sentence 7 where it is; however, the facts in sentence 7 do not relate to either sentence 6, which deals with increased jobs, or sentence 8, which deals with the long-term results of the power loom. The evidence presented in sentence 7 is best presented immediately following sentence 3.

30. E. The first paragraph paints a fairly optimistic and upbeat look at how automation affected the weaving industry of the 19th century by stating that more weaving jobs were created as a result of the increase in automated power looms. But if the writer wants to moderate that optimism, every one of the answers will do that, except for choice E. It is the exception because it harkens back to the means of production before the use of automation; the word "artisans" refers to individuals who create complete works of art or craft. After the spread of automation, artisans could no longer see the result of their labor; they could only help produce one part of the whole. All of the other answer choices do indeed modify or refute the optimism of the first paragraph. Choice A brings up the unjust issue of female workers being forced to work for less money than male workers. Choice B presents the fact that automation also increased child labor in factories, with very young children often working in dangerous conditions. Choice C adds another negative consequence of all the new factory jobs: the workers became indebted to the factory owners. Choice D likewise adds yet another negative example, stating that while factory workers may have had jobs, they were forced to work longer hours, under exhausting conditions.

31. C. The information in this potential addition to the second paragraph may initially appear to be interesting, but it is really only a tangential bit of side information; it should not be added to the paragraph because it is simply not necessary and diverts attention from the flow of the sentences, choice C. Choice A incorrectly votes for adding the sentence, plus the so-called "interesting data" do not really support the writer's argument; it is not relevant. Choice B also erroneously votes for the addition and questionably hints that the paragraph is hindered by its lack of supporting statistics. Even if that were true, the additional sentence, by itself, does not actually support the paragraph. Choice D votes for not adding the new sentence but wrongly claims that it is redundant; in fact, this information is not alluded to anywhere in the paragraph. Choice E correctly indicates "no," but then it goes wrong with the word "unconcerned," which refers to a human emotion, such as being apathetic or indifferent. It makes no sense to say that a sentence can be unconcerned with the writer's argument.

32. B. If the writer wants to relate the sentence to *both* paragraphs, sentence 14 must refer to the content of the first paragraph, even though it is located in the second. Choice B accurately makes the analogous connection between 19th-century factory weavers (in the first paragraph) and 20th-century bank tellers (in the second paragraph) by showing that increased demand equated to increased employment both for factory workers and for bank tellers. Choice A is incorrect because leaving the sentence as it is would not accomplish the writer's goal; as it is, the sentence does not relate to the first paragraph. Choice C tries, but fails, to clarify or identify anything specific from the first paragraph; the vague phrase "other workers" can refer to any workers, not necessarily factory weavers. Choice D is equally vague, claiming that demand will dictate available jobs; like choice C it does not necessarily refer to the specific subject at hand, 19th-century factory weavers and modern bank tellers. Additionally, choice D contains the absolute word "always," which cannot be accurate; surely factors other than just demand affect the number of available jobs. Choice E is irrelevant; the public's perceptions about the effect of demand on employment are not germane to the point in sentence 14. Some test-takers may be distracted by the way that choice E refers to the public's inability to understand how demand affects the job market, an idea that appears in the first paragraph; however, this idea does not flow with the concepts in sentences 13 and 15. Remember to look at the paragraph as a whole when deciding how to revise a sentence.

33. **D.** Choice D provides the best conclusion for this passage because it contains information that is relevant to each of the two paragraphs, and it also summarizes the passage's overall point: that technology and automation interact with society in surprising ways, such as providing more jobs instead of decreasing their number. Choice A begins with a plausible idea, that industry will always face increased automation, but it becomes irrelevant to the passage when it mentions management's need to predict workforce changes. That idea does not appear in the passage and should not suddenly appear in the conclusion. Choice B contradicts the theme of the passage by claiming that one "cannot predict" whether future industries will benefit from increased automation, whereas the passage points clearly to the idea of automation's benefits. Choice C is clearly irrelevant; the idea that economists should note the effect of automation on workers' hours and wages appears nowhere in the passage. Choice E is only slightly relevant to the passage as a whole; the passage does point out that people were wrong when they predicted greater unemployment because of automation, but this is not the passage's overall point; rather, it is a starting point to move the argument forward. Choice E also comes across as being too preachy; the passage is not remonstrating with people about their misperceptions regarding the effects of increased automation.

The draft for questions 34–40 discusses the benefits of handwriting vs. typing.

34. **E.** The first sentence would benefit from revision, especially with its bland "There is . . ." opening phrase, which does not serve as the subject or verb of the sentence. Choice E is the best revision because it begins with a true subject, "debate," and verb, "exists," and drops the redundant phrase about "typing *on a keyboard or other electronic devices.*" Choice A simplifies the original idea too much, ignoring that the issue is a debate about the merits of, not mere preference for, either handwriting or typing. Choice B fails to correct the weak "There is . . ." opening, and it loses the idea of debating the *merits,* merely referring to it as a debate. Choice C magnifies the debate into a controversy and tries to make it even larger by claiming it "is constantly brewing," which is an overstatement of the original. Choice D again drops the idea that the debate is about the merits of handwriting vs. typing, and it engages in exaggeration when it claims that it occurs "all the time."

35. **B.** The first paragraph, with only a single simple sentence, blandly states that a debate over the merits of handwriting vs. typing exists. The paragraph would benefit from the inclusion of more attention-grabbing information, and all choices except choice B offer some interesting ideas. Choice B suggests an explanation of the difference between using a keyboard and a laptop, but this idea is already encompassed in the notion of typing, and thus it is irrelevant to the content of the passage as a whole. The addition of the idea in choice A, a mention of note-taking in an academic setting, would be appropriate because the third paragraph discusses classroom note-taking. Choice C would also be entirely apropos, as the passage fails to provide a thesis statement, and one that clarifies the scope of the passage would certainly help readers follow its progression. Choice D would also pique the reader's interest by providing a brief reference to writing innovations throughout the ages, such as the reed stylus in Sumerian tablets, the rise of the Phoenician alphabet, the Chinese invention of paper, the first codex that produced the first books, the invention of printing, the rise of the ballpoint pen, and, of course, typewriters and modern computers and laptops. Choice E would also make a fitting addition to the first paragraph; the passage discusses the process of handwriting vs. typing, taking notes in a classroom setting, and producing finished products, so setting up the reader's expectations for such topics would be helpful.

36. **D.** The second paragraph describes the physical and mental skills required to write, both by hand and on a keyboard, pointing out the difficulties children face when learning to handwrite vs. the relative ease of simply pressing a key to create a letter on a keyboard. Therefore, it is appropriate to mention that it takes years for children to master handwriting because the paragraph also mentions later how easily they learn typing. Thus, the sentence should not be deleted, choice D. Choice A incorrectly claims the sentence should be removed, and it offers a very poor rationale; the sentence does not distract from the paragraph's content,

but rather, it enhances it. Choice B also incorrectly votes for removing the sentence, and it contradicts the paragraph by claiming it does not present information about learning typing skills; but sentence 6 does so by explaining how easily children can learn to type. Choice C also wants to remove the sentence, and again, it provides a weak reason. Children's learning is the focus of the second paragraph, and, by logical extension, it is related to the rest of the passage. What children learn about handwriting and typing applies to their future writing needs. Choice E votes to keep the sentence, but it offers only an irrelevant reason. Whether or not readers can actually remember children's difficulties in learning to handwrite is unrelated to the content of the sentence and the paragraph.

37. A. Sentence 11, as written, is wordy and repetitive, and choice A simplifies the sentence, reducing it to its bare essence. Changing "those who handwrite notes while in class . . ." to "students who handwrite class notes . . ." clarifies whom "those" refers to, plus the new phrasing reduces "handwrite notes while in class" to "handwrite class notes." The original sentence is repetitive with the phrase, ". . . have to think . . . think about . . ."; choice A reduces and rearranges the second half of the sentence into a much more manageable progression of thoughts: "Students . . . have to think about what is important and how to best articulate it while writing." Choice B may be shorter than the original, but it loses some of the meaning; the sentence is not about who *prefers* handwriting, and the phrase "have to think about the important content" is not equal to the idea that they have to decipher what is important to write down. Choice C misses the point of the original, which does not merely deal with the fact that students who handwrite class notes have to think about what is important, and choice C also exaggerates that idea by claiming it is the only point. Choice D is worse than the original; it creates a longer and more cumbersome sentence while it loses the idea about how to best articulate ideas. Choice E adds an unnecessary and arbitrary value judgment to the original statement by claiming that students who handwrite notes "have a harder task." This idea deviates from the point of the paragraph, which clearly states that the process of thinking before writing notes results in better retention; thus, choice E changes the meaning of the original.

38. C. Choice C appropriately adds the transition "Consequentially" to begin the sentence, and it changes the vague and wordy phrase "What happens is a lack of . . ." to the straightforward ". . . the student has less. . . ." It is also the best revision of all the options because it focuses on the actual subject, "the student" who loses understanding. Choice A suggests leaving the underlined portion as it is; however, the original suffers from vagueness and wordiness, so choice A is not the best option. Choice B is even more vague and awkward than the original; when joined with the end of the sentence, it reads, "A lack of meaningful understanding results and application of information." The sentence *needs* to address that *students* ultimately lose meaningful understanding and application of information, but choice B muddles the meaning entirely. Choice D uses the unclear subject-verb combo, "there is," which is always a poor option. Choice E again drops the concept that students are the ones who lose meaningful understanding and again uses a linking verb, "is." If you have a choice, always try to use action verbs.

39. C. Sentence 15 needs to be moved. Placing it after sentence 10, choice C, provides a better location because it begins to answer the question "Why?" by introducing the idea that handwriting has unique advantages, which will be further explained in the subsequent sentences. Choice A, placing it after sentence 7, makes no sense, because sentence 7 brings up studies that show what happens in brain activity when handwriting, and sentence 8 follows up with a related study. Placing sentence 15 in this location would interrupt this smooth flow of ideas. Choice B, placing it after sentence 8, also makes no sense because sentence 8 introduces the related study, and sentence 9 needs to follow it by explaining the results of the study. Choice D, placing it after sentence 11, is also illogical; sentences 11 and 12 naturally belong adjacent to one another, as one leads into the other. Additionally, placing sentence 15 after sentence 11 would result in an awkward progression of ideas: "Although handwriting is slower for most . . ." followed by "While typing may be faster. . . ." Choice E, leaving it in its current location, is actually a poor choice; currently it is tacked on to the end of the paragraph and brings up the idea of handwriting having advantages before abruptly dropping it. How can we know what those advantages are?

40. B. If you explore the content of the overall passage, you'll see that it addresses the advantages of handwriting far more than it discusses the benefits of typing. It is as if typing gets short shrift; in the second paragraph we learn typing is faster to learn, and in the fifth paragraph we discover that typing helps the finished product and makes for easier editing, but those are the only advantages that are mentioned. Comparatively, we learn much more about the advantages of handwriting. Choice B best addresses this imbalance by suggesting adding more information regarding the specific benefits of typing. Choice A, which suggests complementing the current passage with interviews from those who favor typing class notes, may initially seem like a potentially good answer, but by itself it is too simplistic and potentially biased to counter the overall imbalance in the passage. Choice C would hardly add compelling balance because personal testimony from those who favor typing amounts to mere hearsay in light of the professional studies about handwriting that are presented. Choice D is a viable idea regarding the overall organization of the passage; indeed, sentence 16 stands all by itself and does not have any direct connection to what comes immediately before or after it. However, this question asks about the *balance of ideas,* not just the organization, and the elimination of sentence 16 would not affect the balance of ideas significantly. Choice E is only partially correct; while it is true that the entire passage needs more presentation of the other side of the issue, it would be improper to place it all in the last paragraph.

The draft for questions 41–45 discusses the value of transitional objects for children.

41. D. This passage discusses the important role that transitional objects play in children's lives, and it explains the psychological rationale for such behavior. Choice D crystalizes this idea and best clarifies the writer's main point. While other possible answer choices involve the idea of security, only choice D adds the psychological component, making it the best response. Choice A is too simplistic and overly broad; it merely points out that having a comfort object is important, but it fails to narrow the focus to children and their psychologically appropriate use of security objects, which is the central focus of the passage. Choice B may initially seem like a good choice, but its scope is too narrow because it only mentions a security blanket, while the passage mentions many other forms of transitional objects, and it states blandly that such an object "plays an important role," thus ignoring the psychological importance of such a role in children's growth. Choice C alludes to one minor point of the passage and then tries to magnify it inappropriately. The passage mentions only once that a mother "gradually separates" herself for longer periods of time from her child, but the passage does not indicate that this "creates difficulties," nor does it claim that the mother-child bond is "broken." Choice E takes the main point too far; the passage never asserts that children "*constantly* need assurance. . . ." Also, like all other incorrect responses, choice E ignores the psychological component of the passage.

42. C. All of these answer choices would make appropriate additions that would better develop the passage EXCEPT choice C, which suggests including biographical information about Donald Woods Winnicott. The passage already explains that he was a British pediatrician and psychoanalyst, which is ample information to establish his credentials. If the piece were substantially longer, perhaps more information about Winnicott's studies would be interesting, but this short passage does not need more biographical information. Choice A, adding a definition of the term "transitional object," would be very helpful; as written, the passage offers no such definition, and the reader must infer the meaning of the term. Choice B would also be a helpful addition; currently the passage states that the transitional object serves as a bridge between infancy and childhood, but it does not explain *how* this happens or what psychological purpose it serves. Choice D would definitely help develop the passage; the term "subjective omnipotence" appears suddenly at the end of the second paragraph, and the reader has to grapple with what the term means. Choice E would also help provide appropriate information; currently the passage simply states that the transitional object takes the place of the mother-child relationship, but it neglects to explain how this transformation takes place.

43. B. Choice B does the best job of explaining the logic of how the child substitutes the transitional object for the presence of the mother and, in the process, creates security and safety; without these few extra links, the logic is not complete. Choice A, which favors leaving the sentence as it is, does not explain the logical connections that help provide meaning. Choice C takes the wrong path by claiming the child *can understand* the psychological implications of the transitional object, a complex concept that the child is too young to comprehend. Choice D claims that transitional objects permit children to gain independence faster, but the passage offers no support for such an idea; this is too much of a stretch without any additional evidence. Choice E makes an unwarranted logical leap when it claims that transitional objects encourage children to learn that their mother will not always be there; it makes no sense to claim that the transitional object represents all the components of "mothering" (as stated in the first half of the sentence) and then claim that this object will help children learn that their mother will not always be there.

44. **B.** One common approach that is used in many types of writing is to begin with something that readers will relate to and then return to this idea in the end, bringing the flow of ideas full circle, so to speak. Choice B correctly identifies this technique as the most significant reason that sentence 13 should not be deleted. Choice A also votes for keeping the sentence, but for a poor reason; it is true that the passage relies on readers being able to relate to Linus from the *Peanuts* comic strip, but that does not provide a valid reason for keeping sentence 13. At best it only provides a rationale for introducing Linus in the opening sentence. Choice C incorrectly claims that this information was already established in the passage. While the opening sentence does introduce Linus as having a constant security blanket, that idea alone does not take the extra step of claiming that its name was most appropriate. Choice D states an inaccurate reason for deleting the sentence; on the contrary, this information does move the passage's ideas forward by connecting back to the introductory sentence and by taking us one step beyond, exclaiming the aptness of naming Linus' companion as a security blanket. Choice E also erroneously votes to delete the sentence, by judging it as offering no pertinent information, when it does indeed address the appropriateness of the name "security blanket."

45. **E.** The passage discusses the importance of transitional objects in children's lives, implying it is a fairly universal concept. However, that foundation of universality could be refuted if evidence were presented that shows children who are raised in some other cultures do not have a need for a transitional object; thus, choice E is the best answer. Choice A is incorrect because it merely presents a hypothetical idea of fathers possibly becoming the primary source of comfort, but then it jumps to the unwarranted conclusion that this situation would make any need for transitional objects disappear. This logic simply does not hold up. The information in choice B is irrelevant; whether some children do not need a teddy bear or a security blanket to fall asleep does not refute the passage's overall point about most infants' need for a transitional object. Choice C does not refute the passage but instead reinforces its point. If the transitional object plays an important role in creating security for a child, losing that important object would indeed create stress for the child. Choice D is also irrelevant; a mother's awareness of the role a transitional object plays (the so-called "phenomenon") may or may not help her cope when her child cries, but this idea does not refute the passage as a whole.

Section II: Free-Response Questions

Question 1

Row A: Thesis (0–1 point)	
Scoring Criteria	
0 points for any of the following:	**1 point for**
• Having no defendable thesis. • Only restating the prompt in the thesis. • Only summarizing the issue with no apparent or coherent claim in the thesis. • Presenting a thesis that does not address the prompt.	• Addressing the prompt with a defendable thesis.
Decision Rules and Scoring Notes	
Theses that do not earn this point	**Theses that do earn this point**
• Only restate the prompt. • Are vague or do not take a position. • Equivocate or merely summarize others' arguments. • Simply state obvious facts rather than making a defendable claim.	• Respond to the prompt (rather than restating it) and clearly take a position on the idea that professional athletes are overpaid instead of simply stating pros and cons.

Additional Notes

- The thesis may be one or more sentences that are in close proximity to each other anywhere in the essay.
- A thesis that meets the criteria can be awarded the point whether or not the rest of the response successfully conveys that line of reasoning.
- For a thesis to be defendable, the sources must have at least minimal evidence that could be used as support.
- A thesis may present a line of reasoning, but it is not required to earn a point.

Row B: Evidence AND Commentary (0–4 points)

Scoring Criteria

0 points for	1 point for	2 points for	3 points for	4 points for
• Simply repeating the thesis (if present). • **OR** restating provided information. • **OR** providing fewer than two references to the provided sources.	• Providing evidence from at least two of the provided sources. • **AND** summarizing the evidence without explaining how the evidence supports the thesis.	• Providing evidence from or references to at least three of the provided sources. • **AND** explaining how some of the evidence relates to the thesis, but the line of reasoning may be nonexistent or faulty.	• Providing specific evidence from or references to at least three of the provided sources to support all claims in the line of reasoning. • **AND** explaining how some of the evidence relates to the thesis and supports the line of reasoning.	• Providing specific evidence from or references to at least three of the provided sources to support all claims in the line of reasoning. • **AND** consistently and explicitly explaining how the evidence relates to the thesis and supports the line of reasoning.

Decision Rules and Scoring Notes

Typical responses that earn 0 points:	Typical responses that earn 1 point:	Typical responses that earn 2 points:	Typical responses that earn 3 points:	Typical responses that earn 4 points:
• Are unclear or fail to address the prompt. • May present mere opinion or repeat ideas from a single source.	• Only summarize or describe sources instead of providing specific details.	• Mix specific details with broad generalities. • May contain simplistic, inaccurate, or repetitive explanations that do not strengthen the argument. • Fail to explain the connections between claims and to establish a clear line of reasoning. • May make one point well but fail to adequately support any other claims.	• Consistently offer evidence to support all claims. • Focus on the importance of specific words and details from the sources to build an argument. • Use multiple supporting claims to organize an argument and line of reasoning. • May not integrate some evidence or support a key claim in the commentary.	• Consistently offer evidence to support all claims. • Focus on the importance of specific words and details from the sources to build an argument. • Organize, integrate, and thoroughly explain evidence from sources throughout in order to support the line of reasoning.

Additional Notes

- Writing that suffers from grammatical and/or mechanical errors that interfere with communication cannot earn the fourth point in this row.

Row C: Sophistication (0–1 point)	
Scoring Criteria	
0 points for • Not meeting the criteria for 1 point.	**1 point for** • Exhibiting sophistication of thought and/or advancing a complex understanding of the rhetorical situation.
Decision Rules and Scoring Notes	
Responses that do not earn this point: • Try to contextualize their argument, but make predominantly sweeping generalizations (*"Throughout all history . . ."* OR *"Everyone believes . . ."*). • Only hint at other possible arguments (*"Some may think . . ."*). • Present complicated or complex sentences or language that is ineffective and detracts from the argument.	**Responses that earn this point demonstrate one (or more) of the following:** • Present a nuanced argument that consistently identifies and examines complexities or tension across the sources. • Illuminate the significance or implications of the argument (either the student's argument or the arguments within the sources) within a broader context. • Make effective rhetorical choices that consistently strengthen the force and impact of the student's argument. • Develop a prose style that is especially vivid, persuasive, resounding, or appropriate to the student's argument.
Additional Notes • This point should be awarded only if the demonstration of sophistication or complex understanding is part of the argument, not merely a phrase or brief reference.	

High-Scoring Essay

In recent decades, athletes' salaries have soared, allowing them to collect millions in yearly earnings for merely displaying their physical gifts. Although athletes are arguably the world's most physically gifted individuals, their preposterous salaries are unjustifiable when their jobs are limited to seasonal games intended for purely entertainment purposes. Magnified by the allure of extravagant wealth, athletes become sedated by the extrinsic value of playing their respective sports, which in turn negatively affects society's younger generation. Salaries that run in the ten-millions and even in the hundred-millions are not only excessive, but also unwarranted for individuals who simply play a game for their jobs.

While some sports such as tennis and golf entail all-year-round games, most of the mainstream and high-paying sports, such as basketball, baseball, soccer, and football, are limited to seasons that are played over the course of several months. Especially when athletes are paid on the basis of their performance over a fraction of the year, their absurd salaries do not properly reflect their job's length, no matter what author PK claims in "Athletes Are Underpaid." And although some may argue that athletes must train in the off-season to maintain their peak-condition, it is no different than the unpaid preparation that teachers must sacrifice before each school year. Furthermore, the games in which athletes participate last for an average of three hours per game. It is illogical that athletes are paid in the millions for their performances for a couple of hours per game, when other professions judge individuals' production over the compilation of full day's work. Once again, the preparation that athletes must endure is not a relevant argument, since it is ultimately during the games that fans are entertained. People do not pay for preparation; people pay for the action and pleasure of games.

While society may value sports, consumer choice, according to Gene Callahan, reflects one of the reasons for the rich salaries that athletes receive. However, this fact does not fully account for all of the reasons that athletes' salaries are as such (Source B). Many goods in society are vastly overpriced, and although individuals continue to succumb to outrageous prices by giving in, it may be that society is simply at the receiving end of corruption and inflation. Humans are naturally drawn to what is portrayed as rich and wealthy. It is evident that exorbitant prices for sports venues do not have a proper effect on individuals' decision making, which leads to the fact that society is ultimately submitting to the immoral standards of sports entertainment. This is not limited to American sports at all. In fact, as Source C points out, cricket players in India average $3,612,726 annually, and many European soccer players earn between $1,960,080 (Italy) and $3,184,110 (Britain). It appears the world values sports more than many other commodities.

Some may argue that professional players actually have to sacrifice a great deal to become a pro athlete, but that idea is faulted in the fact that athletes sacrifice no more than other professionals who aspire to become teachers and researchers. Many professions require intense "sacrifice" and yet do not offer the outrageous remuneration professional sports offers. Why should the basketball player's "sacrifice" be worth more than any other professional's? Athletes' salaries are climbing at unprecedented rates, and Source C points out the multi-million dollar salaries athletes receive around the world. Meanwhile, the salaries of prominent government leaders throughout the world seem paltry by comparison: Putin's $136,000, Hollande's $194,251 and Xi Jingping's $22,000 seem like the peanuts sold in NFL stadiums when compared to actual NFL players' salaries (Source A). It boggles the mind that world leaders are compensated only a fraction of professional athletes; after all, which profession is more important? Although athletes may boast amazing and rare skills, million dollar salaries are definitely not reasonable, when their productivity level lies entirely in entertainment purposes. Although athletes encompass elite physical skills, it is nearly impossible to compare their gifts with those of others. Although societal attitudes may be at the root of this imbalance, in which the value of entertainment may supersede the value of life, the disparity in athletes' salaries as compared to most other professional salaries illustrates a self-evident problem. Regardless of deciding where to place the blame for allowing such overpriced salaries, it is clear that athletes receive too much for their supposed sacrifice and production year in and year out.

As athletes continue to receive more than what they are worth, youngsters who delve their interest in modeling their lives after sports superstars are negatively influenced by greed and discontent. The questionable plight of players' unions seeking even greater salaries for athletes combined with the instances in which athletes "opt out of contracts" only to sign bigger and better ones for "stability" purposes elicits a message of insatiability and pure greed (Source E). Youngsters begin with the innocent passion of playing sports—similar to how professional athletes began—but when they are exposed to the attempts of athletes and agents in receiving more and more millions of dollars, they can become corrupted. Athletes who boast contracts that reach up to $252 million dollars are unconditionally blinded by the allure of money (Source E). While their gross incomes are unfair and unjust, their commitment to negotiating for millions of dollars adds an immoral image that unavoidably plagues the rest of society and the younger generation.

Amidst the façade of athletic talent and physical stature, athletes' ridiculous earnings have reached excessive and unprecedented levels that are not warranted, given their limited entertainment-driven performances. The myopia of athletes in merely attempting to find the longest and richest contract further illustrates the pathos of outrageous and disproportionate salaries in the world of sports. After all, it's only a game.

(960 words)

Analysis of the High-Scoring Essay

This essay earns a high score because it is on topic and thoroughly developed. The student begins with an understanding that athletes are indeed "physically gifted individuals" but acknowledges that this gift, coupled with athletes' limited season, does not warrant their multi-million-dollar salaries. The introduction sets up the content and organization of the essay well, demonstrating that the student has planned his or her ideas successfully in advance. The essay definitely earns a point in Row A.

The second paragraph focuses on the aspect that most highly paid athletes only perform for a limited time in a limited season and, therefore, should not receive such exorbitant salaries. Comparing the time athletes train to the time teachers prepare brings the argument to the level of everyman and draws an apt analogy. Certainly an AP Reader can relate to working long hours, but so can every other person who works as hard. By extension, wouldn't all professionals prefer to be paid so handsomely for their preparation? Although this logic demonstrates clear thinking on the student's part, the idea that fans only pay for action and not preparation is not as convincing as it could be. The student would be better served to expand this argument by considering counterarguments and then logically dismissing them.

The next paragraph discusses society's value system and acknowledges the truth that many people in society are willing to pay dearly for those things they deem worthy. The student makes the point even more forceful by discussing that "humans are naturally drawn to what is portrayed as rich and wealthy," intimating that humans do not always know the true value of things; rather, we are influenced by the value judgments of others. The paragraph is further enhanced by exploring sports salaries throughout the globe. This level of analysis demonstrates the maturity of the student.

The following paragraph uses multiple sources from the prompt to compare the actual salaries of many professions. It is as thorough an examination of the data as one could expect in a timed essay. The student continues by addressing the value of certain professions, namely world leaders who carry more important influence, and makes the point that the value of athletes' jobs pales in comparison. The student's comparison of world leaders' salaries to peanuts (sold in stadiums) makes a Reader chuckle, even though the wording is cumbersome. Overall, this paragraph is particularly thorough and convincing in its logical and fact-based presentation and helps earn the essay's high score.

The writer then explores the effect that athletes have on the young, pointing out how young people are so easily influenced by the glitz and glamour of professional athletes. Then, by discussing the example of how an athlete can opt out of a contract in order to sign an even more lucrative one, the student makes a logical connection between the corrupting power of money triumphing over the intrinsic fun of playing a game and how easily a youth's belief system can be swayed by this self-centered behavior. This point is important to all of society, as this student clearly proves. The high quality of the evidence and commentary warrants 4 points in Row B.

The concluding paragraph shows that this student does not run out of steam but rather ends the essay forcefully, using striking phrases such as "the myopia of athletes" and "the pathos of outrageous and disproportionate salaries." The last sentence, concise and pithy, reminds us to place sports into the big picture of society; after all, it is only a game. This concludes the essay with finality, with conviction.

Although this essay does have some flaws, both in minor wording issues and minor lapses in logic, they are not serious enough to keep this essay from receiving a high score. Its overall intelligent presentation and well-developed discussion clearly demonstrate that the student's efforts are worthy of a high score, and it deserves a point in Row C. It should earn an overall score of 6.

Low-Scoring Essay

With the general trend of popularity in sports, athletes have signed contracts worth a lot of money, however, many argue how fair this is despite the fact that athletes have irreplaceable talents and are ultimately paid for the amount of attention they receive. America's emphasis on sports makes the million dollar contracts of athletes just and necessary.

Although there is a disparity in the incomes that athletes earn with the incomes of professionals such as teachers, firefighters and truckers, there are only a limited number of athletes represented in the professional ranks compared to the many individuals in relatively common professions. Given the minority of athletes, the amount of money that they are paid is warranted, if there were as many professional athletes as there were teachers, then it would be vastly unjust, but this is not the case. Furthermore, athletes' talents that they display in their respective sports are unique and unmatchable. After honing their skills for countless years, only a few select individuals who display exceptional athletic abilities are rewarded for their training.

The reasoning behind the rich contracts of athletes is ultimately the valuable God-given talents that athletes have over other individuals. Athletes who grace the covers of magazines and serve as role models for many youngsters are arguably the fittest and most disciplined individuals in society, the achievements that they reach in sports are historically unique and therefore are met with fanatical acceptance through enthusiastic fanfare. People may argue that other professions should receive more incentive for their work, but the fact is that those people should stop putting their money into sports and instead devote it to education

(Source B). Many individuals display insurmountable passion for sports. And in turn are willing to pay the money to see their favorite athletes.

Additionally, unlike most other professions, athletics is distinctive in the fact that athletes are constantly under the scrutiny of the press and the opinions of fans. Athletes are human, they are plagued with a flow of attention. Although attention may have beneficial outcomes, it can also be excruciating and undesirable. Athletes living under this spotlight, sacrifice their personal lives as they continue to perform at high-caliber levels of competition. In turn, the incomes that athletes earn are not merely represented through their accomplishments on the field, but also serve as compensation for the loss of privacy in becoming an athlete.

Given the excitement and exuberance for sports throughout society, athletes are given salaries based on their popular demand. Ultimately, athletes are paid really well all around the world (Source C). With money coming from television, ticket sales and other outlets, athletes' salaries are not generated from nothingness, but in actuality in terms of what fans pay to see these athletes perform. Rather than continuing to deem sports as overpriced, individuals must realize that athletes are simply earning what they are given. Athletes are in reality like every other individual in society and should be given the same rights. When individuals cry afoul regarding contract disputes, athletes are merely exercising the exact rights that other individuals exercise when they seek signing bonuses and other incentives. While the blame continues to revolve around athletes and their supposed extorted earnings, the reality is that athletes are for the most part earning every dollar that they receive. For many individuals, sports is everything, and amidst that fervor, fans are willing to put in the money to watch athletes in action. If people are willing to support athletes, yet criticize them, then the problem lies within the populous of society. The true difference between sports and many other professions is that sports entails a large fan-base. In turn, the revenues coming from sports are immense. Just as any front-office executive, team owners merely reward their players with what the organization earns from yearly revenues.

Inevitably through the uniqueness of athletes' skills and achievements in their respective sports, their grossing salaries that consistently run in the million dollar ranges are both just and reasonable. Professional athletes are rare and given their incredible talents, their rich contracts are merely substantiated from the amount of work that they put in and the passionate fanfare they encounter.

(694 words)

Analysis of the Low-Scoring Essay

This essay, while deceptively lengthy, does not construct a convincing argument, nor does it incorporate the minimum of three sources from the prompt, as directed. Ultimately, this essay demonstrates how a student can write a long essay but basically go nowhere. The language is not particularly striking, and it displays a disturbing number of grammatical and mechanical errors.

The essay begins with a simplistic thesis: that professional athletes justly deserve a large salary because America emphasizes sports. The AP Exam Reader is left wondering where this logic will lead, but the thesis does deserve a point in Row A.

The first body paragraph displays organizational problems, beginning with a discussion of the disparity in the ratio of professional athletes to other professions and then moving into the skills an athlete must hone to succeed. The student also displays gaps in logic—for example, claiming that athletes deserve more money simply because they make up a minority of the workforce. This illogical claim is followed by the equally puzzling remark that if there were as many professional athletes as teachers, "then it would be vastly unjust."

Many of the student's phrases seem hollow and do not help propel the essay forward. For example, some statements, such as "athletes' talents . . . are unique and unmatchable," are simply untrue and really say nothing. The student does include two sources from the prompt but merely uses them to make the point that society values sports without a deeper analysis of how this affects athletes' incomes.

The next brief paragraph does not make a strong argument but merely asserts the claim that, because athletes are "under scrutiny," they deserve more money to compensate for their loss of privacy. However, if the student were to take this argument to its logical conclusion, then many professions would also deserve multi-million-dollar salaries simply because the jobs propel one into the public eye.

The paragraph that follows presents contradictory ideas. The student previously declared that athletes are unique and therefore deserve their high salary but now claims that athletes are "in reality like every other individual in society." Self-contradictory thinking like this cannot help an essay's score. Because the writer only includes two sources from the prompt, the essay automatically earns only 1 point in Row B. If the essay had included even one more source, it would have earned at least 2 points.

The conclusion repeats the essay's main idea, that athletes deserve their salary because they are "rare" and have "incredible talent." But it's a sentiment the Reader has heard before, and so the conclusion offers no food for thought, merely summary.

Finally, take note of how the sentence fragments, run-on sentences, punctuation errors, and frequent verb mistakes distract the Reader from the essay's content. Obviously, it does not earn a point in Row C. Do not let the essay's length deceive you; its many errors, lack of substance and source examples, and logical fallacies should earn a score of 2.

Question 2

Row A: Thesis (0–1 point)	
Scoring Criteria	
0 points for any of the following: • Having no defendable thesis. • Only restating the prompt in the thesis. • Only summarizing the issue with no apparent or coherent claim in the thesis. • Presenting a thesis that does not address the prompt.	**1 point for** • Addressing the prompt with a defendable thesis that analyzes the writer's rhetorical choices.
Decision Rules and Scoring Notes	
Theses that do not earn this point • Only restate the prompt. • Neglect to address the writer's rhetorical choices. • Simply describe or repeat the passage rather than making a defendable claim.	**Theses that do earn this point** • Respond to the prompt (rather than restating it) and clearly articulate a defendable thesis exploring how President Obama's rhetorical strategies help develop his message.

Additional Notes

• The thesis may be one or more sentences that are in close proximity to each other anywhere in the essay.
• A thesis that meets the criteria can be awarded the point whether or not the rest of the response successfully conveys that line of reasoning.
• For a thesis to be defendable, the passage must have at least minimal evidence that could be used as support.
• A thesis may present a line of reasoning, but it is not required to earn a point.

Row B: Evidence AND Commentary (0–4 points)

Scoring Criteria

0 points for	1 point for	2 points for	3 points for	4 points for
• Simply repeating the thesis (if present). • **OR** restating provided information. • **OR** providing mostly irrelevant and/or incoherent evidence.	• Summarizing the passage without reference or connection to the thesis. • **OR** providing mostly general evidence. • **AND** providing little or no explanation or commentary.	• Providing some specific evidence that is relevant to the thesis. • **AND** explaining how some of the evidence relates to the thesis, but the line of reasoning may be nonexistent or faulty.	• Providing specific evidence to support all claims in the line of reasoning. • **AND** explaining how some of the evidence relates to the thesis and supports the line of reasoning. • **AND** explaining how at least one rhetorical choice in the passage contributes to the writer's thesis.	• Providing specific evidence to support all claims in the line of reasoning. • **AND** providing well-developed commentary that consistently and explicitly explains the relationship between the evidence and the thesis. • **AND** explaining how multiple rhetorical choices in the passage contribute to the writer's thesis.

Decision Rules and Scoring Notes

Typical responses that earn 0 points:	Typical responses that earn 1 point:	Typical responses that earn 2 points:	Typical responses that earn 3 points:	Typical responses that earn 4 points:
• Are unclear or fail to address the prompt. • May present mere opinion with little or no evidence.	• Only summarize or restate ideas from the passage without any analysis. • May mention rhetorical devices with little or no explanation or analysis.	• Mix specific details with broad generalities. • May contain simplistic, inaccurate, or repetitive explanations that do not strengthen the argument. • Fail to explain the connections between claims and to establish a clear line of reasoning. • May make one point well but fail to adequately support any other claims.	• Consistently offer evidence to support all claims. • Focus on the importance of specific words and details from the passage to build an argument. • Use multiple supporting claims to organize an argument and line of reasoning. • May not integrate some evidence or support a key claim in the commentary.	• Consistently offer evidence to support all claims. • Focus on the importance of specific words and details from the passage to build an argument. • Use multiple supporting claims with adequate evidence and explanation to organize an argument and line of reasoning. • Explain how the writer's use of rhetorical devices contributes to the student's analysis of the passage.

continued

Additional Notes

• Writing that suffers from grammatical and/or mechanical errors that interfere with communication cannot earn the fourth point in this row.

Row C: Sophistication (0–1 point)	
Scoring Criteria	
0 points for • Not meeting the criteria for 1 point.	**1 point for** • Exhibiting sophistication of thought and/or advancing a complex understanding of the rhetorical situation.
Decision Rules and Scoring Notes	
Responses that do not earn this point: • Try to contextualize the text, but make predominantly sweeping generalizations (*"Throughout all history . . ."* OR *"Everyone believes . . ."*). • Only hint at other possible arguments (*"Some may think . . ."*). • Examine individual rhetorical choices but fail to examine the relationships among varying choices throughout the passage. • Oversimplify textual complexities. • Present complicated or complex sentences or language that is ineffective and detracts from the argument.	Responses that earn this point demonstrate one (or more) of the following: • Explain the purpose or function of complexities or tension in the passage. • Explain the significance of the writer's rhetorical choices for the given rhetorical situation. • Develop a prose style that is especially vivid, persuasive, resounding, or appropriate to the student's argument.

Additional Notes

• This point should be awarded only if the demonstration of sophistication or complex understanding is part of the argument, not merely a phrase or brief reference.

High-Scoring Essay

The whole world was watching and listening as newly elected President Obama stepped up to the microphone on January 21, 2009, representing a campaign that was associated with hope and dignity and change. Traditionally, an inaugural speech is one of inspiration, one of optimism, one of assurance for the future. Indeed, President Obama adheres to this tradition, eloquently and effectively, as he takes the helm as the leader of the United States.

Frequently throughout his remarks, President Obama tactically refers to the past, reminding us of America's strengths during adversity, before looking to the future. He begins by mentioning the forty-three presidents who have come before him, surely establishing his credibility as the new president as he joins those august men. But he does not merely allude to past presidents as a tool to reflect upon himself; he instead immediately segues into the fact that many presidents faced metaphorical "gathering clouds and raging storms," through which the country carried on, thanks to Americans' remaining "faithful to the ideals of our forebears and true to our founding documents." His introduction, therefore, connects to the audience by reminding them of America's past greatness and suggesting more greatness to come. His repetition in the parallel phrasing, "so it has been; so it must be . . ." musically reinforces this goal.

President Obama then explores how this greatness has been achieved, again reaching into American history for examples. He acknowledges that America's greatness has been a hard path, a journey taken by frequently obscure "risk-takers . . . doers . . . makers of things." His repetition of "For us, they packed up . . . and traveled. . . . For us, they toiled . . . and settled . . . endured . . . and plowed. . . . For us, they fought and died. . . ." hammers in the collective idea that Americans overcome hardship, that Americans endure harsh conditions, that Americans sacrifice for their country. Indeed, his powerful diction, parallel construction, and harsh imagery compound his message, ultimately reminding us that we are "bigger than the sum of our individual ambitions, greater than all the differences of birth or wealth or faction." These are the oratorical tools that great speech writers use.

It is interesting to note that his inaugural address continues not by bringing up what problems America faces today, but by probing what questions we ask today. This changes the thrust from negative to potentially positive and influences the way an audience emotionally responds; we do not want to hear about problems in an inaugural address, but we do want to know about what questions we can answer. President Obama acknowledges that our challenges may be new and the way we meet them will also have to be new, but in doing so he again uses the approach of reminding us of our past, how "honesty and hard work, courage and fair play, tolerance and curiosity, loyalty and patriotism," are "old" and "true" forces of progress. Through collectively embracing these values, we want to enthusiastically cheer on America as we jointly work, "giving our all to a difficult task."

The President concludes his oration appropriately with another reference to our history, but this time a very specific one, one often taught in American schools: that of the horrible winter endured by soldiers during the American Revolution in Valley Forge. Reminding us of America's past struggle for "that great gift of freedom," knowing that the struggle was successful in creating a nation that has endured ever since, this allusion to hardship propels the audience to rise to greatness and, "with eyes fixed on the horizon" continue to overcome any new challenges. Emotionally, President Obama has his audience in the palm of his hand as he connects America's past to its present and future, for who can deny that the suffering of those soldiers in the winter of 1777–1778 led to a great and prosperous nation? Who can deny that America as a great and prosperous nation still maintains its place in the world today? Who can deny that we will work hard so that it can continue?

(692 words)

Analysis of the High-Scoring Essay

AP Readers always appreciate and reward well-written, thoughtful essays; this high-scoring essay indeed deserves to be amply rewarded. It begins by arousing a Reader's anticipation, reminding one of the intense public interest that surrounded President Obama's inaugural speech in 2009 and how his campaign was associated with positive ideals: hope, dignity, and change. The student then connects President Obama's optimistic message with previous presidents' addresses, subtly establishing President Obama's credentials. The student completes the introductory paragraph by explicitly claiming that President Obama's speech was both eloquent and effective. It deserves a point in Row A for its defendable thesis.

The second paragraph explores the rhetorical strategy of using historical examples to make a point. While introducing this idea, the student creates a positive connection to the Reader with the phrase "reminding us of America's strengths during adversity." The student understands how Obama's rhetorical strategy of mentioning past presidents establishes "his credibility" without having to use the term "ethos," a word that is so often drilled into AP students. The essay continues by noticing one of the metaphors Obama uses, that of "gathering clouds and raging storms," and connects it to America's ability to overcome hardship. The student then directly states that President Obama's introduction "connects to the audience," because we understand and appreciate his historical allusions. The student also notices President Obama's rhetorical strategy of parallel construction, mentioning that his use "musically reinforces" the speech's goal. Although one might want the student to further develop how this stylistic device enhances the speech, one can reward the student for noticing it and having something accurate to say about its effect.

The essay continues examining President Obama's historical examples, ones that refer not to specific individuals or singular events but to the many "obscure" Americans who helped build the country. The student again notices Obama's parallel construction, and in doing so, the student, in turn, eloquently employs his or her own parallel construction, repeating the phrase "that Americans . . ." three times. The student's phrasing is particularly effective for several reasons: It mirrors the effectiveness of the original speech, and, in the process, it helps prove the student's idea that Obama's speech "hammers in the collective idea" of Americans' success. The student mentions that "powerful diction, parallel construction, and harsh imagery" are tools of great speech writers. This perceptive analysis of how rhetorical strategies help deliver a message is thoughtful and, because of the student's sophisticated style, particularly articulate.

The fourth paragraph discusses a point that not many students notice: how President Obama's choice of exploring questions that America faces, instead of identifying them as problems to be solved, turns something potentially negative into something positive. The student does not merely make this point but continues to explore the effect, pointing out how it influences the way the audience responds. The student again brings up how President Obama uses historical allusions to Americans' fortitude and connects that to audience reaction, claiming that "we want to enthusiastically cheer" as America faces the future.

The student's final paragraph examines how President Obama concludes his speech, again understanding how his historical allusion to the Revolutionary War not only reminds us of our past but also compels us to future greatness. Without having to use the word "pathos," the student claims that "President Obama has his audience in the palm of his hand." The student effectively ends the essay with a series of questions, all using parallel construction with the phrase "who can deny that. . . ." Ending any essay with a series of questions can be risky, because one general bit of advice is that essays should answer questions, not ask them. However, this student's questions are thought-provoking and do not remotely imply that the student does not know the answers. Instead, they are rhetorical questions; we know what the student intends the answers to be. The thorough development of ideas and commentary deserve 4 points in Row B.

Overall, this essay is clearly on topic and well developed. Its organization explores the speech chronologically, walking through it from its introduction to its conclusion. A Reader will be glad that the student did not choose to organize around rhetorical strategies, such as devoting one paragraph to historical allusion, one to parallel construction, and so forth. Although organizing in that fashion may give many students comfort, it is ultimately not as sophisticated as the organization exhibited in this essay. Finally, the student's style is very pleasing, using sophisticated diction and syntax. Any AP Reader will reward this student for what he or she does so well, and a Reader will award this essay with a point in Row C and an overall high score of 6.

Low-Scoring Essay

All presidents give an inaugural speech. Some are great speeches, some are forgettable. President Obama's 2009 inaugural speech was good, making a positive impact on all who heard it or read it today.

Obama talks of unity, something he thinks the nation needs. He thinks the country had strong leaders in the past who helped America. He wants to do the same. In his speech his message is that we have to work hard because "hard work" has "been the quiet force of progress throughout our history."

He uses historical examples to prove his point that "throughout our history" we have worked hard. He talked about Concord, Gettysburg, Normandy, and Khe Sahn, which was during the Vietnam War. These historical examples help prove his point. He also talked about the American Revolutionary War.

He also tries to be uplifting by using phrases like "reaffirming the greatness of our nation" and "vital trust between a people and their government" and "return to these truths" and "with hope and virtue."

President Obama's speech tries to unify the country by using historical examples and uplifting diction.

(183 words)

Analysis of the Low-Scoring Essay

The student who wrote this low-scoring essay appears to appreciate President Obama's inaugural speech, but little more can be said for its presentation. Instead of analyzing *how* the speech's rhetorical strategies develop its message, the student merely paraphrases or directly quotes the speech.

It begins with a short, off-topic introduction that does not clearly address the prompt; instead it claims the speech was "good" and had a "positive impact." The AP Exam Reader of the essay has no idea what criteria the student uses to judge quality or impact. However, its semblance of a defendable thesis, that the "speech was good, making a positive impact on all who heard it or read it today," is adequate enough for a point in Row A. Unfortunately, just as the student claims that "some [speeches] are forgettable," this introduction is also forgettable.

The second paragraph simply tells the Reader what President Obama said, that he spoke of unity and the need for strong leaders. The student does not attempt to identify any rhetorical strategies, let alone analyze how they add effect. Notice the weak wording as the student summarizes the speech's message, claiming that "we have to work hard," misquoting the speech phrase of "hard work." This is both unnecessary and redundant.

In the third paragraph, the student finally identifies a rhetorical strategy, that of using "historical examples," but has no more to say than that they "prove his point." Perhaps one might want to reward the student for knowing that the battle of Khe Sahn occurred during the Vietnam War, but that hardly qualifies as analysis. The comment is as bland as noticing that President Obama "also talked about the American Revolutionary War."

The entire fourth paragraph, consisting of only one sentence, copies four phrases from the speech and claims the President uses them to be "uplifting." Again, sadly, we have no analysis. The poor presentation of evidence and commentary only earns 1 point in Row B.

The one-sentence conclusion merely repeats the three concepts of the three body paragraphs—unity, historical examples, and uplifting diction—and then abruptly ends. Although a Reader wants to reward the student for trying, the essay earns a low score because it is hardly on topic and its paragraph development borders on being anorexic. The essay's organization is not bad, and its language, albeit simplistic, is not riddled with errors. To improve, the student needs to practice connecting what he or she sees in the speech to how its strategies make it more effective. It does not earn a point in Row C. It should earn an overall score of 2.

Question 3

Row A: Thesis (0–1 point)	
Scoring Criteria	
0 points for any of the following:	**1 point for**
• Having no defendable thesis. • Only restating the prompt in the thesis. • Only summarizing the issue with no apparent or coherent claim in the thesis. • Presenting a thesis that does not address the prompt.	• Addressing the prompt with a defendable thesis.
Decision Rules and Scoring Notes	
Theses that do not earn this point	**Theses that do earn this point**
• Only restate the prompt. • Are vague or do not take a position. • Simply state obvious facts rather than making a defendable claim.	• Respond to the prompt (rather than restating it) and clearly evaluate the validity of Franklin's assertion about the ability to justify one's actions through reasoning, instead of simply stating pros and cons.
Additional Notes	
• The thesis may be one or more sentences that are in close proximity to each other anywhere in the essay. • A thesis that meets the criteria can be awarded the point whether or not the rest of the response successfully conveys that line of reasoning. • A thesis may present a line of reasoning, but it is not required to earn a point.	

Row B: Evidence AND Commentary (0–4 points)

Scoring Criteria

0 points for	1 point for	2 points for	3 points for	4 points for
• Simply repeating the thesis (if present). • **OR** restating provided information. • **OR** providing mostly irrelevant and/or incoherent examples.	• Summarizing the passage without reference or connection to the thesis. • **OR** providing mostly general evidence. • **AND** providing little or no explanation or commentary.	• Providing some specific evidence that is relevant to the thesis. • **AND** explaining how some of the evidence relates to the thesis, but the line of reasoning may be nonexistent or faulty.	• Providing specific evidence to support all claims in the line of reasoning. • **AND** explaining how some of the evidence relates to the thesis and supports the line of reasoning.	• Providing specific evidence to support all claims in the line of reasoning. • **AND** providing well-developed commentary that consistently and explicitly explains the relationship between the evidence and the thesis.

Decision Rules and Scoring Notes

Typical responses that earn 0 points:	Typical responses that earn 1 point:	Typical responses that earn 2 points:	Typical responses that earn 3 points:	Typical responses that earn 4 points:
• Are unclear or fail to address the prompt. • May present mere opinion with little or no relevant evidence.	• Only summarize or restate ideas from the passage without any analysis.	• Mix specific details with broad generalities. • May contain simplistic, inaccurate, or repetitive explanations that do not strengthen the argument. • Fail to explain the connections between claims and to establish a clear line of reasoning. • May make one point well but fail to adequately support any other claims.	• Consistently offer evidence to support all claims. • Focus on the importance of specific words and details to build an argument. • Use multiple supporting claims to organize an argument and line of reasoning. • May not integrate some evidence or support a key claim in the commentary.	• Engage specific evidence to draw conclusions. • Focus on the importance of specific details to build an argument. • Use multiple supporting claims with adequate evidence and explanation to organize an argument and line of reasoning.

Additional Notes

• Writing that suffers from grammatical and/or mechanical errors that interfere with communication cannot earn the fourth point in this row.

Row C: Sophistication (0–1 point)

Scoring Criteria

0 points for	1 point for
• Not meeting the criteria for 1 point.	• Exhibiting sophistication of thought and/or advancing a complex understanding of the rhetorical situation.

Decision Rules and Scoring Notes	
Responses that do not earn this point:	**Responses that earn this point demonstrate one (or more) of the following:**
• Try to contextualize their argument, but make predominantly sweeping generalizations (*"Throughout all history . . ."* OR *"Everyone believes . . ."*). • Only hint at other possible arguments (*"Some may think . . ."*). • Present complicated or complex sentences or language that is ineffective and detracts from the argument.	• Present a nuanced argument that consistently identifies and examines complexities or tensions. • Illuminate the significance or implications of the argument (either the student's argument or an argument related to the prompt) within a broader context. • Make effective rhetorical choices that strengthen the force and impact of the student's argument. • Develop a prose style that is especially vivid, persuasive, resounding, or appropriate to the student's argument.

Additional Notes

• This point should be awarded only if the demonstration of sophistication or complex understanding is part of the argument, not merely a phrase or brief reference.

High-Scoring Essay

It is his reason that separates man from the creatures of the wild. Reason also fathers conscience, to act as a counterweight to the volatile animal passions of which his sentience has suddenly made him aware. If this were the only function of reason, to launch conscience, the world could theoretically be a better place. Imagine a society where a criminal, about to rob a hapless victim, stops as his mind reasons out the consequences. Reaching the reasonable conclusion that any punishment would be longer lasting and worse than the immediate benefits of his crime, the robber stops. Unfortunately, in reality, the human mind just does not work this way. Reason is not entirely an agent of good, of conscience. Reason can enter Promethean combat with the conscience it creates and shrewdly invent a means for its owner to justify some of his baser impulses.

Ben Franklin addresses man's propensity to justify and explain away his actions through reasoning, to allow caprices and animal impulses to persist. His Autobiography makes the valid point that once someone has his mind set on doing something, reason frequently acts as a tool to circumvent conscience rather than as an agent of that conscience.

Indeed, virtually any action can be justified through some semblance of reason, no matter how faulty the logic, how heinous the crime. For every violent act, for every deceit, a dozen specious premises rise to the task of denying any wrongdoing by the criminal. For example, study the logic which convinced looters during any recent riots in American inner cities that they were justified in robbing innocent storekeepers. This kind of reasoning, sadly, occurs daily in the minds of humanity.

Empirical approaches to life, from the Socratic Method to Hegelian philosophy, have relied on reason to explain both the natural world and the human response to that world. Moral relativism and "situational ethics" depend on reason of a sort. Proponents of such philosophies insist that man must abandon preconceptions, that he must judge each situation as it happens, and use reason to determine what is morally correct under each set of specific circumstances which arise. But it is not only relativists who look to reason as a means of understanding and reacting to the world. Strict Draconian moral codes find their justification in reason as well. Man's actions, whether representing the "rule of law," or the most liberal definitions of right and wrong, are always defended with arguments paying homage to reason. This holds as true for the Supreme Court justice as for the urban pickpocket . . . whether the subject feels he is doing the will of God and country, or knows he is shrewdly evading responsibility. Reason is the tool of man's shell game with his conscience.

Franklin, then, is essentially correct. After a moment of balancing "between principle and inclination," man seizes upon the "convenience" of being a "reasonable creature, since it enables one to find or make a reason for everything one has a mind to do." What one has a mind to do may be quixotic or craven, vainglorious or altruistic, but whatever the case, man can use reason to nullify the conscience that is its offspring.

(533 words)

Analysis of the High-Scoring Essay

This high-scoring essay begins with a relevant discussion of reason and its function. Introducing the idea that "reason . . . fathers conscience," the student provides a hypothetical example of a robber who stops mid-crime because his reason has convinced him the punishment would exceed the gain. The thesis follows, with the interesting concept that reason can engage in "Promethean combat" with the conscience to justify any human action. The student is obviously linguistically talented; the sophisticated diction and syntax are impressive and set the AP Exam Reader's expectations high for the remainder of the essay.

The next paragraph acknowledges Ben Franklin as the inspiration for this topic and capsulizes Franklin's remarks about reason. This paragraph serves as a direct tie to the essay question, but, although it does not move the essay forward, it does contain a defendable thesis, earning a point in Row A. Fortunately, the next paragraphs are much more impressive.

The third paragraph suggests that humans use reason to justify any kind of action, even immoral actions, and provides another relevant example: looters during recent riots who feel justified in their unlawful actions. The parallel structure in the phrase "no matter how faulty the logic, how heinous the crime" is pleasing to the ear and is another sign of the student's sophisticated writing style.

The fourth paragraph includes a pertinent review of several philosophies and "empirical approaches" that use reason as a way of determining one's actions. This paragraph notes that all those taking positions, from Supreme Court justices to common thieves, use reason to justify actions. The paragraph ends with a somewhat mixed but still effective metaphor: "Reason is the tool of man's shell game with his conscience." This student continues to impress with stylistic sophistication and intellectual panache. High-scoring essays demonstrate the student's ability to think analytically and deeply, avoiding a surface-level presentation, and communicate ideas with mature techniques, just as this essay does. The evidence and commentary deserve 4 points in Row B.

The concluding paragraph returns to Franklin's insight, that humans will always find a reasonable way to explain any action. The student once more uses sophisticated style and diction with phrasing like "quixotic or craven, vainglorious or altruistic." This student possesses the command of language evidenced only in top-scoring essays. This essay might be improved if it recognized Franklin's obviously playful tone and responded in kind, at least to some extent. But, overall, the essay is on topic, philosophically insightful, and intelligently presented, and it provides sufficient convincing examples from real-life situations. While it does not earn a point in Row C, it definitely deserves a high score of 5.

Low-Scoring Essay

Ben Franklin is one of our most important Founding Fourfathers. Like Alexander Hamilton and others who never achieved the presidency, he still had a profound impact on the U.S. His importance is shown in his autobiography, where he discusses vegetarianism and the morality of eating fish among other topics.

Ben Franklin contemplates how people can change their mind about things, such as whether it's O.K. to eat animals that have been alive (like fish). He acknowledges that sometimes people are tempted to do something they might think wrong, just as he was tempted by the delightful smell of fish cooking when he was on a boat trip. Franklin also explains that people use reason to approve their actions. His ideas about reason are right. Man frequently employs reason to back up his deeds, whether they are right or wrong. It seems that everyone can find a way to defend their actions. I have personally seen this trait at work, both in myself and my friends.

By using reason, Franklin proved that eating the fish, even though he believed in vegetarianism before, wasn't wrong after all. In the end, Ben Franklin says that it is a good thing that he is a reasonable creature. He means that he was reasonable enough to be open-minded about eating fish; he changed his mind accordingly after listening to his reason. I think Franklin was correct in this point too. It's important to be open-minded about things and not to eliminate what you're willing to try. Like Franklin, we shouldn't be scared to try something new if our reason can explain it to us.

Thus, Ben Franklin shows that reason is a valid tool in helping man to defend his actions, because without reason his actions might be stuck in the same old ways. He would never try some thing new. And Benjamin Franklin, as he was a great man of our country, is someone to whom that was important.

(325 words)

Analysis of the Low-Scoring Essay

This poorly written essay would score in the low range. The first paragraph is ineffective. It fails to address the question of the validity of Franklin's assertions on justifying one's actions through reasoning. The paragraph lacks a thesis and includes such irrelevant information as the reference to Alexander Hamilton. The student also demonstrates a weak command of language, misspelling words such as "Founding Fourfathers."

The second paragraph improves a bit and approaches the topic. Beginning with a paraphrase of Franklin's fish-eating experience, the student gives an opinion on the validity of using reason. But this thesis is especially weak, merely claiming that Franklin was "right." However, the thesis is sufficient to earn a point in Row A. The student offers no evidence to convince the AP Exam Reader but rather claims only to have personally seen some examples.

The next paragraph discusses the need for one to be reasonable in order to try new things. The student is on shaky ground once again, exhibiting simplistic ideas with no support.

The conclusion merely summarizes the essay and still avoids the topic. This essay deserves a low score because it offers no proof for its assertions, its treatment of the topic is superficial, and its presentation is riddled with errors and unsophisticated diction. It is adequate enough to earn 2 points in Row B but does not deserve a point in Row C. It is a clear example of a score of 3.

Scoring

Use the following worksheet to arrive at a probable final AP grade on Practice Exam 4. Because being objective enough to estimate your own essay score is sometimes difficult, you might give your essays (along with the sample essays) to a teacher, friend, or relative to score, if you feel confident that the individual has the knowledge necessary to make such a judgment and that he or she will feel comfortable doing so.

Section I: Multiple-Choice Questions

$$\underline{\hspace{3cm}} - (\underline{\hspace{3cm}}) = \underline{\hspace{3cm}}$$
right answers   wrong answers   multiple-choice raw score

$$\underline{\hspace{3cm}} \times 1.5 = \underline{\hspace{3cm}} \text{ (of possible 67.5)}$$
multiple-choice raw score   multiple-choice converted score

Section II: Free-Response Questions

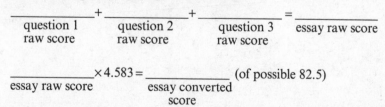

$$\underline{\hspace{2cm}} + \underline{\hspace{2cm}} + \underline{\hspace{2cm}} = \underline{\hspace{2cm}}$$
question 1 raw score   question 2 raw score   question 3 raw score   essay raw score

$$\underline{\hspace{3cm}} \times 4.583 = \underline{\hspace{3cm}} \text{ (of possible 82.5)}$$
essay raw score   essay converted score

Final Score

_____ + _____ = _____ (of possible 150)
    multiple-choice   essay   final
  converted score converted score converted score

Probable Final AP Score

Final Converted Score	Probable AP Score
150–114	5
113–98	4
97–81	3
80–53	2
52–0	1

Glossary

Terms for the Multiple-Choice and Free-Response Sections

Some of the following terms may be used in the multiple-choice questions and/or answer choices or in the free-response section instructions. You might choose to incorporate others into your essay writing—for example, to help identify and explain the effect of a literary device used by an author or to help build your argument.

ad hominem argument: From the Latin meaning "to or against the person," this is an argument that appeals to emotion rather than reason, to feeling rather than intellect.

allegory: The device of using character and/or story elements symbolically to represent an abstraction in addition to the literal meaning. In some allegories, for example, an author may intend the characters to personify an abstraction such as hope or freedom. The allegorical meaning usually deals with a moral truth or a generalization about human existence. Allegory is more commonly used in fiction than in nonfiction.

alliteration: The repetition of sounds, especially initial consonant sounds, in two or more neighboring words (as in "she sells seashells"). Although the term is not usually used in the multiple-choice section, you may want to analyze any alliteration you find in any essay passage. The repetition can reinforce meaning, unify ideas, and/or supply a musical sound.

allusion: A direct or indirect reference to something that is presumably commonly known, such as an event, book, myth, place, or work of art. Allusions can be historical (such as referring to Hitler), literary (such as referring to Kurtz in *Heart of Darkness*), religious (such as referring to Noah and the flood), or mythical (such as referring to Atlas). There are, of course, many more possibilities, and a single work may use multiple layers of allusion.

ambiguity: The multiple meanings, either intentional or unintentional, of a word, phrase, sentence, or passage. Ambiguity can also include a sense of uncertainty or inexactness that a work presents.

analogy: A similarity or comparison between two different things or the relationship between them. An analogy can explain something unfamiliar by associating it with, or pointing out its similarity to, something more familiar. Analogies can also make writing more vivid, imaginative, and intellectually engaging.

anaphora: Deliberately repeating beginning clauses or phrases in sentences to create effect. For example, Winston Churchill famously claimed, "We shall not flag or fail. We shall go on to the end. We shall fight in France. We shall fight on the seas and oceans. We shall fight with growing confidence and growing strength in the air. We shall defend our island, whatever the cost shall be." His repetition of "We shall . . ." creates a rhetorical effect of solidarity and determination. See also *epistrophe,* which is the opposite of anaphora.

anecdote: A short, narrative account of an amusing, unusual, revealing, or interesting event. A good anecdote has a single, definite point and is used to clarify abstract points, to humanize individuals so that readers can relate to them, or to create a memorable image in the reader's mind.

antecedent: The word, phrase, or clause referred to by a pronoun. The antecedent of a pronoun is a noun. The multiple-choice section of the AP exam occasionally asks for the antecedent of a given pronoun in a long, complex sentence or in a group of sentences.

antithesis: A figure of speech involving a seeming contradiction of ideas, words, clauses, or sentences within a balanced grammatical structure. The resulting parallelism serves to emphasize opposition of ideas. The familiar phrase "Man proposes, God disposes" is an example of antithesis, as is John Dryden's description in *The Hind and the Panther:* "Too black for heaven, and yet too white for hell."

aphorism: A terse statement of known authorship that expresses a general truth or moral principle. (If the authorship is unknown, the statement is generally considered to be a folk proverb.) An aphorism can be a memorable summation of the author's point.

apostrophe: A figure of speech that directly addresses an absent or imaginary person or personified abstraction, such as liberty or love, or an inanimate object. The effect may add familiarity or emotional intensity. William Wordsworth addresses John Milton as he writes, "Milton, thou shouldst be living at this hour: England hath need of thee," and John Donne speaks directly to death when he writes, "Death, be not proud."

asyndeton: A deliberate choice to eliminate conjunctions that would normally join phrases or clauses. It creates speed and urgency. For example, "I came. I saw. I conquered" has much more force than "I came, and then I saw, and then I conquered."

atmosphere: The emotional mood created by the entirety of a literary work, established partly by the setting and partly by the author's choice of objects that are described. Even such elements as a description of the weather can contribute to the atmosphere. Frequently, atmosphere foreshadows events. See also *mood.*

caricature: A representation, especially pictorial or literary, in which the subject's distinctive features or peculiarities are deliberately exaggerated to produce a comic or grotesque effect. Sometimes caricature can be so exaggerated that it becomes a grotesque imitation or misrepresentation. Synonymous words include *burlesque, parody, travesty, satire,* and *lampoon.*

chiasmus: A figure of speech based on inverted parallelism. It is a rhetorical figure in which two clauses are related to each another through a reversal of terms. The purpose is usually to make a larger point or to provide balance or order. In classical rhetoric, the parallel structures did not repeat words, such as is found in Alexander Pope's *Essay on Man:* "His time a moment, and a point his space." However, contemporary standards allow for repeated words; a commonly cited example comes from John F. Kennedy's inaugural address: " . . . ask not what your country can do for you—ask what you can do for your country."

clause: A grammatical unit that contains both a subject and a verb. An independent, or main, clause expresses a complete thought and can stand alone as a sentence. A dependent, or subordinate, clause cannot stand alone as a sentence and must be accompanied by an independent clause. Examine this sample sentence: "Because I practiced hard, my AP scores were high." In this sentence, the independent clause is "my AP scores were high," and the dependent (or subordinate) clause is "Because I practiced hard." See also *subordinate clause.*

colloquialism: Slang or informality in speech or writing. Not generally acceptable for formal writing, colloquialisms give language a conversational, familiar tone. Colloquial expressions in writing include local or regional dialects.

conceit: A fanciful expression, usually in the form of an extended metaphor or a surprising analogy between seemingly dissimilar objects. A conceit displays intellectual cleverness due to the unusual comparison being made.

connotation: The nonliteral, associative meaning of a word; the implied, suggested meaning. Connotations may involve ideas, emotions, or attitudes. See also *denotation.*

deductive reasoning: The process of logic in which one takes a rule for a large, general category and assumes that specific individual examples within that general category obey the same rule. For example, a general rule might be that "Objects made of iron will rust." The logician who then encounters a shovel made of iron can assume deductively that the iron shovel will rust just as other iron objects do. Deduction determines the truth about specific examples using a large general rule. See its opposite, *inductive reasoning.*

denotation: The strict, literal, dictionary definition of a word, devoid of any emotion, attitude, or color. See also *connotation.*

diction: Related to style, diction refers to the writer's particular word choices, especially with regard to their correctness, clearness, or effectiveness. For the AP Language and Composition Exam, you should be able to describe an author's diction (for example, formal or informal, ornate or plain) and understand the ways in which diction can complement the writer's purpose. Diction, combined with syntax, figurative language, literary devices, and so on, creates a writer's style. See also *syntax.*

didactic: From the Greek, "didactic" literally means "instructive." Didactic works have the primary aim of teaching or instructing, especially teaching moral or ethical principles.

epistrophe: Deliberately repeating ending clauses or phrases in sentences to create effect. For example, President Lyndon B. Johnson used epistrophe that urged people to come together for a common cause when he addressed the U.S. Congress in 1965: "There is no Negro problem. There is no Southern problem. There is no Northern problem. There is only an American problem. And we are met here tonight as Americans—not as Democrats or Republicans—we are met here as Americans to solve that problem." See also its opposite, *anaphora.*

ethos: From the Greek word for "character," ethos is one of the three rhetorical appeals, coined by Aristotle, that refer to the ways a writer or speaker persuades a reader or an audience. Ethos establishes credibility and believability and sets up trust. The word "ethic" comes from "ethos." See also *logos* and *pathos.*

euphemism: From the Greek for "good speech," euphemisms are a more agreeable or less offensive substitute for generally unpleasant words or concepts. A euphemism may be used to adhere to standards of social or political correctness or to add humor or ironic understatement. Using the term "earthly remains" rather than "corpse" is an example of a euphemism.

extended metaphor: A metaphor developed at great length, occurring frequently in or throughout a work. See also *metaphor.*

figurative language: Writing or speech that is not intended to carry a literal meaning and is usually meant to be imaginative and vivid. See also *figure of speech.*

figure of speech: A device used to produce figurative language. Many figures of speech compare dissimilar things. Figures of speech include the following: *apostrophe, hyperbole, irony, metaphor, metonymy, oxymoron, paradox, personification, simile, synecdoche,* and *understatement.*

generic conventions: This term describes traditions for each genre. These conventions help define each genre; for example, they differentiate between an essay and journalistic writing or an autobiography and political writing. On the AP English Language and Composition Exam, try to distinguish the unique features of a writer's work from those dictated by convention.

genre: The major category into which a literary work fits. The basic divisions of literature are prose, poetry, and drama. However, "genre" is a flexible term; within these broad boundaries are many subdivisions that are often called genres themselves. For example, prose can be divided into fiction (novels and short stories) or nonfiction (essays, biographies, autobiographies, and so on). Poetry can be divided into such subcategories as lyric, dramatic, narrative, epic, and so on. Drama can be divided into tragedy, comedy, melodrama, farce, and so on. On the AP English Language and Composition Exam, expect the majority of the passages to be from the following genres: autobiography, biography, diaries, criticism, and essays as well as journalistic, political, scientific, and nature writing.

homily: This term literally means "sermon," but more informally, it can include any serious talk, speech, or lecture involving moral or spiritual advice.

hyperbole: A figure of speech using deliberate exaggeration or overstatement. Hyperbole often has a comic effect; however, a serious effect is also possible. Often, hyperbole produces irony at the same time.

imagery: The sensory details or figurative language used to describe, arouse emotion, or represent abstractions. On a physical level, imagery uses terms related to the five senses: visual, auditory, tactile, gustatory, or olfactory imagery. On a broader and deeper level, however, one image can represent more than one thing. For example, a rose may present visual imagery while also representing the color in a woman's cheeks. An author, therefore, may use complex imagery while simultaneously employing other figures of speech, especially metaphor and simile. In addition, this term can apply to the total of all the images in a work. On the AP English Language and Composition Exam, pay attention to *how* an author creates imagery and the effect of that imagery.

inductive reasoning: The process of logic that begins reasoning from a specific case or cases and then derives a general rule or prediction that may or may not necessarily be true. It draws inferences from observations in order to make generalizations. Induction uses evidence more than logic when it says, "A, B, and C are true, so D should also be true." This can result in a more uncertain conclusion than the more certain *deductive reasoning*. Inductive arguments are, hence, always open to question because the conclusion is a larger idea than the evidence on which it is based. This breadth allows it to be used where deductive methods may not work—for example, in prediction or invention. One advantage of inductive reasoning is that starting from specifics and building up to a larger generality can be less threatening than starting with the big ideas, which can make inductive arguments more persuasive, as people may understand the process better than a more clinical deduction.

infer: To draw a reasonable conclusion from the information presented. When a multiple-choice question asks for an inference to be drawn from the passage, the most direct, most reasonable inference is the safest answer choice. If an inference is implausible, it's unlikely to be the correct answer. Note that if the answer choice is something that is directly stated in the passage, it is *not* inferred and is, therefore, not the correct answer.

invective: An emotionally violent, verbal denunciation or attack using strong, abusive language.

irony: The contrast between what is stated explicitly and what is really meant; the difference between what appears to be and what is actually true. Irony is used for many reasons, but frequently, it's used to create poignancy or humor. In general, three major types of irony are used in language:

1. In *verbal* irony, the words literally state the opposite of the writer's (or speaker's) true meaning.
2. In *situational* irony, events turn out the opposite of what was expected. What the characters and readers think ought to happen does not actually happen.
3. In *dramatic* irony, facts or events are unknown to a character in a play or piece of fiction but known to the reader, audience, or other characters in the work.

jargon: The specific words or phrases used in a trade, occupation, or field of study, such as sports jargon, medical jargon, police jargon, or military jargon. To the uninitiated, these phrases can sometimes be confusing.

juxtaposition: Placing dissimilar items, descriptions, or ideas close together or side by side, especially for comparison or contrast.

logical fallacy: A mistake in verbal reasoning. Technically, to be a fallacy, the reasoning must be potentially deceptive; it must be likely to fool at least some of the people some of the time. Many types of logical fallacies (which you can easily look up) have been identified, such as *ad hominem argument,* appeals to emotion, bandwagon, begging the question, circular reasoning, hasty generalization, non sequitur argument, post hoc argument, slippery slope, or straw man argument.

logos: One of Aristotle's three rhetorical appeals that refer to the ways a writer or speaker persuades a reader or an audience. Logos, the appeal to logic, means to convince an audience by use of logic or reason, such as citing facts and statistics, historical and literal analogies, or certain authorities on a subject. "Logos" is the Greek word for "word." The word "logic" is derived from "logos." See also *ethos* and *pathos.*

loose sentence: A type of sentence in which the main idea (independent clause) comes first, followed by dependent grammatical units such as phrases and clauses. If a period were placed at the end of the independent clause, the clause would be a complete sentence. A work containing many loose sentences often seems informal, relaxed, and conversational. See also *periodic sentence.*

metaphor: A figure of speech using implied comparison of seemingly unlike things or the substitution of one for the other, suggesting some similarity. For example, consider the title of Carson McCullers' novel *The Heart Is a Lonely Hunter.* Metaphorical language makes writing more vivid, imaginative, thought provoking, and meaningful. See also *simile.*

metonymy: A term from the Greek meaning "changed label" or "substitute name," metonymy is a figure of speech in which the name of one object is substituted for that of another closely associated with it. A news release that claims "the White House declared" rather than "the President declared" is using metonymy. This term is unlikely to be used in the multiple-choice section, but you might see examples of metonymy in an essay passage. See also *synecdoche.*

modes of discourse: This term encompasses the four traditional categories of written texts. See also *rhetorical modes.*

1. Exposition, which refers to writing that intends to inform and demonstrate a point
2. Narration, which refers to writing that tells a story or relates a series of events
3. Description, which refers to writing that creates sensory images, often evoking a mood or atmosphere
4. Argumentation, which refers to writing that takes a stand on an issue and supports it with evidence and logical reasoning

mood: This term has two distinct technical meanings in English writing. The first meaning is grammatical and deals with verbal units and a speaker's attitude. The *indicative* mood is used only for factual sentences—for example, "Joe eats too quickly." The *subjunctive* mood is used for a doubtful or conditional attitude—for example, "If I were you, I'd get another job." The *imperative* mood is used for commands—for example, "Shut the door!" The second meaning of mood is literary, meaning the prevailing atmosphere or emotional aura of a work. Setting, tone, and events can affect the mood. In this usage, mood is similar to tone and atmosphere.

narrative: The telling of a story or an account of an event or series of events.

onomatopoeia: A figure of speech in which natural sounds are imitated in the sounds of words. Simple examples include such words as "buzz," "hiss," "hum," "crack," "whinny," and "murmur." This term usually is not used in the multiple-choice section. If you identify examples of onomatopoeia in an essay passage, note the effect.

oxymoron: From the Greek for "pointedly foolish," an oxymoron is a figure of speech in which the writer groups apparently contradictory terms to suggest a paradox. Simple examples include "jumbo shrimp" and "cruel kindness." This term usually does not appear in the multiple-choice questions, but there is a chance you will see it used by an author in an essay passage or find it useful in your own essay writing.

paradox: A statement that appears to be self-contradictory or opposed to common sense but upon closer inspection contains some degree of truth or validity. The first scene of *Macbeth,* for example, closes with the witches' cryptic remark, "Fair is foul, and foul is fair. . . ."

parallelism: Also referred to as parallel construction or parallel structure, this term comes from Greek roots meaning "beside one another." It refers to the grammatical or rhetorical framing of words, phrases, sentences, or paragraphs to give structural similarity. This can involve, but is not limited to, repetition of a grammatical element such as a preposition or a verbal phrase. A famous example of parallelism begins Charles Dickens' novel *A Tale of Two Cities:* "It was the best of times, it was the worst of times, it was the age of wisdom, it was the age of foolishness, it was the epoch of belief, it was the epoch of incredulity. . . ." The effects of parallelism are numerous, but, frequently, parallelism acts as an organizing force to attract the reader's attention, add emphasis and organization, or simply provide a pleasing musical rhythm. Another famous example comes from the concluding line of Tennyson's poem "Ulysses," as the speaker claims, "To strive, to seek, to find, and not to yield." Many specific terms identify different forms of parallelism, such as *anaphora, asyndeton, epistrophe,* and *symploce.* See also *antithesis* and *chiasmus.*

parody: A work that closely imitates the style or content of another work with the specific aim of comic effect and/or ridicule. As comedy, parody distorts or exaggerates distinctive features of the original. As ridicule, it mimics the work by repeating and borrowing words, phrases, or characteristics in order to illuminate weaknesses in the original. Well-written parody offers insight into the original, but poorly written parody offers only ineffectual imitation. Usually an audience must grasp literary allusion and understand the work being parodied to fully appreciate the nuances of the newer work. Occasionally, however, parodies take on a life of their own and don't require knowledge of the original.

pathos: One of Aristotle's three rhetorical appeals, pathos is a writer's or speaker's attempt to inspire an emotional reaction in an audience—often a deep feeling of suffering, but sometimes joy, pride, anger, humor, patriotism, or any other strong emotion. In its critical sense, pathos signifies a scene or passage designed to evoke the feeling of pity or sympathetic sorrow in a reader or viewer. "Pathos" is the Greek word for both "suffering" and "experience." The words "empathy" and "pathetic" are derived from "pathos." See also *ethos* and *logos.*

pedantic: An adjective that describes words, phrases, or a general tone that is overly scholarly, academic, or bookish.

periodic sentence: A sentence that presents its central meaning in a main clause at the end. An independent clause, it is preceded by a phrase or clause that cannot stand alone. For example, "Ecstatic with my AP scores, I let out a loud shout of joy!" The effect of a periodic sentence is to add emphasis and structural variety. See also *loose sentence.*

personification: A figure of speech in which the writer presents or describes concepts, animals, or inanimate objects by endowing them with human attributes or emotions. Personification is used to make these abstractions, animals, or objects appear more vivid to the reader.

point of view: In fictional literature, this is the perspective from which a story is told. There are two general divisions of point of view, first-person narrator and third-person narrator, and many subdivisions within those. However, on the AP English Language and Composition Exam, the term *point of view* is synonymous with the author's *attitude.*

polysyndeton: Deliberately using many conjunctions to join items in a sentence to create an overwhelming effect. For example, Cormac McCarthy used polysyndeton in this passage from his novel *The Crossing:* "He got the fire going and lifted the wolf from the sheet and took the sheet to the creek and crouched in the dark and washed the blood out of it and brought it back and he cut forked sticks from a mountain hackberry and drove them into the ground with a rock and hung the sheet on a trestlepole. . . ." Notice how joining every action with the conjunction "and" separates and intensifies the actions.

predicate adjective: One type of subject complement—an adjective, group of adjectives, or adjective clause that follows a linking verb. It is in the predicate of the sentence and modifies or describes the subject. For example, in the sentence "My boyfriend is tall, dark, and handsome," the group of predicate adjectives ("tall, dark, and handsome") describes "boyfriend."

predicate nominative: A second type of subject complement—a noun, group of nouns, or noun clause that renames the subject. It, like the predicate adjective, follows a linking verb and is located in the predicate of the sentence. For example, in the sentence "Abe Lincoln was a man of integrity," the predicate nominative is "man of integrity," as it renames Abe Lincoln. Occasionally, this term or the term *predicate adjective* appears in a multiple-choice question.

prose: One of the major divisions of genre, prose refers to fiction and nonfiction, including all its forms, because they are written in ordinary language and most closely resemble everyday speech. Technically, anything that isn't poetry or drama is prose. Therefore, all passages in the AP English Language and Composition Exam are prose. Of course, prose writers often borrow poetic and dramatic elements.

repetition: The duplication, either exact or approximate, of any element of language, such as a sound, word, phrase, clause, sentence, or grammatical pattern. When repetition is poorly done, it bores, but when it's well done, it links and emphasizes ideas while giving the reader the comfort of recognizing something familiar. See also *parallelism.*

rhetoric: From the Greek for "orator," this term describes the principles governing the art of writing effectively, eloquently, and persuasively.

rhetorical modes: This flexible term describes the variety, conventions, and purposes of the major kinds of writing. Sometimes referred to as *modes of discourse,* the four most common rhetorical modes and their purposes are as follows:

1. The purpose of *exposition* (or expository writing) is to explain and analyze information by presenting an idea, relevant evidence, and appropriate discussion. The AP English Language and Composition Exam essay questions are frequently set up as expository topics.

2. The purpose of *argumentation* is to prove the validity of an idea or point of view by presenting sound reasoning, thoughtful discussion, and insightful argument that thoroughly convince the reader. Persuasive writing is a type of argumentation that has the additional aim of urging some form of action. Many AP English Language and Composition Exam free-response questions ask you to form an argument.

3. The purpose of *description* is to re-create, invent, or visually present a person, place, event, or action so that the reader can picture what is being described. Sometimes a writer engages all five senses in description; good descriptive writing can be sensuous and picturesque. Descriptive writing may be straightforward and objective or highly emotional and subjective.

4. The purpose of *narration* is to tell a story or narrate an event or series of events. This writing mode frequently uses the tools of descriptive writing.

rhetorical question: A question that is asked merely for effect and does not expect a reply. The answer is assumed. For example, in Shakespeare's *Julius Caesar,* the character Brutus asks, "Who is here so vile that will not love his country?"

sarcasm: From the Greek meaning "to tear flesh," sarcasm often involves bitter, caustic language that is meant to hurt or ridicule someone or something. It may use irony as a device, but not all ironic statements are sarcastic (that is, intending to ridicule). When well done, sarcasm can be witty and insightful; when poorly done, it's simply cruel.

satire: A work that targets human vices and follies, or social institutions and conventions, for reform or ridicule. Regardless of whether or not the work aims to reform humans or their society, satire is best seen as a style of writing rather than a purpose for writing. It can be recognized by the many devices used effectively by the satirist, such as irony, wit, parody, caricature, hyperbole, understatement, and sarcasm. The effects of satire are varied, depending on the writer's goal, but good satire—often humorous—is thought provoking and insightful about the human condition.

simile: An explicit comparison, normally using "like," "as," or "if." For example, remember Robert Burns' famous lines, "O my love is like a red, red rose / That's newly sprung in June; / O my love is like the melody / That's sweetly played in tune." See also *metaphor.*

subject complement: The word (with any accompanying phrases) or clause that follows a linking verb and complements, or completes, the subject of the sentence by either (1) renaming it or (2) describing it. The former is technically called a predicate nominative, the latter a predicate adjective. See also *predicate nominative* and *predicate adjective* for examples of sentences. This term is occasionally used in a multiple-choice question.

subordinate clause: Like all clauses, this word group contains both a subject and a verb (plus any accompanying phrases or modifiers). But unlike the independent clause, the subordinate clause cannot stand alone; it does not express a complete thought. Also called a dependent clause, the subordinate clause depends on a main clause, sometimes called an independent clause, to complete its meaning. Easily recognized key words and phrases usually begin these clauses—for example, "although," "because," "unless," "if," "even though," "since," "as soon as," "while," "who," "when," "where," "how," and "that." See also *clause.*

syllogism: From the Greek for "reckoning together," a syllogism (or syllogistic reasoning) is a deductive system of formal logic that presents two premises—the first one called major and the second minor—that inevitably lead to a sound conclusion. A frequently cited example proceeds as follows:

- **Major premise:** All men are mortal.
- **Minor premise:** Socrates is a man.
- **Conclusion:** Therefore, Socrates is mortal.

A syllogism's conclusion is valid only if each of the two premises is valid. Syllogisms may also present the specific idea first ("Socrates") and the general idea second ("All men").

symbol: Generally, a symbol is anything that represents or stands for something else. Usually, it is something concrete—such as an object, action, character, or scene—that represents something more abstract. However, symbols and symbolism can be much more complex. One system classifies symbols into three categories:

1. *Natural* symbols use objects and occurrences from nature to represent ideas commonly associated with them (such as dawn symbolizing hope or a new beginning, a rose symbolizing love, a tree symbolizing knowledge).

2. *Conventional* symbols are those that have been invested with meaning by a group (religious symbols, such as a cross or Star of David; national symbols, such as a flag or an eagle; or group symbols, such as skull and crossbones for pirates or the scales of justice for lawyers).

3. *Literary* symbols are sometimes also conventional in the sense that they are found in a variety of works and are generally recognized. However, an individual work's symbols may be more complicated, such as the whale in *Moby-Dick* and the jungle in *Heart of Darkness.* On the AP English Language and Composition Exam, try to determine what abstraction an object symbolizes and to what extent it is successful in representing that abstraction.

symploce: A type of *parallelism* that combines *anaphora* and *epistrophe,* symploce occurs when words or phrases are repeated at both the beginning and at the ending of clauses or verses. President Bill Clinton used symploce in a prayer service at Oklahoma City in 1995 when he said, "When there is talk of hatred, let us stand up and talk against it. When there is violence, let us stand up and talk against it."

synecdoche: A rhetorical figure of speech in which a part of an object represents the whole, or the whole of an object may be used to represent a part. For example, a cowboy who boasts of owning "60 head of cattle" is not referring to their heads alone, but 60 living, whole cows. See also *metonymy.*

syntax: The way a writer chooses to join words into phrases, clauses, and sentences. In other words, syntax refers to the arrangement or order of grammatical elements in a sentence. Syntax is similar to *diction,* but you can differentiate the two by thinking of syntax as referring to groups of words, while diction refers to individual words. In the multiple-choice section of the AP English Language and Composition Exam, expect to be asked some questions about how an author manipulates syntax. In the free-response section, you will need to analyze how syntax produces effects. When you are analyzing syntax, consider such elements as the length or brevity of sentences, unusual sentence constructions, the sentence patterns used, and the kinds of sentences the author uses. The author may use questions, declarations, exclamations, or rhetorical questions; sentences are also classified as periodic or loose, simple, compound, or complex. Syntax can be tricky for students to analyze. First try to classify what kinds of sentences the author uses, and then try to determine how the author's choices amplify meaning—in other words, why they work well for the author's purpose.

theme: The central idea or message of a work, the insight it offers into life. Usually, the theme is unstated in fictional works, but in nonfiction, the theme may be directly stated, especially in expository or argumentative writing. Frequently, a theme can be stated as a universal truth—that is, a general statement about the human condition, society, or humanity's relationship to the natural world.

thesis: In expository writing, the thesis statement is the sentence or group of sentences that directly express the writer's opinion, purpose, meaning, or proposition. Expository writing is usually judged by analyzing how accurately, effectively, and thoroughly a writer has proven the thesis.

tone: Similar to mood, tone describes the writer's attitude toward his or her material, the audience, or both. Tone is easier to determine in spoken language than in written language. Considering how a work would sound if it were read aloud can help identify a writer's tone. Some words describing tone are "playful," "serious," "businesslike," "sarcastic," "humorous," "formal," "ornate," and "somber." As with attitude, a writer's tone in the exam's passages can rarely be described by one word. Expect that an explanation will be more complex. See *attitude* in "Terms for the Free-Response Section," on the next page.

transition: A word or phrase that links different ideas, a transition is used especially, although not exclusively, in expository and argumentative writing. Transitions effectively signal a shift from one idea to another. A few commonly used transitional words or phrases include "furthermore," "consequently," "nevertheless," "for example," "in addition," "likewise," "similarly," and "on the contrary."

understatement: The ironic minimizing of fact, understatement presents something as less significant than it actually is. The effect can frequently be humorous and emphatic. Understatement is the opposite of *hyperbole*. Two specific types of understatement exist:

1. *Litotes* is a figure of speech by which an affirmation is made indirectly by denying its opposite. It uses understatement for emphasis, frequently with a negative assertion. For example, "It was no mean feat" means it was quite hard. "He was not averse to drink" means he drank a lot.

2. *Meiosis,* the Greek term for "understatement" or "belittling," is a rhetorical figure by which something is referred to in terms less important than it really deserves. It describes something that is very impressive with its simplicity. An example is when Mercutio calls his mortal wound a "scratch" in *Romeo and Juliet.*

wit: In modern usage, wit is intellectually amusing language that surprises and delights. A witty statement is humorous, while suggesting the speaker's verbal power in creating ingenious and perceptive remarks. Wit usually uses terse language that makes a pointed statement. Historically, "wit" meant basic understanding. Its meaning evolved to include speed of understanding, and finally (in the early 17th century), it grew to mean quick perception, including creative fancy.

Terms for the Free-Response Section

The following words and phrases have appeared in recent AP English Language and Composition Exam essay prompts. Although what follows is not a comprehensive list of every word or phrase you might encounter, it will help you understand what you're being asked to do for a topic.

argument: In the AP free-response section, this is a global term for one of your essays (also called an argumentation or argumentative essay) in which you will establish an assertion (or group of assertions) and support that idea with evidence and logical explanation. The phrasing in the prompt that you will see on the exam tells you to "write an essay that argues your position [on the specific subject]." See Chapter 2 for a complete discussion of the argument essay.

attitude: A writer's intellectual position or emotion regarding the subject of the writing. In the free-response section, expect to be asked what the writer's attitude is and how his or her language conveys that attitude. Also be aware that, although the singular term "attitude" is used in this definition and on the exam, the passage will rarely have only one attitude. More often than not, the writer's attitude will be more complex, and the student who presents this complexity—no matter how subtle the differences—will appear to be more astute than the student who only uses one adjective to describe attitude. Of course, don't force an attitude for which there is no evidence in the passage; instead, understand that an accurate statement of a writer's attitude is not likely to be a blatantly obvious idea. If it were that simple, the exam committee wouldn't ask you to discuss it.

audience: The person(s) who is reading a text, listening to a speaker, or observing a performance. On the AP English Language and Composition Exam, be aware of who would most likely be eager to read or hear the passage.

concrete detail: Strictly defined, concrete refers to nouns that name physical objects—a bridge, a book, or a coat. Concrete nouns are the opposite of abstract nouns (which refer to concepts like freedom and love). However, as used in the free-response section of the AP English Language and Composition Exam, this term has a slightly different connotation. The directions may read something like this: "Provide concrete details that will convince the reader." This means that your essay should include details from the passage; at times, you'll be allowed to provide details from your own awareness of the world—from your readings, observations, experiences, and so forth.

descriptive detail: When an essay prompt uses this phrase, look for the writer's sensory description. Descriptive details appealing to the visual sense are usually the most predominant, but don't overlook other sensory details. As usual, after you identify a passage's descriptive details, analyze their effect.

device: Devices are the figures of speech, syntax, diction, and other stylistic elements that collectively produce a particular artistic effect.

language: When you're asked to "analyze the language," concentrate on how the elements of language combine to form a whole—how diction, syntax, figurative language, and sentence structure create a cumulative effect.

narrative device: The tools of the storyteller (also used in nonfiction), such as ordering events so that they build to a climactic moment or withholding information until a crucial or appropriate moment when revealing it creates a desired effect. On the essay portion of the exam, this term may also apply to biographical and autobiographical writing.

narrative technique: The style of telling the story, even if the passage is nonfiction. Concentrate on the order of events and on their detail in evaluating a writer's technique.

persuasive device: When asked to analyze an author's persuasive devices, look for the words in the passage that have strong connotations—words that intensify the emotional effect. For example, consider the different connotations in the terms "civil war," "rebellion," and "revolution." In addition, analyze how these words complement the writer's argument as it builds logically. Speeches are often used in this context because they are generally designed to persuade.

persuasive essay: When asked to write a persuasive essay, you should present a coherent argument in which the evidence builds to a logical and relevant conclusion. Strong persuasive essays often appeal to the audience's emotions or ethical standards.

resources of language: This phrase refers to all the devices of composition available to a writer, such as diction, syntax, sentence structure, and figures of speech. The cumulative effect of a work is produced by the resources of language a writer chooses.

rhetorical features: This phrase refers to how a passage is constructed. If you are asked to consider rhetorical features or structure, look at the passage's organization and how the writer combines images, details, or arguments to serve his or her purpose.

rhetorical strategies: This phrase, used to identify one of the three essays you will write in the free-response section of the exam (and sometimes used in the multiple-choice section), is a global term that refers to all the strategies a writer can use. See Chapter 2 for a complete discussion of the rhetorical strategies essay. The term basically encompasses three elements:

1. *Structure,* which refers to the writer's organization
2. *Purpose,* which refers to why the writer wrote the piece and his or her goal
3. *Style,* which is made up of many elements, such as diction, syntax, figurative language, attitude, tone, pacing, selection of detail, and modes of discourse

sentence structure: If appropriate in your essay analysis, look at the type of sentences the author uses. Remember that the basic sentence structures are simple, compound, and complex, and variations are created by combining sentences. Also consider variation (or lack of it) in sentence length; any unusual devices in sentence construction, such as repetition or inverted word order; and any unusual word or phrase placement. As with all devices, be prepared to discuss the effect of the sentence structure. For example, a series of short, simple sentences or phrases can produce a feeling of speed and choppiness, which may suit the author's purpose. This type of analysis is most appropriate for the rhetorical strategies essay prompt.

stylistic devices: An essay prompt that mentions stylistic devices is asking you to note and analyze all of the elements in language that contribute to style—such as diction, syntax, tone, attitude, figures of speech, connotations, and repetition.

synthesis: One of the three essay types you will be asked to write on the essay portion of the AP exam. After reading the given sources that relate to the same issue(s), you will combine, synthesize, and analyze the information from at least three of the sources as you develop your position and your unique perspective on the issue(s). See Chapter 2 for a complete discussion of the synthesis essay.

Past AP Essay Topics

In the following chart, presented in reverse chronological order, you will find a paraphrasing of every AP English Language and Composition Exam essay topic since 2010. Although an exact topic is never reused, when you read this information, you should look for trends and patterns in the essay topics. Examine the different modes the essay category requires. For example, understand the difference between writing a synthesis essay, a rhetorical analysis essay, and an argument essay. Be aware that the real exam will not be printed like this; it will not identify the free-response questions as a synthesis, rhetorical analysis, or argument question, but they will be numbered "Question 1," "Question 2," and "Question 3," respectively.

The topics and question categories are printed in the same order as they appeared on the actual exam for each year.

Year	Question Category	Passage (Title of Passage and Author)/Topic
2019	Synthesis	Large-scale wind power has gained attention as an alternative fuel source, yet establishment of such large-scale wind farms has drawn scrutiny. Develop a position on the most important factors that an individual agency should consider when choosing whether or not to establish a wind farm.
	Rhetorical analysis	The conclusion of Mohandas Gandhi's 1930 letter to Viceroy Lord Irwin, the representative of the British Crown in India, is given. Gandhi presents the reasons he will lead a nonviolent protest against the Salt Act, which imposed taxation on salt, unless the British government changes its unfair policies in India. Analyze the rhetorical choices Gandhi makes as he presents his case to Lord Irwin.
	Argument	The word "overrated" is often used to minimize and discredit ideas. Choose a concept, place, role, etc., that you believe deserves the qualifier "overrated." Then explain your judgment in an essay in which you use appropriate and specific evidence to support your argument.
2018	Synthesis	Eminent domain gives governments the power to acquire private property for public use, based on the assumption that governments have greater legal authority over land than private owners. Develop a position that defends, qualifies, or challenges the idea that eminent domain is productive and beneficial for the public's good.
	Rhetorical analysis	In 1997, Madeline Albright, who served as the United States Secretary of State at the time, delivered the commencement address to Mount Holyoke College, a women's college in Massachusetts. After reading the excerpt, write an essay that analyzes the rhetorical choices Albright makes to present her ideas about America continuing its work in the world to help shape history.
	Argument	A quotation from Anne Morrow Lindbergh's book *Gift from the Sea* explains how choosing the unknown, "with all its disappointments and surprises," can eventually be "most enriching." Using appropriate and specific evidence, develop your position on the value of exploring the unknown.

continued

Year	Question Category	Passage (Title of Passage and Author)/Topic
2017	Synthesis	Consider to what extent the Internet age has changed the role of public libraries, examining their relevance in today's society and any ways in which they might change to meet the needs of a transforming world. Develop a position that discusses the function, if any, that public libraries should serve in the future.
	Rhetorical analysis	In 1960, Clare Boothe Luce, an American journalist and politician, delivered a speech to the Women's National Press Club in which she decried the penchant of the American press for sacrificing journalistic integrity in favor of what is perceived as the public's demand for sensational stories. The introduction to her speech is presented. Analyze how Luce uses her opening to prepare the audience for her message.
	Argument	In an excerpt from *Empire of Illusion,* author Chris Hedges presents the idea that artifice is the most important skill for politicians to use when trying to persuade the public. He points out that successful politicians need to have a narrative, whether it is accurate or not, and that mastering the art of entertainment is essential to being perceived as real and honest; actual sincerity and competency are not necessary, but the appearance of these qualities is. Using appropriate and specific evidence, develop your position on the truthfulness of Hedges' ideas.
2016	Synthesis	English has become the dominant global language in such fields as international finance, science, and politics over the last several decades. Concurrently, learning a foreign language in English-speaking countries has declined. Develop your position on whether monolingual English speakers are at a disadvantage in today's world.
	Rhetorical analysis	The eulogy written by Margaret Thatcher, the former prime minister of Great Britain, and delivered to the American people in honor of former U.S. President Ronald Reagan is presented. Analyze the rhetorical strategies Thatcher uses as she memorializes the leader with whom she had worked closely.
	Argument	In 1891, Irish author Oscar Wilde claimed that disobedience is a virtue that eventually promotes social progress. Using appropriate examples, present your stand on the extent to which you feel Wilde's assertion is valid.
2015	Synthesis	Consider that the intended purpose of honor codes or honor systems in schools, colleges, and universities is to cultivate integrity. Develop a position on whether or not your school should institute, uphold, amend, or abolish an honor code or honor system.
	Rhetorical analysis	An article written by the labor union organizer and civil rights leader Cesar Chavez on the tenth anniversary of Martin Luther King Jr.'s assassination is excerpted. Analyze the rhetorical strategies Chavez uses to present his stand on nonviolent resistance.
	Argument	An anthropologist who studied first-year university students observed that their friendly greetings, such as "How are you?" and "Let's get in touch," were not intended to be literal, but merely polite. Develop your position on the role and value of polite speech within a culture or community with which you are familiar. Use appropriate examples for support.

Year	Question Category	Passage (Title of Passage and Author)/Topic
2014	Synthesis	In light of the fact that many recent college graduates face a dim prospect for employment, develop a position on the value of a college education, given its cost. Consider to what degree college helps students prepare for more than just a job.
	Rhetorical analysis	A letter of advice from Abigail Adams to her son, John Quincy Adams, is reproduced. Her son was traveling with his father, John Adams, who was, at the time, a U.S. diplomat and later the second U.S. president. She urges her son to use adversity to grow, mature, and develop virtue. Analyze the rhetorical strategies Adams uses to offer advice.
	Argument	In 2010, authors Po Bronson and Ashley Merryman published a *Newsweek* article that laments the decline in the public's "creativity quotient" since 1990. The article explores the far-ranging need for creativity in solving many of the world's problems. While explaining your definition of creativity, write a letter to your school board, taking a stand on whether or not the creation of a class in creative thinking is advisable.
2013	Synthesis	Examine what factors any group or agency should contemplate when choosing to create a monument to honor great achievements or deep sacrifice, and also discuss what considerations need to be addressed in the creation of any monument of an event or person.
	Rhetorical analysis	In a passage from Richard Louv's 2008 book, *Last Child in the Woods*, he laments the separation between people and nature. Analyze the rhetorical strategies Louv uses to advance his point.
	Argument	Three positions on the relationship between ownership and one's sense of self are presented. Plato argues that owning material objects damages a person's character. Aristotle counters that owning tangible objects helps to develop moral character. Jean-Paul Sartre suggests that ownership extends beyond the tangible and that to master some skill equates to "owning" it. Develop a position on the relationship between ownership and personality, using examples from your reading, experiences, or observations to support your opinion.
2012	Synthesis	Develop a position on whether or not the delivery days and services of the United States Postal Service should be restructured because of the decreased volume that the post office has faced over the last decade.
	Rhetorical analysis	Opening remarks from President John F. Kennedy's news conference in 1962 are presented. The president criticized the nation's largest steel companies for raising steel prices, and he urged stable prices and wages during a period of economic instability. Analyze the rhetorical strategies President Kennedy used to convey his thoughts.
	Argument	Two different perspectives are presented. William Lyon Phelps, an American educator and writer, states that one can accomplish anything if one has an absolute sense of certainty and powerful beliefs. Bertrand Russell, a British author, mathematician, and philosopher, counters that people need to contemplate their opinions with a degree of doubt. Develop a position on the relationship between certainty and doubt. Use appropriate evidence to support your stand.

continued

Year	Question Category	Passage (Title of Passage and Author)/Topic
2011	Synthesis	Locavores are people who, considering nutrition as well as sustainability, have decided to eat locally grown or produced products as often as possible. Identify the key issues associated with the locavore movement and examine their implications for the community.
	Rhetorical analysis	A speech to the convention of the National American Woman Suffrage Association in Philadelphia on July 22, 1905, is presented by Florence Kelley, a U.S. social worker and reformer who fought successfully for child labor laws and improved conditions for working women. Analyze the rhetorical strategies Kelley uses to convey her message about child labor to her audience.
	Argument	A passage from *Rights of Man,* a book written by the pamphleteer Thomas Paine in 1791 after the American Revolution, is presented. In it he claims one would think that America is least likely to have unity, given that its people are from different backgrounds, speak different languages, and worship different religions; however, he asserts America does have unity, which comes from a government that is based on the needs of society and basic rights of man. Paine asserts that in America, the poor are not oppressed, the rich not privileged, and that taxes are few, resulting in no need for riots. Examine the extent to which Paine's characterization of America holds true today. Use appropriate evidence to support your argument.
2010	Synthesis	Given the pros and cons of modern, fast-paced information technology, evaluate the most important factors that a school should consider before using particular technologies in curriculum and instruction.
	Rhetorical analysis	A 1791 letter is presented from Benjamin Banneker, the son of former slaves who became a farmer, astronomer, mathematician, surveyor, and author, to Thomas Jefferson. Analyze the ways in which Banneker uses rhetorical strategies to argue against slavery.
	Argument	A quotation from Alain de Botton's 2004 book, *Status Anxiety,* posits that, since humorists can say things others cannot or will not, the primary goal of humorists is not simply to entertain but to present "with impunity" ideas that might be "dangerous or impossible to state directly." Defend, challenge, or qualify de Botton's claim about the vital role of humorists in society. Use specific, appropriate evidence to develop your position.

Suggested Reading List

Following is a list of important authors and some of their works that are similar to those used on the AP English Language and Composition Exam. The list is not meant to be all-inclusive or required reading for every student, but reading extensively from works on this list and analyzing the authors' use of language will be excellent preparation for the exam. These works are largely available from reputable libraries and online sources, such as Project Gutenberg (www.gutenberg.org).

Maya Angelou

Gather Together in My Name
The Heart of a Woman
I Know Why the Caged Bird Sings
Singin' and Swingin' and Gettin' Merry Like Christmas
Any of her speeches

Walter Jackson Bate

John Keats
Samuel Johnson

Charles A. Beard

An Economic Interpretation of the Constitution of the United States
The Rise of American Civilization (with Mary R. Beard)

James Boswell

The Life of Samuel Johnson

Van Wyck Brooks

An Autobiography
Days of the Phoenix: The 1920s I Remember
From a Writer's Notebook

Thomas Carlyle

The French Revolution
Past and Present

Bruce Catton

Mr. Lincoln's Army
A Stillness at Appomattox

Winston Churchill

Blood, Toil, Tears and Sweat: The Speeches of Winston Churchill
Europe Unite: Speeches 1947 and 1948
A History of the English-Speaking Peoples
In the Balance: Speeches 1949 and 1950
Marlborough: His Life and Times
My Early Life
Their Finest Hour
Any of his speeches

Charles Dana

Any of his nonfiction

Thomas De Quincey

Confessions of an English Opium-Eater

Frederick Douglass

The Life and Times of Frederick Douglass
My Bondage and My Freedom
Narrative of the Life of Frederick Douglass

Leon Edel

Bloomsbury: A House of Lions
Henry James: A Life
Stuff of Sleep and Dreams
Telling Lives

Dave Eggers

A Heartbreaking Work of Staggering Genius
Zeitoun

Richard Ellmann

Eminent Domain: Yeats among Wilde, Joyce, Pound, Eliot, and Auden

James Joyce

Oscar Wilde

Antonia Fraser

Cromwell

King James I of England

Mary Queen of Scots

The Warrior Queens

The Weaker Vessel

Edward Gibbon

The History of the Decline and Fall of the Roman Empire

Alex Haley

The Autobiography of Malcolm X: As Told to Alex Haley

Lillian Hellman

Scoundrel Time

An Unfinished Woman: A Memoir

William Dean Howells

Years of My Youth

Alfred Kazin

New York Jew

Starting Out in the Thirties

A Walker in the City

Helen Keller

The Story of My Life

Ross King

Brunelleschi's Dome: How a Renaissance Genius Reinvented Architecture

The Judgment of Paris: The Revolutionary Decade That Gave the World Impressionism

Michelangelo and the Pope's Ceiling

Maxine Hong Kingston

China Men

The Woman Warrior

T. E. Lawrence

The Revolt in the Desert

Seven Pillars of Wisdom

Gerda Lerner

The Creation of Patriarchy

The Female Experience: An American Documentary

The Majority Finds Its Past: Placing Women in History

Thomas Macaulay

Critical and Historical Essays

History of England from the Accession of James II

Samuel Eliot Morison

Admiral of the Ocean Sea: A Life of Christopher Columbus

The Growth of the American Republic

The Life and Letters of Harrison Gray Otis, Federalist

John Henry Newman

Any of his nonfiction

Francis Parkman

The Oregon Trail

Pioneers of France in the New World

Samuel Pepys

The Diary of Samuel Pepys

Richard Rodriguez

Days of Obligation: An Argument with My Mexican Father

Hunger of Memory: The Education of Richard Rodriguez

Any of his essays

Mari Sandoz

The Battle of the Little Bighorn

Old Jules

Arthur M. Schlesinger Jr.

The Age of Jackson
The Age of Roosevelt
The Bitter Heritage
Robert Kennedy and His Times
A Thousand Days: John F. Kennedy in the White House

George Trevelyan

English Social History

Barbara Tuchman

Bible and Sword: England and Palestine from the Bronze Age to Balfour
A Distant Mirror: The Calamitous 14th Century
The Guns of August
The March of Folly: From Troy to Vietnam
The Proud Tower: A Portrait of the World Before the War, 1890–1914

Richard Wright

Black Boy (American Hunger)

Anzia Yezierska

The Open Cage
Red Ribbon on a White Horse: My Story

Essays, Fiction, and Criticism

Joseph Addison

Selections From The Spectator, Tatler, Guardian, and Freeholder V1 (edited with Richard Steele)

James Agee

The Collected Short Prose of James Agee
A Death in a Family

Michael Arlen

An American Verdict
The Camera Age: Essays on Television
Exiles

Matthew Arnold

Any of his criticism

Margaret Atwood

Cat's Eye
The Handmaid's Tale
Negotiating with the Dead: A Writer on Writing
Payback: Debt and the Shadow Side of Wealth

Francis Bacon

The Advancement of Learning
The New Atlantis

James Baldwin

Another Country
The Devil Finds Work
The Evidence of Things Not Seen
The Fire Next Time
Go Tell It on a Mountain
If Beale Street Could Talk
Notes of a Native Son

G. K. Chesterton

Heretics
St. Francis of Assisi
St. Thomas Aquinas
The Victorian Age in Literature

Kenneth Clark

Another Part of the Wood

Civilisation

The Other Half

*The Story Behind the Mortgage and Housing
    Meltdown: The Legacy of Greed*

Samuel Taylor Coleridge

Any of his criticism

Arlene Croce

Any of her criticism

Joan Didion

A Book of Common Prayer

Salvador

Slouching Towards Bethlehem

The Year of Magical Thinking

Any of her essays

Ralph Waldo Emerson

Journals and Miscellaneous Notebooks

Any of his essays

Northrop Frye

Anatomy of Criticism

Fearful Symmetry: A Study of William Blake

Fools of Time: Studies in Shakespearean Tragedy

Paul Fussell

Bad: Or, the Dumbing of America

The Great War and Modern Memory

"Thank God for the Atom Bomb" and Other Essays

Nadine Gordimer

Face to Face

My Son's Story

Not for Publication

Telling Times: Writing and Living (1954–2008)

Any of her essays

William Hazlitt

Any of his criticism

Zora Neale Hurston

Dust Tracks on a Road: An Autobiography

Jonah's Gourd Vine

Their Eyes Were Watching God

Ruth Prawer Jhabvala

Heat and Dust

In Search of Love and Beauty

Samuel Johnson

The Lives of the Poets

*The Selected Essays from the Rambler, Adventurer, and
    Idler*

Pauline Kael

5001 Nights at the Movies

I Lost It at the Movies

State of the Art

Hugh Kenner

A Colder Eye

Charles Lamb

Tales from Shakespeare

Any of his essays

Stephen Leacock

Frenzied Fiction

Last Leaves

Winnowed Wisdom

Norman Mailer

Ancient Evenings

The Armies of the Night

The Naked and the Dead

Pieces and Pontifications

Mary McCarthy

Cannibals and Missionaries

Memories of a Catholic Girlhood

"The Writing on the Wall" and Other Literary Essays

N. Scott Momaday
The Names: A Memoir
The Way to Rainy Mountain

Michel de Montaigne
Any of his essays

Vladimir Nabokov
Lectures on Literature
Pnin
Speak, Memory

V. S. Naipaul
Among the Believers: An Islamic Journey
The Return of Eva Peron

Joyce Carol Oates
Contraries: Essays
The Edge of Impossibility
First Person Singular: Writers on Their Craft
New Heaven, New Earth: The Visionary Experience in Literature
On Boxing
Woman Writer

Tillie Olsen
Mother to Daughter, Daughter to Mother
Silences
Tell Me a Riddle
Yonnondio: From the Thirties

George Orwell
Animal Farm
Down and Out in Paris and London
Shooting an Elephant

Cynthia Ozick
Art and Ardor: Essays
The Cannibal Galaxy
The Din in the Head

Walter Pater
Any of his criticism

Adrienne Rich
Of Woman Born: Motherhood as Experience and Institution
On Lies, Secrets, and Silence

John Ruskin
Modern Painters
Praterita: Outlines of Scenes and Thoughts, Perhaps Worthy of Memory in My Past Life
Any of his criticism

George Santayana
The Life of Reason: Or, the Phases of Human Progress
The Sense of Beauty

George Bernard Shaw
The Intelligent Woman's Guide to Socialism and Capitalism
Any of his criticism

Peter Singer
Animal Liberation: A New Ethics for Our Treatment of Animals
Ethics in the Real World: 82 Brief Essays on Things That Matter
How Are We to Live?
The Life You Can Save: Acting Now to End World Poverty
The Most Good You Can Do: How Effective Altruism Is Changing Ideas About Living Ethically

Susan Sontag
"Against Interpretation"
"AIDS and Its Metaphors"
"Illness as Metaphor"
Styles of Radical Will
Regarding the Pain of Others

Richard Steele
Selections From The Spectator, Tatler, Guardian, and Freeholder V1 (edited with Joseph Addison)

John Updike

Assorted Prose

Hugging the Shore: Essays and Criticism

Self-Consciousness

Gore Vidal

Matters of Fact and Fiction

Perpetual War for Perpetual Peace: How We Got to Be So Hated

Reflections Upon a Sinking Ship

Views from a Window: Conversations with Gore Vidal

Alice Walker

In Love and Trouble

You Can't Keep a Good Woman Down

Eudora Welty

The Eye of the Story: Selected Essays and Reviews

The Golden Apples

Losing Battles

One Writer's Beginnings

E. B. White

Essays of E. B. White

One Man's Meat

Oscar Wilde

Any of his criticism

Edmund Wilson

Axle's Castle: A Study in the Imaginative Literature of 1870–1930

The Devils and Canon Barham: Ten Essays on Poets, Novelists, and Monsters

Letters on Literature and Politics

Patriotic Gore: Studies in the Literature of the American Civil War

The Shores of Light

Virginia Woolf

The Common Reader

"The Death of the Moth"

The Moment and Other Essays

Roger Fry: A Biography

A Room of One's Own

Three Guineas

A Writer's Diary

Political Writing and Journalism

Roger Angell

Five Seasons: A Baseball Companion

Late Innings

Once More Around the Park

Hannah Arendt

Between Past and Future

The Human Condition

On Revolution

The Origins of Totalitarianism

Simone de Beauvoir

The Coming of Age

The Prime of Life

The Second Sex

William F. Buckley

God and Man at Yale

The Governor Listeth

On the Firing Line

J. Hector St. John de Crèvecoeur

Letters from an American Farmer

Elizabeth Drew

American Journal: The Events of 1976

The Corruption of American Politics: What Went Wrong and Why

Washington Journal: The Events of 1973–1974

W. E. B. Du Bois

The Autobiography of W. E. B. Du Bois

The Negro

The Souls of Black Folk

Worlds of Color

Nora Ephron

Crazy Salad: Some Things About Women

Wallflower at the Orgy

Frances Fitzgerald

America Revisited

Cities on a Hill

Fire in the Lake

Janet Flanner

Janet Flanner's World: Uncollected Writings, 1932–1975

Men and Monuments

Paris Was Yesterday: 1925–1939

John Kenneth Galbraith

The Affluent Society

Ambassador's Journal

The Anatomy of Power

The Nature of Mass Poverty

Charlotte Perkins Gilman

The Charlotte Perkins Gilman Reader

"Herland"

Ellen Goodman

At Large

Close to Home

Keeping in Touch

Making Sense

Paper Trail: Common Sense in Uncommon Times

Thomas Hobbes

The Citizen: Philosophical Rudiments Concerning Government and Society

Leviathan

Thomas Jefferson

Any of his writings

George Kennan

American Diplomacy, 1900–1950

Democracy and the Student Left

Sketches from a Life

John F. Kennedy

A Nation of Immigrants

Profiles in Courage

Why England Slept

Any of his speeches

Martin Luther King Jr.

Stride Toward Freedom

A Testament of Hope

The Trumpet of Conscience

Any of his speeches

John Locke

An Essay Concerning Human Understanding

Two Treatises of Government

Andy Logan

The Man Who Robbed the Robber Barons

Niccolò Machiavelli

The Prince

John McPhee

The Headmaster

A Sense of Where You Are

H. L. Mencken

The Bathtub Hoax and Other Blasts and Bravos from the Chicago Tribune
A Book of Prefaces
A Choice of Days
H. L. Mencken's Smart Set Criticism
In Defense of Women
Prejudices

John Stuart Mill

On Liberty
The Subjection of Women
Utilitarianism

Thomas More

Utopia

Jan Morris

Destinations: Essays from Rolling Stone

Barack Obama

The Audacity of Hope: Thoughts on Reclaiming the American Dream
Dreams from My Father: A Story of Race and Inheritance
Any of his speeches

Olive Schreiner

The Story of an African Farm

William L. Shirer

Berlin Diary
Nightmare Years
Twentieth Century Journey

Red Smith

The Red Smith Reader
To Absent Friends

Lincoln Steffens

The Autobiography of Lincoln Steffens
The Shame of the Cities
Upbuilders

Alexis de Tocqueville

Democracy in America
The Old Regime and the French Revolution

Calvin Trillin

American Fried
An Education in Georgia
Third Helpings
Uncivil Liberties

Theodore H. White

Breach of Faith: The Fall of Richard Nixon
Fire in the Ashes
In Search of History
The Making of the President: 1960

Tom Wolfe

Any of his essays

Mary Wollstonecraft

Letters Written During a Short Residence in Sweden, Norway, and Denmark
A Vindication of the Rights of Men, in a Letter to the Right Honorable Edmund Burke
A Vindication of the Rights of Woman, with Strictures on Political and Moral Subjects

Science and Nature Writing

Isaac Asimov

The Exploding Suns
In Joy Still Felt (autobiography)
In Memory Yet Green (autobiography)
Until the Sun Dies

Jacob Bronowski

The Origins of Knowledge and Imagination
A Sense of the Future